THE STRATEGY CONCEPT AND PROCESS

THE STRATEGY CONCEPT AND PROCESS:

A Pragmatic Approach

Arnoldo C. Hax

Massachusetts Institute of Technology

Nicolas S. Majluf

Catholic University

of Chile

Prentice Hall, Englewood Cliffs, New Jersey 07632

Library of Congress Cataloging-in-Publication Data

Hax, Arnoldo C.
  The strategy concept and process : a pragmatic approach / Arnoldo
C. Hax and Nicolas S. Majluf.
  Includes index.
  ISBN 0-13-852146-8
  1. Strategic planning. I. Majluf, Nicolas S.
II. Title.
HD30.28.H3885   1991   90-44239
658.4'012—dc20   CIP

Editorial/production supervision and
   interior design: Esther S. Koehn and Brian Hatch
Cover design: Bruce Kenselaar
Manufacturing buyers: Trudy Pisciotti/Robert Anderson

 © 1991 by Prentice-Hall, Inc.
A Division of Simon & Schuster
Englewood Cliffs, New Jersey 07632

Printed in the United States of America

10 9 8 7 6 5 4 3 2 1

ISBN 0-13-852146-8

Prentice-Hall International (UK) Limited, *London*
Prentice-Hall of Australia Pty. Limited, *Sydney*
Prentice-Hall Canada Inc., *Toronto*
Prentice-Hall Hispanoamericana, S.A., *Mexico*
Prentice-Hall of India Private Limited, *New Delhi*
Prentice-Hall of Japan, Inc., *Tokyo*
Simon & Schuster Asia Pte. Ltd., *Singapore*
Editora Prentice-Hall do Brasil, Ltda., *Rio de Janeiro*

Contents

Part II Business Strategy

13 CORPORATE PHILOSOPHY 146

14 STRATEGIC POSTURE OF THE FIRM 153

15 RESOURCE ALLOCATION AND PORTFOLIO MANAGEMENT 161

16 ORGANIZATION AND MANAGERIAL INFRASTRUCTURE: IMPRINTING THE VISION OF THE FIRM 205

Preface

As this century comes to an end, managers are facing challenges of enormous dimensions. The trend toward globalization, which is present in all significant business activities, has resulted in a dramatic increase in the intensity and diversity of competition. A manager today has to understand not only the familiar domestic markets, but also the subtleties of doing business in foreign markets against unfamiliar competitors. The increasing trend toward globalization stems from the pervasive forces of technology, which are reshaping industries and deeply affecting the ways to compete. These two forces of globalization and technology are demanding a new form of leadership. It is essential now that executives feel comfortable with managing changes in a highly dynamic environment and have the capacity to provide a sense of strategic direction to guide the organization constructively into the future.

Paramount to accomplishing this demanding task is for a manager to be able to articulate a vision of the firm with charismatic zeal. This is the essence of leadership: managing strategically by imprinting the vision of the firm throughout the organization.

The central objective of this book is to help managers to bring the vision into a concrete reality. Rather than philosophizing in the abstract about the attributes of leadership, we have adopted a pragmatic approach to strategic management. Our hope is to offer practicing managers and business students a disciplined process that facilitates the formulation and implementation of strategy to allow this demanding task of identifying and imprinting the vision of the firm to become a meaningful reality.

We believe this book, which is the result of years of research work, teaching, and consulting experience, has the following unique attributes to offer its readers:

- *There is a bias toward pragmatism.*
  It is our intent to provide carefully crafted methodologies that facilitate the applications of relevant concepts and tools into strategy development.

xiii

- *It proposes an effective process to facilitate communication.*
  At the heart of strategy resides a willingness to change, to adapt the organization, to improve its competitive position. That change can only be realized if there is a basic consensus among key managers about the central strategic direction of the firm. We believe the strategic process we recommend constitutes a powerful instrument to address all the essential managerial tasks and eventually reach that quality of consensus. Incidentally, consensus does not mean that dissenting views are not tolerated; quite the contrary, a proper strategic planning process will stimulate controversy and the expression of different points of view. But it will also recognize that there is a time to confront and disagree, and a time where differences must be put aside with the emergence of a shared vision agreed upon by all of its key architects.
- *It represents the state of the art of the practice of strategic management.*
  We have made a conscious effort to recognize all key advances in the vast field of strategic management that can assist business executives in addressing the totality of the tasks required to bring a strategic vision to the firm.
- *There is an integrative and comprehensive approach to strategic management.*
  There is no book on strategy, to our knowledge, that has as broad a scope as this book. The essential frameworks that are treated in reasonable depth are: the concept of strategy and the strategy formation process (Part I); the tasks pertaining to the development of business strategy (Part II); the tasks of corporate strategy including the development of organizational and managerial infrastructure, a key concept in strategic management (Part III); and the tasks associated with the development of functional strategy (Part IV).
- *Practical illustrations are offered throughout.*
  In every chapter of the book we have made a constant effort to exemplify with relevant and real-life applications the concept and tools that are described. In particular, we have carried through most of the book the case of AMAX Corporation. Moreover, Part V illustrates the methodology for the development of a strategic plan as a self-contained unit, using the case of Citibank Taipei, a branch of Citibank in the capital city of Taiwan.

Reflecting more specifically about the contributions in each of the book's five parts, we can say the following:

Part I—Strategy and Process. It provides a unified definition of the concept of strategy, as well as suggesting a disciplined step-by-step approach to formalize the development of a strategic plan. The resulting methodology is the first of five guiding frameworks of this book: *A formal strategic planning process* (see Figure 2–2).

Part II—Business Strategy. It covers the core concepts of business strategy: strategic business unit (SBU), mission of the business, industry analysis, competitive positioning, and the tasks required to put together a comprehensive business strategy. This part integrates the two conceptual frameworks proposed by Michael Porter—industry and competitive analysis, and the value chain— as the fundamental constructs to support a business strategy. This is captured in the second guiding framework of this book: *The fundamental elements in the definition of business strategy* (see Figure 3–1).

Part III—Corporate Strategy. Although corporate strategy is vital in defining the vision of the firm, there is no book that has treated in detail the nature of the strategic tasks to be conducted at the corporate level. We recognize ten fundamental activities linked to the development of corporate strategy: the mission of the firm, business segmentation, horizontal strategy, vertical integration, corporate philosophy, special strategic issues, strategic posture of the firm, resource allocation and portfolio management, organization and managerial infrastructure, and human resources management of key personnel. Each of these tasks is treated in significant detail and illustrated accordingly to provide managers with a full understanding of what is needed to construct a corporate strategy and to make it a reality. Two additional guiding frameworks are presented in this part. The first one is *the fundamental elements in the definition of corporate strategy: the ten tasks* (see Figure 8–1). The second one, which captures the organizational and managerial infrastructure issues presented in Chapter 16, is entitled *the fundamental elements of strategic management: imprinting the vision of the firm through formal-analytical and power-behavioral approaches to management* (see Figure 16–1).

Part IV—Functional Strategy. In this deceptively brief part, we cover an immense amount of information to facilitate the development of strategy for all of the key functions of the firm: finance, human resources management, technology, procurement, manufacturing, and marketing. The fifth and last of our guiding frameworks is presented here as *the fundamental elements in the definition of functional strategy* (see Figure 18–3). Chapter 19, in a very compact way, lists the major categories of strategic decisions and the associated measures of performance related to each one of the functional strategies. Finally, Chapter 20 illustrates how to put together a manufacturing strategy, as just one example of the development of a functional strategy.

Part V—Methodology for the Development of a Strategic Plan. The final part of the book is self-standing, so that the reader can benefit from a detailed application of the step-by-step methodology we recommend for the development of the strategic plan, without necessarily reading comprehensively the rest of the book.

We owe a great deal to our colleagues at MIT and elsewhere who have established the solid foundations of strategic management. Their contributions are acknowledged throughout the book. We also have benefited greatly from the work of many of our students at MIT who wrote masters theses and working papers under our supervision. We would especially like to recognize Scott Beardsley, Alain Boutboul, David Burgner, Dexter Charles, Chin-Tain Chiu, John Gray, Lynnet Koh, Marianne Kunschak, Lily Lai, Emmanuel Maceda, Luis Ortega, Kenji Sakagami, Luis Tena-Ramirez, Mark Webster, and Antoinette Williams.

In the production of this book we owe our deepest thanks to Deborah Cohen for an outstanding job of typing, editing and proofreading the many versions of the original manuscript.

CHAPTER **1**

The Concept of Strategy
and the Strategy Formation Process

What is strategy? It seems proper to start a book on strategy by providing its definition. The challenge, however, is not straightforward because there are some elements of strategy which have universal validity and can be applied to any institution, regardless of its nature. Others seem to be heavily dependent not only on the nature of the firm but also on its constituencies, its structure, and its culture. To break this impasse, we find it useful to separate the concept of strategy from the process of strategy formation.

By the concept of strategy, we mean its content and substance. This subject has received a great deal of attention by various authors in the last few decades. Most of them, however, seem to have emphasized a different perspective, providing only a single dimension of this fairly complex concept. We start this book by revisiting the central definitions that have been proposed, and by suggesting an integrative view that, we believe, captures more comprehensively the various dimensions of the concept of strategy. The resultant unified definition can be a useful framework to guide the formulation of strategy for a wide array of institutions. In that sense, it carries a normative character and can be used to gauge the existing versus the desired quality of the strategy formulated in a firm.

The process of strategy formation is much more elusive and difficult to grasp. The first step is to define the key players in charge of formulating and implementing the strategy. Are they supposed to act as a team, or are they going to be divided in independent groups; and if so, how is the information going to flow from one to another? Second, what tasks are those teams going to accomplish, and in which sequence? Is there a calendar that will be driving these efforts, with constant regularity, or will they be acting in a more flexible and ad hoc capacity? To what extent will the process of strategy formation be explicitly stated and communicated to the various constituencies both inside and outside the firm? How disciplined and rational will the resultant process be? Will the process be heavily dependent on formal-analytical tools, or will it be more the result of unorganized deals where bargaining becomes the guiding force? All of these issues are part of the process of strategy formation. Later in this chapter we begin its development, and in Chapter 2 we propose a working

1

framework to support a formal strategic planning process. How to put this process to work is really what this book is all about.[1]

The Various Dimensions in the Concept of Strategy

Strategy can be seen as a multidimensional concept that embraces all of the critical activities of the firm, providing it with a sense of unity, direction, and purpose, as well as facilitating the necessary changes induced by its environment. Reviewing some of the most important works in the field of strategy, we have identified the following critical dimensions that contribute to a unified definition of the concept of strategy.

1. Strategy as a coherent, unifying, and integrative pattern of decisions.

It is quite common to consider strategy as a major force that provides a comprehensive and integrative blueprint for the organization as a whole. Under this perspective, strategy gives rise to the plans that assure that the basic objectives of the total enterprise are fulfilled.[2]

By considering strategy as the pattern of decisions of the firm, we recognize that strategy is an unavoidable construct—it just emerges from what the firm does. We can go into an organization and study from a historical perspective the nature of its decision making and its resultant performance. Strategic patterns can be discerned when detecting major discontinuities in the firm's directions, stemming either from changes in its top management or triggered by important external events that call for strategic repositioning. The resultant "eras" of a firm can be used to analyze the coherence of strategic patterns. It is up to the managers in charge to make those patterns the result of well-defined visions of the firm, or to resort to improvisation and sheer luck. In any event, strategies will emerge willingly or not, leaving footprints of the major steps the firm has taken in the past which might also define its future destination.

2. Strategy as a means of establishing the organizational purpose in terms of its long-term objectives, action programs, and resource allocation priorities.

This is one of the oldest and most classical views of the concept of strategy. The message in this case is that strategy is a way of explicitly shaping the long-term goals and objectives of the organization, defining the major action programs needed to achieve those objectives, and deploying the necessary resources.[3]

Now we are presented with a pragmatic and useful definition of the nature of strategic actions. First, we need to define the long-term objectives of the firm. Hopefully, these objectives have a certain sense of permanence. They are not modified unless external conditions or internal changes call for a reexamination of the long-term commitments of the firm. Nothing could be more destructive and distracting than an erratic reorientation of the firm's objectives, without substantive reasons other than hesitations on the manager's side. Continuous strategic redirections of the firm will end up confusing all its stakeholders, most importantly, its customers and employees.

The desired stability of long-term objectives does not, however, preclude continuous steering and readaptations of the firm's programs. This is accomplished by a reexamination of the strategic action programs, which are more short-term oriented in character, while seeking congruency with long-term objectives.

Finally, this dimension of strategy points to the relevance of resource allocation as the most critical strategic implementation step. The alignment between strategic objectives and programs on the one hand, and the allocation of the human, financial, technological, and physical resources of the firm on the other hand are required in order to assure strategic consistency.

3. Strategy as a definition of the competitive domain of the firm.

It has long been recognized that one of the central concerns of strategy is defining the businesses the firm is in or intends to be in. This places strategy as the basic force that addresses issues of growth, diversification, and divestment.[4]

The key first step in defining a formal strategic planning process is an effective business segmentation. This concept occupies a great deal of attention throughout the book. At this point it is enough to say that most of the strategic attention, both in terms of the formulation and implementation of strategy, resides at the business unit of the firm. Therefore, the basic questions to be addressed are (1) "What businesses are we in?" and (2) "What businesses should we be in?"

If you have never attempted to respond seriously to these questions, you might find them trivial. But we have faced repeatedly great difficulties in extracting a clear-cut answer containing full consensus from an experienced group of managers when these questions are addressed for the first time. There seems to be discrepancies in the criteria defining businesses, in the desired degree of aggregation of the business units, and even in the identification of the responsibilities of those in charge. The issues are further complicated because business segmentation ultimately has enormous impacts in defining the organizational structure of the firm. Consciously or unconsciously, issues of turf and executive responsibilities tend to have a major input in the way those questions are addressed.

Segmentation is the key for business analysis, strategic positioning, resource allocation, and portfolio management. Segmentation explicitly identifies the domain of the firm, clarifying where we are going to be engaged in competitive actions, and how we are going to compete.

4. Strategy as a response to external opportunities and threats, and internal strengths and weaknesses, in order to achieve competitive advantage.

According to this perspective, the central thrust in strategy is to achieve a long-term sustainable advantage over the key competitors of the firm in every business in which it participates. This dimension of strategy is behind most of the modern methodological approaches used to support the search for a favorable competitive position. It recognizes that competitive advantage results from a thorough understanding of the external and internal forces that impact the organization. Externally, we have to identify the industry attractiveness and trends, and the characteristics of the major competitors. This generates opportunities and threats to be reckoned with. Internally, we have to assess the firm's competitive capabilities, which produce strengths and weaknesses that have to be further developed and corrected.

Strategy is needed for organizations to obtain a viable match between their external environment and their internal capabilities. The role of strategy is not viewed as just passively responding to the opportunities and threats presented by the external environment, but as continuously and actively adapting the organization to meet the demands of a changing environment.[5]

From this perspective emerges the fundamental framework of business strategy with three areas of focus: the business unit, as the central subject of analysis; the industry structure, which determines the key environmental trends; and the internal competencies, which define the ways to compete. The long-term objectives, strategic action programs, and resource allocation priorities thus become conditioned to the role that the business unit intends to play within the portfolio of businesses of the firm, the favorable or unfavorable trends of its industry structure, and the internal capabilities needed to be deployed in order to achieve the desired competitive position.

5. Strategy as a channel to differentiate managerial tasks at the corporate, business, and functional levels.

The various hierarchical levels in the organization have quite different managerial responsibilities in terms of their contribution to defining the strategy of the firm. At the corporate level resides those tasks that need the fullest scope to be addressed properly. They deal, primarily, with issues pertaining to the definition of the overall mission of the firm, the validation of proposals emerging from business and functional levels, the identification and exploitation of linkages between distinct but related business units, and the allocation of resources with a sense of strategic priorities. At the business level are all the activities necessary to enhance the competitive position of each individual business unit within its own industry. At the functional level exists the key assignment of developing the necessary functional competencies in finance, administrative infrastructure, human resources, technology, procurement, logistics, manufacturing, distribution, marketing, sales, and services needed to sustain competitive advantage. Recognizing the difference of these managerial roles and integrating harmoniously the resultant efforts is another key dimension of strategy.[6]

Throughout the book, we use the three hierarchical levels as a way to differentiate three distinctive strategic tasks. Unfortunately, the word *hierar-*

chical could be a misleading term, particularly when the current trend is for organizations to flatten their structure rather than depend on rigid hierarchies. We are not necessarily segmenting the strategic tasks according to conventional and orthodox hierarchies. We simply mean to say that regardless of the structure adopted by a firm, there continue to exist three highly differentiated strategic concerns. The first addresses the organization as a whole; we refer to this as the issues pertaining to corporate strategy. The second concern is inherent to the business unit, regardless of where this responsibility resides in the organization—these are the issues pertaining to business strategy. And the third one involves the development of functional capabilities and corresponds to the issues pertaining to functional strategy.

Once again, it might be useful to separate content from process. Content tends to be independent of structure. Looking at the organization as a whole, we use three conceptual levels: corporate, business, and functional. The process of strategy formation, mainly who is going to do what and in which sequence, is highly structure dependent.

> **6.** Strategy as a definition of the economic and noneconomic contribution the firm intends to make to its stakeholders.

The notion of stakeholders has gained importance as an element of strategic concern in the past few years. *Stakeholders* is a term designating everybody who directly or indirectly receives the benefits or sustains the costs derived from the action of the firm: shareholders, employees, managers, customers, suppliers, debtholders, communities, government, and so forth.

This dimension of strategy recognizes the responsibility of the firm in much wider ways than simply maximizing the shareholders' wealth. It views strategy as a means of establishing social contracts—a collection of cooperative agreements entered into by individuals with free will—to produce a process of social interchange that affects a wide variety of constituencies. The final output imprints the kind of economic and human organization the firm is and would like to be. It is a key determinant of both corporate philosophy and organizational culture.

Caring about the stakeholders could be an extremely useful way of putting the central strategic concerns of the firm in a proper perspective. It is obvious that in a profit-making organization, profit becomes an important objective: the proverbial "bottom line." However, it might become a dangerous trap to fall into, if managers look at short-term profitability as the ultimate driving force rather than to the legitimate and deserved reward of a job well done, which emanates from being responsible toward the remaining stakeholders of the firm.

A firm has to recognize that if customers are not properly serviced, eventually another firm will dominate the market with the consequent loss of competitiveness and profitability. Similar arguments can be made for the firm's employees and suppliers; if fair and mutually beneficial relationships are established, constructive associations will result that logically should be translated into enhanced profits. Abusive and unjust associations, that might lead to short-lived financial benefits, could not be sustainable in the long run. Finally, behaving as a good citizen in relationship with the communities in which the firm resides and with other external agencies will likely lead to an enhanced corporate image and the fulfillment of sound social responsibilities.

Toward a Unified Concept of Strategy

The concept of strategy embraces the overall purpose of an organization. It is not surprising, therefore, that many dimensions are required for its proper definition. The ones we have just presented simply emphasize the various components of the concept of strategy, one at a time. All of them are meaningful and relevant and contribute to a better understanding of the strategic tasks. By combining them, we could propose a more comprehensive definition of strategy.

Strategy
1. is a coherent, unifying, and integrative pattern of decisions;
2. determines and reveals the organizational purpose in terms of long-term objectives, action programs, and resource allocation priorities;
3. selects the businesses the organization is in or is to be in;
4. attempts to achieve a long-term sustainable advantage in each of its businesses, by responding properly to the opportunities and threats in the firm's environment, and the strengths and weaknesses of the organization;
5. engages all the hierarchical levels of the firm (corporate, business, functional); and
6. defines the nature of the economic and noneconomic contributions it intends to make to its stakeholders.

From this unifying point of view, strategy becomes a fundamental framework through which an organization can assert its vital continuity, while, at the same time, it forcefully facilitates its adaptation to a changing environment. The essence of strategy thus becomes the purposeful management of change toward the achievement of competitive advantage in every business in which the firm is engaged. Finally, there is a formal recognition that the recipients of the firm's actions are the wide constituency of its stakeholders. Therefore, the ultimate objective of strategy should address stakeholders' benefits, providing a base for establishing the host of transactions and social contracts linking the firm to its stakeholders.

The Strategy Formation Process

Strategy separated from strategy making is academic at best. It is impossible to comprehend the difficulties encountered in formulating and implementing strategy if one ignores the fact that the concept of strategy and the process of making it a reality are inseparable in any actual organizational setting. In fact, the process school of research[7] views strategy as the outcome of three different processes contributing to strategy formation:

- *The cognitive processes of individuals* where the rational understanding of the external environment and internal capabilities of the firm reside.
- *The social and organizational processes* that contribute to the internal communication and the development of a consensus of opinion.
- *The political processes* that address the creation, retention, and transfer of power within the organization.

Within this perspective, the task of the chief executive officer (CEO) is viewed as the administration of these three processes. This requires the CEO to develop a broad vision of what to achieve and to manage a network of organizational forces that lead to the discovery, evolution, and enrichment of that vision.

We discuss now options which are particularly relevant in designing the strategy formation process, and adapting it to the strategic objectives, management style, organizational culture, and administrative processes of a particular firm.

EXPLICIT VERSUS IMPLICIT STRATEGY

Perhaps the greatest controversy surrounding strategy making centers on how explicitly strategy should be communicated both internally within the organization and externally to relevant constituencies. Edward Wrapp, a noted contributor to the business policy field, suggests four strata for the definition of corporate strategy:[8]

Stratum I—Corporate strategy for the annual report. This is a statement which is primarily intended toward the shareholders, and conveys a general sense of direction on where the company is going, as well as a reflection on its past performance. The statement is highly sanitized, with a bias toward presenting a favorable view of the company, heavily edited by the public relations department.

Stratum II—Corporate strategy for the board of directors, financial analysts, and middle managers. This statement is more comprehensive and revealing than Stratum I. It provides information which is more sensitive and addressed to company insiders as well as critical external constituencies that need to be more thoroughly informed. However, the bias still persists in presenting the organization in its best possible standing, intending to assure that intelligent and successful directions are being pursued.

Stratum III—Corporate strategy for top management. This version of strategy is intended to go deeply into the key issues facing the firm and is addressed to the top management team that is expected to fully participate in setting up strategic directions and be responsible for overseeing the implementation efforts. Since the CEO needs the critical support of this group, there is still a positive bias in the way in which issues are framed and information is presented. However, full consideration is given to all of the moves and countermoves needed to strengthen competitive position.

Stratum IV—The CEO's private corporate strategy. The CEO is a critical figure in developing the vision of the firm and carrying this vision to fruitful completion. This stratum recognizes that, regardless of how communicative or participative the CEO management style might be, there is always a remnant of his or her innermost thoughts that are unlikely to be shared with anybody.

Every process of strategy formation has to deal with the probing questions that emerge from the degree of explicitness that is desired to achieve. Wrapp's four levels of strategy point to the enormous influence of the CEO in both shaping and communicating the strategy of the firm, and the various mechanisms that are available to make the process more or less open.

FORMAL-ANALYTICAL PROCESS VERSUS POWER-BEHAVIORAL APPROACHES

Whether the process of strategy formation should be formalized is subject to controversy. On one extreme, there are those who believe in an integrated decision-making process that relies heavily on analytical tools and methodologies to help managers, at all hierarchical levels, to reach a better quality of strategic thinking. Strategy formation is regarded as a formal and disciplined process leading to a well-defined organizational-wide effort aimed at the complete specification of corporate, business, and functional strategies. Those favoring this approach tend to advocate the use of formal planning systems, management control, and consistent reward mechanisms to increase the quality of strategic decision making.[9]

At the other extreme, a second school of management rests on the behavioral theory of the firm and espouses a power-behavioral approach to strategy formation. This school emphasizes multiple goal structures of organizations, the politics of strategic decisions, executive bargaining and negotiation, the role of coalitions in strategic management, and the practice of "muddling through."[10]

These two schools of thought have made significant contributions in increasing our understanding of the central strategic issues. However, neither the formal-analytical nor the power-behavioral paradigms adequately explain the way successful strategy formation processes operate. These taxonomies have been useful in focusing academic research work but neither serves as a normative or descriptive model. To get the best out of strategy making, formal analytic thinking should be combined with the behavioral aspects of management.

STRATEGY AS A PATTERN OF PAST ACTIONS VERSUS FORWARD-LOOKING PLAN

Another element of controversy in strategy making resides in the amount of attention to be given to events through time. Some authors view strategy as exclusively shaping the future direction of the firm; thus, strategy becomes the collection of objectives and action programs oriented at managing the future change of the organization.

Alternatively, strategy is viewed as a pattern of actions emerging from the past decisions of the firm. A leading proponent of this school of thought is Henry Mintzberg who defines strategy as "a pattern in a stream of decisions." According to this view, strategy is deciphered as consistency in behavior, whether or not intended, observed in the past actions of the firm.[11]

The emergence of strategy from the operating decisions of the firm is one of the central issues of strategy making. Thousands of decisions are being made every day in large and complex organizations. The only way to make them consistent is to establish a sense of permanent strategic direction to provide a framework within which those decisions can be made.

Nonetheless, interpreting strategy too rigidly as a pattern revealed in the past stream of decisions might lead to an inability to shape new directions for the firm. In a strict sense, strategy could only become known and explicit ex-post, when, from a historical perspective, it could be deciphered from the continuum of past events. From a managerial point of view, this notion of strategy is clearly impractical. Indeed, strategy is most important when dealing with intended change. Strategy should be formed in cognizance of the past heritage of the firm, but at the same time, be forward looking.

Consequently, strategy making becomes a delicate balance between learning from the past and shaping new courses of action to lead the organization toward a future state which might include a substantial departure from its past conduct.

Deliberate versus Emergent Strategy

A different way to characterize the strategy formation process arises from the definition of deliberate and emergent strategies.[12] A strategy is considered *deliberate* when its realization matches the intended course of action, and *emergent* when the strategy is identified from the patterns or consistencies observed in past behavior, despite, or in the absence of, intention.

These two concepts, especially their interplay, form the basis for a typology to characterize various kinds of strategy formation processes. At one end of this continuum falls the purely deliberate strategy, at the other, the purely emergent. Between these two extremes are strategies that combine varying degrees of different dimensions: openness, participation, CEO's involvement and consensus management, formalization, negotiation, continuity with the past, and orientation toward future change. Also, the type of strategy is affected by the nature of the firm's environment, particularly whether it is more or less benign, controllable, and predictable.

This typology is based on the idea that strategy is formed by two critical forces acting simultaneously: one deliberate, the other emergent. Managers need deliberate strategies to provide the organization with a sense of purposeful direction. Emergent strategy implies learning what works—taking one action at a time in search for that viable pattern or consistency. Emergent strategy means no chaos, but unintended order. Emergent strategy does not have to mean that management is out of control, only that it is open, flexible, and responsive—in other words, willing to learn.

A Typology of Strategy Formation

From our previous discussion it is clear that the relevant dimensions that should be considered in delineating a strategy formation process responsive to the firm's needs are:

Explicit versus implicit strategy
1. The openness and breadth to communicate strategy, both internally in the organization and to all relevant external constituencies;
2. The degree to which different organizational levels participate;
3. The amount of consensus built around intended courses of action, especially the depth of CEO involvement in this effort.

Formal-analytical process versus power-behavioral approach
4. The extent to which formal processes are used to specify corporate, business, and functional strategies;
5. The incentives provided for key players to negotiate a strategy for the firm.

Pattern of past actions versus forward-looking plan
6. The linkage of strategy to the pattern of actions in the past; and
7. The use of strategy as a force for change and as a vehicle for new courses of action.

Deliberate versus emergent strategy
8. The degree to which strategy is either purely deliberate or purely emergent.

Profiling and Diagramming the Concept of Strategy and the Strategy Formation Process

We provide in this section a pragmatic way for performing a diagnosis of the quality of the concept of strategy, and of the process of strategy formation. However, it is important to bear in mind the deep differences between these two notions. We have proposed a single unified definition of the concept of strategy that we feel is universally valid and applicable to any firm, regardless of its nature or its management style. This definition of the concept of strategy can therefore be used in a normative way. Figure 1–1 gives a simple chart that can be used to obtain the existing and desired profiles of the concept of strategy in a firm. The gap between these two profiles is an indication of the kind and intensity of the managerial work to be allocated to the improvement of the strategic capabilities of the firm. It is our opinion that the attributes listed in

FIGURE 1-1. Profile of the Concept of Strategy

	STRONGLY AGREE	AGREE	NEUTRAL	DISAGREE	STRONGLY DISAGREE
1. The decisions of the firm fall into a coherent, unifying, and integrative pattern.					
2. The purpose of the firm is expressed in terms of:					
• Long-term objectives					
• Action programs					
• Resource allocation priorities					
3. The firm:					
• Segments clearly the business it is currently in					
• Recognizes properly those businesses it considers entering					
4. The firm:					
• Understands its major competitors					
• Attempts to anticipate intelligent competitor's moves					
• Has a capacity to adapt dynamically its strategy to environmental changes					
• Recognizes its strengths and weaknesses					
• Attempts to achieve a long-term sustainable advantage over its key competitors in every one of its major businesses					
5. The firm clearly recognizes the different managerial tasks to be addressed at:					
• the corporate level					
• the business level					
• the functional level					
6. The firm defines the economic and noneconomic contribution it intends to make to its stakeholders.					

11

FIGURE 1–2. Profile of the Strategy Formation Process

	STRONGLY AGREE	AGREE	NEUTRAL	DISAGREE	STRONGLY DISAGREE
EXPLICIT VERSUS IMPLICIT STRATEGY					
1. Strategy is openly and widely communicated:					
• Internally to the organization					
• Externally to all relevant constituencies					
2. Strategy is generated through a wide participatory process.					
3. The strategic process is managed to build wide consensus around intended courses of action.					
FORMAL ANALYTICAL PROCESS VERSUS POWER-BEHAVIORAL APPROACH					
4. Strategy is based on a disciplined formal process aimed at the complete specification of corporate, business, and functional strategies.					
5. Strategy is based on negotiation process among all the key players.					
PATTERN OF PAST ACTIONS VERSUS FORWARD-LOOKING PLANNING					
6. Strategy emerges from the pattern of actions in past decisions.					
7. Strategy is mainly a vehicle of change that shapes new courses of action.					
DELIBERATE VERSUS EMERGENT					
8. Strategy is mostly deliberate.					

that figure can be interpreted in a normative sense, by defining a profile skewed to the left as closer to an idealized model of strategy.

The issue is more complex for strategy formation. An enormous number of different ways exist to reach the ideals imbedded in the concept of strategy. This is simply a manifestation of the huge variety present in any social organization. We can say what strategy is, but we cannot propose a universal formula applicable to any conceivable firm facing any kind of environment that would have a general validity. Figure 1–2 provides a chart to facilitate the profiling of the strategy formation process. However, there is no normative paradigm revealed by the profile. The important requirement of the process is that it should be managed consistently in accordance with the overall strategic objectives of the firm, its management style, and its organizational culture. Moreover, the strategy formation process should be integrated with other administrative processes of the firm, particularly management control, information and reward systems, and the organizational structure. Careful integration among managerial processes, structure, and culture is what leads to effective strategic management, a subject which is treated at length in Chapter 16.

There is a great degree of subjectivity in this profiling of the concept of strategy and the strategy formation process. When different individuals and groups in a firm try to assess the characteristics of strategic thinking in the organization, their varying perceptions on this issue can be positively used to transform the strategy formation process in a way that will help to achieve the ideal of strategy as a unifying pattern for the firm.

Notes

1. Our presentation in this chapter follows closely Arnoldo C. Hax and Nicolas S. Majluf, "The Concept of Strategy and the Strategy Formation Process," *Interfaces*, 18, no. 3 (May–June 1988), 99–109.

2. Key proponents of this dimension of strategy are William F. Glueck, *Business Policy, Strategy Formation, and Management Action*, 2nd ed. (New York: McGraw-Hill, 1976) and Henry Mintzberg, "Crafting Strategy," *Harvard Business Review*, 65, no. 1 (July–August 1987), 66–75.

3. The most important proponent of this definition of strategy is Alfred D. Chandler, Jr., in his classical work, *Strategy and Structure: Chapters in the History of American Industrial Enter-* *prise* (Cambridge, MA: The MIT Press, 1962).

4. This concept was early espoused by the Harvard Business School policy group and stated in the influential book written by Edmund P. Learned, C. Roland Christensen, Kenneth R. Andrews, and William D. Guth, *Business Policy: Text and Cases* (Homewood, IL: Richard D. Irwin, 1965).

5. Michael E. Porter has championed the quest for competitive advantage as the central thrust of strategy. In his first book, *Competitive Strategy: Techniques for Analyzing Industries and Competitors* (New York: The Free Press, 1980) he defines a framework to assess the attractiveness of an industry, and discusses generic strate-

gies for effectively positioning a firm within that industry. In his second book, *Competitive Advantage: Creating and Sustaining Superior Performance* (New York: The Free Press, 1985), Michael Porter uses the value chain as a powerful conceptual tool to direct the firm's activities toward enhancing its competitive position.

6. The three levels of strategy have been recognized by many authors in this field, primarily: Kenneth R. Andrews, *The Concept of Strategy* (Homewood, IL: Richard D. Irwin, 1980); H. Igor Ansoff, *Corporate Strategy* (New York: McGraw-Hill, 1965); and George A. Steiner and John B. Miner, *Management Policy and Strategy* (New York: Macmillan, 1977). Richard F. Vancil and Peter Lorange, "Strategic Planning in Diversified Companies," *Harvard Business Review*, 53, no. 1 (January–February 1975), 81–90, were the first in proposing a formal planning process to describe the interactions of these three managerial levels. Arnoldo C. Hax and Nicolas S. Majluf, *Strategic Management: An Integrative Perspective* (Englewood Cliffs, NJ: Prentice Hall, 1984a) and "The Corporate Strategic Planning Process," *Interfaces*, 14, no. 1 (January–February 1984b), 47–60 developed a thorough methodology to facilitate the disciplined formulation of strategies at the corporate, business, and functional levels.

7. For a presentation of the process school of strategic research, see Joseph L. Bower and Yves Doz, "Strategy Formulation: A Social and Political Process," in *Strategic Management: A New View of Business Policy and Planning*, eds. C. W. Hofer and Dan Schendel (Boston, MA: Little Brown and Co., 1979).

8. See Kenneth R. Andrews, "Corporate Strategy as a Vital Function of the Board," *Harvard Business Review*, 59, no. 6 (November–December 1981), 174–184; and H. Edward Wrapp, "Good Managers Don't Make Policy Decisions," *Harvard Business Review*, 62, no. 4 (July–August 1984), 8–21.

9. Primary proponents of the formal-analytical strategy school are H. Igor Ansoff, *Implanting Strategic Management* (Englewood Cliffs, NJ: Prentice Hall, 1984); Arnoldo C. Hax and Nicolas S. Majluf, 1984a, 1984b; Peter Lorange, *Corporate Planning: An Executive Viewpoint* (Englewood Cliffs, NJ: Prentice Hall, 1980); Michael Porter, 1980, 1985; and Boris Yavitz and William H. Newman, *Strategy in Action: The Execution, Politics and Payoff of Business Planning* (New York: The Free Press, 1982).

10. Major proponents of the power-behavioral strategy school are: Richard M. Cyert and James G. March, *A Behavioral Theory of the Firm* (Englewood Cliffs, NJ: Prentice Hall, 1963); Charles E. Lindblom, "The Science of Muddling Through," *Public Administration Review* (Spring 1959), pp. 79–88; Herbert A. Simon, *Administrative Behavior: A Study of Decision-Making Processes in Administrative Organizations* (New York: The Free Press, 1976); and H. Edward Wrapp, "Good Managers Don't Make Policy Decisions," 1984, op. cit.

11. For a review of Mintzberg's work, see: Henry Mintzberg, "Patterns in Strategy Formation," *Management Science*, 1976, pp. 934–948; and Henry Mintzberg and James A. Waters, "Of Strategy Delivered and Emergent," *Strategic Management Journal*, 6, no. 3 (July–September 1985), 257–272.

12. See Mintzberg and Waters, "Of Strategy Delivered and Emergent," 1985, op. cit.

CHAPTER 2

A Formal Strategic Planning Process

The art and science of strategic planning reside in balancing the various polar dimensions of the strategy formation process: explicit versus implicit strategy; formal-analytic processes versus power-behavioral approaches; strategy as a pattern of past actions versus forward-looking plans; and deliberate versus emergent strategy. None of these extremes adequately characterizes the way successful strategic planning processes operate. Nonetheless, it is legitimate to ask what should be the components of a disciplined and formal approach to strategic planning, aimed at improving the overall capabilities of the firm to operate in an intensive competitive environment. The answer to this question is what we refer to as a formal strategic planning process. Deciphering that answer draws most of the attention in this book.

The strategic planning process is a disciplined and well-defined organizational effort aimed at the complete specification of a firm's strategy and the assignment of responsibilities for its execution. It is a complex matter to describe this process in general terms because it depends on the particular characteristics of each firm. The planning process appropriate for a single business firm with a purely functional organizational structure is quite different from one suitable for addressing the strategic tasks of a highly diversified global corporation. There are, however, basic commonalities found in the formal planning process of most business firms, whose adequate recognition can help in their specification. These are the hierarchical levels participating in the process, the planning tasks at each one of these levels, and the sequence in which the tasks should be executed.

Hierarchical Levels of Planning

A formal planning process should recognize the different roles to be played by the various managers within the business organization in the formulation and execution of their firm's strategies. There are three basic conceptual hierarchical levels which have always been identified as the essential layers of any formal planning process: corporate, business, and functional levels.

At the corporate level reside the decisions which, by their nature, should be addressed with full corporate scope. These are decisions that cannot be decentralized without running the risk of committing severe suboptimization errors. Those who operate at lower levels of the firm do not have the proper vantage point to make the difficult trade-offs required to maximize the benefits for the corporation as a whole, mainly when confronted with situations that affect adversely their own unit in the organization. It should be noticed that the decision maker at the corporate level is not necessarily the isolated CEO. Depending, among other things, on the management style of the CEO, corporate strategies might be shaped and implemented by the core team of top executives.

At the business level reside the main efforts aimed at securing the long-term competitive advantage in all the current businesses of the firm. Business managers are supposed to formulate and implement strategic actions congruent with the general corporate directions, constrained by the overall resources assigned to the particular business unit.

Finally, functional strategies not only consolidate the functional requirements demanded by the composite of businesses of the firm but also constitute the depositories of the ultimate competitive weapons to develop the unique competencies of the firm.

In the vast majority of American business firms the strategic attention is almost solely concentrated at the business level. This management practice has severe limitations and, to a great extent, could be the cause of the recent erosion of American competitiveness in the world. The lack of a corporate vision deprives the firm of the necessary leadership to consolidate its overall activities, and to guide the difficult trade-offs between long-term development and short-term profitability. Similarly, treating the key managerial functions strictly with a short-term operational bias weakens the competitiveness of the firm. It is clear that all of the key functions—finance, human resources, technology, procurement, production, marketing, distribution, and services—need to be dealt with strategically. This means that we ought to have external intelligence to understand how competitors are deploying functional resources that will allow the firm to respond with the necessary functional skills to enhance its competitive position.

These three hierarchical levels are apropriate for the design of the formal planning process in most business firms; however, in some special conditions, these levels should be either expanded or contracted. In the case of a firm engaged in a single business, with a functional organizational structure, only the corporate and functional levels might be required. For a totally decentralized multidimensional firm, in which every division has its own business with autonomous functional support, only the corporate and business hierarchical levels will suffice. On the other hand, when dealing with a large diversified corporation, additional hierarchical levels need to be added, both for simple span of control reasons as well as to facilitate the identification and exploitation of synergism across distinct but related businesses. Frequently, those related businesses are clustered under the supervision of a coordinating executive, such as sector vice president or group manager. The resultant additional hierarchical levels could indeed have distinct and important strategic responsibilities that the planning process has to recognize formally.

Another critical dimension to be added to the hierarchical planning levels of the firm is the international perspective. Whenever the firm is actively engaged in international business, a regional as well as a country manager might emerge as a central actor in defining and executing the firm's strategy. In fact, the coordination required between world-wide product managers, functional managers, and country managers is one of the toughest managerial challenges that can greatly be enhanced by a planning process which formally recognizes the additional international levels.

The final issue worth commenting on has to do with the identification of the managers participating at each hierarchical level. The proper answer to this question depends very heavily on the type of organizational structure and managerial style existing in the firm. The prevailing notion, however, is that each level should incorporate all of the key managers who can contribute to the formulation of the individual strategies being discussed, and whose concurrence is vital for their successful implementation. The concept of the *linking-pin*[1] could be of value in illustrating the participation of different managers at each of the hierarchical levels. As illustrated in Figure 2–1, the corporate level is composed of the CEO and key business and functional managers. A given business manager has two roles. One assists in shaping corporate direction,

FIGURE 2–1. The Role of Linking-Pin Managers in the Various Hierarchical Planning Levels

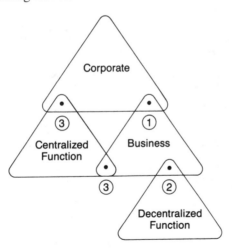

Manager ① is the linking-pin between corporate and business levels.

Manager ② is the linking-pin between a business level and a fully decentralized function.

Manager ③ has two different linking-pin roles as a centralized functional manager. One role forces coordination with the corporate level, and the other with all of the businesses that need the functional support.

and the other translates the corporate initiatives into his or her own business strategy; thus, the designation of linking-pin to that managerial role. Similarly, functional managers could act as linking-pins from either corporate or business levels to their own individual functional strategy.

In Figure 2–2, we present a model for the formal strategic planning process which recognizes the three essential layers of managerial decision making. It also serves to illustrate the different nature of planning tasks undertaken by each level, and a possible sequence for the execution of those tasks. Individual responsibilities have to be assigned at all levels in the organization, for developing, implementing, and controlling the proper strategic tasks.[2]

FIGURE 2–2. A Formal Strategic Planning Process

Hierarchical Levels of Planning	Structural Conditioners	Planning Cycle		
		Strategy Formulation	Strategic Programming	Strategic and Operational Planning
Corporate	① - - ▸ ②	⑥	⑨	⑫
Business	③ - - - ▸ ④	⑦	⑩	
Functional		⑤	⑧	⑪

① (a) Vision of the firm: mission of the firm, business segmentation, horizontal and vertical integration, corporate philosophy, special strategic issues
  (b) Managerial infrastructure, corporate culture, and management of key personnel

② Strategic posture and planning guidelines: corporate strategic thrusts, planning challenges at corporate, business, and functional levels, and corporate performance objectives

③ The mission of the business: business scope, ways to compete, and identification of product-market segments

④ Formulation of business strategy and broad action programs

⑤ Formulation of functional strategy: participation of business planning, concurrence or non-concurrence to business strategy proposals, broad action programs

⑥ Consolidation of business and functional strategies, portfolio management, and assignment of resource allocation priorities

⑦ Definition and evaluation of specific action programs at the business level

⑧ Definition and evaluation of specific action programs at the functional level

⑨ Resource allocation and definition of performance measurements for management control

⑩ Budgeting at the business level

⑪ Budgeting at the functional level

⑫ Budgeting consolidations, and approval of strategic and operational funds

Planning Tasks and Their Sequence of Execution

Regarding the nature of the planning tasks, it is important to distinguish activities which have a more permanent character. Although planning is a continuous process repeated year in and year out in the life of an organization, there are certain basic conditions that seem to be more permanent and are not significantly altered in each planning cycle. We have referred to them as the structural conditioners of the firm and they are represented in Figure 2–2 by the vision of the firm, the managerial infrastructure, corporate culture, management of key personnel, and the mission of the business.

At the same time, there are three major tasks which need to be updated and revised at every planning cycle: strategy formulation, strategic programming, and strategic and operational budgeting. These tasks are described in more detail in Figure 2–2.

The definition of strategy resulting from formal planning is expressed as a hierarchy of objectives that is progressively specified in the twelve steps of this process, from very broad guidelines to very detailed action plans. Each level and each unit in the organization can find in the definition of strategy a declaration, a piece of information, a goal, or an action plan that appeals directly to them. The explicit definition of a strategy must reflect a widely shared vision of the current potential and future projection of the firm. Parts II, III, and IV of this book are devoted to a full description of the planning tasks at the three hierarchical levels.

With regard to the execution sequence of the planning tasks, the essence of the message portrayed in Figure 2–2 is that planning is neither a top-down nor a bottom-up process. It is a much more complex activity requiring a strong participation of the key managers of the firm. Here objectives are proposed from the top, and specific programmatic alternatives are suggested from business and functional levels. It is a process that, properly conducted, generates a wealth of individual commitments and personal participation from everybody who has a definitive say in sharpening the direction of the firm. It is a rich communication device where the key managers have an opportunity to voice their personal beliefs about the conduct of businesses of the firm and offer a valuable joint experience as well as an educational opportunity to be shared by key participants.

Tom MacAvoy, former president of Corning-Glass Works, once said that the most important role of a CEO was to identify, develop, and promote "the one hundred centurions." In the old Roman empire, the centurion was a soldier who received instructions from the Caesar and was sent to remote lands. The Caesar knew that regardless of the number of years he would take for his task, the centurion would always be fighting for the Caesar's interests. If the planning process has any definitive objective and basic influence, it is to develop a strong esprit de corps among the one hundred centurions of the firm.

Formal strategic planning constitutes a powerful contribution to enhance managerial understanding and decision making. Among the most salient accomplishments we could cite the following:

1. **The planning process helps to unify corporate directions.** By starting the process with a proper articulation of the vision of the firm, subsequently extended by the mission of each business, and the recognition of functional competencies, the planning process mobilizes all of the key managers in the pursuit of agreed-upon and shared objectives. This unifying thrust could be very hard to accomplish without the formalization and discipline of a systematic process.

2. **The segmentation of the firm is greatly improved.** The formal planning process enriches significantly the firm's segmentation by addressing the recognition of the various strategic focuses of attention—corporate, business, and functional—and their representation in the organizational structure. This process centers on seeking business autonomy oriented toward serving external markets and recognizing horizontal and vertical integration to fully realize the firm's potential.

3. **The planning process introduces a discipline for long-term thinking in the firm.** The nature of the managerial tasks is so heavily dependent on taking care of an extraordinary amount of routine duties that unless a careful discipline is instituted, managerial time could entirely be devoted to operational issues. By enforcing upon the organization a logical process of thinking, with a clearly defined sequence of tasks linked to a calendar, planning raises the vision of all key managers, encouraging them to reflect creatively on the strategic direction of the businesses.

4. **The planning process is an educationl device and an opportunity for multiple personal interactions and negotiations at all levels.** Perhaps the most important of the attributes of a formal strategic planning process is that it allows the development of managerial competencies of the key members of the firm, by enriching their common understanding of corporate objectives and businesses, and the way in which those objectives can be transformed into reality. In other words, the most important contribution of the planning process is the process itself. A mere by-product is the final content of the "planning book." The engaging communicational efforts, the multiple interpersonal negotiations generated, the need to understand and articulate the primary factors affecting the business, and the required personal involvement in the pursuit of constructive answers to pressing business questions are what truly make the planning process a most vital experience.

Avoiding the Limitations of Formal Strategic Planning

In spite of its many contributions, the corporate strategic planning process has limitations that, if not properly recognized, could destroy its effectiveness.

RISK OF EXCESSIVE BUREAUCRATIZATION

One of the inherent risks in formalizing any process is to create conditions which impose a bureaucratic burden on an organization, stifling creativity, and losing the sense of the primary objectives intended by that process. Planning could become an end in itself, transformed into a meaningless game of filling in the numbers and impairing the strategic alertness which is the central concern of planning.

It may be difficult to maintain strong vitality and interest in a process which is time consuming and repetitive. Often, the initial stages of introducing a well-conceived planning process in an organization is accompanied with an exhilarating challenge generating a strong personal commitment and enthusiasm. As time goes by, the threat of the planning process becoming a routine bureaucratic activity is very real.

There are several ways to prevent this undesirable situation. One is not to force a revision of all the steps of the planning process outlined in this writing; instead, one might conduct a comprehensive and extensive strategic audit, say every five years. In the interim, managers should deal simply with minor upgrading of strategies and programs.

Another approach is to identify selectively, each year, the planning units that deserve more careful attention to the planning process, either because of changes in environmental conditions or internal organizational issues. This discriminatory emphasis could help to avoid spending unnecessary efforts on businesses which do not require such attention.

A third organizational device to prevent bureaucratization is to select a planning theme each year, which will require the attention of all key managers in their annual planning effort. Possible theme choices are globalization, new manufacturing process technologies, the value of the firm's products to customers, alternative channels of distribution, productivity improvements, information technology questions, and product quality.

LACK OF AN INTEGRATION WITH OTHER FORMAL MANAGEMENT SYSTEMS

Planning cannot be viewed as an isolated activity. Rather, it is part of a set of formal managerial processes and systems whose aim is to improve the understanding of managers in identifying and executing the organizational tasks.

There is an inherent danger in an organization which decides to implement its strategic planning process with a heavy planning department. Although there are legitimate activities that it could undertake such as collecting the external information, serving as catalyst in the planning process, and assuming an educational role to facilitate the understanding of planning methodologies, it is crucial to realize that planning is done by line executives and not by planners. Moreover, the establishment of heavy planning departments might tend to isolate the planning process from the mainstream of managerial decisions.

Strategic management, as we discuss in Chapter 16, is the response that is offered as a way to integrate all managerial capabilities within corporate values and corporate culture to assure effective strategic thinking at all levels in the organization.

GRAND DESIGN VERSUS LOGICAL INCREMENTALISM

An issue that has been raised is whether creative strategic thinking can ever emerge from a formal disciplined process. Some go even further and question whether it is desirable to commit to a rational grand scheme as a way of projecting the organization forward. A leading scholar who casts a serious doubt on the merits of formal planning is James Brian Quinn.[3] He regards formal planning as an important building block in a continuously evolving structure of analytical and political events that combine to determine overall strategy. He states that the actual process used to arrive at a total strategy, however, is usually fragmented, evolutionary, and largely intuitive. He claims that in well-run organizations, managers proactively guide streams of actions and events incrementally toward a strategy embodying many of the principles of formal strategies. But top executives rarely design their overall strategy, or even its major segments, in the formal planning cycle of the corporation. Instead they use a series of incremental processes which build strategies largely at more disaggregated levels and then integrate these subsystem strategies step by step for the total corporation. The rationale behind this kind of incremental strategy formulation is so powerful that it, rather than the formal system planning approach, seems to provide an improved normative model for strategic decision making.

We believe that the notion of logical incrementalism is not necessarily contradictory to a well-conceived corporate strategic planning process. By that we mean a process which is supported in the corporate values of the organization, that is participatory in character, which has a sense of vision given from the top but shared by all key managers, and which allows for meaningful negotiations to take place within an organizational framework. This process does not blindly set up long-term objectives, but rather expresses a sense of desired long-term direction and is incrementally attempting to adjust its course of action with a strategic posture in mind.

FORMAL PLANNING VERSUS OPPORTUNISTIC PLANNING

Formal planning systems represent an organized way of identifying and coordinating the major tasks of the organization. If all the planning capabilities were to be dependent entirely on the formal planning structure, the firm would be in a highly vulnerable position, unable to face unexpected events not properly foreseen within the assumptions underlying the strategy formation process. Therefore, coexisting with formal planning, there is another form of planning referred to as *opportunistic planning*. In Figure 2–3 a comparison is presented of the characteristics of formal and opportunistic planning.

Since opportunistic planning is triggered by unexpected events and is concentrated normally in a more narrow segment of the corporate activities, it seems unlikely that the triggering event affects all the businesses of the corporation. The key capability essential for the prompt response to the external event is the existence of *slack*. Often, organizations assign untapped financial resources to be quickly mobilized at the discretion of the corresponding manager to meet the unforeseen emergency. This is a form of financial slack. Yet more important is what we might call organizational slack. By that we mean the availability of human resources which are not overly burdened by their program commitments, so that they can absorb additional duties without experiencing a severe organizational constraint.

There is a need to balance the weight of these two coexisting planning processes. Organizations which rely exclusively on formal planning could trap themselves in unbearable rigidities. On the other hand, a firm whose decision-making capability rests entirely on purely opportunistic schemes will be constantly reacting to external forces, without having a clear sense of direction. The answer lies in a good compromise between these two extremes. A proper dose of formal planning provides the broad strategic planning framework with-

FIGURE 2–3. The Characteristics of Formal and Opportunistic Planning

FACTORS	FORMAL PLANNING	OPPORTUNISTIC PLANNING
Timing	Systematic process that follows a prescribed calendar	Responses to unexpected emergencies of opportunities and threats
Scope	Corporate-wide	Usually concentrated on a segment of the corporation
Purpose	Attempts to develop a coordinated and proactive adaptation and anticipation to changes in the external environment, while seeking internal effectiveness and efficiency	It is based on existing capabilities that permit slack and flexibility to respond to unplanned events

out binding every action of the enterprise, while opportunistic planning allows for creative responses to be made within that organized framework.

A CALENDAR-DRIVEN PLANNING PROCESS IS NOT THE ONLY FORM OF A FORMAL PLANNING SYSTEM

Implicit in the sequence of steps that we use to describe the formal corporate strategic planning process is the notion of a calendar-driven system. In fact, many American corporations have adopted variations of this type of planning approach. This, however, is not the only way of addressing a disciplined formalization of the planning activities. The most important alternative to the calendar-driven system is a program-period planning process, instituted in organizations such as IBM and Texas Instruments (TI).

The essence of this process consists in allowing for program initiatives to be generated at any time during the year, as opposed to waiting for the prescribed timing in which broad and specific strategic action programs are supposed to be formulated. It is necessary, however, at a given point in time, to consolidate all the program proposals into a meaningful integrated document. This is what is referred to as period planning. In that way, period planning becomes a mechanism for adding up all the technical and business proposals which are part of program planning, integrating them in a consistent way.

Program-period planning processes are specially suited for organizations which face a high degree of technical complexity with a rapid pace of change, dealing primarily with an integrated business, such as IBM and TI. In those cases, program planning is focused on either product development or productivity improvements in a functional area, while period planning is characterized by its regular, calendar-driven sequence of events.

HIERARCHIES SHOULD NOT BE AN OBSTACLE FOR THE DEVELOPMENT OF STRATEGIC CAPABILITIES

The advent of information technologies is producing enormous impacts in the modern organization, whose ultimate implications are extremely difficult to grasp at this point. What we now know is that the corporate structure is becoming more compact. The information, which was traditionally collected and presented to the company's top managers by its middle managers, is now being obtained and presented by computers and communication networks. As a result of this, the middle levels in the management hierarchy are contracting, structure is becoming more compact, and the work force is becoming more diverse and enterprising. Networks are beginning to substitute the conventional role of the managerial hierarchy. The traditional roles of boss and subordinates, with their associated flow of vertical communications, are being replaced by the notions of networking and group working. Effective coordination across lateral networks is becoming more crucial to understand the firm of the future than the managerial hierarchy, which may become either invisible or irrelevant.[4]

Within this context, one should interpret our strategic tasks at the corporate, business, and functional levels not as a rigid hierarchical sequence of actions, but rather as useful conceptual paradigms that address different focuses of attention which we believe are central to run a business firm now as well as in the future.

Notes

1. Rensis Likert, *The Human Organization* (New York: McGraw-Hill, 1967).

2. An initial version of a strategic planning process presented in Figure 2–2 was proposed by Richard F. Vancil and Peter Lorange, "Strategic Planning in Diversified Companies," *Harvard Business Review*, 53, no. 1 (January–February 1975), 81–90. The full specification of the strategic tasks implicit in that process was developed by Arnoldo C. Hax and Nicolas S. Majluf, *Strategic Management: An Integrative Perspective* (Englewood Cliffs, NJ: Prentice Hall, 1984).

3. James Brian Quinn, *Strategy for Changes—Logical Incrementalism* (Homewood, IL: Richard D. Irwin, 1980); James Brian Quinn, "Formulating Strategy One Step at a Time," *The Journal of Business Strategy*, 1, no. 3 (Winter 1981), 42–63; James Brian Quinn, Henry Mintzberg, and Robert M. James, *The Strategy Process: Concepts, Context, and Cases* (Englewood Cliffs, NJ: Prentice Hall, 1988).

4. Tom Malone, a computer scientist and organizational psychologist at MIT is developing a new field which he refers to as "coordination theory" to study the impact that information is causing in organizations. For a discussion of coordination theory and its implications, the reader is referred to Thomas W. Malone, JoAnne Yates, and Robert I. Benjamin, "Electronic Markets and Electronic Hierarchies," *Communications of the ACM*, 30 (1987), 484–497; Thomas W. Malone and Stephen A. Smith, "Modeling the Performance of Organizational Structures," *Operations Research*, 36, no. 3 (May–June 1988), 421–436.

CHAPTER 3

Business Strategy: The Core Concepts

Out of the three hierarchical levels that we recognize as the central foci for strategic thinking in an organization—the corporate, business, and functional levels—the business level is the core of managerial actions. Business strategy attracts prime executive attention, and many of the concepts and methodologies required to understand the business strategic tasks are also central to the comprehension of corporate and functional strategic issues. Because of these practical as well as pedagogical considerations, we have chosen to start the more in-depth discussion on the content and process of strategy at the level of the business unit.

There are two central concepts essential to achieving a solid understanding of a well-rounded business strategy: the definition of a strategic business unit, and the choice of a business competitive strategy.

The Concept of Strategic Business Unit

A highly demanding and challenging question we need to address at the start of the planning process is: What businesses are we in and intend to be in? This is the question of business segmentation which normally requires an enormous amount of knowledge and expertise to be properly answered. In order to undertake this task we have to define the unit of analysis, which is referred to as *strategic business unit* (SBU).

An SBU is an operating unit or a planning focus that groups a distinct set of products or services sold to a uniform set of customers, facing a well-defined set of competitors.

Notice that the external dimension (that is, customers and markets) is the relevant perspective for the recognition of SBUs. This stems from the fact that the essence of strategy deals with positioning the business so as to respond effectively to a customer need in a superior way to the competitor's offering.

The Choice of Business Competitive Strategy

There are two key sets of factors in deciding how to position the business within its competitive environment: (1) factors that determine the attractiveness of the industry pertaining to the business, as measured primarily by its long-term profitability prospects; and (2) factors that determine the relative advantage of the business with respect to competitors in the industry.

The first set of factors is normally external to and uncontrollable by the firm. Its analysis, referred to as *environmental scanning*, leads us to recognize the industry attractiveness and competitors' behavior.

The second set of factors, which corresponds to the actions controllable by the firm, allows us to comprehend how the business can develop unique and sustainable competitive advantages. Its analysis, labeled *internal scrutiny*, is basically supported by a thorough understanding of the activities represented in the business units' value chain.

In what follows, we elaborate on these core concepts, and we comment on how they contribute to the task of developing a superior position for the business unit, which is the ultimate objective of business strategy.

The Strategic Business Unit

The concept of a strategic business unit first originated in 1970, when Fred Borch, as Chairman of General Electric (GE), decided to break the GE businesses into a set of autonomous units, following a recommendation made by McKinsey and Company. GE had evolved from a company restricted to the electrical motors and lighting businesses into a conglomerate of activities spanning a wide variety of industries. Complexity increased as size, diversity, international scope, and a spectrum of technologies began to impose an unprecedented challenge to GE's top managers.

Confronted with this formidable task, GE's answer was to break down the businesses of the firm into independent autonomous units that could be managed as viable and isolated business concerns. Those entities were labeled strategic business units (SBU). The original intent of the business segmentation undertaken by GE was to provide the SBU general manager with complete independence from the rest of the businesses of the firm. The SBU had its own well-defined market segments and the SBU manager had all the resources available to define and carry out a successful strategy with full autonomy. The SBU concept has produced a long-lasting influence in the way companies design, develop, and implement formal strategic planning processes.[1]

A similar approach for business segmentation has been proposed by the management consulting firm Arthur D. Little, Inc. (ADL). They define an SBU as a business area with an external marketplace for goods or services, and for which one can determine independent objectives and strategies. To accomplish the business segmentation, ADL suggests the use of a set of clues grounded on conditions in the marketplace rather than on internally shared resources, such as sharing of manufacturing facilities, common technology, or joint distribution channels. Once again, the emphasis on segmentation is articulated in terms of the external environment, attempting to establish the roots of business identification in the behavior of competitors, instead of being driven by internal functional arrangements. The clues which ADL offers to define an SBU are:

1. **Competitors:** The business unit should have a single set of competitors.
2. **Prices:** All products belonging to a business unit should be affected similarly by price changes.
3. **Customers:** Business units should have a single set of well-defined customers.
4. **Quality/Style:** In a properly defined business unit, change in quality and style affects products similarly.
5. **Substitutability:** All products in a business unit should be relatively close substitutes. Also, there should be no clear substitute in different business units, as this would signal the need to unify products in the same unit.
6. **Divestment or Liquidation:** All products belonging to a given business unit should be able to stand alone as an autonomous viable economic entity if divested.

The first four clues indicate that a set of products belongs to a given SBU whenever it faces a single set of competitors and customers, and is similarly affected by price, quality, and style changes. If this is not the case, the set of products might be split into more than one SBU to focus more sharply its strategic actions. Moreover, all products in an SBU should be close substitutes of one another. Finally, an SBU could probably stand alone if divested.[2]

Interrelationship Across Strategic Business Units

As the previous definitions proposed by GE and ADL testify, the initial concept of an SBU presupposes a sense of autonomy and independence. As the concept started to be more fully recognized, accepted, and implemented in a variety of business firms, the issue of independence began to be seriously contested. There are a number of reasons why breaking businesses into autonomous units is not feasible. First, a firm primarily engaged in a single or a dominant business activity with a purely functional organizational structure cannot be broken into totally independent segments. This is a prevalent situation in small enterprises, and it is commonly observed in medium-sized and large organizations in process-oriented industries characterized by high levels of vertical integration.

Our inability to establish autonomous entities in those cases, however, does not preclude the firm from participating in a plurality of external markets, each one possessing distinct opportunities and demanding different competitive efforts. We have to manage a situation in which there is no easy match between the functional organizational structure and the strategic focus for different market segments.

Another important exception to the definition of independent business units is the firm which can be broken into highly distinct businesses, but if those units were to be managed in a totally autonomous way, unacceptable inefficiencies would result. We can identify situations where different units, in order to be run effectively, have to share common resources like manufacturing facilities, distribution channels, technology, or other functional support. Ignoring these potentials would deprive the organization of significant benefits to be derived from shared experiences and economies of scale. Another form of interrelationship is the existence of shared concerns, like common geographical areas and key customer accounts.[3]

Consequently, a thorough discussion of business segmentation has to consider the implications of managing the synergies resulting from potential interrelationships across business units. This is the all important subject of horizontal strategy, which is presented in Chapter 11 as one of the key corporate strategic tasks. In the meantime, the following considerations are important to bear in mind.

1. An SBU is intended to serve an external market, not an internal one. This means that an SBU should have a set of external customers and not just serve as an internal supplier.

2. An SBU should have a well-defined set of external competitors, with respect to whom we are attempting to obtain a sustainable advantage.

3. The SBU manager should have sufficient independence in deciding the critical strategic actions. This does not mean that the SBU manager could not share resources such as manufacturing facilities, sales force, procurement, services, technologies, and the like from other business units existing in the firm. It simply means that the SBU manager is free to choose from where to obtain the necessary resources and how to compete effectively.

4. If the three conditions just stated are met, an SBU becomes a genuine profit center, totally accountable for the profitability as opposed to becoming either a cost center or an artificial profit center where profit is measured through transfer price mechanisms.[4]

5. Finally, an SBU does not have to be a well-defined organizational unit with a line manager in charge to be regarded as a legitimate SBU. In an organization structured along functional lines participating in a variety of markets and facing several distinct sets of competitors, it could not be feasible to match the SBU segmentation with the organizational structure. In those cases, the SBU still could be the central focus for strategic analysis. But the SBU manager would simply play a coordinating role, seeking the necessary resources from the various organizational units of the firm, none of which might report directly to him or her.

The Fundamental Elements in the Definition of a Business Strategy

Figure 3–1 displays a framework that identifies the major tasks conducted in a formal business strategic planning process. Having resolved the question of

FIGURE 3–1. The Fundamental Elements in the Definition of a Business Strategy

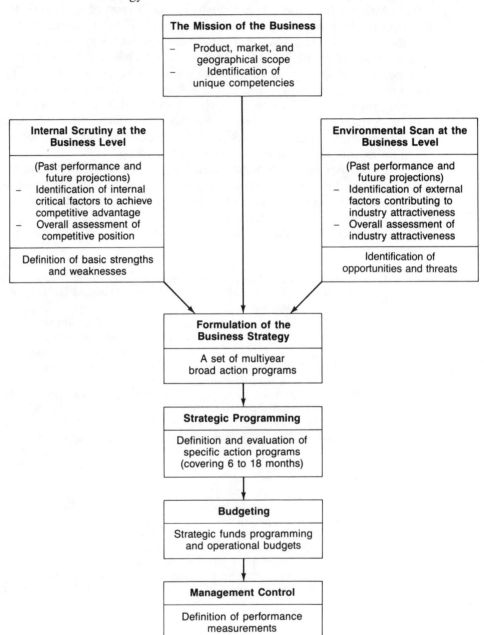

SBU definition, the first task consists in defining the *mission of the business*, expressed in terms of its product, market, and geographical scope, and a way to develop the necessary unique competencies that will assure a sustainable competitive advantage. Then we face the two central analytical tasks: *the environmental scan* which leads to the identification of opportunities and threats; and the *internal scrutiny*, which defines the basic strengths and weaknesses at the SBU level. When these three core activities are properly done, they naturally lead to the *formulation of the business strategy*, supported by a set of multiyear broad and specific action programs. The corporation will evaluate those programs, allocate resources, make a formal commitment through the agreed-upon budget figures, and define the performance measurements needed to carry out an intelligent strategic management control. By adhering to this framework, the business strategy becomes the end product of a thoughtful process that includes an environmental scan and an internal scrutiny, and requires a previous articulation of the business mission.

Notes

1. For a historical overview of General Electric's strategic planning system, see the case: General Electric Company, "Background Note on Management Systems: 1981," Case #181-111 (Boston, MA: Harvard Business School, 1981).

2. For a description of Arthur D. Little's strategic planning approach, see: Arthur D. Little, Inc., *A System for Managing Diversity* (Cambridge, MA: December 1974); Arthur D. Little, Inc., *Discovering the Fountain of Youth: An Approach to Corporate Growth and Development* (San Francisco, CA: 1979); Arthur D. Little, Inc., *A Management System for the 1980s* (San Francisco, CA: 1980); and Arnoldo C. Hax and Nicolas S. Majluf, *Strategic Management: An Integrative Perspective* (Englewood Cliffs, NJ: Prentice Hall, 1984).

3. The cornerstone to identify shared resources opportunities is the value-added chain, which covers all stages of business activities from product development to delivery of the finished product to the final customer. A careful treatment of the value chain and its implications for business strategy is presented in Chapter 6.

4. These four criteria for the definition of an SBU were originally stated by William E. Rothschild, "How to Insure the Continuous Growth of Strategic Planning," *The Journal of Business Strategy*, 1, no. 1 (Summer 1980), 11–18.

4

The Mission of the Business

The expression of the business purpose, as well as the required degree of excellence to assume a position of competitive leadership, is an essential first step in the formulation of a business strategy. This overall statement of business direction is what we refer to as the mission of the business.

The primary information that should be contained in a statement of mission is a clear definition of current and future expected business scope. This is expressed as a broad description of the products, markets, and geographical coverage of the business today and within a reasonably short time frame, commonly three to five years. The statement of business scope is informative not only for what it includes; it is equally telling for what it leaves out.

The specification of current and future product, market, and geographic business scope is focused at determining the changes that the business is expected to sustain. The mission statement should allow for a broad enough definition of business scope in order to detect modifications in the industry trends, the repositioning of competitors in terms of products, markets, geographical coverage, and the availability of new substitutes. The contrast between current and future scope is an effective diagnostic tool to warn against myopic positioning of the business.

The other important piece of information that should be contained in the mission statement of a business is the selection of a way to pursue a position of either leadership or sustainable competitive advantage. A mission statement which includes a definition of its current and future components is presented in Figure 4–1 for AMAX Corporation, a widely diversified metals and energy company based in Greenwich, Connecticut, which operates on a world-scale basis. It shows an intended movement toward diversification from commodity to noncommodity products, from durables to nondurables and services, and from major world markets (which are saturated) to less developed countries with high-growth potential. The way to achieve competitive leadership is as a low-cost producer. Another important aspect is the need to reduce financial risk by lowering the debt-to-equity ratio, and to hedge volatile price swings by managing the corporate position in commodity futures.

One approach to obtain a meaningful statement of a business mission is to engage the key managers associated with the SBU in an exercise for coming to terms with a description of current and future business characteristics. We

FIGURE 4–1. Mission Statement of AMAX, Inc.

	CURRENT	FUTURE
Product Scope	• Commodity metals • Fossil fuel energy products	• Expand to noncommodity differentiated products in both metals and energy
Market Scope	• Metals, automotive and steel industries • Energy, utilities and residential consumers	• Expand to nondurable consumer products • Expand to the service industry, through consulting or operations management to reduce recessionary impact
Geographic Scope	• Europe • Australia • North America	• Concentrate on Latin America and East Africa to help reduce further erosion of U.S. markets
Way to Achieve Competitive Leadership	• Dedicated exploration and development of quality mines containing high grade ores in order to be a low-cost producer • Significant marketing presence	• Intensify low-cost production • Develop marketing and R&D efforts to evolve new products and market niches • Manage economic and financial risk

SOURCE: John C. Gray, *The Strategic Planning Process Applied to a Natural Resource-Based Firm*, unpublished Masters thesis, Sloan School of Management, MIT, 1984. Reprinted by permission of John C. Gray.

have found useful, at times, to break those managers into two groups as equally balanced as possible, assign them the task of defining the mission, and request that they report their conclusion to the full assembly. It should not come as a surprise to know that often groups are unable to coincide with a statement of the current mission, let alone what future directions should be. Normally, the hottest issue of contention is the identification of what leads to a truly competitive advantage. By examining the sources of disagreement and by debating the essential components of the mission statement, it is possible to engage in a rich communication process, focusing on the heart of what the business should be now, and the major challenges residing in the future.

Occasionally, the full enumeration of products, markets, and geographical scopes could become unmanageable and uninsightful. This is often the case when dealing with a major business enterprise, where the mere cataloguing of the elements of the mission would consume an enormous amount of time, without adding much to the strategic intelligence of the business positioning. In those instances, we have found it preferable to leave aside a description of a full mission statement, and rather to concentrate on the identification of the strategic challenge derived from *changes* in the business mission. This requires a qualified managerial team having, as part of their common background, an amply shared understanding of the current business state, so they can focus their attention in detecting the necessary changes that must be brought to each

FIGURE 4-2. Significant New Challenges in the Mission
of a High-Tech Business

Changes in Product Scope	Reduce overlapping of existing product lines Protect low-end of product range from foreign competitors Develop new products based on our proprietary technology Broaden product lines for data processing Develop software products
Changes in Market Scope	Achieve a presence in consumer markets Retain presence in industrial markets world-wide Penetrate markets which become standard (e.g., IBM PC)
Changes in Geographic Scope	Become a significant player in Japan Develop further position in Europe Explore opportunities in Southeast Asia and China
Changes in Technology Scope	Incorporate emerging new technologies in design and manufacturing of products for the industrial markets Couple responsibilities for design and manufacturing in products for data processing Produce technology for software development
Changes in Ways to Compete	Rationalize world-wide manufacturing strategy to get more flexibility and lower costs Look for alliances in Europe and Japan Stress service as a competitive weapon Work with the customer in the technical solution to their problems Speed up cycle time for design and manufacturing

dimension of the business mission, in order to enhance its competitive position. Figure 4-2 provides an example of such a statement. Notice that it adds a technology scope dimension to the mission that is a useful extension for companies in which technology plays a central competitive role.

Even if one opts for addressing the full description of the mission statement, it is highly valuable to summarize the strategic challenge resulting from expected changes in the mission in a format similar to that presented in Figure 4-2. This is particularly helpful for the development of broad and specific action programs, aimed at responding to the desired changes in the business mission, at a later stage of the strategic planning process.

Determination of Product-Market Segments

A useful way to perform a further analysis in the product- and market-scope dimensions of the business mission statement is exemplified in Figure 4-3. The resultant matrix emphasizes the different alternatives for growth within a product-market scope. The existing products in the existing markets constitute the current business. To seek growth opportunities within that context, the firm has to resort to expansion in sales volume, geographical extensions, or market-share improvements; all of these alternatives are labeled *market penetration* in Figure 4-3. Extending the existing product line into existing markets is the

FIGURE 4–3. Determination of Product-Market Segments and Alternative Growth Strategies

PRODUCT ⟍ MARKET	EXISTING	NEW
EXISTING	Market penetration	Market development
NEW	Product development	Diversification

SOURCE: H. Igor Ansoff, *Corporate Strategy*, New York: McGraw-Hill, 1965. Used with permission.

product development alternative, while seeking new markets for the existing product line is referred to as *market development*. Finally, the development of new products into new markets represents the entry into new businesses, which is the *diversification* strategy.

An accepted practice is that the role of the business manager is limited to identify and fully exploit the potential extensions of current business into adjacent product and market opportunities. It is not the business manager's responsibility to pursue diversification strategies; rather, this task resides entirely at the corporate level. Consequently, the subject is more thoroughly treated when analyzing the corporate strategic tasks in Chapter 9.

5

Environmental Scan at the Business Level

One of the trademarks of modern planning approaches is its external orientation. Not many years ago, planning used to be a purely internally driven activity. This is no longer so. Today we have to address ourselves to the careful appreciation of environmental trends leading to an understanding of the attractiveness of the industry in which the business resides. We should be alert to all developments in our industry, especially to the behavior of competitors. Only a deep knowledge of the structural characteristics of the industry in which we operate and a sound awareness of competitors' actions can generate the high-quality strategic thinking required for the healthy long-term development of a firm.

Definition of Industry

An industry can be defined as a group of firms offering products or services which are close substitutes of each other. Thus, the boundaries of the industry are determined from a user's point of view. The relevant question is: which are the products that an individual trying to satisfy a certain need is willing to consider in his or her buying decision? The answer is: all products which, in the eyes of the individual, perform approximately the same function. Speaking more technically, we could answer that close substitutes are products with high cross elasticities of demand. This can be understood more easily if we think of two products, and only one of them suffers a price increase; close substitutability implies a transfer of the demand from the more highly-priced product to the other one.

Definition of
Industry and Competitive Analysis

Industry and competitive analysis is an orderly process which attempts to capture the structural factors that define the long-term profitability prospects of an industry, and to identify and characterize the behavior of the most significant competitors.

Four basic methodologies to perform this analysis are the subject of our attention in this chapter:

- Porter's framework for the structural analysis of industry
- Environmental scan at the business level based on external factors analysis
- Strategic groups analysis
- The financial statement analysis framework

Structural Analysis of Industries: The Five-Forces Model

In order to select the desired competitive position of a business, it is necessary to begin with the assessment of the industry to which it belongs. To accomplish this task, we must understand the fundamental factors that determine its long-term profitability prospects because this indicator embodies an overall measure of industry attractiveness.

By far, the most influential and widely used framework to evaluate industry attractiveness is the five-forces model proposed by Michael E. Porter.[1] Essentially, he postulates that there are five forces which typically shape the industry structure: intensity of rivalry among competitors, threat of new entrants, threat of substitutes, bargaining power of buyers, and bargaining power of suppliers. These five forces delimit prices, costs, and investment requirements, which are the basic factors that explain long-term profitability prospects, and henceforth, industry attractiveness. Figure 5–1 illustrates that the generic structure of an industry is represented by the main players (competitors, buyers, suppliers, substitutes, and new entrants), their interrelationship (the five forces), and the factors behind those forces that help to account for industry attractiveness.

INTENSITY OF RIVALRY AMONG THE INDUSTRY COMPETITORS

The rivalry among competitors is at the center of the forces contributing to industry attractiveness. Out of the many determinants of rivalry presented in the figure, four of them stand out: industry growth, the share of fixed cost to the total value added of the business, the depth of product differentiation, and the concentration and balance among competitors. If an industry exhibits high growth, low relative fixed cost, a wide variety of differentiating capabilities, and a high degree of concentration, then it is most likely that healthy profitability opportunities will become available to most participants in the industry. The opposite is also true. Think, for instance, in the domestic airline carriers

FIGURE 5–1. Elements of Industry Structure: Porter's Five-Forces Model

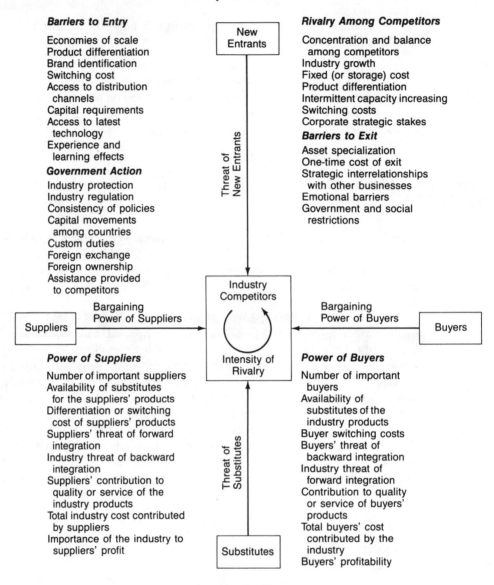

Barriers to Entry

Economies of scale
Product differentiation
Brand identification
Switching cost
Access to distribution
  channels
Capital requirements
Access to latest
  technology
Experience and
  learning effects

Government Action

Industry protection
Industry regulation
Consistency of policies
Capital movements
  among countries
Custom duties
Foreign exchange
Foreign ownership
Assistance provided
  to competitors

Rivalry Among Competitors

Concentration and balance
  among competitors
Industry growth
Fixed (or storage) cost
Product differentiation
Intermittent capacity increasing
Switching costs
Corporate strategic stakes

Barriers to Exit

Asset specialization
One-time cost of exit
Strategic interrelationships
  with other businesses
Emotional barriers
Government and social
  restrictions

New Entrants

Threat of New Entrants

Industry Competitors

Intensity of Rivalry

Bargaining Power of Suppliers

Bargaining Power of Buyers

Suppliers

Buyers

Threat of Substitutes

Substitutes

Power of Suppliers

Number of important suppliers
Availability of substitutes
  for the suppliers' products
Differentiation or switching
  cost of suppliers' products
Suppliers' threat of forward
  integration
Industry threat of backward
  integration
Suppliers' contribution to
  quality or service of the
  industry products
Total industry cost contributed
  by suppliers
Importance of the industry to
  suppliers' profit

Power of Buyers

Number of important
  buyers
Availability of
  substitutes of the
  industry products
Buyer switching costs
Buyers' threat of
  backward integration
Industry threat of
  forward integration
Contribution to quality
  or service of buyers'
  products
Total buyers' cost
  contributed by the
  industry
Buyers' profitability

Availability of Substitutes

Availability of close substitutes
User's switching costs
Substitute producer's profitability
  and aggressiveness
Substitute price-value

SOURCE: Adapted from Michael E. Porter, *Competitive Advantage,* New York: The Free Press, 1985.

industry after deregulation, where the four factors just mentioned established conditions which create a largely unattractive base for most of its participants.

It is to be expected that these four factors become dominant determinants of competitive rivalry. First, if the industry is growing aggressively, there are opportunities for everyone involved, and the resultant bonanza produces a source of unlimited prosperity.

Second, fixed costs seem to have an almost psychological impact on the way businesses are managed. When a firm is confronted with high fixed costs, the breakeven point raises to a significant fraction of full capacity. If that level of operation is not achieved, the most common reaction is to offer the customer very favorable conditions to boost demand, disregarding the consequences that this action might have on the overall industry performance. Think, for example, of an airline running a regular schedule between Boston and San Francisco, with a Boeing 747 aircraft. After 100 scheduled flights are completed half-full, the burden of absorbing overhead costs may become a major obsession. This may prompt the airline managers to undertake options like price cutting, the offering of all kinds of frills, and other competitive moves intended to capture passengers, despite the detriment to the overall industry performance.

Third, product differentiation is a most critical factor in the determination of competitive rivalry. Nothing could be more devastating to industry profitability than the "commodity syndrome." A commodity is a product or service that cannot be differentiated. That means that no one can legitimately claim that what it is offering to its customers is superior to an equivalent offering from other competitors. If that is truly the case, a customer decision depends entirely on price; and that means war. When the product features are such that its characteristics fit those of a commodity—such as primary metals—the major strategic challenge is to escape this competitive trap. This means that every effort should be undertaken to differentiate the product, drawing on properties other than its intrinsic attributes. Creative thinking would always identify opportunities for competitive advantage in service, financial conditions, delivery lead time, image, marketing skills, customer responsiveness, and whatever other critical attributes are seen as unique in the eyes of the final customer.

And finally, we have the issue of concentration and balance. It is by far more desirable to participate in an industry with just four major competitors capturing 85 percent of the market, with a homogeneous competitors philosophy (even if we are not the leading firm), than in an industry with hundreds of players, equally balanced, and with very different competitive perspectives (as is the case of too many diverging international players).

The rationale for this preference is clear. In the first option, we are not likely to expect great surprises. The rules of the game are explicitly or implicitly spelled out. We would be living in a gentle oligopoly, where not a single competitor would have an incentive to undertake a move that, although beneficial to its own position in the short term, is likely to produce adverse consequences for everybody in the long run. This form of constrained behavior is absurd when a larger number of quite diverse players converge in the competitive arena.

These are just four of what we regard as the central determinants of the intensity of rivalry among competitors. Other factors included are:

Intermittent Overcapacity

In industries where capacities are added in large increments such as steel and office space in big cities, the overall supply of the industry tends to go through cycles, alternating periods of large idle capacity, and of insufficient supply that sends prices through the roof. When the incentives of high prices trigger a simultaneous reaction in many competitors, they generate another spurt of larger added capacity, giving rise again to a new cycle of deterioration of the whole industry profitability.

Brand Identity

This constitutes an important source of differentiation and, therefore, firms try to establish solidly their brands in the market. Brand recognition by consumers is eagerly sought by most companies, and they spend dearly for it. But there are some firms who introduce generic products to the market, attacking the position of fairly differentiated competitors and eroding their profitability base. Numerous examples can be found in over-the-counter pharmaceutical products as well as supermarket products, where generic items are sold at significantly discounted prices with respect to well-recognized brand names.

Switching Costs

The easier it is for customers to switch products in a given industry, the higher is the intensity of rivalry. Therefore, it is not surprising that firms might adopt strategies to either make switching difficult, as normally pursued by computer manufacturers, or to provide incentives for customers not to switch, which is the intent of the frequent-flyer programs sponsored by most airlines.

Exit Barriers and Corporate Stakes

A very high exit barrier is a formidable contributor to the deterioration of industry attractiveness in mature and declining markets. When the industry is in the last stages of its life cycle, it is normal to expect a shrinkage in the number of competitors, since opportunities become insufficient to sustain the full roster of participants that were attracted under better structural conditions. However, if exit is very hard or nearly impossible, which is the case when asset specialization and one-time cost of exit are particularly high, an orderly decline is unrealizable. A serious profitability erosion ensues for all competitors.

Not only tangible factors contribute to ease of exit. Sometimes, even more important are the so-called emotional barriers, as well as strategic interrelationships with other businesses and government and social restrictions, all of which would either prevent or seriously delay the exit decision. Finally, there are firms who deliberately seek to perpetuate themselves in an industry beyond its financial soundness, just with the purpose of becoming a "competitive harasser." This tends to happen when firms are *multipoint competitors*, that is, face each other in a variety of industries with broadly different relative strengths. As an example, consider three well-known financial firms whose individual strengths are rooted in completely different foundations: Merrill Lynch (originally regarded as a brokerage firm), American Express (formerly in the travel-recreation-leisure industry), and Citicorp (a leading U.S. bank with global reach). They are actually or potentially facing each other in a wide variety of industries, such as retail banking, investment and asset management, international banking, travel-financial and communication, and insurance. In the case of multipoint competitors, a firm which faces a serious attack at the core of its central business might counterattack in an area which is of little significance for itself but is critical to that competitor. The competitive-harrasser business could therefore be used to provide a signal to another competitor about the destructive nature of excessive aggressiveness.

THREAT OF NEW ENTRANTS

On many occasions, the most critical strategic issue for a given firm does not reside in understanding the existing set of competitors and achieving an advantage over them, but in directing the attention to possible and sometimes inevitable new entrants. This was precisely the case many years ago for AES, a Canadian firm which was then the world leader in stand-alone word processors, and whose distribution branch in the United States was Lanier. It was clearly recognized at that point that the industry was about to attract some of the most formidable firms in the United States, such as Wang, Digital Equipment Corp., and IBM. Under those conditions, attempting to raise entry barriers or to seek a comfortable niche in which to develop a unique competence becomes the central thrust of a firm's strategy.

This leads us to one of the most important concepts of strategy: the concept of entry barriers and its relationship with the profitability of the industry. Entry barriers are the result of a wide variety of new factors, including economies of scale, product differentiation, intensity of capital requirements, ease of access to distribution channels, to critical raw materials, and to latest technology, relevance of learning effects, and degree of government protectionism. Entry barriers also result from some factors that were already present as determinants of rivalry: brand identity and switching costs.

High entry barriers are fundamental to explain a sustained level of strong profitability. A strategy conducive to raising entry barriers to an industry is expected to generate abundant long-term payoffs. Porter proposed a very simple scheme, presented in Figure 5–2, to reflect on the combined impact of exit and entry barriers on the profitability of an industry. High profitability comes with high entry barriers, and stability is brought by low exit barriers.

FIGURE 5–2. The Impact of Entry
and Exit Barriers
Over Industry Profitability

Exit Barriers

		Low	High
Entry Barriers	High	High and stable profits	High, but possibly unstable profits
	Low	Low and stable profits	Low and unstable profits

Consequently, the ideal situation is precisely one with high entry barriers and low exit barriers. Unfortunately, these conditions are seldomly met simultaneously because the factors that contribute to raise entry barriers at the same time increase exit barriers.

It is clear, then, that when a firm is already in an industry, a high entry barrier is much preferred. In that way the business is protected from a strong competition easily coming in and wiping out its benefits. But there is a less evident situation. Suppose a firm is not yet in an industry but it is considering entering. Is it better to have high or low entry barriers? When we confront our students with this quandary, there is always one or more who would answer that low entry barriers are to be preferred. The reply to the students is, more or less, along the following lines:

"Well, a minute ago I asked you for your preferences for entry barriers when you were in an industry; you said high, and everyone agreed on that answer. Now, you are telling me that when you are outside the industry you would like it low, but as soon as you enter, you would realize that you would rather be in a high entry barrier industry. How do you reconcile this discrepancy?" In time, the true answer emerges: "What you always want is high entry barriers. And when you are weighing the option of entering an industry, you still prefer very high entry barriers for everybody . . . but you." That is the trick. What is needed is to have unique capabilities, not transferable to competitors, that can make entry easy for the firm and unacceptably difficult for everybody else. A typical example of this kind of situation is IBM entry in the personal computer industry.

THREAT OF SUBSTITUTES

It is not only the firms participating in the industry and the potential newcomers that are central forces in determining industry attractiveness; we have to add firms offering substitutes which can either replace the industry products and services or present an alternative to fulfill that demand. Substitutes could affect in different ways the attractiveness of an industry. Their mere presence establishes a ceiling for industry profitability whenever there is a price threshold after which a massive transfer of demand takes place. A famous example that emphasizes this point is the conversion from steel to aluminum cans in the American beer and soft-drinks industry. The steel producers kept raising their prices, without giving enough attention to the fact that aluminum prices were not escalating as rapidly. Eventually, a point was reached where the one-time conversion cost was made attractive for the beer and soft-drink manufacturers.

The impact that the threat of substitution has on industry profitability depends on a number of factors, such as availability of close substitutes, user's switching cost, aggressiveness of substitutes' producers, and price-value trade-offs between the original products and its substitutes.

The lesson to be derived from this force is that substitutes are far from being an externally irrelevant factor. They constitute a primary component of a well-conceived strategic analysis.

BARGAINING POWER OF SUPPLIERS AND BUYERS

In the original model of industry structure prepared by Porter, he treats the power of buyers and suppliers as mirror images of one another. This becomes patently clear from examining the factors that contribute to the inherent power in these two cases.

Power of Suppliers	*Power of Buyers*
• Number of important suppliers	• Number of important buyers
• Availability of substitutes for suppliers' products	• Availability of substitutes for the industry products
• Differentiation or switching costs of suppliers' products	• Buyers' switching costs
• Suppliers' threat of forward integration	• Buyers' threat of backward integration
• Industry threat of backward integration	• Industry threat of forward integration
• Suppliers' contribution to quality or service of the industry products	• Contribution to quality or service of buyers' products
• Total industry cost contributed by suppliers	• Total buyers' costs contributed by the industry
• Importance of the industry to suppliers' profit	• Buyers' profitability

Porter's wording, "bargaining power of suppliers and buyers," suggests that there is a threat imposed on the industry by an excessive use of power on the part of these two agents. Porter can be interpreted as indicating that a proper strategy to be pursued by a business firm will have, as a key component, the attempt to neutralize suppliers' and buyers' bargaining power. In today's world, that message is, at best, controversial. The Japanese firms have given us lesson after lesson on the significance of treating suppliers as central partners, whose relationship has to be nurtured and strengthened, so as to become an extension of the firm itself. Moreover, buyers are the most important constituency of the firm, to be treated not as rivals, but as the depositories of a long-lasting friendly relationship based on performance and integrity.

TWO ILLUSTRATIONS OF THE STRUCTURAL ANALYSIS OF INDUSTRIES: ENGINEERING POLYMERS AND SEMICONDUCTORS

The model just presented has an ability to communicate very rapidly and effectively the principal issues that must be recognized in assessing the attractiveness of an industry. To convey that message, we have selected two brief examples. One deals with the engineering polymers industry, that are groups of polymers to which engineering equations can be applied, as products are designed and developed.[2] These materials are capable of sustaining high loads and stresses, and performing under stringent environmental conditions over long periods of time. Members of this family include: nylon, polycarbonates, acetyl, and others. The Du Pont company has played a major role in this industry, having invented many of the products that comprise it. Its major competitor, both in the United States and world markets, is General Electric. A brief summary of Porter's five-forces framework applied to this industry is given in Figure 5–3. Later in this chapter we contrast the different strategies followed by General Electric and Du Pont.

The second example describes the state of the semiconductor (computer chips or integrated circuits) industry, which has been very successful as a result of the electronic technology boom.[3] Today, semiconductors are the basis for innovations in everyday products such as television, cars, personal computers, toys, and VCRs; and also in many scientific, industrial, and military applications such as missile, mainframe computers, airplanes and radars. Over the past twenty-five years, the industry has grown to U.S. sales of $11.5 billion. Some major product categories in the industry are microprocessors, memories, logic, custom/semi-custom, and application specific integrated circuits (ASIC). Important players in the market are National Semi-Conductors (NSC), INTEL, LSI Logic, Analog Devices, NEC, Fujitsu, Motorola, Toshiba, Texas Instruments (TI), Philips, Matsushita, and Advanced Micro Devices (AMD).

Figure 5–4 presents a brief summary of the attractiveness of this industry, as described by Porter's model.

PROFILING THE INDUSTRY ATTRACTIVENESS

To assist managers with a comprehensive step-by-step analysis of the industry attractiveness, we find it useful to provide some disciplined methodology. The first approach simply consists of detailing each one of the factors contributing

FIGURE 5–3. Porter's Five-Forces Model Applied to the Engineering Polymers Industry

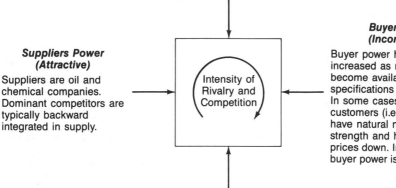

Entry Barriers (Attractive)

Potential entrants face significant barriers to entry, including investment costs (plants are highly capital intensive) and patent protection on many products, as well as extensive product qualification requirements.

Suppliers Power (Attractive)

Suppliers are oil and chemical companies. Dominant competitors are typically backward integrated in supply.

Intensity of Rivalry and Competition

Buyers Power (Inconclusive)

Buyer power has gradually increased as more products become available, and specifications more stringent. In some cases, very large customers (i.e. Ford, GM) have natural negotiating strength and have driven prices down. In other cases, buyer power is not significant.

Substitutes (Unattractive)

In the early stages of the industry, there were no significant replacements. As it matures, however, substitution is increasingly a factor. Traditional rivals, such as aluminum, have become more competitive in order to preserve their markets. In addition, upscale commodity polymers threaten the low end as they also improve. Differentiation is becoming more important.

Intensity of Rivalry and Competition (Attractive)

The industry is still very much a gentleman's oligopoly, as low-cost producers are also price leaders. Both Du Pont and GE are lowest-cost producers, but follow quality-differentiated strategies to justify high prices. It is also helpful that these leaders–for the most part–do not compete head-on with their products. Competition then is not to attack each other, but to attempt to capture most of the industry growth, so price wars are typically avoided.

Conclusion: The industry is still fairly attractive, and can be characterized as being in the growth "shape-out" stage. We already see consolidation as dominant players exercise their market power.

Source: Emmanuel P. Maceda, *Strategic Analysis: Du Pont Company, Engineering Polymers Division,* unpublished student paper, Sloan School of Management, MIT, 1988. Reprinted by permission of Emmanuel P. Maceda.

FIGURE 5-4. Porter's Five-Forces Model Applied to the Semiconductor Industry

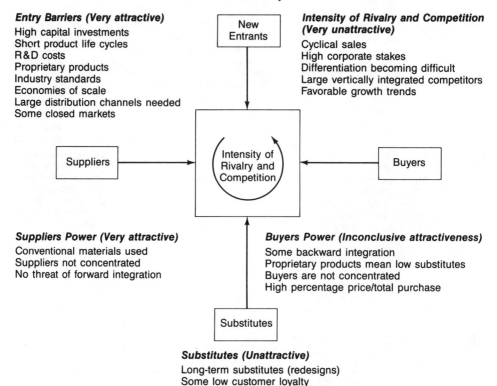

Entry Barriers (Very attractive)
High capital investments
Short product life cycles
R&D costs
Proprietary products
Industry standards
Economies of scale
Large distribution channels needed
Some closed markets

Intensity of Rivalry and Competition (Very unattractive)
Cyclical sales
High corporate stakes
Differentiation becoming difficult
Large vertically integrated competitors
Favorable growth trends

New Entrants

Suppliers → Intensity of Rivalry and Competition ← Buyers

Suppliers Power (Very attractive)
Conventional materials used
Suppliers not concentrated
No threat of forward integration

Buyers Power (Inconclusive attractiveness)
Some backward integration
Proprietary products mean low substitutes
Buyers are not concentrated
High percentage price/total purchase

Substitutes

Substitutes (Unattractive)
Long-term substitutes (redesigns)
Some low customer loyalty

Conclusion: The industry can be classified as attractive, despite intense rivalry. The changes taking place favor consolidation into larger firms, which have the substantial resources necessary to commit expensive R&D throughout the cycles of the industry.

SOURCE: Scott Beardsley and Kenji Sakagami, *Advanced MicroDevices: Posed for Chip Greatness,* unpublished student paper, Sloan School of Management, MIT, 1988. Reprinted by permission of Scott Beardsley.

to Porter's industry structure framework. Figure 5–5 illustrates the way to construct a systematic profile of the industry attractiveness, both analyzing its current state as well as its future trends. The example provided in the figure is the magnesium industry from the perspective of AMAX, Inc. Figure 5–6 gives a final summary of the contribution the major forces make to the magnesium industry attractiveness, now and in the future. For the sake of brevity, we do not comment on the rationale behind the assessment of each factor, but we encourage the reader to try to follow the example closely.

The industry attractiveness analysis that we have just presented allows us to detect those industry factors that affect us favorably, which represent *op-*

FIGURE 5–5. AMAX, Inc.—The Magnesium Business: Environmental Scan at the Business Level

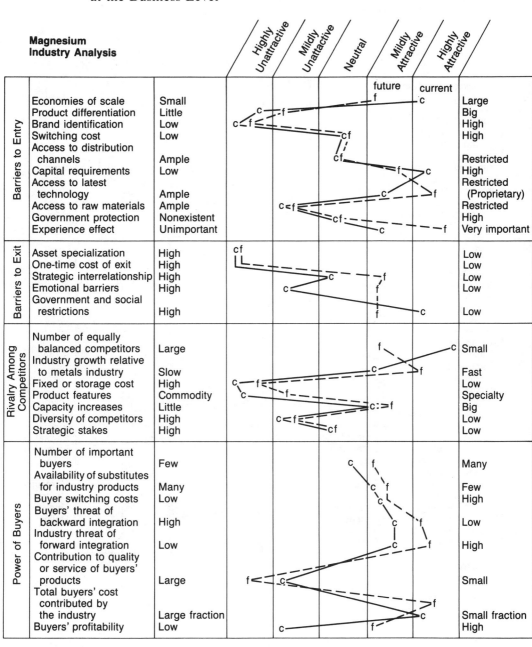

c = current
f = future

(continued)

FIGURE 5–5. AMAX, Inc.—The Magnesium Business: Environmental Scan at the Business Level (continued)

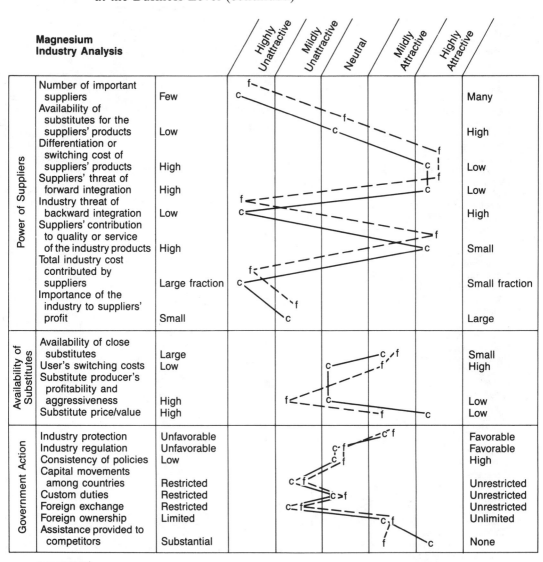

c = current
f = future

SOURCE: Gray (1984).

portunities, and those factors which constitute adverse impacts or *threats*. It is useful at this point of the analysis to articulate more explicitly the key opportunities and threats uncovered so far. Figure 5–7 provides a summary listing of the opportunities and threats exercised on the magnesium division of AMAX, Inc.

FIGURE 5–6. AMAX, Inc.—The Magnesium Division: Summary of the Environmental Scan

Industry Attractiveness

	CURRENT			FUTURE		
	Low	Medium	High	Low	Medium	High
Barriers to entry		X			X	
Barriers to exit		X			X	
Rivalry among competitors		X			X	
Power of buyers	X			X		
Power of suppliers		X			X	
Availability of substitutes	X				X	
Government actions			X			X
Overall assessment		X			X	

SOURCE: Gray (1984).

FIGURE 5–7. AMAX, Inc.–The Magnesium Division: Identification of Environmental Opportunities and Threats

OPPORTUNITIES

1. Good market growth potential due to strong government and industry energy conservation and transportation programs which should create demand for light-weight metals.
2. Resource is abundant and currently available.
3. New technology is being developed to reduce production costs to help magnesium compete against other metals, i.e., aluminum.
4. New product developments and new markets are opening up.
5. Currently, there are only a few significant magnesium producers, and they are all profit oriented.
6. Demand for aluminum increases beyond the aluminum industry's capacity and buyers begin substituting available magnesium in their products.

THREATS

1. Aluminum industry expands its capacity and forces aluminum prices to remain relatively low.
2. Future possibility of Third World countries entering the magnesium market providing excess capacity for nonprofit reasons or sophisticated global scale firms exploiting low-cost labor in those countries.
3. New and currently unknown technology may make magnesium noncompetitive in certain high-growth markets, e.g., the structural and consumer products areas.

SOURCE: Gray (1984).

FURTHER COMMENTS ON THE FIVE-FORCES MODEL

The Firm Should be Judged Against the Standards of the Industry
The combined effect of the forces affecting an industry might create either a significantly depressed environment, where most firms are doing poorly, or an inherently attractive set of conditions that benefits most of the industry players. Examples of the latter in the late 1980s were soft drinks, tobacco, publishing, medical services, financial services, health-care services, apparel, and office products and equipment. Examples of the former in the same time period were metals, coal, industrial and farm equipment, petroleum refining, and airlines.[4] Therefore, the performance of the firm has to be judged against that of the industry standard in order to really appreciate the value added at the firm level and the competencies of its managers.

Not All Forces are Equally Important
As it happens with any complex evaluation where a host of critical factors is included in the final analysis, it is important to bear in mind that not all the forces, and for that matter the factors contributing to these forces, have an equal weight. It could very well be that many factors add to an unattractive position, and yet, when judged from its entirety, the industry still presents an overall attractive picture. This simply reinforces the notion that this kind of analysis cannot be carried out in a mechanistic way. It has to be supported by a thorough and sophisticated understanding of the critical factors which contribute the most as determinants of industry attractiveness. These are the central issues that we need to grasp fully and deserve preferential attention when we decide on the best competitive position of the firm within that industry, and when we consider possible ways, if feasible, to alter industry structure. This becomes apparent in the case of the semiconductor industry summarized in Figure 5–4, where in spite of the intensity of rivalry within the industry and an equally unattractive impact of substitutes, the final conclusion was that the industry presented quite appealing opportunities for larger firms with substantial resources.

The Dynamic Nature of Industry Structure
Perhaps the only statement that one could make with certainty about the structure of an industry is that it will change, most likely, in unpredictable ways. That by no means invalidates the significance of a carefully done industry analysis, but it serves to reinforce the fact that there is an inherent dynamics in industry structure that we should recognize and attempt to cope with to the best of our abilities. Therefore, despite the criticality and importance of the analysis of the existing structural conditions of an industry and its competitive implications, it has to be followed up with an attempt to recognize the most likely future trends, and the opportunities and threats imbedded in those

changes for the business firm. Occasionally, scenario planning is used as a way of configurating meaningful future structural alternatives which could help the organization to prepare itself to either take advantage of optimistic scenarios or to seek protection against pessimistic ones.

In the last decade, technology and innovation have deeply affected the ways to compete, and have been responsible for creating new industries and significantly changing the structure of existing ones. Perhaps none of the existing technologies can match the potential impact that information technology has in reshaping industry structure and in transforming the nature of businesses and firms. We are living in the information revolution, where computer and communications technologies are affecting every facet of our society.

Information technology can offer endless opportunities for a firm to achieve competitive advantage. A company can use information technology to build barriers to entry, to build in switching costs, to completely change the basis of competition, to change the balance of power in supplier relationships, or to generate new products.

We are now in the midst of the "third wave" of computer applications: providing information to middle and top managers. As a result of powerful trends in hardware, software, and communications technology, as well as data availability, managers today have increasingly cost-effective hardware, user-friendly software systems, enhanced communications capabilities, and access to data that allows them to be better informed than ever before. A host of applications has been made possible by these technological changes, including robotics in the factory, decision-support systems for middle managers, executive data bases, electronic mail systems, and interorganizational systems within corporations.[5]

A CENTRAL DILEMMA: WHEN TO COMPETE AND WHEN TO COOPERATE

We have indicated already that Porter's model represents industries as a battlefield or a power game, with conflicting and clashing forces. The mere selection of the wording of the model is quite revealing. It talks about *rivalry* among competitors, *threats* of new entrants, *threats* of substitutes, and bargaining *power* of both suppliers and buyers. All of these account to one major message: The business world is tough and competitive. To survive, you have to be better than the best and be prepared to annihilate your opponents and destroy their power base.

As we all know, this conflicting and antagonistic climate does not necessarily explain the most effective or even the most common ways to compete. In the recent past, those firms which are truly smart at conducting their businesses have learned a very important lesson: You need to know when and how to compete, but also, and even more importantly, you need to know when and how to cooperate.

Today, *strategic alliances* represent one of the buzzwords for business. They are formal coalitions between two or more firms, for short- or long-term ventures, born out of opportunistic or permanent relationships that evolve into a form of partnership among players. Some of these alliances, under the more traditional rules, could correspond to agreements among competitors with conflicting interests, and they were prohibited in the United States until very recently, by antitrust legislation, forcing American firms to seek covenants only with overseas companies.

These alliances include joint ventures, licensing agreements, supply agreements, venture capital initiatives, joint partnership acquisitions, and many other forms of cooperation. All approaches share the common objective to eliminate or significantly reduce confrontation among competitors, suppliers, customers, potential new entrants, and substitute producers. Certainly, the completion of these alliances is intended to create better conditions for all partners involved through technology acquisition and shared scale economies, access to new markets, raw materials, and components, response to pressures by local governments, and the establishment of agreements for global standardization of products, to mention just the most common among a limitless field of opportunities.

A remarkable example of global strategic alliances is the contrast between the 1965 world automotive industry (Figure 5–8) and the 1985 map of global strategic partnerships in that industry (Figure 5–9). In 1965, the industry was well defined on a geographic basis, with three major centers of activity in the United States, Japan, and Europe. Out of all the competing firms, only GM, Ford, and Chrysler had overlapping interests in just two of these regions. Moreover, there were not formal relationships among any of the major players. It is striking to look at the world auto industry twenty years later. It is no longer feasible to either separate the geographical scope of the industry participants or to follow up closely the enormous amount of alliances that have been established across the board. Not only that, but the dynamic of change in the industry is so overwhelming it would take a full-time industry expert to be totally up to date with the extensive amount of interfirm agreements which are taking place almost daily.

Environmental Scan at the Business Level
Based on External Factors Analysis

The environmental scan at the business level attempts to identify the degree of attractiveness of the industry in which the business belongs. We just covered extensively the five-forces model, whose foundations are anchored in industrial organization.

Another methodology that we have found useful is based on the identification of those critical external factors considered to be the central determinants of industry attractiveness in the opinion of key managers of the busi-

FIGURE 5–8. 1965 World Automobile Industry

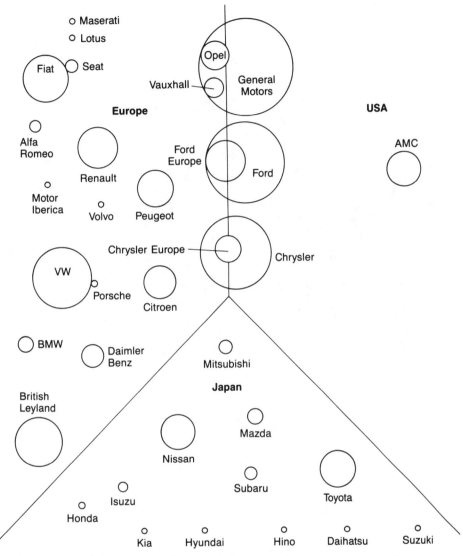

SOURCE: David A. Burgner, *Global Strategy: A Systematic Approach,* unpublished Masters thesis, Sloan School of Management, MIT, 1986. Reprinted by permission of David A. Burgner.

ness. Although this methodology might seem exceedingly subjective and heavily dependent upon the sound judgment of the managers involved, it has the advantage of committing them to a serious reflection to identifying the most critical structural issues and their future trends.

Managers are required to engage in a totally fresh exercise for deeply probing the identification of those issues which are considered truly significant, and to concentrate their efforts in the assessment of their influence over the

FIGURE 5–9. 1985 Map of Global Strategic Partnerships in the World Automobile Industry

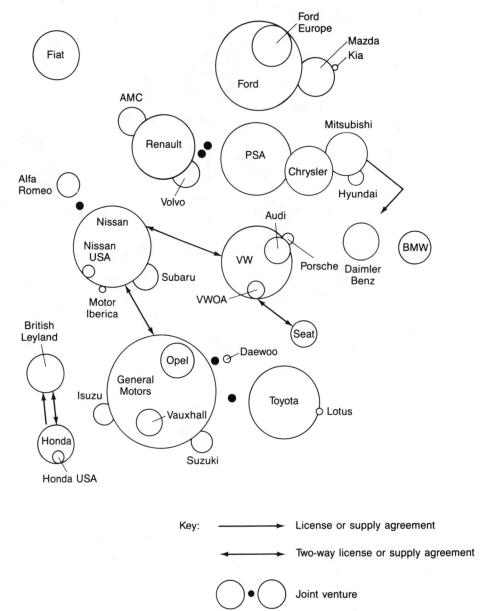

Key:

→   License or supply agreement

←——→   Two-way license or supply agreement

Joint venture

Equity holding

Parent   Daughter

SOURCE: Burgner (1986).

industry attractiveness. This inquiry also serves as an effective communication device among top managers, which generates a broad consensus among them, and leads to a collective enrichment of their business understanding. At the same time, it prevents any mechanistic treatment of this all important strategic question.

If it were desirable to enrich the conceptual framework used by the managers engaged in the identification and assessment of these critical external factors, one could expose them previously to the principles of industrial organization, or to the essence of the five-forces model; or, better yet, to provide them with a list of suggested external factors such as the ones exhibited in Figure 5–10. The rules of the game, however, are that these frameworks or lists are just springboards for the articulation of their own ideas that should be applied pragmatically to their idiosyncratic environment.

The resultant methodology can be summarized as follows:

1. Identify the critical external factors which impact business attractiveness for the business unit.
2. Evaluate the degree of attractiveness of each one of those factors, both for the current state and future projections, leading to a profile of the industry as the one presented in Figure 5–10. A summary of the overall industry assessment can be prepared as portrayed in Figure 5–11.
3. Extract from the analysis the key opportunities and threats associated with the business unit.

Strategic Groups Analysis

The industry analysis carried forward so far considers all participating firms in a unique pack, implicitly assuming that they share some characteristics, just by the fact of pertaining to the same industry. For a primary level of analysis, this is a good approximation, but it is not enough if we are interested in understanding more deeply the structural qualities of an industry. On a second level of analysis, we need to recognize that firms are not homogeneous. Consequently, to gain a more profound knowledge of the forms of competition, we must perform a subsequent stage of industry representation aimed, this time, at identifying the *strategic groups*. These groups correspond to aggregations of firms that include in a unique set those competitors that follow a common or similar strategy along well-defined dimensions. We can say then that groups collect firms which are relatively homogeneous according to the way they compete.

Porter suggests the following dimensions to identify differences in firm strategies within an industry: specialization, brand identification, push versus pull marketing approach, channel selection, product quality, technological leadership, vertical integration, cost position, service, price policy, financial and operating leverage, relationship with parent company, and relationship to home and host government.[6] We should try to locate in the same group all firms with comparable characteristics and following a similar competitive strategy.

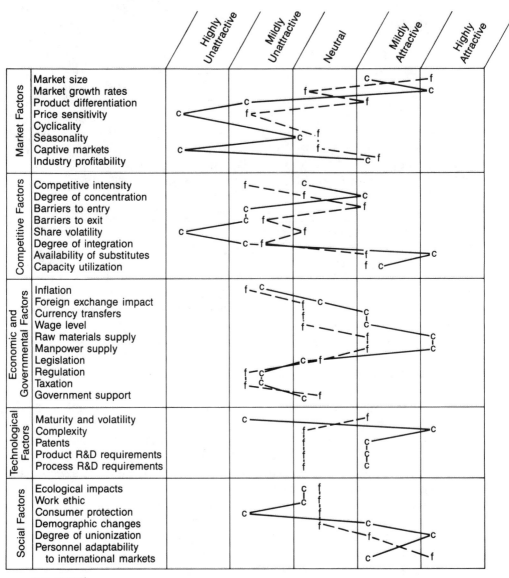

FIGURE 5–10. Illustration of an Industry Attractiveness Profile Based on External Factors Analysis

c = current
f = future

At this more detailed level of analysis, we could still apply the five-forces model to recognize the different degrees of attractiveness within the strategic groups in a process that might be referred to as industry analysis within an industry. Thus, the firm will have higher profits if it is located in a strategic group with the best combination of high *mobility barriers*, insulation from

FIGURE 5–11. Overall Assessment of Industry Attractiveness Based on External Factors Analysis

Industry Attractiveness

	CURRENT			FUTURE		
	Low Att.	Medium Att.	High Att.	Low Att.	Medium Att.	High Att.
Market factors			X			X
Competitive factors		X			X	
Economic and governmental factors			X		X	
Technological factors			X		X	
Social factors		X				X
Overall assessment			X		X	

intergroup rivalry and substitute products, and strong bargaining power with adjacent industries. Notice that the concept of entry barriers, applicable to the industry as a whole, has been replaced by mobility barriers, which capture the difficulty that a strategic group within an industry has to penetrate into an adjacent strategic group.

The structure within an industry consists of the configuration of strategic groups including mobility barriers, size and composition, strategic distance, and the relative market interdependence.

Essentially, the concept of strategic grouping is a very pragmatic approach aimed at cataloguing firms within an industry in accordance to the way they have chosen to seek competitive advantage. This segmentation is useful when one faces a high diversity of competitive positions in a fairly complex and heterogeneous industry. Typical examples of this situation are global industries with a wide variety of players, some being totally international and some purely local.

A useful tool that can guide the separation of strategic groups in an industry is the so-called *strategic mapping*. This is a two-dimensional display that helps to explain the different strategies of firms. Those dimensions should not be interdependent because otherwise the map would show an inherent correlation.

The two most common dimensions that are used for a strategic mapping purpose are the breadth of the product line and the degree of vertical integration. They allow us to separate firms which have a full coverage of product lines and, at the same time, are fully self-reliant from those firms which are focusing on a very narrow line and concentrating in a short range of the value-added chain. Figure 5–12 illustrates alternative strategic positionings of different competitors on those two dimensions.

To recognize the various strategic groups within an industry, we need to identify the critical explanatory variables that help to discriminate competitive positioning. This is an art more than a science, despite the numerous good-quality statistical efforts in this area. Therefore, we limit ourselves to providing

FIGURE 5–12. Strategic Groups Defined
in Generic Terms: An Illustration

Degree of Vertical Integration

	Low	High
Full Line	• Assembler • Very close to suppliers • Most likely a differentiated market coverage	• Full line • Vertically integrated • Most likely a low-cost competitor
Narrow Line	• Narrow line • Assembler • High price • High technology • High quality	• Highly focused • Highly automated • Low-cost production

(Breadth of Product Line — vertical axis label)

illustrations that might guide the reader into an understanding of this difficult task.

Our first example has to do with the investment banking industry in the middle 1980s in the United States.[7] In order to separate the various firms competing in that industry, we have chosen the following two dimensions: brand identification and product leadership.

With regard to *brand identification*, the industry can be classified into three tiers, characterized by prestige, type of client served, and special product and service expertise. The first tier includes firms that typically serve the investment banking needs of the largest corporations in the United States. They are among the best capitalized, with firmly established client relationships and extensive distribution systems. The second tier is formed by firms who have strong retail operations with some institutional business, serving smaller companies with smaller debt rating, and are not widely dispersed geographically. The third tier is composed by discount or retail brokers and smaller investment banks that serve the needs of small companies.

Regarding *product leadership*, there are firms known as great innovators, such as First Boston, a pioneer in interest rate swaps, collateralized mortgage obligations (CMO), public zero-coupon bonds, merger and acquisition strategies, and aggressive entry into international banking. In contrast, there are those who prefer to be followers, the most notable being Goldman Sachs. They are not great innovators but are masters at taking the innovations of others and perfecting them to the point where they have become one of the best at founding new services or products.

Figure 5–13 shows the strategic groups using the U.S. markets as a base, while Figure 5–14 shows the groups using the Eurobonds (international markets) as the base. The size of the circles represents the combined market share of firms in a strategic group within relevant markets.

Just as entry barriers protect the industry as a whole, mobility barriers protect the strategic groups. However, these mobility barriers are greater along

FIGURE 5–13. Strategic Groups Analysis of U.S. Investment Banks (93% of market) in the U.S. Underwriting Market

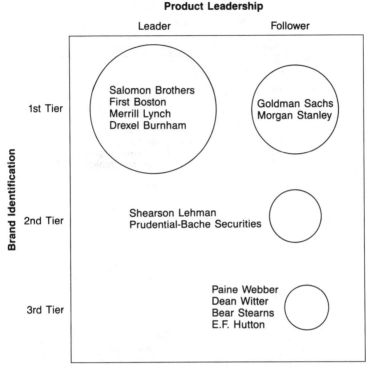

Product Leadership

Note: Circle size proportional to market share

SOURCE: Dexter H. Charles, *International Commercial Banks Take on Wall Street, An Analysis and Evaluation,* unpublished Masters thesis, Sloan School of Management, MIT, 1986. Reprinted by permission of Dexter H. Charles.

the vertical dimension (brand identification) than along the horizontal dimension (product leadership). Moving along the horizontal dimension can be achieved to a large extent through raiding the personnel of competitors. In contrast, moving between tiers is very difficult. Factors that determine a firm's tiering are its history, culture, contact and public prestige, clients, and so on. In many respects, investment banking is a snobbish industry.

In both the U.S. and international markets there is room for new entrants to create new strategic groupings. From comparing Figures 5–13 and 5–14, Wall Street is not as well represented in the international market. As a result, a new entrant may find easier going in this market.

Our second example is drawn from the world-wide telecommunications equipment industry.[8] We have selected one of the most popular frameworks to characterize strategic groups within a global industry.[9] It uses configuration and coordination of the value-added activities of the firm as the key elements of strategic mapping. The *configuration* dimension addresses the degree of geographical dispersion of the various activities performed by the business firm

FIGURE 5–14. Strategic Groups Analysis of U.S. Investment Banks (36% of market) in the Eurobond Underwriting Market

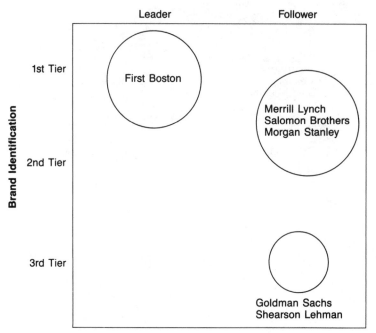

1985 Total = $134,401 Billion

Product Leadership

Note: Circle size proportional to market share

SOURCE: Charles (1986).

in a global setting. The *coordination* dimension identifies the degree of centralization that is imposed to properly integrate the activities of the firm.

Figure 5–15 lines up the major players of the world-wide telecommunications equipment industry according to these two criteria. The framework allows us to split the competing firms into four strategic groups. In the bottom-left quadrant, there are those firms which are either purely domestic or country-centered multinational corporations, which manage the subsidiaries as totally independent entities. In the upper-left corner, we identify those firms which are heavily centralized, but yet their presence covers a multitude of geographical locations. This is typical of foreign direct investments, with a high degree of centralized control from headquarters. In the bottom-right corner, we find those firms which are simply exporting from a home base with a completely decentralized marketing strategy. Finally, in the upper-right corner, we encounter those companies pursuing a global strategy, maintaining a centralized coordination from a headquarters position.

A second framework to identify global strategic groups is based on the

FIGURE 5–15. Configuration and Coordination of Activities
of Telecommunications Equipment Firms

Configuration

	Multiple Location	Single Location
Centralized	*High foreign investment with strong control* • GTE • Siemens	*Pure global strategy* • AT&T • Northern Telecom
Decentralized	*Country-centered multinational corporations or domestic firms* • GEC • Hassler (Swiss) • Plessey • STA (Swedish) • ITT Europe • TUN (West German)	*Export-based strategy with decentralized marketing* • LM Ericsson • Hitachi • NEC • CIT-Alcatel • Fujitsu

SOURCE: Lynnet Koh, *Strategic Analysis of the Worldwide Telecommunications Industry,* unpublished Masters thesis, Sloan School of Management, MIT, 1986. Reprinted by permission of Lynnet Koh.

breadth of the product line and the global geographical coverage as the two discriminant dimensions.[10] The resultant categorization is presented in Figure 5–16, which segments the firms into five different strategic groups. Firms that offer a broad product range in a global setting can be differentiated by their strategic positioning into either attempting to achieve global cost leadership or global differentiation. Those firms retaining a global scope with a narrow range of products are pursuing a niche strategy through global segmentation. Broad product lines at a country level can normally be explained exclusively in terms of protectionist policies of the local country. And finally, a narrow range at the country level is the residue that belongs to local firms pursuing a limited competitive position responding to national interest or taste.

Figure 5–17 illustrates the five strategic groups just described within the context of the consumer electronic industry in the mid-1980s. It is upsetting to see the limited role played by American firms RCA and Zenith, which not so long ago were important international players and are now relegated to an insignificant global role. It is also interesting to observe the strategic positioning of the European firms, which are benefitting from a highly protected national environment. However, in the late 1980s this situation is not expected to prevail because changes are fast paced. The Korean and Taiwanese firms are seeking a global positioning from a narrow product line. The key issue with respect to those firms is whether the magnitude of mobility barriers will allow them to easily move into a broad range of products, where they will be facing the most stable Japanese and Dutch competitors.

FIGURE 5–16. Global Strategic Groups:
Five Strategic Alternatives
for a Global Company

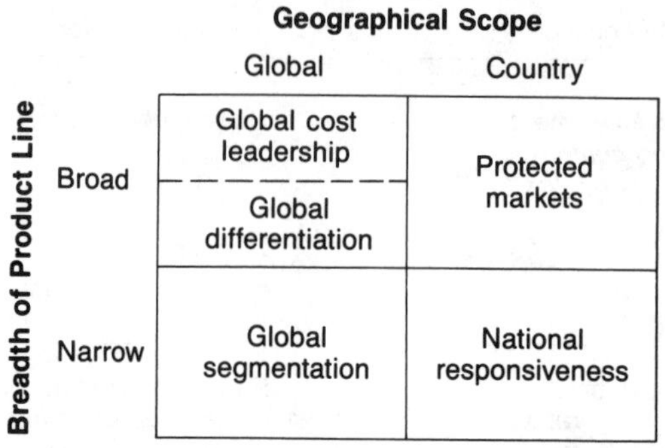

Geographical Scope

	Global	Country
Broad	Global cost leadership ——————— Global differentiation	Protected markets
Narrow	Global segmentation	National responsiveness

Breadth of Product Line

FIGURE 5–17. An Illustration of Global
Strategic Groups: The
Consumer Electronic
Industry in the Mid-1980s

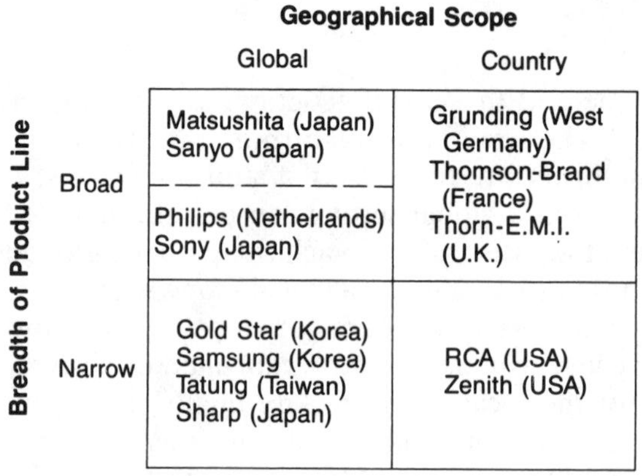

Geographical Scope

	Global	Country
Broad	Matsushita (Japan) Sanyo (Japan) ——————— Philips (Netherlands) Sony (Japan)	Grunding (West Germany) Thomson-Brand (France) Thorn-E.M.I. (U.K.)
Narrow	Gold Star (Korea) Samsung (Korea) Tatung (Taiwan) Sharp (Japan)	RCA (USA) Zenith (USA)

Breadth of Product Line

The Financial Statement Analysis Framework

In this section, we cover a methodological approach to gather quantitative intelligence at the level of the firm, based on financial statements analysis. One of the most widely distributed sources of information of all firms in any industry are the set of three financial statements—balance sheet, income statement, and statement of changes in the financial position—and the 10K reports, which must be made public periodically by all major corporations. It is only natural, then, to make use of that information for gaining certain understanding of the competitive position of different firms in an industry. The appropriate technique to perform this task has been known for many years, and it is called *financial statement analysis* (FSA).

There are two basic procedures to make these figures more easily comparable among different competitors: (1) define common-size financial statements, and (2) perform a financial ratio analysis. Let us review these procedures now.[11]

DEFINITION OF COMMON-SIZE FINANCIAL STATEMENTS

Corporations in an industry are normally of quite different size. Therefore, to say that accounts receivable in firm A are larger than in firm B does not carry too much information. One simple transformation to make financial statements comparable across all firms in an industry is to standardize all of them to a common size, usually 100. In Figure 5–18 we present the common-size balance sheet and income statement for a group of companies in the pharmaceutical industry. We can see, for example, that for Squibb Corp., cash and marketable securities are comparably low, while long-term debt is comparatively high. Also, its income after taxes is the lowest in the industry. This procedure helps us to identify when a player departs from the norms prevailing in the industry and allows us to raise questions with regard to what may be considered as abnormal behavior.

FINANCIAL RATIO ANALYSIS

This is the most extensively used form of financial statement analysis. The ratio analysis is aimed at characterizing the firm in a few basic dimensions considered fundamental to assess the financial health of a company. They are usually categorized in five types:

- Liquidity ratios
- Leverage-capital structure ratios
- Profitability ratios
- Turnover ratios
- Common stock security ratios

Liquidity Ratios
A liquid firm is one that can meet short-term financial obligations without much of a problem when they fall due. This ability is normally measured in terms of three different ratios:

$$\text{Current ratio} = \frac{\text{Current assets}}{\text{Current liabilities}}$$

FIGURE 5–18. Common-Size Statements for a Group of Companies in the Pharmaceutical Industry

A. COMMON-SIZE BALANCE SHEET (%)

	Abbott Labs	Bristol Myers Co.	Syntex Corp.	Smith-Kline Corp.	Eli Lilly & Co.	Merck Co.	Searle Co.	Squibb Corp.	Group Mean
ASSETS									
Cash and Marketable Securities	5	17	20	21	9	10	20	8	14
Accounts Receivable	16	26	15	21	22	19	19	21	20
Inventories	18	23	19	16	23	22	12	20	19
Other Current Assets	6	5	2	1	3	0	3	5	3
Net Plant and Equipment	31	23	35	31	35	41	26	25	31
Investments and Other Assets	24	6	9	10	8	8	20	21	13
	100	100	100	100	100	100	100	100	100
LIABILITIES AND EQUITY									
Accounts payable	5	7	8	8	4	13	15	17	8
Other Current Liabilities	31	23	17	17	24	10	18	6	18
Long-Term Debt	9	4	12	10	2	7	8	20	10
Deferred Tax & Other Liabilities	6	3	0	0	5	4	6	4	4
Stockholders' Equity	49	63	63	65	65	66	53	53	60
	100	100	100	100	100	100	100	100	100

B. COMMON-SIZE INCOME STATEMENT (%)

	Abbott Labs	Bristol Myers Co.	Syntex Corp.	Smith-Kline Corp.	Eli Lilly & Co.	Merck Co.	Searle Co.	Squibb Corp.	Group Mean
REVENUES	100	100	100	100	100	100	100	100	100
EXPENSES									
Cost of Goods Sold	55	38	35	31	39	39	33	41	39
Research & Development	5	4	9	8	8	8	9	6	7
Marketing, G&A Expenses	22	42	38	32	30	27	38	36	33
Interest Expense	0	0	0	1	1	1	0	3	1
Other Expense	1	0	0	2	1	1	4	5	2
Tax	6	7	4	8	7	9	6	2	6
Income After Tax	11	9	14	18	14	15	10	7	12
	100	100	100	100	100	100	100	100	100

SOURCE: Adapted from Marianne Kunschak and Luis F. Tena-Ramirez, "Strategic Management for a Pharmaceutical Company: A Case Study," 1983. Reprinted by permission of Marianne Kunschak and Luis F. Tena-Ramirez.

This is just a ratio between short-term assets and short-term liabilities. *Current assets* are made up of cash, short-term marketable securities, accounts receivable, inventories, and prepaid expenses. *Current liabilities* are made up of accounts payable, dividends, taxes due within one year, and short-term bank loans.

$$\text{Quick ratio} = \frac{\text{Cash} + \overset{\text{Short-term}}{\text{marketable securities}} + \overset{\text{Accounts}}{\text{receivable}}}{\text{Current liabilities}}$$

This is a more stringent definition of liquidity which is commonly called the acid test. Among the short-term assets only the most liquid ones are included, leaving aside inventories and prepaid expenses.

$$\underset{\text{interval (days)}}{\text{Defensive}} = \frac{\text{Cash} + \overset{\text{Short-term}}{\text{marketable securities}} + \overset{\text{Accounts}}{\text{receivable}}}{\text{Projected daily operating expenditures}}$$

This ratio is an estimate of the total number of days of operation that can be financed with the most liquid of short-term assets (also called defensive assets).

Projected daily operating expenditures can be estimated by adding together cost of goods sold; excise taxes; marketing, administrative, and general expenses; interest expenses; and other expenses; and then deducting depreciation and deferred tax and dividing that figure by 365 (days of the year).

The values of these three ratios for a group of companies in the pharmaceutical industry are presented in Figure 5–19 on page 66. It can be observed that in all three measures, Abbott Labs presents the most critical condition, while Squibb appears well protected for fulfilling its short-term obligations, at least as reflected by the current and quick ratios.

Due to the importance of cash and marketable securities as a source to meet operative expenditures and other cash demands, three additional financial ratios are sometimes used to define the *cash position* of the firm.

$$\frac{\text{Cash} + \text{Short-term marketable securities}}{\text{Current liability}}$$

$$\frac{\text{Cash} + \text{Short-term marketable securities}}{\text{Sales}}$$

$$\frac{\text{Cash} + \text{Short-term marketable securities}}{\text{Total assets}}$$

FIGURE 5–19. Liquidity Ratios for a Group of Companies in the Pharmaceutical Industry

	ABBOTT LABS	BRISTOL MYERS CO.	SYNTEX CORP.	SMITH-KLINE CORP.	ELI LILLY & CO.	MERCK CO.	SEARLE CO.	SQUIBB CORP.	GROUP MEAN
Current ratio	1.22	2.38	2.23	2.28	2.40	2.04	2.40	2.29	2.20
Quick ratio	0.59	1.35	1.35	1.49	1.69	1.09	1.73	1.32	1.33
Defensive intervals(days)	97	135	135	206	220	179	222	126	165

SOURCE: Adapted from Kunschak and Tena-Ramirez (1983). Reprinted by permission of Marianne Kunschak.

Obviously, the greater the value of these ratios, the better the cash position of the firm.

Moreover, increasing emphasis is being given to the capacity of the firm for generating cash. Since most firms do not report directly cash-flow information in their financial statements, additional computations have to be made to figure out "working capital from operations" and "cash flow from operations." These two concepts allow us to compute the following financial ratios which introduce both working capital and cash flow.

$$\frac{\text{Working capital from operations}}{\text{Sales}}$$

$$\frac{\text{Working capital from operations}}{\text{Total assets [average]}}$$

$$\frac{\text{Cash flow from operations}}{\text{Sales}}$$

$$\frac{\text{Cash flow from operations}}{\text{Total assets [average]}}$$

Leverage-Capital Structure Ratios

These ratios measure the use of leverage in the firm (debt versus equity capital) and the ability it has to fulfill its long-term commitments with debtholders. These are the most commonly used ratios:

$$\text{Leverage of long-term debt} = \frac{\text{Long-term debt}}{\text{Shareholders' equity}}$$

$$\text{Leverage of total debt} = \frac{\text{Current liabilities} + \text{Long-term debt}}{\text{Shareholders' equity}}$$

These two leverage ratios measure the number of debt dollars (either long term or total debt) per equity dollar

$$\text{Times interest earned} = \frac{\text{Operating income}}{\text{Annual interest payments}}$$

where: Operating income = Sales − (Cost of goods sold + Excise tax + Marketing, administrative, and general expenses).

This ratio measures the number of times that interest payments could be covered by operating income (profit before interest and taxes). The larger the ratio, the more certain is the ability of the firm to make its interest payments, and consequently, the lower the risk borne by debtholders.

In Figure 5–20 (see page 69) we present the leverage-capital structure ratios for a group of companies in the pharmaceutical industry. Abbott Labs appears again as the most levered company with a 0.93 ratio of total debt to equity and it is closely followed by Squibb with a 0.84 ratio. Curiously enough, Squibb shows to be very liquid in the short run, but rather illiquid in the long run, with earnings only four times interest payments.

Another debt-service ratio that has been proposed takes into consideration the portion of the annual interest payments covered by cash flow, as follows:

$$\frac{\text{Cash flow from operations}}{\text{Annual interest payments}}$$

Profitability Ratios
Profitability ratios measure the ability of the firm to generate profits. There are different measures of profitability, three being the most widely used:

$$\frac{\text{Return on}}{\text{total assets}} = \frac{\text{Net income after tax} + \text{Interest expenses} - \text{Tax benefits of interest expenses}}{\text{Total assets}}$$

This is a measure of the profitability of the business, independent of the source of financing.

$$\frac{\text{Return on}}{\text{equity}} = \frac{\text{Net income after taxes available to common shareholders}}{\text{Common shareholders' equity}}$$

This ratio measures the profitability of the firm to common shareholders, that is, to equity owners. Interest payments are deducted this time from the measure of profit in the numerator.

$$\text{Sales margin} = \frac{\text{Revenues} - \text{Operating expenses}}{\text{Revenues}}$$

This is a measure of the operating profit in relation to revenues from sales.

In Figure 5–21 (see page 69) we present the profitability ratios for a group of companies in the pharmaceutical industry. What is most noticeable in this table is the low sales margin of Squibb Corp. Over total assets, the return is quite comparable with most corporations, except for Smith-Kline

FIGURE 5-20. Leverage-Capital Structure Ratios for a Group of Companies in the Pharmaceutical Industry

	ABBOTT LABS	BRISTOL MYERS CO.	SYNTEX CORP.	SMITH-KLINE CORP.	ELI LILLY & CO.	MERCK CO.	SEARLE CO.	SQUIBB CORP.	GROUP MEAN
Long-term debt / Shareholders' equity	0.18	0.07	0.16	0.11	0.03	0.11	0.33	0.39	0.17
Total debt / Shareholders' equity	0.93	0.59	0.54	0.50	0.46	0.46	0.76	0.84	0.64
Times interest earned	3.2	9.4	4.4	15.8	13.1	11.2	5.3	4.0	8.3

SOURCE: Adapted from Kunschak and Tena-Ramirez (1983). Reprinted by permission of Marianne Kunschak.

FIGURE 5-21. Profitability Ratios for a Group of Companies in the Pharmaceutical Industry

	ABBOTT LABS	BRISTOL MYERS CO.	SYNTEX CORP.	SMITH-KLINE CORP.	ELI LILLY & CO.	MERCK CO.	SEARLE CO.	SQUIBB CORP.	GROUP MEAN
Return on total assets	0.12	0.13	0.14	0.20	0.14	0.15	0.11	0.12	0.14
Return on shareholders' equity	0.21	0.20	0.20	0.30	0.20	0.22	0.17	0.10	0.20
Sales margin (5-year average)	0.44	0.62	0.63	0.66	0.61	0.62	0.67	0.53	0.60

SOURCE: Adapted from Kunschak and Tena-Ramirez (1983). Reprinted by permission of Marianne Kunschak.

Corp. which shows very high profitability in all three indices. But the return on equity is only half the level of other corporations, and the sales margin is still lower. This points again to the capital structure problem, and most likely to an inadequate production-cost structure.

Turnover Ratios

Turnover ratios are also called efficiency ratios because they measure performance in the utilization of assets. The most popular ratios are:

$$\frac{\text{Total assets}}{\text{turnover}} = \frac{\text{Sales}}{\text{Average total assets}}$$

This ratio indicates the number of times that "assets are sold" in a stated period.

$$\frac{\text{Average collection}}{\text{period (days)}} = \frac{\text{Average (net) accounts receivable}}{\text{Daily sales}}$$

This is the average number of days required for the collection of payments on credit sales.

$$\text{Inventory turnover} = \frac{\text{Cost of goods sold}}{\text{Average inventory}}$$

In this case the ratio refers to the number of times that "inventories are sold."

In Figure 5–22 (see page 71) we present the turnover ratios for a group of companies in the pharmaceutical industry. This time Squibb shows the lowest efficiency indicators, with only 0.81 for asset turnover (low sales compared to assets) and 3.9 for inventory turnover (too much inventory for the prevailing level of sales). Also a collection period of over 100 days speaks of credit terms more generous than other firms in the industry. Is this an intended policy or is it just the result of poor collection practices?

Common Stock Security Ratios

Financial analysts often express some of the information contained in the financial statements on a per-share basis. This is done in order to capture information which is central for the equityholders to judge the firm's performance. The most commonly used of these ratios are:

$$\text{Earnings per share (EPS)} = \frac{\text{Net income available for common}}{\text{Number of shares outstanding}}$$

FIGURE 5-22. Turnover Ratios for a Group of Companies in the Pharmaceutical Industry

	ABBOTT LABS	BRISTOL MYERS CO.	SYNTEX CORP.	SMITH-KLINE CORP.	ELI LILLY & CO.	MERCK CO.	SEARLE CO.	SQUIBB CORP.	GROUP MEAN
Total asset turnover	1.06	1.49	0.96	1.15	0.96	1.00	0.86	0.81	1.04
Average collection period (days)	56	57	56	67	83	68	79	101	68
Inventory turnover	5.8	6.3	5.3	6.3	4.1	4.6	7.3	3.9	5.5

SOURCE: Adapted from Kunschak and Tena-Ramirez (1983). Reprinted by permission of Marianne Kunschak.

$$\text{Book value per share} = \frac{\text{Shareholders' equity}}{\text{Number of shares outstanding}}$$

$$\text{Dividends per share} = \frac{\text{Dividends paid on common}}{\text{Number of shares outstanding}}$$

$$\text{Dividend yield} = \frac{\text{Dividends per share}}{\text{Price per share}}$$

$$\text{Market-to-book value (M/B)} = \frac{\text{Price per share}}{\text{Book value per share}}$$

A highly relevant measurement for assessing the economic performance of a firm in terms of value creation is the market-to-book value ratio, which is discussed extensively in Chapter 15. In Figure 5–23, we provide the trend of M/B values for Squibb Corporation, Smith-Kline (an outstanding performer within its industry), and the drug industry average. The differences observed in these ratios constitute evidence on the actual investment opportunities of the firms, as suggested by:

1. Squibb's M/B ratio experiences an important increase in 19X5, when new and quite profitable products were introduced by the company.
2. Smith-Kline's M/B ratio is very high, though it shows a persistent downward trend that could be explained by the prompt expiration of a valuable patent (Tagamet).
3. The average M/B ratio for pharmaceutical companies is relatively high, which indicates a favorable comparison with alternative investment opportunities.

Other Measures of Performance

Besides the five categories of financial ratios we have described, often it is useful to include other performance measurements particularly critical in a given

FIGURE 5–23. The M/B Ratio for Squibb Corporation, Smith-Kline Corporation, and the Pharmaceutical Industry

	19X1	19X2	19X3	19X4	19X5
Squibb Corporation	1.88	1.85	1.32	1.38	1.99
Smith-Kline	6.32	5.71	5.34	4.61	3.73
Drug industry (world-wide)	2.00	1.88	1.76	1.89	2.19

SOURCE: Adapted from Kunschak and Tena-Ramirez (1983). Reprinted by permission of Marianne Kunschak.

industry. For instance, for high-technology firms, comparative measures pertaining to R&D expenses could be quite significant. Likewise, for firms with high capital intensity, it could be interesting to observe the ratio of capital investment over sales. In most industries, the firm's growth compared to the industry growth is an important indicator of the changes of relative market share for each of the competitors. Figure 5–24 shows additional measures of performance which were considered significant for a group of companies in the pharmaceutical industry. The data associated with sales growth and relative market share positioning (company growth versus industry growth) present Smith-Kline and Syntex Corporation as those gaining competitive positioning more aggressively. All other companies seem more or less to maintain their existing shares. It is clear from the figures that the pharmaceutical industry is exceedingly high in the intensity of R&D expenditures. Abbott Laboratories stands alone as the lowest spender in R&D, among the group of companies being considered. This should be a matter of concern for them.

DEFINING THE STANDARD OF COMPARISON: CROSS-SECTIONAL VERSUS TIME-SERIES ANALYSIS

To interpret fully the meaning of a ratio we need standards of comparison. For example, it is a commonly held belief to think that a corporation with a liquidity ratio of 2 or more and a quick ratio of 1 or more could be considered liquid. But these absolute standards are very hard to justify. For that reason, the preferred two methodologies to define standards for the interpretation of common-size statements and financial ratio analysis use relative indicators. These methodologies follow.

The *cross-sectional analysis* takes all firms in an industry at a given point in time and allows the comparison of their relative standing. The usual reference selected in this case is the mean or the median for the group of industries. Figures 5–18 through 5–22 and 5–24, which correspond to illustrations of cross-sectional analysis of both common-size statements and financial ratios, include the group mean in the final column.

In the case of *time-series analysis*, the interest is centered on the evolution of an indicator through a period of many years, so the criteria for analysis are not only the behavior of selected indicators for the competitors in the industry, but also the pattern shown by all indicators through time, including the average or median for the group of firms. For example, in Figure 5–25 on page 75 we present the return on equity and return on total assets for Squibb Corporation and for the industry average between 19X1 and 19X5. In this period, Squibb shows a persistent deterioration of these two indicators, being more pronounced in the return-on-equity ratio. It is interesting to notice that in 19X1, Squibb presented an average profitability as measured by those two indicators, but in all other years it is markedly below the average.

FIGURE 5–24. Other Measures of Performance for a Group of Companies in the Pharmaceutical Industry

Growth Performance Measures Five-Year Average (19×1 Through 19×5)	ABBOTT LABS	BRISTOL MYERS CO.	SYNTEX CORP.	SMITH-KLINE CORP.	ELI LILLY & CO.	MERCK CO.	SEARLE CO.	SQUIBB CORP.	GROUP MEAN
Average sales growth %*	16	9.4	19	23	13	9	5.3	14	14
19×5 Sales growth %*	18	14	26	17	12	12	17	18	17
R&D expenses as % of sales	5	9.1	9.1	7.4	8.1	8.2	8	6.1	8
Capital investment/sales	6.5	4.1	8	9.7	7.3	8.7	8.4	6.1	7
Company growth/industry growth*	1.04	0.99	1.1	1.12	1.03	1.03	0.97	0.96	1.03

*Real dollars

SOURCE: Kunschak and Tena-Ramirez (1983), pp. 41, 43, 44, 45. Reprinted by permission of Marianne Kunschak.

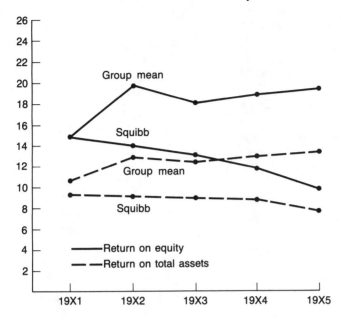

FIGURE 5–25. Profitability Ratios for Squibb and a Group of Companies in the Pharmaceutical Industry

Notes

1. The five-forces model for industry attractiveness is presented in detail in Michael E. Porter, *Competitive Strategy* (New York: The Free Press, 1980). The foundations of the model are rooted in the field of industry organization. For an introduction to the principles of this field, the reader is referred to Richard E. Caves, *American Industry: Structure, Conduct, Performance*, 6th ed. (Englewood Cliffs, NJ: Prentice Hall, 1987); and F. M. Scherer, *Industrial Market Structure and Economic Performance*, 2nd ed. (New York: Houghton Mifflin, 1980). For a comprehensive application of this model to a wide variety of industries, see Walter Adams, *The Structure of American Industry*, 7th ed. (New York: Macmillan, 1986).

2. The presentation of the engineering polymers industry follows Emmanuel P. Maceda, *Strategic Analysis: Du Pont Company, Engineering Polymers Division*, unpublished student paper, Sloan School of Management, MIT, 1988.

3. The discussion of the semiconductor industry is based on Scott Beardsley and Kenji Sakajami, *Advanced MicroDevices: Posed for Chip Greatness*, unpublished student paper, Sloan School of Management, MIT, 1988.

4. The industries mentioned as examples of high and poor profitability sectors were identified from the *Forbes Annual Report* in the January 11, 1988 issue.

5. For a further discussion of the strategic impact of information technologies, the reader is referred to: James I. Cash, Jr. and Benn R. Konsynski, "IS Redraws Competitive Boundaries," *Harvard Business Review* (March–April 1985), 134–142; F. Warren McFarlan, "Information Technology Changes the Way You Compete," *Harvard Business Review* (May–June 1984), 98–103; Gregory L. Parsons, "Information Technology: A New Competitive Weapon," *Sloan Management Review* (Fall 1983); Michael E. Porter and Victor E. Millar, "How Information Gives You Competitive Advantage," *Harvard Business Review* (July–August 1985), 149–160; and John F. Rockart and Michael S. Scott Morton, "Implications of Changes in Information Technology for Corporate Strategy," *Interfaces*, 1, no. 14 (January–February 1984), 84–95.

6. For an additional reference of the strategic groups concept, the reader is referred to Michael E. Porter, *Competitive Strategy* (New York: The Free Press, 1980); and Kathryn Rudie Harrigan, *Strategic Flexibility* (Lexington, MA: Lexington Books, 1985).

7. The example of the investment banking industry is taken from Dexter H. Charles, *International Commercial Banks Take on Wall Street, An Analysis and Evaluation*, unpublished Masters thesis, Sloan School of Management, MIT, 1986.

8. This example is drawn from the work of Lynette Koh Sui Lin, *Strategic Analysis of the Worldwide Telecommunications Industry*, unpublished Masters thesis, Sloan School of Management, MIT, 1986.

9. For a further discussion of the configuration-coordination framework, see Michael E. Porter, *Competition in Global Industries* (Boston, MA: Harvard Business School Press, 1986).

10. Porter, *Competition in Global Industries* (1986), op. cit.

11. For a comprehensive review of financial statement analysis, see George Foster, *Financial Statement Analysis*, 2nd ed. (Englewood Cliffs, NJ: Prentice Hall, 1986).

6

Internal Scrutiny at the Business Level

We have indicated before that there are two key issues regarding the choice of a business competitive strategy. One is the attractiveness of the industry in which the business is placed, assessed primarily by its long-term profitability prospects. The other is the set of factors that determines the competitive position the business will adopt in order to gain a sustainable competitive advantage. It is the second subject that becomes the central concern of this chapter.

In order to examine systematically the ways available to a business to achieve a long-lasting competitive advantage, it is not possible to look at the firm's activities as a whole. Rather, it is necessary to disaggregate a business unit into strategically relevant stages to take into full account all of the tasks that are conducted to add value. These tasks include: product development and design, production, distribution, marketing, sales, services, and the many forms of support required for the smooth operation of a business. A valuable framework to accomplish this objective is the *value chain,* whose implications to achieve competitive advantage have been thoroughly explored by Porter.[1]

The Value Chain

The focus of analysis of the value chain is the SBU. The underlying principle is that all of the tasks performed by a business organization can be classified into nine different broad categories. Five of them are the so-called *primary activities,* and the other four are labeled *support activities.* A full representation of the value chain is given in Figure 6–1.

The primary activities are those involved in the physical movement of raw materials and finished products, in the production of goods and services, and in the marketing, sales, and subsequent services of the outputs of the business firm. To some extent, they can be thought of as the classical managerial functions of the firm, where there is an organizational entity with a manager in charge of a very specific task, and with full balance between authority and responsibility. The support activities, however, are much more pervasive. As their name indicates, their essential role is to provide support not only to the

FIGURE 6–1. The Value Chain

SOURCE: This setup for the value chain was suggested by Michael E. Porter (1985), op. cit.

primary activities, but to each other. They are composed by the managerial infrastructure of the firm—which includes all processes and systems to assure proper coordination and accountability—human resource management, technology development, and procurement.

It is easy to see that those support activities are spread out around the whole business organization. The responsibility for financial, human, and technological resources of the business do not reside exclusively with the controller, personnel, and R&D manager, respectively. They are central matters of concern to all of the key managers, regardless of their range of immediate authority. Likewise, procurement is an activity that permeates far beyond the centralized purchasing function.

Perhaps the only point worth stressing is the role that technology is playing in business firms today. Not long ago, technology was regarded as the exclusive province of the R&D managers, not much different from what a manufacturer manager's role is today. Now, particularly with the advent of information technology, this activity is truly pervasive and affects the way to achieve competitive advantage in all of the key managerial tasks of the firm.

Figure 6–2 provides a brief description of both primary and support activities.

Since the value chain is composed of the set of activities performed by the business unit, it provides a very effective way to diagnose the position of the business against its major competitors, and to define the foundation for actions aimed at sustaining a competitive advantage. As opposed to the forces which determine the industry attractiveness to the business, which are largely external and uncontrollable by the firm, the activities of the value chain constitute the foundation of the controllable factors to achieve competitive superiority. Their analysis leads us to identify the critical success factors that are central to compete, and to understand how to develop the unique competencies which provide the basis for sound business leadership.

FIGURE 6–2. Definition of Activities in the Value Chain

PRIMARY ACTIVITIES

Inbound Logistics
Receiving, storing, materials handling, warehousing, inventory control, vehicle scheduling, and returns to suppliers.

Operations
Transforming inputs into final product form (e.g., machining, packaging, assembly, equipment maintenance, testing, printing, and facility operations)

Outbound Logistics
Distributing the finished product (e.g., finished goods warehousing, material handling, delivery vehicle operation, order processing, and scheduling)

Marketing and Sales
Induce and facilitate buyers to purchase the product (e.g., advertising, sales force, quoting, channel selection, channel relations, and pricing)

Service
Maintain or enhance value of product after sale (e.g., installation, repair, training, parts supply, and product adjustment)

SUPPORT ACTIVITIES

Procurement
Purchasing of raw materials, supplies, and other consumable items as well as assets

Technology Development
Know-how, procedures, and technological inputs needed in every value chain activity

Human Resource Management
Selection, promotion, and placement; appraisal; rewards; management development; and labor/employee relations

Firm Infrastructure
General management, planning, finance, accounting, legal, government affairs, and quality management

A final comment has to do with the designation of value. The value generated by a business chain is measured by the total revenues collected by the buyers' payment for the business output. Added value is created whenever the buyers' contribution exceeds the total cost resulting from the completion of all the activities in the chain. The word *margin* at the end of the chain intends to capture precisely the difference between the total value generated and the aggregated cost of the value activities.

ILLUSTRATION OF THE VALUE CHAIN: U.S. TELECOMMUNICATIONS INDUSTRY

To show the communicational power of the value chain and its effectiveness for contrasting various competitive positions of different business firms in a given industry, we have chosen to compare AT&T, NYNEX, and IBM value chains in the telecommunications industry.[2] AT&T is a dominant firm in U.S. telecommunications, NYNEX is one of the leading Bell operating companies serving the New York and New England area, and IBM is a growing force in this industry.

The telecommunications industry today is in a state of flux, due to the rapid progress in technology and changes in the regulatory and competitive environment. The increasing technological sophistication in many telecommunication networks has expanded the range of products being offered. It has also increased the pressures on major players to maintain their technological edge as a competitive tool. There are three classes of products: public networks (for example, telephone lines, satellites), customer-premise equipment (CPE, ranging from answering machines to sophisticated PBXs), and value-added network services (VANs, like electronic mail, videotext, voice messaging).

Figures 6–3, 6–4, and 6–5 present the value chains for the three corporations. It is fascinating to contrast their different competitive strength. AT&T has a nation-wide presence, a strong technological and procurement leadership through Bell Labs and Western Electric, the strongest telecommunications

FIGURE 6–3. Value Chain for AT&T

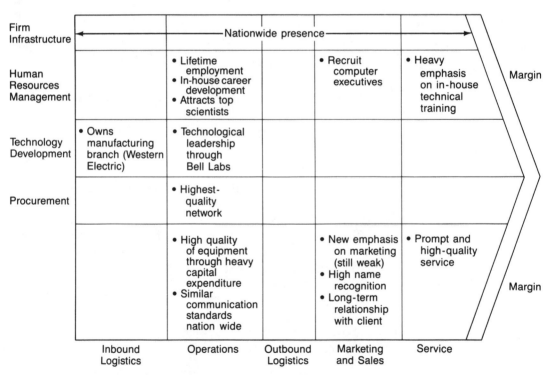

Firm Infrastructure					
	← Nationwide presence →				Margin
Human Resources Management		• Lifetime employment • In-house career development • Attracts top scientists		• Recruit computer executives	• Heavy emphasis on in-house technical training
Technology Development	• Owns manufacturing branch (Western Electric)	• Technological leadership through Bell Labs			
Procurement		• Highest-quality network			
		• High quality of equipment through heavy capital expenditure • Similar communication standards nation wide		• New emphasis on marketing (still weak) • High name recognition • Long-term relationship with client	• Prompt and high-quality service
	Inbound Logistics	Operations	Outbound Logistics	Marketing and Sales	Service

SOURCE: Mark A. Webster, *Strategic Analysis of AT&T, NYNEX and IBM in the Telecommunications Industry*, unpublished student paper, Sloan School of Management, MIT, 1988. Reprinted by permission of Mark A. Webster.

FIGURE 6–4. Value Chain for NYNEX

Firm Infrastructure					
	←———————— Regional Monopoly ————————→				
Human Resources Management	• Recent change in employee attitudes (less job security)		• Hold sales force responsible for client satisfaction		Margin
Technology Development	• New software products		• Better use of customer database		
Procurement	• Free to use any supplier it wants to				
	• Introduced innovative equipment from outside suppliers • High-quality network through heavy capital investment	• Sales and distribution centers close to customers	• Use of Bell logo • Focus on top 1000 corporate customers • International focus (Europe)	• Prompt and high-quality service	Margin
	Inbound Logistics	Operations	Outbound Logistics	Marketing and Sales	Service

SOURCE: Webster (1988).

network, and a great reputation for high-quality service. NYNEX enjoys a regional monopoly, freedom to use any suppliers, proximity to the customer, as well as a service image. IBM is attempting to position itself in this important industry using its enormous world-wide reputation for excellence in computers, that gives it easy access to most major corporations. Its alliance with ROM and MCI, and its strong capabilities in software and hardware technologies, provide IBM a solid foundation to launch a competitive assault in telecommunications.

It is hard to predict the final competitive position of these three corporations in the telecommunications industry. It will depend eventually on a variety of outside factors, such as government regulation, technological development, evolution of customers' expectations, and most importantly the exact scope of the market in which the three firms compete. There are two trends which seem to define this scope: the blurring of the computer and communications industry into a still nebulous information society, and the trend toward globalization of major markets.

FIGURE 6-5. Value Chain for IBM (in telecommunications)

	Inbound Logistics	Operations	Outbound Logistics	Marketing and Sales	Service	
Firm Infrastructure	◄───── Multidomestic Presence ─────►					Margin
	◄───── Access to Most Major Corporations ─────►					
Human Resources management		• Lifetime employment • In-house career development		• All employees think in marketing terms	• In-house technical training	
Technology Development		• Strong R&D resources	• Strong software capability			
Procurement	• Owns Rolm, CPE manufacturer					
		• Leading computer technology used in-house • Partnership with MCI		• Strong reputation for excellence • Already sells to most major corporations • Experienced sales force	• Extensive buyer training	Margin
	Inbound Logistics	Operations	Outbound Logistics	Marketing and Sales	Service	

SOURCE: Webster (1988).

Generic Competitive Strategies

The analysis that we have been conducting so far of the segmentation of the business, assessment of industry attractiveness, and evaluation of competitive capabilities through the value chain activities has as sole objective the definition of the business position in the industry. The idea is to seek a competitive advantage, which means enjoying a sustainable level of profitability above the industry average.

Porter states that a business can enjoy a competitive advantage exclusively by one of two basic generic strategies: cost leadership or differentiation.[3] A final understanding of whatever strengths and weaknesses a business could have relative to its competitors can only be explained either by a relative cost advantage or a differentiation capability. Both of these generic ways to compete are born from the businesses' abilities to understand and deal with the five forces of industry structure and the exploitation of internal capabilities anchored in the value chain activities.

These two generic ways to compete can be combined with the market scope in which the firm attempts to achieve competitive advantage. The resultant alternatives lead to three generic strategies, depending on whether the firm is seeking a competitive position in the overall industry, or whether it will concentrate its activities on a narrow market scope. These generic strategies are overall cost leadership, differentiation, or focus and can be described as follows:

1. *Overall cost leadership* requires aggressive construction of efficient-scale facilities, vigorous pursuit of cost reductions from experience, tight costs and overhead control, avoidance of marginal customer accounts, and cost minimization in areas like R&D, service, sales force, advertising, and so on.
2. *Differentiation* calls for creating something that is perceived *industry-wide* as being unique. Approaches to differentiation can take many forms: design or brand image, technology, features, customer service, dealer network, or other dimensions.
3. *Focus* consists of concentrating on a particular buyer group, segment of the product line, or geographic market. As with differentiation, focus may take many forms. Although the low-cost and differentiation strategies are aimed at achieving those objectives industry-wide, the entire focus strategy is built around servicing a particular target very well, and each functional policy is developed with this in mind.

Figure 6–6 shows how these strategies relate to the breadth of the strategic scope. As the figure clearly indicates, even when selecting a narrow market scope the two basic strategies to achieve competitive advantage are cost leadership and differentiation.

SOURCES OF UNIQUE COMPETENCIES

Having agreed on the two basic ways of achieving competitive advantage, cost leadership and differentiation, the question that remains is how to pursue a systematic process for a thorough diagnosis and a prescription for developing competitive capabilities. One answer to that question is based in the value chain.

Cost leadership, by definition, implies that the SBU establishes a position that has a significant cost advantage over all of its competitors in the industry. To achieve such a position, we have to understand first the critical activities in

FIGURE 6–6. The Three Generic Strategies

		Competitive Advantage	
		Lower Cost	Differentiation
Market Scope	Broad	Cost leadership	Differentiation
	Narrow	Cost focus	Differentiation focus

the SBU value chain that are the sources for cost advantage, and then to deploy the necessary capabilities to excel in one or more of them.

Differentiation implies that the business unit has to offer something unique, unmatched by its competitors, that is valued by its buyers beyond offering simply a lower price. Once again, it is necessary to understand the potential central sources of differentiation stemming from the activities of the value chain, and the deployment of the necessary skills to enable those potentials to be realized.

What is important to realize is that virtually every activity in the value chain is a potential source to pursuing either cost leadership or differentiation. At the same time, not all of them have the same significance in achieving the desired competitive advantage. Therefore, the process of selecting a competitive position starts with an understanding of the industry structure, the selection of the appropriate generic strategy, and the identification of the crucial activities within the chain that will allow the business to achieve the corresponding sustainable advantage.

THE ENGINEERING POLYMERS EXAMPLE REVISITED

In the previous chapter we presented the industry attractiveness analysis for the engineering polymers industry. Now we describe briefly the competitive position of some of its key players.

We have indicated already that GE and Du Pont are dominant firms, both domestically and globally. For many years, GE has been experiencing higher growth and, as a result of this, GE overtook Du Pont in the United States in the mid-1970s. And in the mid-1980s, they surpassed them on a global basis.[4]

GE's move into plastics in the early 1960s was a backward integration into materials from their appliance business. Because of this background, they have always been very attuned to marketing, and satisfying customer needs has been key to their strategy. In part, under the leadership of Jack Welch, a Ph.D. chemical engineer and its current CEO, GE achieved dominance in the engineering polymers industry by:

- a commitment to large investment in production and R&D
- focused attention on market needs
- concentration in globalization of the markets
- a commitment to maintain and increase market share

Welch's innovative, entrepreneurial, and risk-taking style was vastly different from the stodgy corporate culture that characterized Du Pont management. GE's competitive advantage is illustrated in its value chain in Figure 6–7.

FIGURE 6–7. GE's Competitive Advantage: Sources of Differentiation

Firm Infrastructure	Top Management Support (Welch is CEO)					
Human Resources Management	• Superior training		• Use of commission sales incentives			Margin
Technology Development	• Best alloy technology		• Best applications engineering support • Best market research			
Procurement			• Excellent product positioning			
	• High-quality production • Excellent conformance to specifications	• Flexible delivery capability	• Extensive advertising • Strong focus on high-growth areas	• High sales force coverage • Strong personal relation-ships • Extensive credit (GE Credit)	• Easy-to-use products • Extensive training of customers	Margin
	Inbound Logistics	Operations	Outbound Logistics	Marketing	Sales	Service

- In GE's value chain, their source of differentiation in recent years has been primarily in the marketing/sales area.
- In their future strategy, they expect to emphasize technology development and investment in R&D.
- As they begin to face real competition in their products, they will begin to focus more on generating cost advantages as well.

SOURCE: Maceda (1988).

On the other hand, Du Pont's early formula for success was based on R&D and innovation:

- invest in research
- invent new products
- obtain patent protection
- manufacture it safely with a high level of quality
- sell everything that could be made at monopoly prices to a waiting market

The stream of inventions would become household words, and many of them were plastics and polymers. Du Pont created such products as cellophane, nylon, acetal, Teflon, Dacron, Mylar, and many others. The monopolies created, however, attracted the concern of the U.S. government, and the company had several brushes with antitrust situations in the 1950s and 1960s.

With GE's competitive pressures, and growth slowing down in the 1970s, Du Pont's next step to maintain high returns was to look toward manufacturing. Investment in technology, development of maximum-scale economies, and location of plants abroad positioned Du Pont as the low-cost manufacturer of its products. Figure 6–8 illustrates the sources of Du Pont's competitive advantage through a value-chain analysis.

A close inspection and comparison of the value chains prevailing in the current situation, and shown in Figures 6–7 and 6–8, allow us to draw an interesting conclusion from this case: we observe a convergence of the firms' strategies. Du Pont, the technology company, is being forced to enhance its marketing capabilities; and GE, the marketing company, is being driven toward an improvement of its technological skills. In the end, both firms find themselves

FIGURE 6–8. Du Pont's Competitive Advantage: Sources of Cost Leadership

Firm Infrastructure	History and Tradition of Du Pont in Plastics and Materials					
Human Resources management	• Paternalistic culture guarantees security, attracts highest-quality scientists		• Best training, integrating sales and technical service			
Technology Development	• Best polymer R&D • Global scale R&D/Technology		• Extensive commitment to process development. Recognized for R&D of customers' manufacturing processes			
Procurement	• Lowest-cost raw materials			• Quality image		
	• Direct supply	• Largest scale economies • Highest product physical properties • High yield, low defects	• Extensive warehouse network • Rapid delivery guaranteed	• Quality image • Horizontal integration of marketing with other Du Pont SBUs	• Strong sales force	• Replacement guaranteed • Best customer process training • Highest technical service coverage
	Inbound Logistics	Operations	Outbound Logistics	Marketing	Sales	Service

• In manufacturing, Du Pont has developed lowest cost position through exploitation of the learning curve. There is also extensive horizontal and vertical integration of products across different divisions and departments since most materials have the same building blocks, and Du Pont is basic in almost everything.

• The majority of their advantage has been in research, technology, and manufacturing. The current strategy is to develop strength in the marketing and sales area to compete better with GE.

SOURCE: Maceda (1988).

in the enviable position of having a sound low cost base and at the same time enjoying differentiated products.

Methodology to Perform the Internal Scrutiny at the Business Level

We have discussed already the basic concepts behind the task of defining the competitive position for a business. We propose now a systematic and disciplined approach to guide a manager through all the necessary steps to perform the internal scrutiny at the business level. This process attempts to identify the major strengths and weaknesses of the firm against its most relevant competitors.

The internal scrutiny is supported by the following tasks:

- Identification of the most relevant SBU's competitors
- Determination of critical success factors; that is, those capabilities controllable by the firm in which it has to excel for the SBU to achieve a long-term sustainable competitive advantage and a profitability level above industry standards.
- Development of a competitive profile for the SBU, by measuring the business strengths and weaknesses against each of the most relevant competitors.
- Preparation of the summary assessment and identification of overall strengths and weaknesses associated with the SBU.

IDENTIFICATION OF THE MOST RELEVANT COMPETITORS

A relevant competitor is one who fulfills one or more of the following conditions:

- From a market point of view
  - It has a high market share.
  - It has experienced a sustained market growth.
  - It earns high levels of profitability with regard to the industry average.
  - It has demonstrated an aggressive competitive attitude against your entire business or important segments of your business.
  - It has a highly vulnerable position against your own competitive actions.

- From a functional point of view
  - It has the lowest cost structure.
  - It has the strongest technical base.
  - It has the strongest marketing.
  - It offers the best product quality.
  - It shows the highest level of vertical integration.
  - It exhibits the highest level of capacity utilization.

FIGURE 6–9. The Most Relevant Competitors to the Magnesium Business of AMAX

COMPETITORS	1983 SALES (000s tons)	1983 MARKET SHARE	ESTIMATED 1983 PRODUCTION COST RANKING
Dow Chemical	75	37.5	2nd
Norsk Hydro (Norway)	33	16.5	1st
Northwest Alloys*	16	8.0	4th
Chromasco (Canada)	10	5.0	N.I.**
Sofrem (France)	11	5.5	N.I.
Siam (Italy)	12	6.0	N.I.
Magnachrome (Yugoslavia)	5	2.5	N.I.
Others	7	3.5	N.I.
AMAX Magnesium	31	15.5	3rd
Total for the Market	200	100	—

*Northwest Alloys utilizes a substantial amount of this production internally.
**Not included.
Note: Financial data for competitors of the magnesium division are not available, but in general terms the period since 1980 has not been profitable for any of the producers because an over-supply situation caused production cutbacks. Due to the depressed world market for magnesium, sales growth stagnated or was negative over the past three years.

SOURCE: Gray (1984).

Any sound strategy has to be supported by a thorough understanding of the firm's most relevant competitors, since a business strategy aims at achieving a sustainable advantage over them. Unless this is derived from a sound intelligence gathering, we would be playing the business game blindly. Figure 6–9 provides the list of the key competitors of AMAX magnesium business, with a few comparative indicators. Normally, it is important to collect as much quantitative and qualitative information as required to construct a well-rounded overall competitive profile. The financial statement analysis framework, which we discuss in Chapter 5, constitutes a sound first step in this direction.

SELECTING THE CRITICAL SUCCESS FACTORS AND DEVELOPING A COMPETITIVE PROFILE

The value-chain concept is a valuable framework to organize the tasks undertaken at the business level. It serves as a guideline to perform a diagnosis of current strengths and weaknesses, and to identify the capabilities to be mobilized to achieving competitive advantage. However, its categories are still too broadly defined. They do not incorporate enough detailed content to facilitate the selection of the critical success factors leading to the identification of key strengths and weaknesses of the SBU.

FIGURE 6–10. Assessment of the Competitive Standing of AMAX's Magnesium Business against Dow Chemical

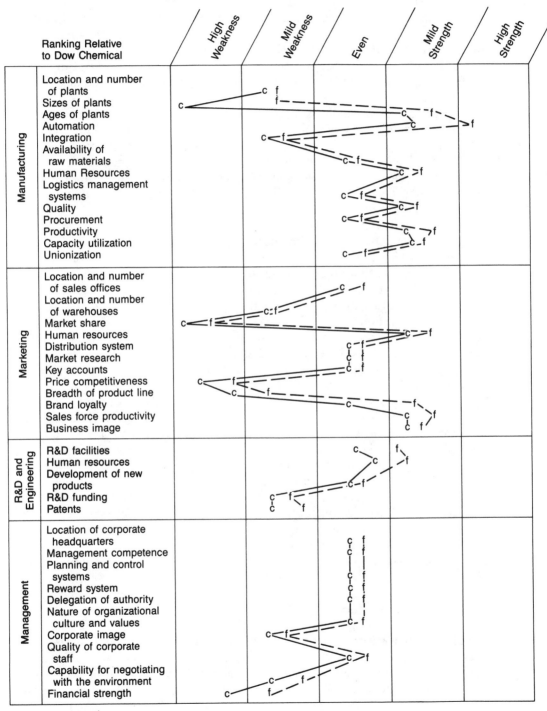

c = current
f = future

SOURCE: Gray (1984).

A pragmatic approach to conduct the internal scrutiny at the business level is to look at the business in its entirety with a very broad perspective. As with the environmental scan, the top business managers can be called on to provide an initial overall assessment of the business position. The group could be asked first to identify those central competitive skills that are the foundation for determining the business position in its industry. Second, the managers could be asked to agree on a diagnosis of the current situation, and third, to define collectively a desired state of the future competitive positioning of the business.

At this point, it might be useful to recognize an important, but somehow subtle, distinction between the projections and future trends of the industry attractiveness in which the business resides, which are truly forecasts because we are dealing with uncontrollable factors external to the firm, and the desired competitive state of the business in the upcoming future. This desired state is based on the development of unique competencies resting in activities controllable by the firm.

This approach to internal scrutiny serves three very important purposes. One, by no means the least important, is to provide the proper forum and process by which top managers could enrich each other's understanding of the ways to compete, share their insights and experiences in running the business, and reach, hopefully, a consensus on the tasks to be faced. The second objective is to produce a rich overall assessment of the current business standing, with a proper recognition of the existing strengths and weaknesses, the most promising potentials, and the challenges to be assumed for their realization. And the third and final end is generating a commitment toward the business future development, which will involve the recognition of the specific functional tasks that are necessary to support the business strategy.

In this approach, strategy is spelled out only at a very broad level. This leads to a subsequent stage when performing the functional strategic tasks of the expounding of all the necessary details at the functional level, and the consolidation of all functional strategies aimed at supporting not just one SBU, but the full portfolio of businesses of the firm.

This form of internal scrutiny is illustrated in Figure 6–10 for the magnesium business of AMAX. The figure displays those factors judged to be critical for the business competitive position, and provides an assessment of its current and desired state, using as standard of comparison Dow Chemical, AMAX's most important competitor.

Figure 6–11 provides a very brief summary of the key competitors' standing. Figure 6–12 exhibits an overall assessment of the magnesium business within its industry. Finally, Figure 6–13 distills the major strengths and weaknesses of AMAX's magnesium business, as a whole.

An alternative approach for doing the internal scrutiny at the business level is to carry out an in-depth rigorous functional analysis for the business in question. This option could be desirable when dealing with an SBU that is totally decentralized and maintains full functional autonomy. If this is not the case, we might be better off by retaining at this level a rather broad competitive

FIGURE 6–11. Summary Assessment of AMAX's Five Major Competitors' Strengths and Weaknesses in the Magnesium Industry

COMPANY	STRENGTHS	WEAKNESSES
Dow Chemical	a. Largest market share b. Strong parent company to share resources in finance, R&D, and marketing	a. Oldest plant and equipment b. Old process technology c. May not have corporate backing to update or increase capacity
Norsk Hydro	a. New process technology b. Highly qualified operating personnel c. Low-cost hydro electricity d. Low-cost producer in the industry e. Close to European markets	a. Government ownership
Northwest Alloys	a. Vertically integrated with Alcoa aluminum company–locked in market b. Good corporate resources	a. Poor process b. High costs c. Low-quality product d. Little R&D
Chromasco	a. Small enough, so that incremental production increases will add significantly to its bottom line b. Low-cost hydro and taxes in Ontario	a. Small market share b. Higher processing costs c. Little R&D and marketing
Sofrem	a. Government-sponsored high level of resources	a. High-cost process b. Poor marketing and R&D

SOURCE: Gray (1984).

FIGURE 6–12. Overall Assessment of Business Strength for AMAX's Magnesium Business

	CURRENT			FUTURE		
	Low	*Medium*	*High*	*Low*	*Medium*	*High*
Manufacturing	X				X	
Marketing		X			X	
R&D and engineering		X				X
Management	X			X		
Overall assessment	X				X	

SOURCE: Gray (1984).

FIGURE 6–13. Overall Assessment of AMAX's Competitive Strength Compared to Its Competitors

---

MAJOR STRENGTHS

1. Low-cost manufacturing processing system due to location
2. Low energy costs at plant location
3. Human resources
4. R&D and marketing ability

MAJOR WEAKNESSES

1. Small size of current facilities
2. Vulnerable to energy cost increases in the future
3. May have environmental concern in future
4. Threat of competition through new substitute materials

SOURCE: Gray (1984).

perspective, reserving for later on the exhaustive multifunctional analysis. We address the functional strategic thrusts in Part IV, where we come back to this subject.

Notes

1. The value chain, as a way of achieving competitive advantage, is thoroughly examined in Michael E. Porter, *Competitive Advantage* (New York: The Free Press, 1985).

2. The telecommunications industry example follows Mark A. Webster, *Strategic Analysis of AT&T, NYNEX and IBM in the Telecommunications Industry,* unpublished student paper, Sloan School of Management, MIT, 1988.

3. Porter, *Competitive Advantage* (1985), op. cit.

4. As before, the presentation of the engineering polymers industry follows Emmanuel P. Maceda, *Strategic Analysis: Du Pont Company, Engineering Polymers Division,* unpublished student paper, Sloan School of Management, MIT, 1988.

7

The Development of Business Strategy

All the previous analyses conducted so far, the mission of the business, the environmental scan to determine industry attractiveness, and the internal scrutiny to identify competitive strengths, should lead to an intelligent formulation of the business strategy. This is captured in Figure 3–1 which describes the fundamental elements in formal business strategic planning.

A business strategy can be defined as a well-coordinated set of action programs, aimed at securing a long-term sustainable advantage. These action programs should respond to the desired changes in the business mission, properly address the opportunities and threats revealed by the environmental scanning process, and reinforce the strengths as well as neutralize the weaknesses uncovered in the internal scrutiny.

The business programs are defined at two different levels of specificity: broad action programs typically covering a multiyear planning horizon, which are normally understood to represent the long-term strategic objectives of the SBU; and specific action programs, covering a six- to eighteen-month period, which represent the tactical support needed for the realization of the strategic objectives.

All of these programs, broad and specific, often involve functional commitments, transforming a business strategy in the articulation of properly integrated multifunctional activities. Furthermore, the final output of the business strategy is translated into a budget, a document of enormous significance because it carries with it a final agreement for implementation, and counts with the approval of all key participants.

There are three primary categories of information which are part of a well-designed business plan, to be submitted by the SBU managers to corporate managers for its final sanctioning and resource allocation assignments. The first is a *narrative* concerning key descriptive elements of the SBU and including a statement of the set of broad and specific action programs. An example of that type of information is provided in Figure 7–1 for the magnesium business unit of AMAX. The second is the *budget*, and the third is the definition of *performance measurements* for management control.

FIGURE 7–1. Summary of AMAX Magnesium Business Strategy

BUSINESS: Magnesium

MISSION STATEMENT

To produce competitively high-quality magnesium products at the Rowley, Utah, plant and to sell the products on a world-wide basis. Marketing in conjunction with R&D will develop additional products and markets with improved price elasticity characteristics and market scope to assume future improved and sustainable profitability.

INDUSTRY PERSPECTIVE

A. Market Overview

Total available market: The free world market for magnesium in 1983 is estimated to be 200,000 tons. The total production capacity is 295,000 tons. Market growth has been 1% per annum during the 1970s.

B. Market Trends

Future growth of the magnesium market is expected to be 6% per annum due to lower relative costs of magnesium compared to aluminum and other metals, to shortages of aluminum forecasted for the mid-1980s, to more aggressive magnesium marketing, and the elimination of buyer resistance resulting from having only one major producer in the 1980s.

C. Competitive Environment

1. Narrative:
   The magnesium industry is a highly concentrated industry with 3 major producers in the United States comprising 61% of the free world market; 77.5% of the total free market is produced by only 4 producers. The largest producer makes up 41% of the total market.
2. Competitive Profile and Market Share:
   The free world magnesium competitors and their estimated market share in 1983 are:

Dow Chemical	37.5%
Norsk Hydro	16.5%
AMAX	15.5%
North West Alloys (Alcoa)	8.0%
Siam (Italy)	6.0%
Sofren (France)	5.5%
Chromasco (Ontario)	5.0%
Magnachrome (Yugoslavia)	2.5%
Furukawa (Japan)	1.5%
U.B.E. Kosan (Japan)	1.5%
Bresmay (Brazil)	0.5%
	100.0%

BUSINESS DESCRIPTION

A. Markets and Distribution

AMAX, in 1983, had 15.5% of the free world market. It is establishing itself as a reliable producer of high-quality magnesium and is gaining a strong presence in the marketplace through superior technical customer service. Major market segments include aluminum alloys, ferro alloys, metal reduction, powder, structural, desulphurizing, sheet and plate extrusion, and anodes. It is in the structural, desulphurization, and cast anodes areas that AMAX plans to concentrate its marketing efforts to increase demand for its products.

B. Products-Technology Scope

The products in the magnesium business are ingot, powder, sheet and plate extrusions, and cast anodes. Through marketing efforts, AMAX should realize more demand for sheet and plate extrusions and cast anodes in the future. Process technology is changing and significant improvements have been made to the magnesium electrolytic cell to increase productivity and significantly reduce costs.

FIGURE 7–1. (continued)

C. Manufacturing

Current production capacity is constrained at 38,000 tons per year. Resource base from the Great Salt Lake is unlimited. Energy costs are low because of solar evaporation in the Salt Lake area and low relative electrical energy costs in Utah. To make further economic gains in the future, larger economies of scale are required to amortize the large fixed cost of the operation.

INDUSTRY ATTRACTIVENESS AND BUSINESS STRENGTH

Current and future position of the magnesium business

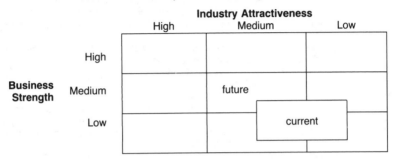

Approved priority for resource allocation: Maintain selectively

ENVIRONMENTAL SCAN

A. Opportunities

1. High potential relative market growth
2. Abundant resources available
3. New process technology to reduce costs
4. New markets and products to expand demand capacity
5. Few competitors—all profit oriented
6. Good opportunity for aluminum substitution

B. Threats

1. Aluminum industry expands its capacity or achieves technological improvements and forces aluminum prices to remain low relative to magnesium, i.e., magnesium prices will be above 1.5:1 magnesium to aluminum.
2. Future possibility of Third World countries entering the magnesium market providing excess capacity for nonprofit reasons.
3. New and currently unknown technology, i.e., glass-reinforced polyester plastics may make magnesium noncompetitive in certain high-growth markets, such as the structural and consumer products area.

INTERNAL SCRUTINY

A. Strengths

1. AMAX is positioned to capture an increased market share through technically marketing magnesium.
2. Cost of production is favorable due to location, resulting in low energy costs and solar evaporation.
3. AMAX's internal proprietary development of new cell technology will serve to further reduce costs and maintain competitiveness.

B. Weaknesses

1. Current production capacity at Rowley plant is too low and does not capitalize on economies of scale.
2. Current energy supply contracts are not adequate to ensure reliable long-range production plans.
3. Current emission levels of HCl, chlorine, and other effluents may become increasingly subject to more pollution control measures in the future.

FIGURE 7–1. Summary of AMAX Magnesium Business Strategy (continued)

BROAD ACTION PROGRAMS

A. Achieve Low-Cost Production

Specific Action Programs:

1. Expand Rowley Plant Capacity
   (a) Resources Requested: N/A (a list of labor and capital required should be included)
   (b) Statement of Benefits: Through plant expansion economies of scale will be achieved causing a 40% increase in production of magnesium. Upon completion of expansion, plant will produce 45,000 tons per year, which was original plant design.
   (c) Statement of Performance and Goals: Achieve a 45,000 tons-per-year capacity; achieve expected economies of scale
   (d) Milestone: Complete, by mid-1986
   (e) Priority: Absolutely first priority
2. Technology Gains in the Process
   (a) Resources Requested: N/A (a list of labor and capital required should be included)
   (b) Statement of Benefits: Continued research into more efficient magnesium production processes, i.e., improved cell design will reduce energy required; reduce maintenance cost, and increase productivity of the cell.
   (c) Statement of Performance and Goals: Reduce energy costs of cell, reduce maintenance costs of cell, increase current cell productivity
   (d) Milestone: Mid-1986
   (e) Priority: Highly desirable
3. Methods and Functions Gains in Efficiency
   (a) Resources Requested: N/A (a list of labor and capital required should be included)
   (b) Statement of Benefits: Reduce fixed and variable operating costs
   (c) Statement of Performance and Goals: Through the establishment of human resource programs to improve labor efficiency and effectiveness, and improved asset utilization program, total operating costs will be reduced.
   (d) Milestone: December 1985
   (e) Priority: Desirable

B. Magnesium Market Development

Specific Action Programs:

1. Market Penetration in Specific Growth Areas
   (a) Resources Requested: N/A (a list of labor and capital required should be included)
   (b) Statement of Benefits: To ensure AMAX participates in growth areas of magnesium market such as die casting, cathodic protection, and desulphurization in the steel market.
   (c) Statement of Performance and Goals: To increase market share in the structural, metal reduction, desulphurizing, and cast anode market segments from 1984 to 1985; to increase sales in these areas at a rate greater than the market growth rate
   (d) Milestone: December 1985
   (e) Priority: Absolutely first priority
2. Initiate New Market Developments
   (a) Resources Requested: N/A (a list of labor and capital should be included)
   (b) Statement of Benefits: To generate new customer and industry sales for magnesium; to establish AMAX as a reliable supplier of magnesium with a strong technical support and service division, which in turn will generate increased sales
   (c) Statement of Performance and Goals: To become customer technical-service leader in the magnesium industry; to increase market share in new market areas such as the computer industry, and increase market penetration in the automotive structural markets
   (d) Milestone: Mid-1986
   (e) Priority: Highly desirable

FIGURE 7–1. (continued)

3. Forward Integration
   (a) Resources Requested: N/A (a list of labor and capital required should be included)
   (b) Statement of Benefits: To determine if AMAX should pursue vertical integration into the magnesium powder and extrusion—sheet and plate—product lines, which are currently contracted
   (c) Statement of Performance and Goals: Completion of cost-benefit-risk analysis with conclusions as to AMAX's position of entering forward vertical integration into the magnesium business
   (d) Milestone: January 1987
   (e) Priority: Desirable
               C. Assure Future Business Position
Specific Action Programs:
1. Development of Long-Range Energy Contracts
   (a) Resources Requested: N/A (a list of labor and capital required should be included)
   (b) Statement of Benefits: To ensure the economic viability of the Rowley operation in the future
   (c) Statement of Performance and Goals: To negotiate a long-term agreement with the energy utilities to guarantee the supply and long-term economies of the required energy supply
   (d) Milestone: January 1985
   (e) Priority: Highly desirable
2. Technology Improvements to Reduce Environmental Impact
   (a) Resources Requested: N/A (a list of labor and capital required should be included)
   (b) Statement of Benefits: To ensure the long-term viability of AMAX's Rowley operation
   (c) Statement of Performance and Goals: To ensure the magnesium plant operation complies with government environmental control targets and is in keeping with AMAX's corporation reputation as a good corporate citizen in minimizing its impact on the environment
   (d) Milestone: Mid-1986
   (e) Priority: Highly desirable

SOURCE: Gray (1984).

Budgeting

Budgets represent projections of revenues and costs normally covering one or more years. The *master budget* of a firm includes all those activities whose monitoring is judged to be important for a healthy development of the firm's businesses; among them are sales, manufacturing, administrative activities, investment, and cash management. Figure 7–2 provides a schematic view of the primary elements in a master budget.

Efficiency standards with regard to all of the firm's activities are implicit in the budgetary projections. The estimated productivity figures used to set budgetary targets are commonly based on standards of performance derived from historical observations, internal data drawn from the firm's experience, and external figures obtained from financial statements of competitors. A properly defined budget calls for not only the use of historical data, but also for the establishment of commitments that emerge from a strategic plan.

Thanks to many years of experience with the formulation of budgets, this

FIGURE 7–2. A Schematic Representation of a Master Budget

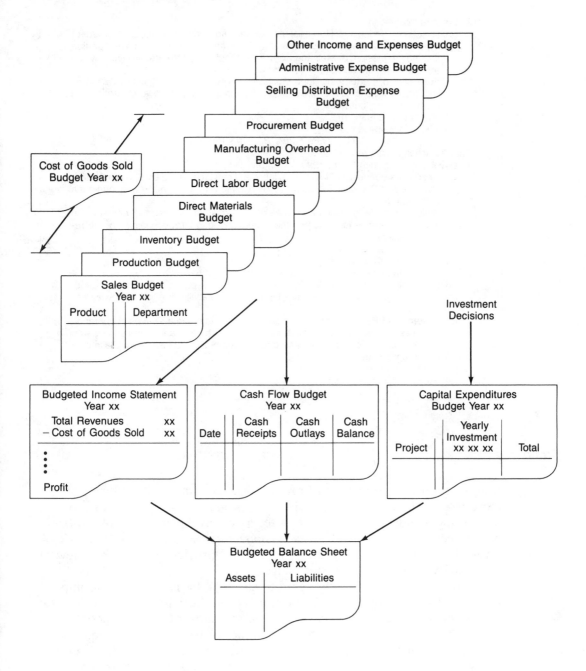

process has been under continuous refinement and new mechanisms for defining the budget have appeared. For example, *flexible budgets* permit the original standards being used to measure performance to be modified with the changes in the actual level of operations. Also, *zero-base budgeting* (ZBB) establishes a set of very comprehensive rules to force managers to justify their budgetary allocations from ground zero, rather than defining the new budget in an incremental way.[1]

The result of the business planning process leads toward the development of an *intelligent budget* which is not a mere extrapolation of the past into the future, but an instrument that contains both strategic and operational commitments. Strategic commitments pursue the development of new opportunities which very often introduce significant changes in the existing business conditions. Operational commitments, on the other hand, are aimed at the effective maintenance of the existing business base.

A way to break this dichotomy within the budget is to make use of strategic funds and operational funds to distinguish the role that those financial resources will have. *Strategic funds* are expense items required for the implementation of strategic action programs whose benefits are expected to be accrued in the long term, beyond the current budget period.[2] *Operational funds* are those expense items required to maintain the business in its present position.

There are three major components of strategic funds:

1. Investment in tangible assets, such as new production capacity, new machinery and tools, new vehicles for distribution, new office space, new warehouse space, and new acquisitions.
2. Increases (or decreases) in working capital generated from strategic commitments, such as the impact of increases in inventories and receivables resulting from an increase in sales; the need to accumulate larger inventories to provide better services; increasing receivables resulting from a change in the policy of loans to customers, and so on.
3. Developmental expenses that are over and above the needs of existing business, such as advertising to introduce a new product or to reposition an existing one; R&D expenses of new products; major cost reduction programs for existing products; introductory discounts, sales promotions, and free samples to stimulate first purchases; development of management systems such as planning, control, and compensation; certain engineering studies, and so on.

It is important to recognize these three forms of strategic funds. Although all of them contribute to the same purpose, namely, the improvement of future capabilities of the firm, financial accounting rules treat these three items quite differently. Investment is shown as an increase in net assets in the balance sheet and as annual expenses through depreciation in the profit and loss statement. Increases in working capital also enlarge the net assets of the firm, but they have no annual cost repercussion. Developmental expenses are charged as expenses in the current year income statement and have no impact on the balance sheet. Since there are no immediate profitability results derived from

FIGURE 7-3. Summary of Financial Information and Strategic Funds for an SBU

Business: _____

Numbers in $, except where indicated	HISTORY				CURRENT YEAR		PROJECTION				
	19__	19__	19__	19__	Actual	Budget	19__	19__	19__	19__	19__
Total Market											
Market Share (%)											
Company Sales											
– Operating Cost of Goods Sold											
Gross Operating Margin											
– Sales, General, & Administrative Expenses											
*Operating Margin											
– Strategic Expenses											
SBU Margin											
– Taxes											
SBU Net Income											
+ Depreciation											
* – Capital Investments											
* – Increases in Working Capital											
Contribution/Request of Funds to the Corporation											

* Items contributing to strategic funds

these strategic funds, it is important to make a manager accountable for the proper and timely allocation of those expenditures using performance measurements related to the inherent characteristics of the action programs they are attempting to support.

If the business has developed a sound strategy, it will be easy to see how the key performance variables begin to improve with the years. What is more difficult is to measure the short-term contribution of a multitude of programs requiring strategic expenses. Often, it is necessary to resort to project-management type of control mechanisms, centered in cost and time efficiency, as the only way to measure the quality of the implementation of strategic funds.

Figure 7–3 presents a simple format to provide basic financial information related to the SBU operating base, including also a specification of strategic funds necessary for its further development.

Definitions of Performance Measurements for Management Control

THE RELATIONSHIP BETWEEN PLANNING AND CONTROL

Planning and control are management activities intrinsically linked. On the one hand, the planning effort results in the definition of fundamental tasks for the SBU and represents serious organizational commitments. Therefore, it could be unthinkable to terminate the process without setting in motion the proper mechanism to allow for the monitoring of those commitments. On the other hand, the control process is centered in analyzing the results of the planned activities, evaluating their performance, diagnosing their merits, and taking corrective actions when needed, which amounts to a redefinition of plans.

These arguments clearly state the dependency and mutual reinforcing of the planning and control processes. Normally, the linking bridge that joins planning and control is the budget as the depository of the standards against which performance should be measured.

MONITORING THE COMMITMENTS EMERGING FROM THE BUSINESS PLAN

We indicated that the business plan is basically expressed in terms of a set of both broad and specific action programs, representing a critical set of tasks that should be subjected to proper control. This is the primary reason why broad action programs, ample in scope but producing some ambiguity in their description, are supported by a set of specific action programs. As their name implies, specific programs should be defined in fairly concrete terms to make

FIGURE 7–4. Definition of Broad and Specific Action Programs with Indications for Management Control

BROAD ACTION PROGRAMS	SPECIFIC ACTION PROGRAMS	RESOURCES REQUESTED	STATEMENT OF BENEFITS	STATEMENT OF PERFORMANCE AND GOALS	MILESTONES	RESPONSIBLE MANAGER

their control practicable. Figure 7–4 provides a format that could contribute the base for a sound description of action programs for management control purposes.

The additional commitments from a financial nature that emerge from a business plan are normally addressed in the budget, and it is relatively straightforward to monitor and control them. Once more, it is worthwhile insisting on the importance to pay particular attention to the operational results of the business, as well as to the proper allocation of strategic funds. This is the reason behind the categorization of financial results presented in Figure 7–3, which unambiguously captures these two dimensions of operational and strategic expenses.

Finally, there are a host of other variables defined in the business plan which might be desirable to control in an explicit way. Foremost among them are the critical success factors, particularly those linked to the central activities of the value chain, needed to achieve competitive advantage. They could lead to a rich set of indicators, comprising another important set of variables of the business strategic control system.

From a practical and pedagogical point of view, it is better to postpone the subject of a properly designed management control system until we can address it as one of the central corporate strategic tasks. This is so because the business unit not only should monitor its own individual performance, but it should be responsive to those tasks and measurements which are perceived as relevant by the top managers of the firm. Moreover, the proper design of a strategic control system is a task that by far exceeds the limited business scope; and, therefore, it constitutes a central corporate task which cannot be delegated at a business level. Chapters 14 and 16 readdress the subject of management control from the corporate level.

Notes

1. For further references on flexible budgets and zero-base budgeting, see Paul J. Stonich, et al., *Zero-Base Planning and Budgeting* (Homewood, IL: Dow Jones-Irwin, 1977); Charles T. Horngren and George Foster, *Cost Accounting: A Managerial Emphasis*, 6th ed. (Englewood Cliffs, NJ: Prentice Hall, 1987); Robert S. Kaplan and Anthony A. Atkinson, *Advanced Management Accounting*, 2nd ed. (Englewood Cliffs, NJ: Prentice Hall, 1989).

2. The concept of strategic funds was first advanced by Richard F. Vancil, "Better Management of Corporate Development," *Harvard Business Review*, 50, no. 5 (September–October 1972), 53–62, and Paul J. Stonich, "How to Use Strategic Funds Programming," *The Journal of Business Strategy*, 1, no. 2 (Fall 1980), 35–50.

CHAPTER 8

Corporate Strategy: The Core Concepts

Strategic Tasks at the Corporate Level

In Chapter 2 we provided an overall discussion about the components of a disciplined and formal strategic planning process, which distinguishes three levels of decision making—corporate, business, and functional. In this part, we address the tasks that reside entirely at the corporate level. These tasks have enormous significance because they are the fundamental mechanisms allowing top management to provide a sense of vision and leadership. Undoubtedly, the most powerful individuals within an organization reside at its top. They have the duty to guide the organization into a better future by exercising their power intelligently, ethically, and inspiringly. Not only should top managers be the primary architects of that vision, but they should also be able to communicate it to all levels of the organization, transmitting a contagious sense of enthusiasm. We hope that by systematizing the strategic tasks at the corporate level, we might contribute to a better understanding of the major initiatives that pertain to top managers, as well as to facilitate the proper execution of these tasks. However, we fully realize that the style of top managers, particularly the one of the CEO, is the most significant factor that influences the formulation, delivery, and execution of these managerial activities.

On a more pragmatic dimension, the central issue behind the strategic corporate tasks is the question of how to add value at the corporate level. It is not just a matter of leadership, but it is also the simple economic fact that a conscious effort has to be made by corporate managers to take advantage and exploit economies of scale and scope across the businesses of the firm. This is the pursuit of that old challenge: The whole should be greater than the sum of its parts. The acid test is whether the businesses of the firm are benefiting from being together, or if they would be better off as separate and autonomous units. If the latter is the case, corporate managers are not fulfilling their role, and they are destroying instead of creating value.

What constitutes a corporate task; that is to say, which are the tasks that, by their sheer nature, cannot be delegated to any lower level in the organization? The answer seems to be pretty clear. Corporate tasks are those that need the full firm's scope to be properly addressed. If delegated at a lower level, managers will not be able to make the trade-offs between the benefits received by their own unit and the adverse effects to other units within the firm. With that criterion in mind, we have identified ten tasks at the corporate level that we analyze in this part of the book.

1. The mission of the firm: choosing competitive domains and the way to compete.
2. Business segmentation: selecting planning and organizational focuses.
3. Horizontal strategy: pursuing synergistic linkages across business units.
4. Vertical integration: defining the boundaries of the firm.
5. Corporate philosophy: defining the relationship between the firm and its stakeholders.
6. Special strategic issues: identifying current key subjects of strategic concern.
7. Strategic posture of the firm: identifying strategic thrusts; corporate, business, and functional planning challenges; and corporate performance objectives.
8. Portfolio management: assigning priorities for resource allocation and identifying opportunities for diversification and divestment.
9. Organizational structure and administrative systems: adjusting the organizational structure, managerial processes, and systems in consonance with the culture of the firm to facilitate the implementation of strategy.
10. Human resources management of key personnel: selection, development, appraisal, reward, and promotion.

The methodology presented here to support each individual corporate task has two main purposes. The first aim is to provide a diagnosis of the conditions prevailing within each key strategic area, by searching for those situations that require prompt attention and making managers confront difficult decisions, rather than providing immediate answers to fairly complex issues. In essence, we are cataloguing all the critical issues the organization faces, from the perspective of its top managers. It is only in the definition of a strategic posture for the firm where the formulation and execution of strategic programs are passed on to the individuals who are more equipped to become responsible for their completion.

The second objective of the methodology is to purposely concentrate on change. We are required repeatedly to contrast the existing state of the firm against its future or desired state. If a significant change is detected, an equally significant strategic task emerges. The heart of strategy is the management of change. In an extreme situation, where there are no differences between the existing and desired states of the organization, there would be no real strategic tasks to perform. In this case, corporate executives become absorbed solely in the management of continuity.

The Fundamental Elements in the Definition of Corporate Strategy

We can organize the corporate strategic tasks in a way which is patterned after the strategic planning framework. Essentially, the framework consists of first identifying the focus of strategic attention. This could be the firm, business, or managerial function. Then external intelligence relative to the entity that we are analyzing must be gathered. This is what we have referred to as the environmental scanning process. Finally, we reflect on how to position the entity being analyzed within its environment, so as to achieve competitive advantage. Figure 8–1 places the corporate strategic tasks within such a framework. As shown in the figure, we have broken the tasks into four different clusters. The first one is labeled *the vision of the firm,* which intends to provide a fundamental statement of purpose of the organization as a whole. This is described in terms of the mission of the firm, its business segmentation, horizontal strategy, vertical integration, corporate philosophy, and whatever other special strategic issues are regarded as critical. *The strategic posture* serves as the central vehicle to communicate the critical action programs that summarize all of the key strategic questions the organization has to face. This includes the corresponding assignment of responsibilities and the definition of overall performance measurements. *Portfolio management* is the instrument for resource allocation. And finally, under the label *managerial infrastructure*, we have included the tasks more directly related to the implementation of strategy: the design of the organizational structure and administrative systems, and the management of key personnel.

The discussion and analysis of these tasks are the object of the remaining chapters in this part of the book. We turn now to the presentation of a methodology to perform the environmental scan at the corporate level, which is a critical input for the realization of all central corporate decisions.

Environmental Scan at the Corporate Level

The environmental scan attempts to diagnose the general health of the industrial sectors relevant to the businesses in which the corporation is engaged. It concentrates on assessing the overall economic, political, technological, and social climates that affect the corporation as a whole. This assessment has to be conducted first from a historical perspective to determine how well the corporation has mobilized its resources to meet the challenges presented by the external environment. And then, with a futuristic view in mind, the environmental scan attempts to forecast future trends in the environment and seek a repositioning of the internal resources to adapt the organization to those environmental trends.

The output of the environmental scan normally starts with an economic scenario which exhibits the most likely trends affecting the next planning cycle. A call for the development of contingency plans addressing either optimistic

Figure 8–1. The Fundamental Elements in the Definition of Corporate Strategy: The Ten Tasks

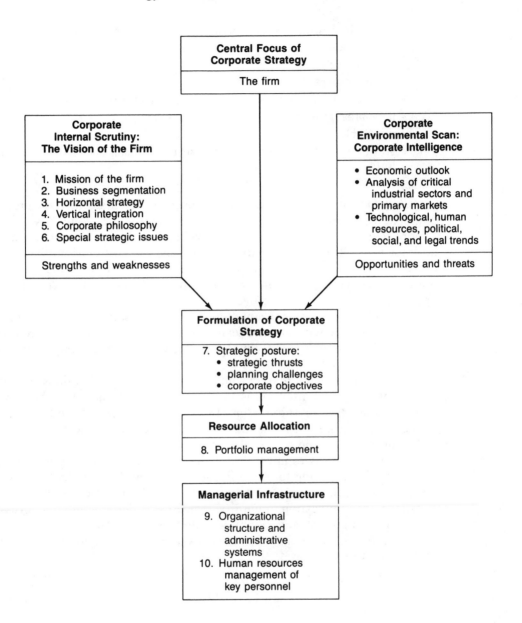

or pessimistic departures from this most likely trend may also be added. Topics to be included in this economic scenario are:

- economic growth: GNP and major influencing factors
- inflation rate
- prime interest rate
- unemployment
- overview of foreign markets and foreign exchange rates considerations
- population growth in critical geographical areas
- disposable income
- growth of critical industrial sectors, such as housing, defense, health, and so forth.

A second important component of the environmental scan is the projection of global trends in the primary markets in which the firm competes. Although a more detailed industry and competitive analysis has to be conducted at the business level, it is important to provide some macro-trends mutually agreed upon by corporate officers and key business managers in order to assure a sense of overall consistency in the formulation of business strategies and action programs.

For a firm competing in a high-technology environment, an essential third ingredient of the environmental scanning process is a thorough analysis of the change of pace of emerging technologies and the threats and opportunities this situation creates for the firm.

Besides economic, market, and technological considerations, a question that deserves special attention is the availability and quality of the supply of human resources. For some firms, this is the most critical and constraining resource. Therefore, it is essential to understand the composition and trends of key professional and technical skills.

Finally, the environmental scan has to address more subtle but often crucial issues pertaining to the political, social, and legal environments. Concrete items which are central to most business firms are regulatory issues, questions of unionization, minority concerns, environmentalists' pressures, public opinion groups, community activities, and so forth.

Figures 8–2 through 8–5 summarize the environmental scan conducted for AMAX Corporation.

FIGURE 8–2. AMAX, Inc.: Environmental Scan at the Corporate Level

U.S. Economic Overview

	PAST YEARS				CURRENT YEAR	FUTURE PROJECTIONS				
	80	81	82	83	1984	85	86	87	88	89
GNP growth (%)	(0.3)	2.6	(1.9)	3.4	5.4	2.9	3.4	1.0	2.8	4.8
Inflation rate (CPI)	12.4	8.9	3.9	3.3	5.2	6.2	7.0	5.7	4.7	6.2
Unemployment (%)	7.0	7.5	9.5	9.6	8.3	7.4	8.2	7.9	7.3	7.3
Disposable personal income	0.2	2.5	1.4	3.8	3.3	2.7	2.6	2.9	—	—
Prime rate (%)	15.3	18.9	14.9	10.8	11.0	12.7	11.6	10.5	10.0	11.0
Growth of critical industrial sectors: (a) Fixed investment business (b) Residential business	(2.2) (20.1)	3.6 (4.9)	(3.8) (10.9)	0.1 40.1	7.7 9.7	6.3 (7.2)	7.2 1.4	2.0 (15.0)	(1.5) 5.4	6.5 (9.7)
Corporate net profits	(16.8)	(11.1)	(23.5)	13.4	19.4	4.5	(16.3)	7.1	16.6	—
U.S. population (millions)	228.0	230.0	232.0	234.0	237.0	239.0	241.0	244.0	—	—

Note: Growth rates derived from U.S. Economic Forecast Citicorp, January 1984, and the Economic Indicators, December 1983. Prepared for the Joint Economic Committee by the Council of Economic Advisors.

SOURCE: Gray (1984).

FIGURE 8–3. AMAX, Inc.: Environmental Scan at the Corporate Level

Growth in Primary Markets

	PAST YEARS				CURRENT YEAR	FUTURE PROJECTIONS				
	80	81	82	83	1984	85	86	87	88	89
1. Housing	(21.0)	6.2	(17.0)	59.4	—	(14.8)	5.6	(15.0)	5.4	(9.7)
2. Automotive sales-domestic	(19.5)	(6.1)	(6.5)	19.0	13.3	(1.3)	(1.2)	(9.3)	10.3	6.7
3. Steel ingot production	(25.1)	0.4	(41.0)	13.2	19.6	11.1	8.2	(10.0)	10.0	0.0
4. Business fixed investment										
(a) structures	3.5	10.9	2.4	(7.6)	1.7	4.5	7.2	20.0	(1.5)	6.5
(b) equipment	3.4	2.0	(9.2)	3.7	10.2	7.0	7.1	2.0	(1.5)	6.5

Note: Growth rates derived from U.S. Economic Forecast Citicorp, January 1984, and the Economic Indicators, December 1983. Prepared for the Joint Economic Committee by the Council of Economic Advisors.

SOURCE: Gray (1984).

FIGURE 8-4. AMAX, Inc.: Environmental Scan at the Corporate Level

Broad Assessment of Basic External Factors

	PAST	FUTURE	MAJOR OPPORTUNITIES AND THREATS
Economic Overview	• Declining markets relative to industrial production since 1972 in metals business	• Continued declining markets in metals relative to economy, but some businesses able to grow individually	• 1984–86 growth and profitable period before next recession • Inflation will remain low • Economic outlook favorable for 2 years on demand side, but supply side overcrowded
Primary Market Overview	• Declining relative markets due to more efficient use of materials in end products	• Declining relative markets but slower decline due to positive market upswings	• Capital spending stronger, will be greatest opportunity • Greatest threat is recession before 1986 extending beyond a 1–2 year period
Technological Trends	• Downsizing end products, i.e., autos cut ± 1,000 lb./car metal • Aerospace industry building fewer products; more efficient design and capability	• Continuation of downsizing but not so fast • Light-weight substitutes for steel take advantage of design efficiencies	• Steel substitutions in end products, i.e., magnesium, aluminum • New developments in markets require higher quality, less weight • Higher gross profits created by innovative marketing
Supply of Human Resources	• Has not been a problem	• May be minor problems starting up mines with people on layoff	• Threat may be shortage of trained miners upon startup of mines in the industry
Political Events	• Devaluation of currencies in Third World	• U.S. dollar remains relatively strong • Trend of Third World to export their resources will continue	• Problems competing against Third World companies, which are not motivated by profitability and tend to ignore basic supply/demand for product
Social and Legal Issues	• National control of natural resources, i.e., Canada and Mexico • Pollution and environmental regulations and issues	• Socialization trend continues in countries with more industry-government interface • Pollution control regulations more stringent and costly	• U.S. has less regulation on business than other countries • Cost of doing business will increase due to pollution control regulations • Opportunities in waste management, consulting, and pollution control will expand

SOURCE: Gray (1984).

FIGURE 8-5. AMAX, Inc.: Environmental Scan at the Corporate Level—U.S. Market

Definition of Alternative Planning Scenarios

	OPTIMISTIC	PESSIMISTIC
1. General Description	• Federal deficit becomes controllable • Capital durable goods market improves • Oil prices fall, reducing cost of producing capital goods	• Federal deficit increases, driving rates up • Oil prices rise • Capital goods market falls

2. Economic Outlook
  • GNP-Growth
 	
  • Inflation Rate
	• GNP growth rate does not recede in 1986–87
	• Inflation rate less than 10%/year
		• GNP growth rate stops in 1985–86 and remains negative for more than 1 year
		• Inflation exceeds 10%/year

3. Growth in Primary Markets
  • Automotive
  • Capital Goods
  • Housing
	• Strong growth in all primary markets	• Temporary strong growth, followed by a downturn in growth due to early recession and suppressed capital goods growth

4. Relevant Critical Factors
  • Technology
 	
  • Political
 	
  • Social
	• Metal development competes successfully against nonmetals
	• No further government intervention with business in Third World
	• Pollution control will not cause plants to shut down and government and company will resolve differences
		• Rapid development in nonmetal/composite products vs. metals
		• Continued nationalization of foreign companies by Third World governments
		• Pollution control and environmental concerns affect business by forcing higher operating costs, causing some plant shutdowns

SOURCE: Gray (1984).

CHAPTER 9

The Mission of the Firm

The mission of the firm is a statement of the current and future expected product scope, market scope, and geographical scope as well as the unique competencies the firm has developed to achieve a long-term sustainable advantage. A mission statement of Citicorp, which adheres to this definition, is presented in Figure 9–1.

The subject of the mission of a business is treated in Chapter 4. All of the comments made there are immediately transferable at the level of the firm, and therefore, they are not repeated here. The major difference resides in the degree of aggregation of the firm's mission statement and its much richer significance.

Establishing the mission of the firm is the first major corporate task in the planning process. It constitutes the initial effort that provides top managers with an opportunity to reflect seriously on the current status of the overall firm activities, and to reach consensus with regard to the desired changes they would like to carry into the future. The declaration made explicit in the mission statement contains an inherent definition of priorities for the strategic agenda of the firm, and simultaneously it identifies the major opportunities for growth and those capabilities that have to be enhanced to achieve a superior competitive advantage. As such, it provides basic guiding principles and a set of expectations that are going to condition the rest of the strategic activities at all managerial levels of the firm. The proper amount of detail to be used in addressing each component of the mission clearly depends on the complexity of the firm and, primarily, in its degree of diversification. In highly diversified multinational firms, the statements of product and market scope should be carried out at the level of an industry; and the geographical scope might be described by listing the countries in which the firm operates or serves. Much finer details could be both feasible and useful in a less complex organization.

FIGURE 9-1. The Mission Statement of Citicorp

Summary Statement

The premise of Citicorp's mission is to offer an array of products and services to all of its market segments primarily where a customer need has been established. Its entry into the lucrative consumer market has begun to show signs of positive returns, while the corporate market continues to remain a highly profitable segment with strong demands for many of the products and services Citicorp offers. Its technological capabilities and its global communications network are and will continue to be significant driving forces behind many new products. Citicorp will also continue its active participation in legislative reform since many of the laws in existence today preclude its activities in various product-market and geographical segments within the United States.

	CURRENT	FUTURE
PRODUCT SCOPE:	• To provide consumer and institutional financial services which include credit extension, electronic cash management, foreign trade services, foreign exchange, savings and checking vehicles, credit cards, equipment leasing, fund-raising and investment advisory services, securities underwriting, distribution and trading, and venture capital • Build products and services generating fee-based revenue • Package the right mix of financial services	• Expand product scope by delivering a broader range of integrated financial services • Continue fee-based emphasis • Differentiate basic product delivery through innovation, product expertise, and global communications • Capitalize on lead position in foreign exchange, multinational finance packaging, international payments, and electronic banking
MARKET SCOPE:	• Market scope involves offering products and services to consumers, governments, private corporations, and financial institutions through a global, communications network • Identified consumer market as a major strategic thrust in the mid-1970s • Consolidated business approach towards funds flow intermediation within the world capital markets	• Capitalize on investment made in the consumer market through expansion with market share growth; provide for attractively priced funds and new opportunities • Leverage the communications network in order to identify and participate in new markets • Maximize participation in the world's capital market—identification of product and market combinations
GEOGRAPHICAL SCOPE:	• Geographical scope extends to 96 countries in Asia, Australia, Middle East, Africa, Caribbean, Central and South America, Europe, and North America	• Maximum growth potential: Western Hemisphere and Asia • Continuing expansion of the geographic boundaries of banking within the United States

FIGURE 9–1. (continued)

| WAYS TO ACHIEVE COMPETITIVE LEADERSHIP: | • Establish a global communications network connecting domestic and international branches and offices as well as major financial centers
• Reorganize the institutional business into one entity bringing together a unified business approach
• Make substantial investments in the consumer market to increase market share, capitalize on profitable opportunities, and lower funding costs
• Consolidate business segments involved in off-balance-sheet financial intermediation to provide for increased share of a $15-trillion world credit pool.
• Invest heavily in technology involving computer and telecommunications research
• Establish a legal focus to seek regulatory changes, which will improve ability to compete in all market segments | • Exploit advantage of global communications network
• Increase market share, efficiency, and product and service expertise
• Foster technological innovations to promote lower costs, fee revenue business, and profitability
• Develop the ability to understand the cost dynamics of the business and become a low-cost supplier of financial services
• Continue major emphasis on legislative process to remove restrictive regulatory barriers |

SOURCE: Antoinette M. Williams, "A Strategic Planning Process: The Case of Citicorp and Its Commercial Finance Subsidiary," 1983. Reprinted by permission of Antoinette M. Williams.

Alternatives for Growth and Diversification: A Guide to Assess the Future Scope of the Firm

Growth is the dominant force that drives future changes in the mission statement. The patterns of growth in the American industry have been well documented by the prominent business historian Alfred D. Chandler, Jr., in *Strategy and Structure* (The M.I.T. Press, Cambridge, MA, 1962). The major generic alternatives for growth are depicted in Figure 9–2. After the introduction of a successful product, the first logical strategy to follow is that of expanding the existing business within its current product-market structure. This can be accomplished by further penetration leading to increased sales volumes and geographical expansion, including perhaps international coverage. More-

FIGURE 9–2. Alternatives for Growth and Diversification: A Guide to Assess the Future Scope of the Firm

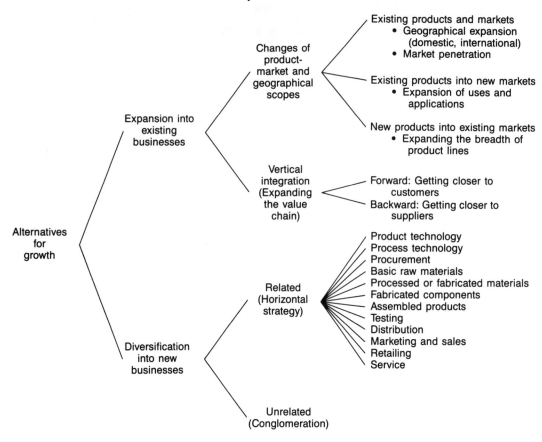

over, extensions of the existing market and product breadths are basic strategies for growth in existing businesses.

The second major strategy available to firms is vertical integration, which is an attempt at increasing value added within a given business base. There are two forms of vertical integration: forward, which leads the firm closer to its customers; and backward, which moves it closer to its suppliers.

A logical next step is to seek entry into new businesses via diversification. The nature of the diversification could be either related or unrelated, the latter type conducive to what is referred to as conglomeration. Related diversification is supported by expertise residing in one or more stages in the value chain. Thus, the firm could attempt to enter into new businesses, where the key for success can be traced back to one or more of the following stages of value added in which the firm currently excels: product and process technology, procurement, basic raw materials, processed or fabricated materials, fabricated components, assembled products, testing, distribution, marketing and sales, retailing, and services.

All of these alternatives for growth can be achieved either through internal development or acquisition. The pursuit of internal development has the advantage of establishing a strong base with deep cultural consistency. The obvious advantage of acquisition is its speedy and expedient accessibility to skill and competency not available internally to the firm. Acquisition prevails in the execution of unrelated diversification.

The selection of the strategies for growth as well as the intensity to carry out each one of them requires the exercise of a high level of judgment. There are clear dangers in not pursuing a strategy of extending the product line, for example, when competitors are including various features to differentiate their products. However, there are also serious problems in going too far in product-line extension, when product differences only contribute to increased inventory and lower productivity without adding significant value to the business.

Even more difficult is designing a proper strategy of vertical integration. If one is too aggressive in implementing a forward integration strategy, one could antagonize its own customers and pay dearly for it. Likewise, a backward integration strategy might result in severe negative responses on the part of one's own suppliers. Yet if key competitors seek a strategy of value-added maximization, it would be hard to compete if vertical integration is not properly undertaken. And then, there is always the risk that your own customers integrate backwards or the suppliers integrate forward. This subject is more thoroughly treated in Chapter 12.

We have found that a discipline enforced by carefully analyzing each one of these strategies for growth contributes to the quality of the overall assessment of the opportunities available to a firm. This framework could generate alternatives to be subjected to a careful economic analysis, ultimately leading towards a preferred strategic direction for a firm.

CHAPTER **10**

Business Segmentation

The cornerstone of the strategic planning process is the segmentation of the firm's activities into business units. This is a subject that already received a fair amount of attention in Chapter 3. We defined the strategic business unit (SBU) as an operating unit or a planning focus that sells a distinct set of products or services to a uniform set of customers, facing a well-defined set of competitors. Also, we identified the basic criteria for SBU definition, and we commented about the nature of interactions that normally exist across business units.

We are revisiting this subject now, because the business segmentation to be undertaken by top managers is a task of critical importance for a firm. Its completion has implications which go far beyond the identification of the focuses of attention of the planning process, although that is its ultimate purpose. Most of the analysis, formulation, and implementation of strategic activities has the SBU as the central concern. In fact, when defining the business units, top managers are creating the domains in which the strategy of the firm will become explicit. This is a powerful way of conveying the sense of direction and priorities that will lead the overall managerial decision-making process. It is a manifestation of the perspective selected by the firm to compete in the markets in which it participates.

The importance of having a thorough understanding of the key dimensions that could be legitimate candidates for business segmentation is clear. The first, and most obvious, is the set of products of the firm. In fact, most organizations have a natural tendency to define SBUs according to product lines, simply because they are the tangible outputs of managerial activities. Without denying the importance of products as a key to segmentation, they do not carry a sense of exclusiveness or might not even be the most relevant. In some specific circumstances, markets, functions, and geographical areas could be equally valid dimensions of business segmentation because of the significance that they bring to strategic positioning.

Another important aspect of business segmentation is that it does not have to be based on one single predominant criterion. Most likely, we will have an array of product, market, functional, and geographical dimensions to take into consideration. The essence of segmentation is the identification of all matters demanding focused strategic attention. Consequently, we may well end up with a selection of critical areas which are not mutually exclusive, but have partially overlapping focuses of attention. That is to say, the resultant business segments may imply a fair amount of double counting. For example, the segmentation process might finish with the identification of an array of exhausting world-wide products as definition of critical businesses. Moreover, we might include perhaps Japan and Financial Services as two additional SBUs—where some or all of the previously identified products converge—simply because of the critical importance of that country and market, respectively. Even a function, such as technology, could become the basis for SBU segmentation because of its potential to act as a springboard for important new business development.

We can assert then that segmentation is a complex and dynamic representation of the organizational purpose. This segmentation evolves and is reflected in those matters selected as focuses of organizational attention in the form of units or special areas of concern identified in the process of strategy formation.

Matching Organizational Structure and Business Segmentation

Business segmentation is strongly influenced by the principles commonly used for designing the organizational structure of a firm. The central question in organizational design is how to identify key *responsibilities* representing the major tasks of the organization and allocate the proper levels of *authorities* to facilitate the use of the necessary resources to execute the assigned tasks. The process that leads toward the final organizational structure of the firm is only possible through the wise exercise of a large number of trade-offs and compromises. Because of the inherent limitation of span of control, one has to identify just a very few critical dimensions as basis for the primary segmentation of organizational tasks. This is what one normally observes in the first echelon of the organization chart of a firm. But the process of segmentation does not end there. It continues to flow through finer and finer segmentation, until we have a subordinate hiearachy incorporating all of the critical dimensions that address the overall allocation of responsibilities and authorities.

Likewise, the business segmentation process is applied at different hierarchical levels in the organization. There is a span of control issue when identifying businesses from the corporate perspective. The resultant number of SBUs should not be so large as to impair the ability of top managers to understand the broad characteristics of each business and effectively contribute to their proper management. By necessity, therefore, the corporate segmentation in a large firm is rather broad and aggregated.

Normally, the resultant SBUs are thus composed of a plurality of products and markets which have to be properly identified by a secondary segmentation taking place at the business level. This segmentation provides the necessary intelligence for the SBU manager to establish meaningful priorities for the development of each individual segment. This may mean possible abandonment of some of them in order to concentrate all of the business competencies in a more narrowly focused market.

Although the two processes of business segmentation and organizational structure design do not have the same final objective, they are strongly linked. One could argue that a complete match between business segmentation and organizational structure is highly desirable. This match would greatly facilitate the formulation and implementation of strategy, the congruency between operational and strategic commitments, and the resultant accountability in both modes. Whenever organizational and business segmentations do not result in a perfect alignment, a significant ambiguity regarding the strategic and operational responsibilities is generated. In this case, considerable efforts would have to be made to match strategy and structure.

To summarize, there are two extreme alternatives in relation to the congruency between business segmentation and organizational design. At one end of the spectrum, we face situations where business units are entirely autonomous, totally self-sufficient with regard to the necessary functional support, and the organizational structure coincides entirely with the business segmentation. This is the case of a fully decentralized diversified business firm, where the criteria for organizational and business segmentation are the autonomous SBUs. This kind of structure requires a relatively minor amount of coordinating effort across the business units.

At the other end of the spectrum, we face a situation with a complete mismatch between the tasks that determine the organizational design and the business focuses that lead to a proper business segmentation.

Let us take an example which is close to our daily experiences: the organizational structure of the Massachusetts Institute of Technology (MIT) Sloan School of Management. As Figure 10–1 indicates, we are structured according to conventional functional disciplines: management science; economics, finance, and accounting; and behavioral and policy sciences. This is central for us because those dimensions represent our professional backgrounds, allowing us to communicate directly with our peers in the academic environment. These are equivalent to the functional capabilities in a conventional business firm. Now, one could ask, what businesses are we in? The answer is none of the above, simply because those are internal dimensions dealing with inputs as opposed to outputs, and centered in capabilities as opposed to external markets and competitors. Our businesses are represented by our major teaching and research programs: the master's program, the doctoral program, the undergraduate program, a wide variety of executive programs, and a number of research initiatives which are aimed at providing services to well-defined sets of customers in direct competition with some of the finest academic institutions of the world. How do we reconcile this discrepancy between the organizational structure segmentation and the business definition? For one, it is central for us to retain our disciplinary base: economists talking to economists (and we have three Nobel laureates in the faculty), computer scientists talking to computer scientists, and so on. The answer is to establish strong coordinating mechanisms which cut across those disciplinary boundaries. Thus, we have a variety of administrative officers and faculty chairpersons in charge of over-

FIGURE 10–1. Organizational Structure of MIT Sloan School of Management

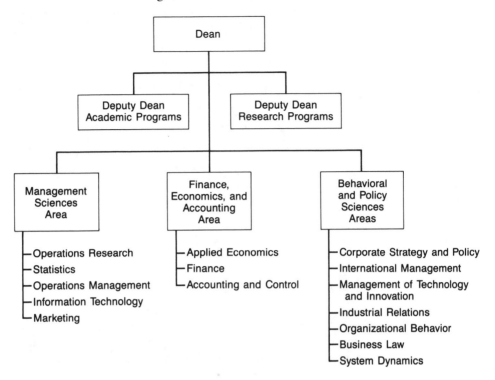

seeing the quality and integrity of "our businesses," and drawing the necessary human resources from the specific functional areas. Against all conventional wisdom, this does not represent a matrix organization because we do not have a dual-boss system. The line and the power are clearly on the functional side. Although the business dimension is absolutely central to the successful development of our institution, it is to a great extent a truly coordinating activity subordinated to the objectives of the functional disciplines. This might sound paradoxical given the attention that external markets and competitors deserve, but it is a fundamental reflection of our culture and a clear expression of the strategic priorities that we promote at MIT.

This example provides us with a simple illustration of the kind of issues that are created when business segmentation does not coincide with the way the organizational structure is designed. When this is the case, we need to put in place an infrastructure of horizontal coordinating mechanisms. The most common among them are assigning a manager as liaison, formation of task forces and committees, appointing either temporary or permanent coordinating managers, or recognizing formally the dual responsibilities and authorities by means of a matrix organization.

FIGURE 10–2. Business Segmentation and Assignment of Managerial Responsibility

BUSINESS UNIT	RATIONALE FOR SEGMENTATION	RESPONSIBLE MANAGER

Making Explicit the Business Segmentation

Regardless of the final dimensions selected to resolve the way the business segmentation process is conducted, it is important that top managers reach a final consensus on the resultant business units, its rationale for segmentation, and the identification of the individuals responsible for the formulation and implementation of the corresponding business strategy. Figure 10–2 presents a form to summarize the required information. As a final note, it is interesting to report that it is normally rather hard to achieve a rapid consensus on business segmentation among top managers of the firm. This tends to underscore the inherent complexity associated with this task, as well as the centrality of carrying it through to a successful completion.

CHAPTER 11

Horizontal Strategy

Having segmented the businesses of the firm, the critical question to be resolved is the extent to which potential synergism across businesses could be identified and properly exploited in order to add value beyond the simple sum of independent business contributions. This activity is the distinctive form in which a diversified firm enhances its competitive advantage, and it is the heart of the development and implementation of horizontal strategy. Since its managerial scope embraces the totality, or at least a partial group of businesses of the firm, it is defined in our context as a corporate task. Depending on the specific organizational structure of the firm, it could reside exclusively at the level of top corporate officers or be shared with other high-ranking managers of the firm at the group or sector echelons.

For many organizations, the appropriate pursuit of horizontal strategy becomes one of the most critical ways to establish a superior competitive position. This is particularly so when the firm's strategy stems from a unique competency residing, normally, in one stage of the value chain which has permitted the company to enter successfully in a wide variety of business enterprises, all of which share that particular resource. Countless companies can be cited as examples to stress this point. Among them are the original strategy of Procter & Gamble exploiting its clout in distribution, particularly through supermarket chains; Texas Instruments using electronic technology to support a large array of industrial consumer products; and Corning Glass Works, with a similar wide-range coverage of products, all of them sharing specialty glass technology. Even a company as widely diversified as General Electric can legitimately claim that all of their businesses are stemming from what Jack Welch refers to as the three circles of excellence: the traditional "core" business, the high-technology businesses, and the service businesses.

Most top managers today are keenly aware of the importance of carefully developed horizontal strategies. If a firm does, in fact, possess opportunities for exploiting synergism across businesses and is incapable of doing so, it is literally throwing away what could become a source of significant competitive strength. Moreover, horizontal strategies do not tend to emerge spontaneously. This is because the organizational structure of the firm tends to promote a vertical flow of information but seldomly generates on its own the lateral communications which are needed for grasping horizontal opportunities. In fact, we could say that the natural response of a vertical organization is to impede and oppose the support of horizontal interrelationships. This is due to a wide variety of factors, such as asymmetric benefits, protection of turf, conflicts over priorities, biased incentive systems, cultural and managerial differences, and excessive decentralization forces.

What we conclude from these comments is: (1) that horizontal strategy could become an important strategic concern, and (2) that it will not materialize unless there exists a determined will to make it happen. In this chapter, we reflect on the guiding principles that facilitate the formulation of horizontal strategies, as well as the organizational mechanisms that can be used to assure their implementation.[1]

Interrelationship Among Business Units

Horizontal strategy is a set of coherent long-term objectives and action programs aimed at identifying and exploiting interrelationships across distinct but related business units. Therefore, a crucial first step in the definition of horizontal strategy is to identify the sources of possible interrelationships. Porter proposes three types of possible interrelationships:

- Tangible interrelationships, arising from opportunities to share activities in the value chain.
- Intangible interrelationships, involving the transference of management know-how among separate value chains.
- Competitor interrelationships, stemming from the existence of rivals that actually or potentially compete with the firm in more than one business unit.

Tangible interrelationships are the easier to detect and capitalize. The sources of competitive advantage that they support are founded on the actual sharing of concrete assets or managerial capabilities in one or more activities of the value chain. It is not surprising, therefore, that tangible interrelationships constitute the most likely sources for horizontal strategy development.

Going back to the concept of generic strategies, a tangible interrelationship can either be used to obtain cost leadership, often by means of economies of scale and scope or to improve the differentiating capabilities of businesses. However, sharing activities of the chain brings additional costs such as cost of coordination and cost of compromising, resulting from suboptimal decisions for one particular business, compared with what could have been done with a completely independent management of that business. Another added cost is the cost of inflexibility resulting from the inability to respond to environmental changes as quickly as a competitor without the burden of strong critical masses in some activities of the value chain.

In order to simplify the analysis of tangible interrelationships, Porter combines the value-chain activities into five categories: managerial infrastructure including central administrative functions, financial management, and human resources management; technology; procurement; manufacturing; and marketing. Figures 11–1 through 11–5 summarize the major sources of tangible interrelationships according to those five categories, list possible forms of sharing, comment on the potential competitive advantage to be gained, and provide an indication of the costs to be borne.

FIGURE 11–1. Infrastructure Interrelationships

SOURCE OF INTERRELATIONSHIP	POSSIBLE FORM OF SHARING	POTENTIAL COMPETITIVE ADVANTAGE	COMPROMISE COST
Common firm infrastructure needs	Shared accounting Shared legal department Shared government relations Shared hiring and training	Smaller support staff Lower costs Critical mass to attract top-level managers	Need for coordination is higher People may have differing interests Conflicts may occur more often Needs of different types of people
Common capital	Shared raising of capital Shared cash utilization	Lower cost of financing	Increased complexity leads to higher overhead

SOURCE: Alain C. Boutboul, *A Framework for Analyzing Acquisition and Divestitures Decisions,* unpublished Masters thesis, Sloan School of Management, MIT, 1986. Reprinted by permission of Alain C. Boutboul.

FIGURE 11–2. Technology Interrelationships

SOURCE OF INTERRELATIONSHIP	POSSIBLE FORM OF SHARING	POTENTIAL COMPETITIVE ADVANTAGE	COMPROMISE COST
Common product technology	Joint technology development	Lower product or process costs Larger critical mass in R&D	Technologies are the same, but the trade-offs in applying the technology are different among business units
Common process technology		Enhanced differentiation	
Common technology in other value activities			
One product incorporated into another	Joint interface design	Lower interface design cost Higher differentiation	A nonstandard interface reduces the available market
Interface among products			

SOURCE: Boutboul (1986).

FIGURE 11–3. Procurement Interrelationships

SOURCE OF INTERRELATIONSHIP	POSSIBLE FORM OF SHARING	POTENTIAL COMPETITIVE ADVANTAGE	COMPROMISE COST
Common purchased inputs	Joint procurement	Lower cost of input	Input needs are different in terms of quality or specifications, leading to higher cost than necessary in business units requiring less quality
		Improved input quality	Technical assistance and delivery needs vary
		Improved service from vendors in terms of responsiveness, holding of inventory, conditions of sale	Centralization can reduce the information flow from factory to purchasing, and make purchasing less responsive

SOURCE: Boutboul (1986).

FIGURE 11–4. Manufacturing Interrelationships

SOURCE OF INTERRELATIONSHIP	POSSIBLE FORM OF SHARING	POTENTIAL COMPETITIVE ADVANTAGE	COMPROMISE COST
Common location of raw materials	Shared inbound logistics	Lower costs	Plants are located in different areas
Identical or similar fabrication process	Shared component fabrication	Lower costs	Needs for component design and quality differ
Identical or similar assembly process	Shared assembly facilities	Better capacity utilization; lower costs	Less flexibility Different needs
Identical or similar testing/quality control procedures	Shared testing/quality control	Lower testing costs	Testing procedures and quality standards differ
Common factory support needs	Shared indirect activities	Lower cost Improved quality	Different needs More difficult to manage a larger work force

SOURCE: Boutboul (1986).

It might be useful, both as a diagnostic mechanism and as a strategy formulation device, to examine the degree to which the value-chain activities are shared by the full set of products or businesses of the firm. This technique is referred to as *strategic field theory*. Figure 11–6 illustrates Procter & Gamble's

FIGURE 11–5. Marketing Interrelationships

SOURCE OF INTERRELATIONSHIP	POSSIBLE FORM OF SHARING	POTENTIAL COMPETITIVE ADVANTAGE	COMPROMISE COST
Common Buyer	Shared brand name	Lower advertising cost Reinforcing product images	Product images are inconsistent Buyer is reluctant to purchase too much from one firm Diluted reputation if one product is inferior
	Shared advertising	Lower advertising cost Greater leverage in purchasing advertising space	Appropriate media or messages are different Advertising effectiveness reduced by multiple products
	Shared promotion	Lower promotion costs	Appropriate forms and timing of promotion differ
	Cross selling of products to each other's buyers	Lower cost of finding new buyers Lower cost of selling	Product images are inconsistent or conflicting Buyer is reluctant to purchase too much from one firm
Common channel	Shared channels	Higher bargaining power Lower infrastructure cost	Too much dependency on channel Channel unwilling to allow a single firm to account for a major portion of its sales
Common geographic market	Shared sales force	Lower selling cost Better sales force utilization	Different buyer purchasing behavior Different types of sales person is more effective
	Shared service network	Lower servicing costs More responsive servicing Better capacity utilization	Different in equipment necessary to make repairs Different needs of buyers
	Shared order processing	Lower order processing costs Better capacity utilization	Differences in the form and composition of typical orders Differences in ordering cycles

SOURCE: Boutboul (1986).

FIGURE 11-6. Procter & Gamble Strategic Field

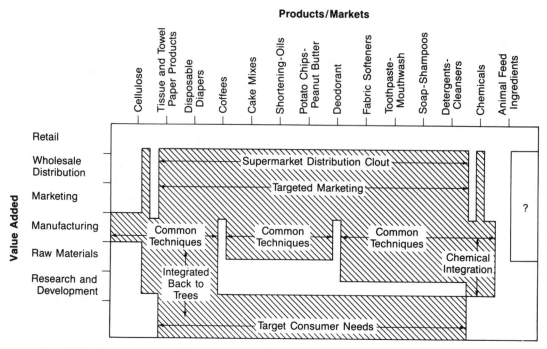

SOURCE: Walker W. Lewis, "The CEO and Corporate Strategy in the 80's: Back to Basics," 1984. Reprinted by permission of The Institute of Management Sciences, Providence, RI.

strategic fields, and it shows quite clearly that Procter & Gamble brings powerful skills in distribution, marketing, manufacturing, and R&D strengths to a wide variety of apparently unrelated businesses.

Intangible interrelationships lead to competitive advantage through sharing managerial skills among different value chains. They involve interactions across independent SBUs that are placed in different industries, but retain generic similarities; like:

- same generic strategy
- same type of buyers
- similar configurations of the value chain (e.g., value chains in different countries)
- similar important value activities (e.g., relationships with government)

Intangible interrelationships can also be an important source in seeking cost advantage or in gaining differentiation capabilities. However, they are much more difficult to apprehend and exploit. Because of the wide array of similarities existing across value chains of different business units, it is impossible to provide a full cataloguing of all types of interrelationships. Instead, careful attention to the nature of the value chains of the firm's business-units constitutes an effective source of analysis from which intangible interrelationship opportunities might emerge.

Figures 11–7 and 11–8 show the most important sources of tangible and intangible interrelationships across the primary business units of AMAX, Inc. In Figure 11–7 we observe a strong need for corporate involvement in the areas of mining technology, R&D, and human resources management to assure that the sources of commonality among businesses are properly exploited. This is also valid, to a lesser extent, in the areas of marketing and sales, and exploration. Figure 11–8 stresses the importance of establishing coordinating mechanisms to exploit intangible interrelationships in the metal industry, where competition from foreign government control sources is widespread. Opportunities for transferring know-how across geographical areas, both domestically and internationally, are of the highest priority among all businesses except coal and fertilizer. There also seems to be opportunities for sharing skills through commonality of major clients and industries, for example, Bethlehem Steel and the steel industry, respectively. Finally, all of the business units share a declining consumption rate relative to GNP, which places them in the same generic industry environment, calling for a common managerial approach.

Competitors' interrelationships exist when a firm competes with diversified rivals in more than one business unit. Multipoint competitors necessarily link industries together because actions toward them in one business may have implications in another.

The presence of multipoint competitors expands the scope of competitive analysis. This time, rather than searching for opportunities to share resources and skills to enhance one's own competitive position, the focus is on retaliatory actions that we could undertake in response to the overall competitive standing of a rival firm. The clearest example of this kind of issue arises in global competition. When Michelin successfully penetrated the American market with radial tires, Goodyear was confronted with a very difficult strategic response. Fighting Michelin aggressively in the U.S. markets had very asymmetric consequences for both players with Michelin having little to lose, and Goodyear being threatened in the primary source of its profitability. Goodyear's answer to this puzzle was to retaliate aggressively in the French market. This strategic action, besides the ultimate financial implications that it might generate, has the purpose of providing a signal to a competitor that sets up the rules of the game. What we have described is a "turf" battle: Michelin was charging into Goodyear's "profit sanctuary." A smart response was for Goodyear to do likewise and charge against Michelin's profit sanctuary.

Multipoint competitors are important because they might force us to consider different forms of retaliation in jointly contested industries, as well as providing opportunities to exploit our overall corporate position vis-à-vis a multipoint competitor.

FIGURE 11-7. AMAX, Inc.: Tangible Interrelationships

VALUE-CHAIN ACTIVITIES	MOLYB	NICK	TUNG	COPP	Ld/Zn	SILV	SPECIALTY METAL	IRON	ALUM	MAGN	OIL & GAS	FERT	COAL
Product R&D	X	X	X	X	X	X	X			X			
Process R&D	X	X	X	X	X	X	X	X	X	X		X	X
Purchasing of Raw Materials													
Transportation of Raw Materials													
Exploration	X		X	X				X			X		X
Mining Technology and Mining Operation Know-How	X		X	X	X	X		X					X
Marketing	X	X	X	X	X								
Sales	X	X	X	X	X								
Distribution													
Human Resources	X	X	X	X	X	X	X	X	X	X	X	X	X

Note: X indicates sharing

Key:
Molyb Molybdenum Copp Copper Alum Aluminum
Nick Nickel Ld/Zn Lead/Zinc Magn Magnesium
Tung Tungsten Silv Silver Fert Fertilizer

SOURCE: Gray (1984).

FIGURE 11-8. AMAX, Inc.: Intangible Interrelations

SOURCE OF INTERRELATIONSHIP	MOLYB	NICK	TUNG	COPP	Ld/Zn	SILV	SPECIALTY METAL	IRON	ALUM	MAGN	OIL & GAS	FERT	COAL
Major Clients	X	X	X				X	X	X	X			
Domestic Areas (U.S.)	X	X	X	X	X	X	X	X	X	X			
Major Geographic International Areas	X	X	X	X	X	X	X	X	X	X	X		
Industries	X	X	X	X	X		X	X	X	X			
Foreign Government Controlled Production	X	X		X	X	X			X		X	X	
Declining Consumption Rate Relative to GNP	X	X	X	X	X	X	X	X	X	X	X	X	X

Note: X indicates sharing
Key:
Molyb Molybdenum   Copp Copper   Alum Aluminum
Nick Nickel   Ld/Zn Lead/Zinc   Magn Magnesium
Tung Tungsten   Silv Silver   Fert Fertilizer

SOURCE: Gray (1984).

Configuration of Activities of the Value Chain: The Case of the Telecommunications Equipment Industry World-Wide

A key decision to be made in the development of a horizontal strategy is to decide on the physical configuration of the value chain. Depending on the potential that exists for achieving primarily economies of scale and scope, it could be advantageous to centralize one activity in a single location, or to disperse it across multiple areas in the world. This choice often leads to profound differences in the managerial systems required to integrate the resulting administrative tasks. Thus, the issues of *configuration* of the value chain, and *coordination* of the value activities represent key design questions of an horizontal strategy.

In order to provide a concrete illustration of the important issues of configuration and coordination surrounding the deployment of a horizontal strategy, we have chosen the world-wide telecommunications equipment industry as a core study.[2]

The telecommunications equipment industry world-wide is large and fast growing. In 1986, world-wide sales in this industry were close to $30 billion. The industry is very heavily concentrated with five firms supplying more than half of total demand. The leading competitors are the following:

FIRM	1985 WORLD-WIDE MARKET SHARE (%)	COUNTRY OF ORIGIN
AT&T Technologies, Inc.	20	U.S.
ITT	12	U.S.
L. M. Ericsson	7	Sweden
Siemens	6	West Germany
GTE	6	U.S.
NEC	4	Japan
OKI	4	Japan
Hitachi	4	Japan
Fujitsu	4	Japan

Market sales of telecommunications equipment falls into four major categories: cable, main-exchange switchgear, transmission equipment, and station equipment. All of these products complement each other and are required in a balanced mix for the development of a telecommunications equipment network. The issues that affect the configuration and coordination for the overall industry are summarized in Figure 11–9. It is apparent that the central activities providing the foundation for horizontal strategy are research and development; components manufacturing; assembly, testing and quality control; and marketing, distribution, and sales. Figure 11–10 presents the main advantages and disadvantages for a centralized configuration and a high coordination in each one of the respective value activities. The resulting analysis allows us to conclude that R&D and components manufacture would have the highest potential for sharing resources across all businesses. This imposes a high pressure to

FIGURE 11–9. Factors Affecting Configuration and Coordination in the World-wide Telecommunications Equipment Industry

FACTORS FAVORING CENTRALIZED CONFIGURATION	• The existence of unexploited economies of scale beyond the size of national markets • Rising R&D, production, logistics, and distribution economies • Lowering of trade barriers • Falling of transport costs • Homogenizing of marketing systems, business practices, and infrastructure • Falling communication and coordination costs and increasing speed and scope of communication technology • Homogenizing of product needs among countries • Flexible manufacturing allows production of multiple varieties in a given facility
FACTORS FAVORING HIGH COORDINATION	• Computerization of manufacturing process and other coordination among activities • Greater mobility of buyers internationally • More multinational and global buyers

Source: Koh (1986).

centralize these activities in one or very few world locations, and to exercise a high degree of coordination to reap the resulting benefits. On the other extreme, assembly, and marketing, distribution, and services present little potentials for economies of scale and scope, and, therefore, there is little pressure to concentrate and integrate those activities. Somewhere in between resides the testing and quality control activity, where some regionalization and coordination appears to be advantageous.

The reader might want to go back to Chapter 5, where we use the same example to illustrate the concept of strategic groups. Figure 5–15 divides the players in the telecommunication equipment industry—using the configuration and coordination dimensions—into four distinct competitive groups.

Organization and Managerial Infrastructure for Horizontal Strategy

We said in the introduction of this chapter that the vertical nature of flows prevailing in the conventional organizational structure is an impediment to the proper execution of horizontal strategy. Therefore, to assure successful implementation, we need to create horizontal mechanisms that cut across the existing organizational units of the firm. There is a wide variety of ways to adapt the organizational structure, the administrative processes and systems, and even the culture of the firm to be more responsive to the demands of horizontal strategy.

There are two important critical dimensions for deciding the proper design

FIGURE 11–10. Factors Affecting Configuration and Coordination in the Main Activities of the Value Chain of the World-wide Telecommunications Equipment Industry

ACTIVITIES OF THE VALUE CHAIN	CENTRALIZED CONFIGURATION		HIGH COORDINATION	
	Advantages	Disadvantages	Advantages	Disadvantages
R&D	• Go down the learning curve faster • Gain economies of scale and scope • Gain protection against leakage of technology to outsiders	• Failure to respond to heterogeneous local product needs • Failure to respond to government requirements in some countries	• Bargaining advantages with governments • Share know-how and learning • Better serve multinational buyers	• Government restrictions on flow of information • Coordination costs • Organizational difficulty in achieving transfer of technology among subsidiaries
Components Manufacturing	• Gain scale economies • Go down the learning curve faster	• Transport and storage costs • No hedge against the risks of single site • Unable to encourage nationalistic purchasing	• Share know-how and learning • Bargaining advantages with governments	• Coordination costs • Government restrictions on the movement of components
Assembly	• Better quality control	• Higher costs • Failure to respond to heterogeneous local product needs • Failure to respond to local government requirements • Failure to encourage nationalistic purchasing	• Share know-how and learning • Flexibility in responding to competitors • Respond to changes in comparative advantage among countries	• Coordination costs • Government restriction on flows of goods and information
Testing and Quality Control	• Some economies • Some learning curve effects	• Failure to differentiate product in final production stages to address local market segments • Failure to encourage nationalistic purchasing • Failure to respond to government requirements	• Share know-how and learning • Solidify brand reputation of the product throughout the world	• Coordination costs
Marketing, Distribution, and Sales	• Standard marketing policies world-wide • Solidify brand reputation world-wide	• Failure to respond to heterogeneous local product needs • Failure to encourage nationalistic purchasing • Failure to respond to government requirements	• Solidify brand reputation world-wide • Better serve multinational buyers • Gain flexibility in responding to competitors	• Coordination costs • Organizational difficulty in achieving cooperation among subsidiaries • May not respond well to heterogeneous local conditions

of an organizational structure: segmentation and coordination. From a segmentation point of view, we can define formal units within the organization whose primary roles are that of assuring horizontal responsiveness among businesses. This is commonly done by grouping distinct, yet related, businesses within clusters, and assigning the management of those businesses to a group or sector manager, whose primary role is the integration of key activities common to the subordinated businesses.

Whenever segmentation alone is not enough, we have to resort to lateral coordinating mechanisms, the most popular among them being the creation of liaison roles, task forces, committees, integrating managers, and matrix relationships, which allow preservation of a dual focus of managerial attention: one pertaining to business development, and the other concerned about identifying and exploiting lateral synergism.

Another device which has proven to be enormously effective in reinforcing horizontal strategic commitment is the intelligent use of key managerial processes and systems available to the firm: planning, control, communication and information, and reward systems.

The planning process, when properly instituted, can become a powerful integrative instrument, which facilitates the recognition of the critical tasks confronted by the firm, and the achievement of a healthy consensus on how to go about the execution of those tasks. Within the numerous encounters, retreats, and analytical sessions that are intrinsic to a well-run planning process, there are many opportunities to address sharing resources and concerns, and to develop the proper commitment to carry on the demanding obligations imposed by a horizontal strategy.

The management control system is the key for monitoring, evaluating, and reformulating the action programs which emerge from the planning process. When horizontal strategies are an important part of the overall strategic blueprint of the firm, the control system should properly identify the way to follow up the shared responsibilities, and to assure that their execution reaches a healthy congruency. A key consideration in this respect, is the development of performance measures and procedures which stimulate the intended behavior on the part of all managers involved. Transfer price systems, make-or-buy policies, revenue and cost allocation procedures, and capital budgeting systems for joint projects are just a handful of examples of mechanisms that could make or break the kind of climate needed for cooperative behavior among independent managers.

Communication and information systems are also key elements to support the horizontal structure. Not only do they constitute the backbone for facilitating the flow of information across all of the organizational entities, but they can become the central vehicles to instill the desired sense of direction, and to resolve conflicts whenever they emerge. Managing the interface of a variety of independent businesses, functions, and geographical areas—including, possibly, a wide number of countries with completely different cultural backgrounds—requires enormous communication and informational skills, and extraordinary wisdom to reconcile legitimately different points of view. The communication process becomes the foundation for the negotiations that have to take place in order to develop constructive relationships among a wide variety of heterogeneous players. Facilitating that process is an indispensable factor in the successful execution of a horizontal strategy. This also calls for the dissemination or acceptance of clear procedures for conflict resolution, including direct access to top managers entrusted with the authority for sanctioning eventual appeals.

The rewards and human resources management system are the final, but perhaps the most important of all of the managerial processes available to firms to facilitate horizontal integration. Rewards are key for motivating people, and motivation shapes behavior. Therefore, it is imperative to recognize the complexities of rewarding individuals not only for actions that belong to their own private domain, but also for those that reside outside their scope of authority, but bring in positive results for the overall organization. Moreover, human resource practices pertaining to selection, promotion, placement, appraisal, management development, and employee relations can truly facilitate the intended collaboration across business units. Among the most commonly used practices in that regard, we can mention: personnel rotation, organization-wide selection and training of personnel, promotional practices that encourage broad experiences, and personnel development programs with ample scope.

Some Final Comments

We have not exhausted the issue of horizontal strategy. There is still much to be said with regard to the role that lateral interrelationships play in diversification strategies, as well as in supporting vertical integration decisions. In Chapter 9, we alluded to the importance of the value chain as a way of suggesting alternatives for growth linked to related diversification. In the next chapter we address the important question of vertical integration, which refers to the extent of the activities that a firm chooses to perform internally. That decision depends upon the degree in which value activities can be shared by the business units of the firm. We are leaving for the next chapter a description of an integrative methodology that allows us to consider the interaction of horizontal and vertical issues.

Notes

1. Often in this chapter we rely for our presentation on Michael E. Porter's able treatment of this subject. Michael E. Porter, *Competitive Advantage: Creating and Sustaining Superior Performance* (New York: The Free Press, 1985).

2. The description of the telecommuni-

cations equipment case study already started in Chapter 5, and it is based on Lynette Koh, *Strategic Analysis of the Worldwide Telecommunications Equipment Industry*, unpublished master thesis, Sloan School of Management, MIT (1986).

CHAPTER 12

Vertical Integration

Vertical integration involves a set of decisions that, by the nature of their scope, reside at the corporate level of the organization.[1] These decisions are threefold:

1. Defining the boundaries a firm should establish over its generic activities on the value chain (the question of make versus buy or integrate versus contract).
2. Establishing the relationship of the firm with its constituencies outside its boundaries, primarily its suppliers, distributors, and customers.
3. Identifying the circumstances under which those boundaries and relationships should be changed to enhance and protect the firm's competitive advantage.

This set of decisions is of critical importance in defining what the firm is and is not, what critical assets and capabilities should reside irrevocably within the firm, and what type of contracts the firm should establish to deal with its external constituencies.

We have conceptualized the firm as a chain of activities that relates to the administration, production, distribution, and marketing of the goods and services that constitutes its primary outputs. The degree of ownership the firm chooses to exercise on these activities will eventually determine the breadth and extent of its vertical integration. To decide this question, the firm has to weigh carefully the economic, administrative, and strategic benefits against the costs resulting from vertical integration. As indicated earlier, this is a question that goes far beyond the simple economic analysis of make or buy decisions. It also involves issues of flexibility, balance, organization, market incentives, and capabilities for managing the resulting enterprise.

Characterization of Vertical Integration

Before entering into more substantive discussions on the advantages and disadvantages of vertical integration and the ways to achieve it, we provide a few definitions to characterize and measure the vertical integration of the firm

137

through four dimensions: direction, degree of integration and forms of ownership, breadth, and extent.

1. The *direction of vertical integration* recognizes two different ways of adding value to the inputs and outputs of the firm, respectively: *backward*, which means getting closer to suppliers by incorporating into the firm a given input to the current core; and *forward*, which involves a greater proximity to customers by putting a given output of the core under the firm's umbrella. These two forms of vertical integration are sometimes referred to as upstream and downstream extensions, respectively.

2. *The degree of integration and forms of ownership* are defined for each one of the important inputs and outputs of the firm. The categories used to describe vertical integration according to this dimension are the following:

● *Full integration*

A firm which is fully integrated backward on a given input satisfies all the needs for that particular input from internal sources. Likewise, when a firm is fully integrated forward for a given output, it is self-sufficient in providing internally the demand for that product or service. Fully integrated companies have complete ownership of their assets.

● *Quasi-integration*

Quasi-integrated firms do not have full ownership of all of their assets in the value chain related to a given input or output. Rather, they resort to several mechanisms to assure steady relationships with its external constituencies, which reside somewhere in between long-term contracts and full ownership. Prevalent forms of quasi-integrations are joint ventures or alliances, minority equity investments, loans, loan guarantees, licensing agreements, franchises, R&D partnerships, and exclusivity contracts.

● *Tapered integration*

Tapered integration represents a partial integration, backward or forward, that makes the firm dependent on external sources for the supply of a portion of a given input, or for the delivery of a portion of a given output. For the fraction of the input or output that the firm handles internally, it can resort to either a full integration or a quasi-integration mode of ownership.

● *Nonintegration*

A firm which decides not to integrate on a given input or output depends completely on external providers for its necessary support. The commitments that facilitate the reliance on those external parties are normally drafted in terms of contracts which represent joint responsibilities but no internal integration. Common forms of contracts are competitive bids, long-term contracting, and rent of assets.

The degree of backward integration can be measured by the percentage of requirements of a particular input that the firm secures from internal sources. Similarly, the degree of forward integration for a given output can be measured by the percentage of it that is transferred directly to an organizational unit adjacent to the core of the firm.

3. *The breadth of integration* measures how broadly or narrowly the firm depends on its own internal sources for all of its important inputs and outputs. Breadth can be measured as the fraction of value provided by the internal inputs or outputs of the firm with regard to the total value of its internal and external transactions, for a given organizational unit.

4. *The extent of integration* refers to the length of the value chain housed by the firm, whether it is limited to just a few stages or if it covers the whole array. One way of measuring the extent of integration is through the fraction of the final value of a product or service that is added by the firm.

Benefits and Costs of Vertical Integration

As any other crucial decision that has significant strategic importance, vertical integration is affected by complex trade-offs. All of the benefits that support a movement toward increased vertical integration have to be balanced against potential costs. The final decisions as to the direction, degree, breadth, and extent of vertical integration have to be undertaken based not only on numerical computations of the financial consequences of those decisions, but with a broader understanding of the strategic implications of the competitive standing of the firm.

To save the reader from a lengthy commentary on detailed factors that support and discourage vertical integration, we simply present Figures 12–1 and 12–2 with a listing of benefits and costs related to vertical integration decisions.

The major benefits of vertical integration can be classified into four categories: (1) *cost* to internalize economies of scale and scope, and avoid transaction costs from imperfect markets; (2) *defensive market power* which provides autonomy of supply or demand, and protection of valuable assets and services; (3) *offensive market power* which allows access to new business opportunities, new forms of technology, and differentiation strategies; and (4) *administrative and managerial advantages* rising from a more simplified managerial infrastructure when basic tasks are brought inside as opposed to outside the firm.

Those benefits have cost counterparts which represent barriers to vertical integration. The deterrent factors can be grouped also under four major labels: (1) *cost* represented by increased overhead and capital investment requirements, and the inability to reach operational breakeven; (2) *flexibility loss* resulting from the difficulties to respond quickly to changes in the external environment because of being locked into a more rigid position than competitors when vertical integration is higher; (3) *balance penalties* resulting from underutilized capacities or unfulfilled demands originated from drastic changes in demand patterns; and (4) *administrative penalties* derived from the burden of managing a more complex and heterogeneous set of activities.

FIGURE 12–1. Benefits from Vertical Integration

COST REDUCTIONS

- Internalize economies of scale resulting in a cost lower than outside suppliers and distributors
- Avoid high transaction costs from many sources; e.g., expensive physical transfer of goods and rendering of services, writing and monitoring contracts with external providers, excessive coordination, and heavy administrative burden
- Eliminate cost penalties from unpredictable changes in volume, product design, or technology that the firm requires to introduce in contracts with providers
- Generate economies from combined operations, sharing of activities, and maintenance of a stable throughput in a long stretch of the value chain

DEFENSIVE MARKET POWER

- Provides autonomy in supply or demand that shields the firm from foreclosure, unequitable exchange relationships, and opportunistic behavior and overpricing on the part of upstream or downstream providers of goods and services
- Gets for the firm protection of valuable assets and know-how from unwanted imitation or diffusion
- Allows the retention of exclusive rights to the use of specialized assets
- Protects the firm from poor service provided by external suppliers that may have special incentives to favor competitors
- Guards against important attributes being degraded, distorted, ignored, or impaired by sloppy distribution, marketing, or service operations
- Raises entry or mobility barriers

OFFENSIVE MARKET POWER

- Increases opportunities for entering new businesses, upstream or downstream
- Makes new forms of technology available for existing business base
- Promotes strategy of differentiation through the control of the interface with final customers
- Improves market intelligence
- Facilitates a more aggressive strategy to gain market share

ADMINISTRATIVE AND MANAGERIAL ADVANTAGES

- Impose throughout the firm a market discipline through direct dealing with providers, up and downstream
- Increase the interchange of information with external sources
- Ameliorate the need of a heavy organizational structure and large bodies of personnel

---

Conceptual Frameworks for Vertical Integration

There are two frameworks particularly helpful in guiding managers to a better understanding of vertical integration decisions. The first one, proposed by Gordon Walker, uses two basic dimensions as the key to analyze these kinds of issues: the qualifications of the buyer relative to best outside suppliers, and the degree of strategic risk associated with sourcing from an outside supplier. Qualifications of the inside and outside sources are determined by their capabilities to meet specific performance criteria such as price, delivery, quality,

FIGURE 12-2. Costs of Vertical Integration

COST INCREASE

- Increased operating leverage implies a greater fraction of fixed costs and a correspondingly greater business risk
- Higher capital investment requirements
- Possibility of increased overhead costs

FLEXIBILITY LOSS

- Flexibility to diversify is reduced
- Ability to tap different distributors and suppliers is curtailed
- Harder to compete when the environment takes a negative turn
- Higher exit barriers and larger volatility in earnings
- Great difficulties in getting rid of obsolete processes

BALANCE REQUIREMENTS

- Vertical integration forces the firm to maintain a balance among the various stages of the value chain because otherwise external shocks might produce cost penalties on several counts: excess capacities and unfulfilled demand simultaneously

ADMINISTRATIVE AND MANAGERIAL PENALTIES

- Vertical integration forces the use of internal incentives (as opposed to market incentives), which are more arbitrary in character and might produce strong distortion if not properly applied
- Vertical integration could affect adversely the flow of information to the firm from either customers or suppliers
- Vertical integration may impose an additional burden in the organizational structure, managerial processes, and systems in order to deal effectively with increased heterogeneity and complexity

---

and technological leadership. Strategic risk has three components: (1) *appropriation risk* represented by the ability of the firm to appropriate the rent generated by its assets; (2) *diffusion risk* corresponding to the possibility of unwanted imitation and the difficulties of protecting the know-how of the firm when external vendors are used; and (3) *degradation risk* refers to the deterioration of product characteristics and service to clients when distribution and sales are not the responsibility of the firm. Figure 12–3 represents the alternatives for vertical integration decisions associated with different combinations of strategic risk and buyer qualification.

The second framework for vertical integration, proposed by David Teece, exploits even further the concepts of rent appropriation just described. It postulates that the ability of the firm to appropriate the rent depends on two main factors: (1) *regimes of appropriability* or the ability to maintain exclusive know-how or effective legal protection of key value activities of the firm; and (2) the *access to complementary assets* which are those required to manufacture and commercialize a product in addition to the assets owned by the firm. Complementary assets can be classified into three different groups: (1) *generic* when assets are widely available and can serve the needs of many firms; (2) *specialized*

FIGURE 12–3. Strategic Risk vs. Buyer Qualification Matrix
for Vertical Integration Decisions

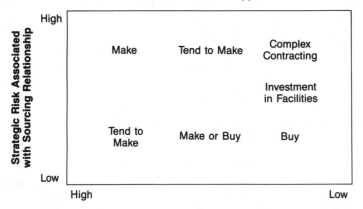

SOURCE: Gordon Walker "Strategic Sourcing, Vertical Integration and Transaction Costs," *Interfaces*, 19, 3, May–June 1988, pp. 62–73.

when the firm is fully dependent for its smooth operation on the use of a scarce asset, but this asset can easily be modified to serve other needs; and (3) *co-specialized* when it is a specialized asset that cannot be modified to serve other needs.

The implications for vertical integration and contracting options, which are derived from these concepts, are clearly spelled out in the flow chart given in Figure 12–4. This indicates that the firm has to integrate vertically whenever a number of conditions are fulfilled simultaneously: complementary assets are specialized, the appropriability regime is weak (it does not offer enough protection from copying and imitation), specialized assets are critical, the cash position allows for an investment, and the firm finds itself in a favorable position with regard to competitors. Otherwise, the firm would have to negotiate part of its share of profits away to contract for the required access to specialized complementary assets.

The main lessons to be learned with regard to vertical integration are that:

- Critical complementary assets must be owned (mainly when they are specialized for the needs of the firm), unless there is a cash constraint. In this last case, the firm should try to form a partnership with at least a minority position.
- When critical complementary assets are not owned, the firm should secure early access to them, mainly when its product is not protected by a tight regime of appropriability (it is an easy matter to copy it), and when the capacity of complementary assets is in short supply and may become a bottleneck.

FIGURE 12–4. Selecting Between Vertical Integration and Contracting Options

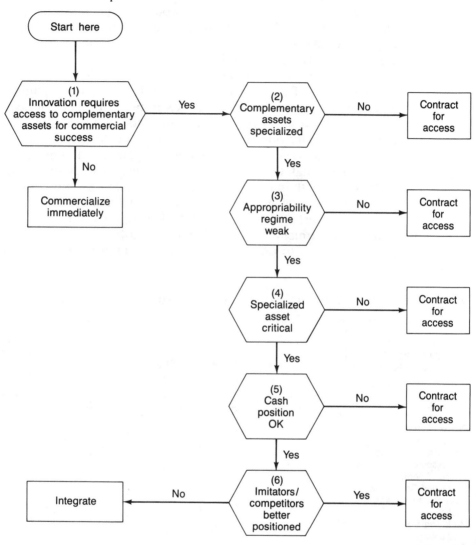

SOURCE: David J. Teece, ed., *The Competitive Challenge: Strategies for Industrial Innovations and Renewal.* (Cambridge, MA: Ballinger Publishing Co., 1987), p. 204.

A Methodology for Linking Horizontal Strategy and Vertical Integration

Horizontal strategy and vertical integration are very closely linked. An individual business unit which is considering extending its value chain might conclude that it is both infeasible and uneconomical due to its own reduced scope.

However, when the issue of adding another value activity is considered from the overall point of view of the firm, it might be perfectly affordable and desirable to add that activity because it would be shared by a large number of business units. That is the central linking element between vertical integration decisions which extend the activities of the value chain and horizontal strategies which share activities across businesses within the value chain.

Be aware that the interrelationships between business units and activities in the value chain, if exhaustively examined, lead us into a significant combinatorial problem. Every business unit has to be confronted with one another in each value activity to detect the potential for synergisms and the ways of exploiting them. This obviously can be done, but the task is such that it can only be performed by staff analysts or business planners. It is not an assignment that can be meaningfully addressed by top managers in an organization.

Therefore, with full knowledge of this technique's limitations, we favor a simple way of identifying potentials for horizontal and vertical integration opportunities, as presented in Figure 12–5. This is a deceptive figure because it tends to convey a highly structured and easy task. This is far from being the case. First, we have to reflect on the current state of the firm's activities, and

FIGURE 12–5. Identification of Horizontal and Vertical Integration Opportunities

STAGES OF VALUE CHAIN	BUSINESS UNITS								OVERALL DEGREE OF HORIZONTAL INTEGRATION	
									Current H M L	Desired H M L
Product R&D Process R&D Basic Raw Materials Processed or Fabricated Raw Materials Fabricated Components Assembled Products Testing Marketing & Sales Distribution Retailing Service										
OVERALL DEGREE OF VERTICAL INTE-GRATION — Current H M L										
Desired H M L										

Use the following code to fill the form:
C = Current: Activity developed by the SBU or another unit of the firm
F = Future: Potential for horizontal and vertical integration opportunities

Key:
H = High
M = Medium
L = Low

attempt to identify for each stage in the value chain the existing breadth or coverage of each activity across the business units. This effort leads to an assessment of the overall degree of vertical integration by business unit, and the current degree of exploitation of horizontal strategy across business entities. The next task is to reflect on the desired changes. We could proceed by analyzing the desired degree of vertical integration by business unit, and then capture how these expectations can be supported by the sharing of value-chain activities across business units from the pursuit of meaningful horizontal strategies.

The chart clearly is an oversimplified way of addressing horizontal and vertical integration, yet we believe it contains the heart of the issues to be resolved in the proper reconfiguration of this critical decision.

Note

The primary sources for the topic of vertical integration that we have used throughout the chapter are: Kathryn Rudie Harrigan, *Strategic Flexibility: A Management Guide for Changing Times* (Lexington, MA: Lexington Books, 1985); Robert H. Hayes and Steven C. Wheelwright, *Restoring our Competitive Edge: Competing through Manufacturing* (New York: John Wiley & Sons, 1984); Michael E. Porter, *Competitive Strategy: Techniques for Analyzing Industries and Competitors* (New York: The Free Press, 1980); Gordon Walker, "Strategic Sourcing, Vertical Integration and Transaction Costs," *Interfaces*, 19, (May–June 1988), 62–73; and David J. Teece, "Profiting from Technological Innovations: Implications for Integration, Collaboration, Licensing, and Public Policy," David J. Teece, ed., *The Competitive Challenge: Strategies for Industrial Innovations and Renewal*, (Cambridge, MA: Ballinger Publishing Co., 1987).

13

Corporate Philosophy

Corporate philosophy is a rather permanent statement, articulated primarily by the CEO, addressing the following issues:

1. The relationship between the firm and its primary stakeholders—employees, customers, shareholders, suppliers, and the communities in which the firm operates.
2. A statement of broad objectives of the firm's expected performance, primarily expressed in terms of growth and profitability.
3. A definition of basic corporate policies with regard to issues such as management style, organizational policies, human resources management, financial policies, marketing, and technology.
4. A statement of corporate values pertaining to ethics, beliefs, and rules of personal and corporate behavior.

The corporate philosophy has to provide a unifying theme and a vital challenge to all organizational units, communicate a sense of achievable ideals, serve as a source of inspiration for confronting daily activities, and become a contagious, motivating, and guiding force congruent with the corporate ethic and values. The corporate philosophy is a statement of basic principles that sets apart those firms which have been able to articulate it in a positive manner from those which lag behind in this respect.

An individual working for a firm has to become an active collaborator in the pursuit of the corporate purposes; he or she must share the vision of the firm and feel comfortable with the way it is translated or expressed in traditions and values. The behavior of individuals is conditioned by this framework and they must intimately sense that by following these guidelines, they are fulfilling their most personal needs for achievement. The corporate philosophy is a personal drive for their own lives.

It is interesting to observe that those firms that have taken the time to truly reflect on the essence of their purpose and communicate it in writing through a public statement of corporate philosophy tend to produce documents that look very much alike. A cynical interpretation of this convergence of principles might be that they are empty of any significance—the so-called motherhood-and-apple-pie values—which do not convey any meaning for individual behavior. Normally, the reality is quite the opposite. These firms really adhere to a code of conduct which goes far beyond a narrow expectation of profitability, and project the firm as a public entity with full acceptance of a wide range of societal responsibilities.

The best way to convey the communicational power of philosophy statements is to provide concrete illustrations. We have chosen two very different organizations, Analog Devices (Figure 13–1) and Citicorp (Figure 13–2), as two good examples of forceful declarations of corporate philosophy.

FIGURE 13–1. The Statement of Corporate Philosophy of Analog Devices, Inc.

CORPORATE PURPOSE AND SCOPE OF BUSINESS

Our purpose is to search continuously for opportunities where we can make unique or valuable contributions to the development and application of analog and digital signal processing technology. In so doing, we strive to offer our customers products that improve the performance, quality and reliability of their products, and thereby increase the productivity of human and capital resources, and contribute generally to upgrading the quality of life and the advancement of society.

Our primary product focus is on monolithic integrated circuits manufactured on semiconductor processes developed by and proprietary to Analog Devices. We also manufacture hybrid circuits and assembled products, including components and board-level subsystems and systems.

Our customers consist primarily of original equipment manufacturers (OEMs) who incorporate Analog's products into a wide variety of instruments and systems. The Company's served markets include laboratory and industrial automation, defense/avionics, telecommunications, transportation, computer peripherals, and selected high-end consumer products. We pursue business in these markets on a world-wide basis.

OUR EMPLOYEES

Our employees' personal motivation and interests are primarily related to ascending needs for security, safety, purpose, recognition, identity, and the realization of one's full potential. Our corporate goals are thus best achieved in an environment that encourages and assists employees in the achievement of their personal goals while helping Analog Devices achieve its goals. We therefore seek to offer our employees a challenging and stable work environment where they can earn above average compensation for above average performance and contribution to the Company. It is our policy to offer unrestricted opportunity for personal advancement irrespective of race, creed, color, sex, national origin, age, or disability.

Our objective is to build mutual respect, confidence and trust in our personal relationships based upon commitments to integrity, honesty, openness, and competence. Our policy is to share Analog Devices' success with the people who make it possible.

OUR CUSTOMERS

Satisfying our customers' needs is fundamental to our survival and our prosperity. These needs can best be understood in terms of the support we lend our customers in helping them meet their objectives with the minimum use of their resources. Thus, our goal must be to provide superior, easy to use, reliable products that conform to specifications and offer innovative solutions to our customers' problems. We must back up these products with excellent product literature and strong customer service that includes highly effective applications assistance, quick response to inquiries, and dependable delivery. We must work hard at understanding our customers' businesses so that we may anticipate *their* needs and enhance *their* effectiveness. We wish to be major suppliers to our key customers and to establish long lasting business relationships based on quality, performance and integrity.

OUR STOCKHOLDERS

Our responsibility to our stockholders is to satisfy their desire for a secure and liquid investment that provides an attractive rate of return. Our objective is to consistently earn a return on invested capital that is well above average for all manufacturing companies and comparable to the most successful companies in our industry. By achieving consistent growth with a high return on capital we can offer our stockholders an attractive opportunity for capital appreciation.

OUR SUPPLIERS

Our suppliers are partners in our efforts to develop market share by fulfilling our customers' needs. This requires that we be open and frank about our plans and requirements as they would affect our suppliers. It also requires that we seek to understand the constraints placed upon our suppliers by their technology, cost structure, and financial resources. We place strong emphasis on associating with suppliers who are financially stable, competent, and honest and who are consistent in meeting their delivery and quality commitments to us.

OUR COMMUNITY

Our goal is to be an asset to every community in which we operate by offering stable employment and by lending effort and support to worthy causes. We encourage our employees to take an active interest in their communities and contribute their efforts toward making their communities better places to live and work. We make a special effort to aid and support those universities and colleges that are an important source of scarce resources.

GROWTH

Growth is an important means by which we satisfy the interests of our employees, our stockholders, and our customers. High caliber people look for opportunities for personal development and advancement which can best be achieved in a growth environment. Our stockholders are looking for an above average return, which is much more likely to be achieved by a growth company.

To achieve growth we continuously search out and focus on application for our products and technology that have above average long-term potential. We also continuously broaden the range of our products and technology, mostly through internal development.

PROFIT

Profit generated by our business is the primary source of the funds required to finance our growth. Without growth and profits we cannot achieve our corporate objectives. Our financial goals are to generate profit after tax and return on capital comparable to the best-performing companies in our industry and—without taking unreasonable risks—self-fund our growth.

MARKET LEADERSHIP

Our goal is to obtain the largest share of each market segment we serve. We believe the key to achieving market share is to enter growth markets early with superior, innovative products, and to provide a high level of quality and customer service. Our markets are world-wide in scope, and our objective is to achieve comparable penetration in every major geographical market.

FIGURE 13–1. (continued)

QUALITY

Customer satisfaction, and thus our success, is critically dependent on dependable delivery of high quality products and services. A high quality product or service is one that is delivered when promised and performs as specified under all intended operating conditions throughout its intended life.

The achievement of high quality begins with product planning, but it must also be an integral part of product design and the design and implementation of manufacturing processes. High quality depends upon the commitment of all employees to the on-time production of defect free products and services.

High quality is not a static condition. It is susceptible to continuous improvement through systematic identification and elimination of causes of errors and variances, through development of improved designs and processes and through education and training. Continuous improvement of quality leads not only to greater customer satisfaction but also to higher productivity and lower costs.

The concept of quality improvement is applicable to every area of the Company, including marketing, customer service, finance, and human resources, as well as manufacturing and engineering. Every employee should be committed to quality improvement and should be determined to "do it right the first time and do it better the next time."

SUMMARY

Achieving our goals for growth, profits, market share, and quality creates the environment and economic means to satisfy the interests and needs for our employees, stockholders, customers, and others associated with the firm. Our success depends on people who understand the interdependence and congruence of their personal goals with those of the Company, and who are thus motivated to contribute toward the achievement of these goals.

SOURCE: Analog Devices, Inc., "Corporate Objectives." Reprinted by permission of Analog Devices, Inc., Norwood, MA.

FIGURE 13–2. An Annotated Statement of Corporate Philosophy for Citicorp

---

I. RELATIONSHIP WITH STAKEHOLDERS

Citicorp maintains that its relationship with its customers is its primary focus, for without customers the corporation recognizes that it would not be able to meet the needs of its employees, stockholders, or its communities at large.

Its relationship with its employees can be described as tough but fair, where one's intelligence, wit, and energy, without regard to race, sex, or creed can become the driving force in predicting how far one can move within the corporation.

Citicorp's commitments to its many publics can be recognized in its Public Issues Committee's underlying principle that its business franchise is grounded in the support of its corporate constituencies, and in the belief that its social responsibility is to provide to its customers the highest quality of services.

The mandate of the Public Issues Committee is to ensure that the public interest is maintained both in the performance of Citicorp's business roles and in the achievement of a more competitive business environment.

Its role during 1981 provided for the continued review of bank policies of public interest and appropriate policy guidance. More specifically, it reviewed the bank's Equal Employment Opportunity and Affirmative Action goals and accomplishments, and reviewed the goals and strategies of external affairs. In summary, the Committee confirmed the concept that public confidence in the corporation's performance, commitment to good corporate citizenship, and achievement of legal and regulatory relief for the industry are all critically linked.

II. BROAD CORPORATE OBJECTIVES

As Citicorp looks ahead towards the future by moving through the decade of the 1980s its efforts will be guided by its broad framework of corporate goals:

- Citicorp is not interested in being the largest financial institution, only one of the most profitable.
- It will endeavor to provide all financial services which the customer requires.
- The broad network is considered a major asset because of the expertise and knowledge it gives the institution, and Citicorp is committed to its enlargement domestically and world-wide.
- The customer of today wants a package of services as has been shown by the success of Merrill Lynch's Cash Management Account. Citicorp needs to develop additional thrusts for the business to meet this kind of customer demand.
- Finally, Citicorp will keep standing by its stock of human capital upon which, in the last analysis, its success depends and in this spirit will continue to promote its employees purely on the basis of performance and opportunity.

III. CORPORATE POLICIES

We present now the components of Citicorp's policies. Particularly for purposes of this study, management style, human resources, and technological policies will be highlighted.

Management Style

Citicorp's management style cannot be summarized into one all-embracing description, but can be traced back to various approaches which complement each other in contributing to the growth of the company. There are managers who prefer to be more hands-on while others are more conceptual and yet others who are more administrative. Many managers, however, can be described as sporting an aggressive style which allows for a willingness to take chances and bring new ideas into fruition.

Managerial resources are vital to Citicorp's attainment of financial leadership and therefore it is committed to a system where talented and able people are identified, tracked, and given opportunities to develop their skills and take on greater responsibility.

This system involves consistent line management reviews of performances and career development plans of each officer from every organizational level.

Human Resources

Citicorp views the ability to hire and train highly qualified people as one of its major challenges for the future. In the words of the Chairman of the Board, "This institution owes its realization to the capabilities of its people. I've said repeatedly that people are the only game in town. We have assembled the largest body of talent that has ever existed in the financial services industry."

Its personnel policies can be defined by way of five basic principles which are exemplified as the Citicorp approach:

- To provide the climate and resources that will enable all staff to advance on merit as far as their talents and skills will take them, without regard to age, color, handicap, marital status, national origin, race, religion, sex, or veteran status
- To offer pay and benefits that are fair and competitive
- To make certain that ideas, concerns and problems are identified and that two-way communication is effectively maintained
- To provide an environment that identifies, encourages, and rewards excellence, innovation, and quality customer service
- To remember always that respect for human dignity is fundamental to our success

In addition, the Personnel Planning Committee which was recently formed has as its task, the responsibility of ensuring that Citicorp's personnel policies and programs keep in step with changes in the internal and external environments. Even though the committee

FIGURE 13–2. (continued)

will focus on compensation, personnel policy, and staff relations, its review will encompass the full range of personnel activities.

Technological Policies

Citicorp's commitment to pursuing advancements in technology has been in existence for a long time. Even though the corporation does not consider itself a high technology company as in the case of IBM, it maintains that high technology will pervade the financial services industry.

Inherent in this commitment is the establishment of the corporate Technology Committee which is chartered with identifying and taking advantage of opportunities in telecommunications and data processing markets while maintaining a decentralized, line-driven management philosophy.

Futhermore, Citicorp recognizes that its customers will be looking for information-based services on a global scale and in order to respond technology will become a major force.

IV. CORPORATE VALUES

Citicorp's success can be attributed to a strong set of central values which are shared experiences of Citibankers across the globe. First, its innovative character rests in a strong tradition of creativity, uniqueness, and a dauntless approach to solving problems. Second, Citibankers share a passion to excel with an energetic commitment to be first in whatever needs to be done. Third, integrity is a cherished quality where honesty and respect for individuals both internally and externally are exemplified through its people relationships.

The Corporation's global expansion developed an appreciation for decentralization in decision making. Citibankers are expected to make decisions and solve problems wherever they are assigned without a central decision-making authority. It is through this decentralization that Citicorp has assured diversification in risk taking.

To an unusual extent, the Corporation has taken a great deal of chances on its people by giving them opportunities to lead, an opportunity to make mistakes, grow, develop and test new ideas.

Finally, Citicorp can be characterized for its uniquely open style and informality in its communications.

SOURCE: Antoinette M. Williams, "A Strategic Planning Process: The Case of Citicorp and Its Commercial Finance Subsidiary," 1983. Reprinted by permission of Antoinette M. Williams.

Methodology for a Diagnosis of Corporate Philosophy

Although we have indicated that a corporate philosophy represents permanent values, it is useful to undertake occasionally a deep revision of every single one of the tasks that shape corporate strategy. The corporate philosophy is not an exception. The methodology that we use for this purpose is portrayed in Figure 13–3. The way to proceed is to solicit from the top managers of the organization a brief description of the existing condition of the various elements that are part of the expression of corporate philosophy. Having done that, we turn our attention toward the changes that seem to be desirable along the same dimensions. As we have indicated with the previous corporate tasks, our intent is to capture the need to change and to translate those desires into statements of strategic thrusts.

FIGURE 13–3. Framework for Analyzing Changes of Corporate Philosophy

	EXISTING	DESIRED
RELATIONSHIPS WITH STAKEHOLDERS Employees Customers Shareholders Suppliers Communities		
BROAD CORPORATE OBJECTIVES Growth Profitability		
CORPORATE POLICIES Management Style Organizational Policies Human Resources Management Finance Marketing Manufacturing Technology		
CORPORATE VALUES Ethics Beliefs Rules of Personal and Corporate Behavior		

Whenever this process leads to the identification of significant modifications of the current corporate philosophy, we normally face a task of unquestionable difficulty, since they most likely force adaptations of deeply ingrained attitudes and cultural values.

CHAPTER 14

Strategic Posture of the Firm

The strategic posture of the firm is a set of pragmatic requirements developed at the corporate level to guide the formulation of corporate, business, and functional strategies. It is expressed primarily through the formulation of corporate strategic thrusts; corporate, business, and functional planning challenges; and corporate performance objectives. As shown in Figure 8–1, principal inputs to define a strategic posture of the firm are the vision of the firm and the corporate intelligence. These have been the subjects of discussion in Chapters 8 through 13.

Corporate Strategic Thrusts and Planning Challenges

The corporate strategic thrusts constitute a powerful mechanism to translate the broad sense of directions the organization wants to follow into a practical set of instructives to all key managers involved in the strategic process. We define strategic thrusts as the primary issues the firm has to address during the next three to five years to establish a healthy competitive position in the key markets in which it participates.

Strategic thrusts should contain specific and meaningful planning challenges for each of the business units of the firm. In addition, depending on the nature of the organizational structure, the strategic thrusts could also contain challenges addressed at the corporate level as well as some key centralized functions.

The process of collective reflection on the strategic thrusts by a group of top managers, conducive to listing these primary issues, assigning priorities and identifying responsible individuals in charge of responding to those thrusts, represents a major advance in the strategic thinking of the firm. On the surface, it may sound like a relatively simple and straightforward exercise. This is far from being the case. The formulation of strategic thrusts permits raising the central questions the firm should address for a meaningful strategic development. Once the strategic thrusts are stated and agreed on, we have established

153

an important part of a coherent and relatively stable framework to conduct the strategic planning process.

There is significant power in the actions set in motion by the definition of strategic thrusts. Regardless of the individual concerns and situational issues residing at every level in the organization, we know that those managers who have been entrusted with the responsibility of responding to strategic thrusts will have to produce proper answers to those questions, mobilizing every unit in the organization in the desired overall direction. This provides an opportunity for all competencies and talents in the organization to be thoroughly applied in the pursuit of clearly established lines of action. It is a most constructive procedure to call for the maximum participation of all individuals in the firm. For example, suppose that one issue considered critical at a given point in time is the excessive maturity of the firm's businesses. A thrust demanding the identification of new business opportunities will create a flare of energy to be channeled into this question. Although there is no guarantee that an edict of that sort will necessarily solve that particular problem, at least it assures that all key managers will search for alternatives to be contributed to its solution, will report on their finding, and will communicate to their peers the result of their probes. In other words, it will generate a challenge and a sense of urgency to a strategic concern that otherwise could have continued to be neglected.

We should realize that the strategic thrusts are the depository of all of the previous analytical processes that need to be conducted at the corporate level. Prior to stating the central issues that should be part of the strategic thrusts, it is useful to compile the desired changes detected in previous corporate tasks which legitimately generate a call for further attention. Examples are changes in the mission of the firm, changes in the definition of some of its businesses, activities stemming from horizontal strategy, changes induced by vertical integration strategies, changes in corporate philosophy, and whatever other special strategic issues have been captured so far. These are the elements that are part of the corporate internal scrutiny. Similarly, the strategic thrusts should address the opportunities and threats uncovered in the corporate environmental scanning process. These are responses stemming from the economic outlook, the analysis of the critical industrial sectors and primary markets of the firm, and either favorable or unfavorable trends of technological, human resources, political, social, and legal nature.

Figure 14–1 illustrates in a very succinct way the statement of strategic thrusts for AMAX, Inc., and the assignment of planning challenges to the organizational levels in charge of responding to those thrusts. The statement also includes relevant measures of performance intended to monitor the operational and strategic results associated with each thrust. Notice that there is a priority assigned to those planning challenges, depending on the level of intensity of the necessary participation required. It could be beneficial to expand the description of each thrust to allow for a better communication of the issues to be covered.

The chart containing strategic thrusts can be read in three different ways. First, we could analyze the overall set of issues identified to check whether, as a set, they really capture the totality of the strategic initiatives facing the

FIGURE 14–1. Statement of Strategic Thrusts, Assignment of Planning Challenges, and Definition of Performance Measures for AMAX, Inc.

| STRATEGIC THRUSTS | CORP. LEVEL | GROUP LEVEL | BUSINESSES | | | | FUNCTIONS* | | | | | | PERFORMANCE MEASURES |
			Metals	Oil and Gas	Fertil-izers	Coal	Fin.	H.R.	Tech.	Proc.	Manf.	Mrktg.	
Divest nonstrategic business units	1		2			1	1						Present a plan for $100M to the Executive Committee by June 30
Reduce costs by gains in efficiency and cost reduction programs			1	1	1	1		2	2	2	1		5% reduction on average at end of year
Increase investment in strategic areas	1		1	2	1	1	1			2		2	Present a plan for $100M to the Executive Committee by June 30
Develop new marketing expertise in strategic areas	2	2			2	1						1	Increase market share by 1% before October 30 through introduction of products in new markets
Reduce debt/total capital ratio	1						1				2		A 25% debt-to-total-capital ratio should be achieved by the end of the year
Upgrade senior managers to think in terms of external environment as well as financial and operational issues	2							1					Prepare special program for April 15
Reduce costs by restructuring organization and reducing overhead	1	2					2						5% reduction on average at the end of the year

Code: 1 = Key role in formulation and implementation; 2 = Important support and concurrence; 3 = Minor involvement.
*Functions included: Finance, Human Resources, Technology, Procurement, Manufacturing, Marketing.

SOURCE: Adapted from Gray (1984).

corporation, and the extent to which they really represent a forceful and impacting challenge. This is a check for completeness and aggressiveness.

Second, we can read each thrust horizontally to make sure that we have properly identified the organizational units and managers who should be involved in formulating the action programs addressing each thrust, as well as supporting their implementation. If we have a situation where too many organizational entities are forced to participate in a central way, we might need to institute a coordinating mechanism such as a task force, a committee, or a coordinating manager to allow those organizational units to operate in an integrated way. Incidentally, the density of the chart gives us a sense of the degree of centralization or fragmentation that exists in these key strategic responsibilities of the firm.

And third, we can read this chart vertically to detect the role assigned to each individual organizational unit. This allows us to spot potential bottlenecks and the criticality of the involvement of each unit. To some extent, that also gives us another check of completeness. For example, suppose that we know that human resources are a very important strategic factor in the firm as a whole, and yet, when we look at the challenges assigned to that unit, we find a very passive and secondary role. This indicates a mismatch between the existing description of the thrust and its intent.

Corporate Performance Objectives

Corporate objectives are quantitative indicators of the overall performance of the firm. Typically, companies choose to express corporate objectives via a selective number of indices predominantly of a financial nature.

Although there is no universal set of such indices, we can classify them into two major categories. The first includes quantitative financial measures that relate to size, growth, profitability, capital markets, and a host of other financial variables. These performance evaluators are of the greatest importance because they address objectives which are central to the short-term well-being of the firm, as well as its long-term survival and development. Also, the financial standing of the firm and its position in the capital markets constitute parameters of undeniable managerial significance. American managers have often been criticized for paying excessive attention to the response of capital markets and being obsessed by short-term (even quarterly) financial performance. Without denying the importance of financial performance, managers should aim at having a balance between short- and long-term consequences, acting in a way that does not distort one of these dimensions in favor of the other. Figure 14–2 lists suggested performance variables to measure this category of financial indicators. We attempt to contrast current and past performance, and to set up objective targets for the short and the long term.

Various considerations serve as a base to arrive at a numerical expression of those targets: (1) the historical performance achieved by the corporation; (2) the projected trends expected from the existing and new business lines; and

Figure 14–2. Corporate Performance Objectives: Size, Growth, Profitability, Capital Markets, and Other Financial Measures

PERFORMANCE INDICATORS	PAST YEARS 19×1	PAST YEARS 19×2	PAST YEARS 19×3	CURRENT YEAR 19×4	OBJECTIVE TARGETS Short Term	OBJECTIVE TARGETS Long Term
SIZE Sales / Assets / Profits / Market value / Number of employees						
GROWTH Sales / Assets / Profits / Market value / Number of employees						
PROFITABILITY Profit margin / Return on assets (ROA) / Return on equity (ROE) / Spread ($ROE - k_E$)						
CAPITAL MARKETS Dividend yield (Dividend/Price) / Total return to investors / Price/Earning ratio (P/E) / Market-to-book value ratio (M/B) / Payout (Dividend/Earning) / Price per share (P) / Book value per share (B)						
LIQUIDITY Current ratio / Quick ratio / Defensive interval / Cash position / Working capital from operations / Cash flow from operations						
LEVERAGE Debt-to-equity ratio / Short-term vs. Long-term debt / Times interest earned / Cash flow vs. Interest payments						
TURNOVER Total assets turnover / Average collection period / Inventory turnover						
OTHER FINANCIAL Bond rating / Beta / Cost of equity capital (k_E) / Cost of debt / Weighted average cost of capital						

(3) the financial position of the firm's competitors. It is important to recognize the financial performance of the key competitors not only from the perspective of comparative analysis, but also because firms in the same industry attract the same group of investors in the capital markets.

These corporate performance objectives should not be applied indiscriminately to every business of the firm but should be adjusted to recognize the

FIGURE 14–3. Financial Corporate Performance Objectives for AMAX, Inc.

PERFORMANCE INDICATORS	PAST YEARS			CURRENT YEAR	OBJECTIVES
	1980	1981	1982	1983	1984–86
1. Sales Size (M$) Growth (%)	2,949 3.0	2,799 (5.0)	2,415 (13.7)	2,285 (5.3)	Sales growth will not be an objective since divestiture will play an important role
2. Profits Size (M$) Growth (%)	470 28.8	231 (50.8)	(390) (268.8)	(205) 47.4	Profits should grow at a real rate exceeding the rate of inflation
3. Assets Size (M$) Growth (%)	5,276 34.0	5,449 3.3	5,090 (6.6)	4,724 (7.2)	Asset size will be reduced by divestitures
4. Capital structure long- term debt/equity Long-term debt/total capital	57.4 37.0	56.7 36.0	71.5 41.7	73 42	 25%
5. ROE	22.1	8.5	—	—	12–15%
6. ROA	11.3	7.5	—	—	10–12%
7. Turnover Ratios Assets (%) Times interest earned	64 4.8	52.2 2.3	45.8 (0.5)	 (3)	 >2 times
8. Earnings per share ($)	7.48	3.31	(6.53)	N.A.	
9. Dividends as a % of earnings (Payout)	32	73	—	—	
10. Average-market-to- average-book value	1.25	1.32	1.03	0.85	
11. P/E ratio range	8–5	21–11	—	—	

SOURCE: Gray (1984).

different contribution they make to the short- and long-run performance of the firm.

Figure 14–3 illustrates the financial corporate performance objectives for AMAX.

The second major category of corporate performance objectives is oriented at measuring the overall efficiency of the managerial functions of the firm, particularly human resources, technology, procurement, manufacturing, and marketing. Incorporating these functional measures at the corporate level is relevant whenever we deal with centralized functions. Otherwise, the functional measures should become part of either divisional or business performance

FIGURE 14–4. Corporate Performance Objectives for Centralized Functions

		PAST YEARS			CURRENT YEAR	OBJECTIVE TARGETS	
PERFORMANCE INDICATORS		19x1	19x2	19x3	19x4	Short Term	Long Term
HUMAN RESOURCES MANAGEMENT	Job satisfaction Job performance Turnover Absenteeism Motivation Job security Career prospects Psychological stress Safety health conditions Income						
TECHNOLOGY	Rate of technological innovation R&D productivity Rate of return in R&D investment Resources allocated to R&D Rate of new products introduction Technology-based diversification Royalties or sales of technology Cycle time of product development						
PROCURE-MENT	Cost Service Quality Vendor relationships						
MANU-FACTURING	Cost Delivery Quality Flexibility New products introduction						
MARKETING	Product strategy Distribution Price strategy Promotion and advertising						

This table suggests performance criteria for each function. Specific quantitative indicators must be defined to fit the particulars of a firm.

indicators, depending on where the function resides within the organization. Figure 14–4 on page 159 lists functional indicators in a format quite similar to the one we use for financial corporate performance. The figure limits itself to broad criteria to evaluate these functions, leaving the exact specification of quantitative indices to be decided in accordance with the particular circumstances of the firm. Part IV of the book deals extensively with functional strategy. The reader is referred to that part for a better treatment of functional issues.

Resource Allocation
and Portfolio Management

After all the proposals related to corporate, business, and functional programs are completed, a major task that inevitably resides at the corporate level is the allocation of limited resources to attend the wide array of requests coming from the lower levels of the firm. In most organizations, top managers face the difficult decision of having to discriminate among the proposals that are finally submitted because the financial, technological, and human resources available to the firm are not sufficient to support every proposed initiative. This fact of life is the fundamental reason why resource allocation is a truly centralized decision that cannot be delegated to lower echelons of the firm. Besides, this calls for the identification of criteria to allow the organization to make the best possible use of the available restricted resources.

In business firms, the bottom line for resource allocation is *value creation*. In financial terms, it means that the profitability enjoyed by the economic entity—the firm, the business, or a project—should exceed its cost of capital.

The cost of capital is a concept that has involved technical ramifications. However, from a simple point of view it represents the required rate of return of a given investment, and it consists of two components. One is the risk-free rate, namely, an opportunity available to any investor that guarantees without any uncertainty a return. In the United States, the normal measures of risk-free rates are Treasury bills and government bonds. Having been assured that level of profitability, a rational investor would only consider additional investment alternatives if they could generate a higher level of return. This additional level of profitability fundamentally depends on the inherent risk of the financial investment option, and it is called risk premium. Thus, the cost of capital is simply the risk-free rate of return plus a risk premium. Figure 15–1 presents a procedure to estimate the cost of equity capital by using the capital-assets pricing model.

Although this is a simple economic concept, we often find that managers do not recognize the significance of economic profitability as a yardstick in measuring the financial performance of every individual unit of the firm. Obviously, accounting profitability—meaning that the businesses are in the black—is not enough. Economic value is only created when the businesses of

161

FIGURE 15–1. Estimate of the Cost of Capital Using the Capital-Assets Pricing Model

---

The cost of equity capital may be estimated as:

$$k_E = \text{risk-free rate} + \text{risk premium} = r_f + \beta_E \times (r_m - r_f)$$

1. *Risk-free rate $= r_f$*
   The risk-free rate corresponds to the return on an investment that offers a sure return. Normally, it is estimated as the return on government-backed Treasury bills.
2. *Risk premium*
   The risk premium may be estimated as the product of two terms:

$$\text{Risk premium} = \left\{ \begin{array}{c} \text{Volatility} \\ \text{of the equity} \\ \text{cash flow} \end{array} \right\} \times \left\{ \begin{array}{c} \text{Average risk premium} \\ \text{for the capital} \\ \text{markets} \end{array} \right\}$$

2.1 *Average risk premium $= (r_m - r_f)$*
   The average risk premium for the capital markets has been estimated to be about 9%. The term r_m represents the average return of the market.
2.2 *Volatility $= \beta_E$*
   The volatility is a coefficient that measures the inherent risk of an equity cash flow. When the volatility is 1, the risk is equivalent to the average in the market.
   The volatility coefficient for a given business can be estimated from historical market returns for the firm or for other firms in the same industry. Volatility estimates for specific companies are provided by Merrill Lynch, and other financial firms. In the following table we present a summary of the relative riskiness of different industries as measured through their β-coefficients.

The β-Coefficient of Different Industries*

Industry	Beta
Electronics components	1.49
Crude petroleum and natural gas	1.07
Retail department store	0.95
Petroleum refining	0.95
Motor vehicle parts	0.89
Chemicals	0.88
Metal mining	0.87
Food	0.84
Trucking	0.83
Textile mills products	0.82
Paper and allied products	0.82
Retail grocery stores	0.76
Airlines	0.75
Steel	0.66
Railroads	0.61
Natural gas transmission	0.52
Telephone companies	0.50
Electric utilities	0.46

---

*These are assets betas. The effect of financial leverage has been removed.

SOURCE: Richard A. Brealey and Stewart C. Myers, *Principles of Corporate Finance,* 3rd ed. (New York: McGraw-Hill, 1988), p. 182.

the firm and the firm as a whole enjoy profitability levels which exceed that of their respective cost of capital.

If we consider the definition of return on equity:

$$\text{ROE} = \frac{\text{Profit after interests and taxes}}{\text{Equity}}$$

we can assert that:

Accounting profitability results when $ROE > 0$,

Economic profitability results when $ROE > k_E$,

where k_E is the cost of equity capital.

Thus, *spread* $(ROE - k_E)$ is positive.

Sources of Value Creation

When economists talk about perfect competitive markets, there always seems to be a tendency to emphasize the long-term equilibrium conditions that result from perfect competition. In this world of perfect balance of supply and demand, there are no real sources of economic returns that can legitimately exceed the cost of capital. When perceived from that dimension, the true objective of a strategy is to break the economic equilibrium law. It is to search for windows of opportunity that might position the firm in a unique competitive advantage which can legitimately allow it to claim economic rents beyond those resulting from perfect competition. Rather than living in this long-term equilibrium condition, the central purpose of strategy is, first, to identify opportunities to create disequilibrium, and then to protect and sustain those conditions as long as possible. This is the essence of a long-term sustainable competitive advantage.

Throughout the book, we have been addressing the sources of competitive advantage—which now we are labeling sources of value creation—and the mechanisms to exploit them. The winning formula is very simple. It consists in understanding the opportunities available in the industries in which we participate, and then developing internally—primarily through value-chain mechanisms—the necessary competencies to allow us to achieve a singular competitive position.

Alan Shapiro, a finance professor, when talking about corporate strategy and capital budgeting decisions, concludes that there are five basic lessons to achieve excess return:[1]

1. Investments structured to fully exploit economies of scale are more likely to be successful than those that are not.

2. Investments designed to create a position at the high end of anything, including the high end of the low end, differentiated by quality or service, will generally be profitable.

3. Investments aimed at achieving the lowest delivered cost position in the industry, coupled with a pricing policy to expand market share, are likely to succeed, especially if the cost reductions are proprietary.

4. Investments devoted to gaining better product distribution often lead to higher profitability.

5. Investments in projects protected from competition by government regulation can lead to extraordinary profitability. However, what the government gives, the government can take away.

These are indeed sobering lessons which emphasize important sources for competitive advantage, such as economies of scale, product differentiation, cost advantage due to learning curve, proprietary technology, and monopoly control of low-cost raw materials; advantages of new entrants in deregulated industries mainly when a new technology becomes available, access to distribution channels, and government protection.

Measuring the Contribution to Value Creation

There are a wide number of methodologies available to assess the attractiveness of any form of economic activity at the level of the firm, the business unit or a project. We review briefly the most important ones.

THE DISCOUNTED CASH-FLOW MODEL

There is no question that the best methodology available to assess the economic value of the firm, a business unit belonging to the firm, or a project within an individual business unit is to compute the net present value (NPV) of the expected future cash flows generated, discounted at an appropriate rate, and adjusted for inflation and risk. The discount rate is, in fact, the cost of capital associated to the entity.[2]

The advantages and disadvantages of discounted cash-flow models and the mechanics of calculation are well known and have received wide attention. We assume that the reader is familiar with this basic concept. Because of the orientation of the book, we concentrate on methodologies more directly applicable to strategic assessment of businesses within the context of the firm's overall portfolio.

THE MARKET-TO-BOOK VALUE MODEL (M/B)

A meaningful proxy for the value of the equity of the firm in a country with an efficient capital market, such as the one prevailing in the United States, is given by the market value of the common stock. The assumption is that the market price of common shares represents a consensus of the present value assigned by investors to the expected cash flow streaming from the assets the firm has already in place, as well as from investments the firm will have the opportunity to make at some time in the future, once the interest payments to debtholders have been subtracted.

Therefore, within an efficient capital market setting, the objective of the firm equates to maximizing the market value of equity, provided that the capital structure of the firm has already been defined. A broader objective would be the maximization of shareholders' wealth, considering the capital structure as one of the decision variables.

The market value of a firm's common shares is an indicator that can assist managers both in assessing the shareholders' wealth, as well as in measuring its economic and financial performance vis-à-vis other firms in its industry. It is not surprising, therefore, that managers carefully observe long-term trends in the capital market as an ultimate guide for the managerial success of business firms. On the other hand, excessive concern in day-to-day movements of stock market indicators has been repeatedly stated as one of the most negative forces pressuring American managers to inappropriate short-term orientation. Therefore, there seems to be a paradox in the capital-market messages to the manager. But this is not so. There is plenty of evidence that the market does reward long-term performance, and penalizes erratic behavior intended to hide unfavorable developments in the short run.

The preceding considerations make highly desirable the use of evaluation methodologies in which the market price of the common shares plays an essential role, while retaining the legitimacy of the NPV approach. The M/B model represents such a tool.

The M/B model is a blend of two different perspectives of the firm. In the denominator, the book value of the firm's shares provides the accountant's perspective, which corresponds to the historical measurements of resources contributed by shareholders. In the numerator, the market value of the firm's shares gives the investor's perspective, which corresponds to an assessment of future payments generated from the assets the firm has already in place and from the investments the firm would have the opportunity to make at some time in the future. Therefore, the M/B ratio can be equated to:

$$\frac{\text{Expected future payments}}{\text{Past resources committed}}$$

The basic message of the M/B model can be summarized as follows:

- If M/B is equal to 1, the future payments are expected to yield a fair return on the resources committed. The firm is neither creating nor destroying value.
- If M/B is greater than 1, there is an excess return. The firm is creating value for the shareholders.
- If M/B is less than 1, the return is under the benchmark provided by the market. The firm is destroying value for its shareholders.

When we refer to book value, we assume that all distortions induced by accounting rules have been corrected, mainly the ones produced by inflation and the charges of certain investments as expenditures in one period (most notably R&D and advertising).[3]

THE RELATIONSHIP BETWEEN PROFITABILITY AND GROWTH

Two of the most relevant measures of corporate performance are growth and profitability. Although there are strong interactions between these two concepts, very often growth and profitability goals are set up completely independent of one another. This is a major logical flaw. There is a close association between profitability and growth as measured by spread $(ROE - k_E)$, market-to-book value (M/B), and net present value (NPV). The relationships are exhibited in Figure 15–2.

When a business is profitable, it means that its return on equity exceeds its cost of equity capital (spread is positive) which implies that the business is creating value (therefore, M/B is greater than 1) and the corresponding discounted cash flow produces a positive net present value (NPV positive). Under those conditions, growth will significantly contribute to create value at a compounding rate, and the greater the growth, the greater the value created. Exactly the opposite is true when the business is unprofitable, in which case spread is negative, M/B is less than 1, net present value is also negative, and growth is a damaging contribution that helps in accelerating the value destruction process. The optimal strategy for ongoing businesses that are generating a return on equity below the cost of capital is to minimize growth, or even better, to disinvest and have a negative growth. In that way, market value is maximized. Eventually, the best strategy could be liquidation, particularly if the permissible disinvestment rates are very small. Finally, when the business is at breakeven (spread is zero, M/B equals 1, and net present value is also zero) growth does not help nor hinder value creation.

FIGURE 15–2. Relationship Between Profitability and Growth

	PROFITABILITY OF THE FIRM OR BUSINESS		
	Profitable	*Break Even*	*Unprofitable*
SPREAD = $ROE - k_E$ M/B NPV	positive greater than 1 positive	0 1 0	negative less than 1 negative
CONTRIBUTION OF GROWTH TO VALUE CREATION	growth creates value	growth does not create nor destroy value	growth destroys value

FACTORS AFFECTING THE MARKET VALUE
OF THE FIRM

Previously, we have reflected on the sources behind the acquisition of a competitive advantage which, in turn, should be translated in an increased market value of the firm. From a strictly financial point of view and without going into elaborate arguments, these sources can be explained in terms of three critical factors that determine market value: the size of spread, the rate of reinvestment of the firm's profits, and the number of years during which a firm will enjoy a favorable spread. We comment on them now.

The Size of the Spread $= ROE - k_E$

Economic profitability is achieved when the return on equity enjoyed by the firm exceeds its cost of equity capital. This concept can be captured in a single measurement, which is the spread. Obviously, the greater the spread, the greater the economic profitability and, therefore, the greater the market value.

The value of k_E represents the cost of equity capital of the firm. This is a fundamental parameter that is characteristic of each business unit. It depends on the general condition of the economy, the situation of the industry in which the business operates, and the particular policies used by the firm in managing the business. A procedure to estimate the cost of equity capital is based on the so-called capital-assets pricing model (CAPM), and is presented in Figure 15–1.

The Rate of Reinvestment of the Firm's Profits $= p$

The profits of the firm can be assigned either as dividends to its shareholders or reinvested in profitable opportunities available within the firm. The reinvestment rate (p) is the critical determinant for the growth of the firm. Let us define growth as the fraction of reinvested profits to the existing equity base of the firm:

$$\text{growth} = \frac{\text{profits reinvested}}{\text{equity}}$$

In order to get the relationship between growth and profitability, we can simply multiply and divide the right-hand side of this expression by profits:

$$\text{growth} = \frac{\text{profits reinvested}}{\text{profits}} \times \frac{\text{profits}}{\text{equity}}$$

This leads us to the relationship which links growth with the reinvestment rate and profitability:

$$g = p \cdot ROE$$

where:

$$g = \text{growth in equity}$$

$$p = \text{profit reinvestment rate}$$

$$ROE = \text{return on equity}$$

In turn, ROE can be expressed as a function of ROA as follows (see appendix at the end of the chapter).

$$ROE = ROA + \frac{D}{E} [ROA - k_D (1 - T_C)]$$

where

$$D = \text{total debt}$$

$$E = \text{total equity}$$

$$k_D = \text{debt interest rate before tax}$$

$$T_C = \text{corporate tax rate}$$

Therefore, growth can be expressed as:

$$g = p \cdot (ROA + \frac{D}{E} [ROA - k_D (1 - T_C)])$$

This expression represents a first cut of the *maximum-sustainable growth*[4] that assumes a stable debt-equity ratio and dividend-payout policy, as well as a fixed overall rate of return on assets and cost of debt. Although a coarse approximation, this number might represent a guide for corporate growth that should be considered at the corporate level.

There are many variations of alternative expressions for the maximum-sustainable growth. Our aim has been to present the simplest of those expressions in order to stress the underlying concept that a firm faces an upper bound in its objectives for future growth when the financing policy does not consider the issuing of new shares.

The Number of Years During Which a Firm Will Enjoy a Favorable Spread = n
As we indicated when discussing the sources of value creation, a positive spread is an anomaly for a firm operating in conditions of perfect competition because in the long run the market conditions will make the spread nil. The reason, however, for finding economic opportunities with positive profitability is be-

cause of the ability of the firm to sustain a form of competitive advantage that gives access to excess returns. This is what we refer to as the window of a profitable investment opportunity, and its duration is measured by the value n. Obviously, the larger this value, the more the firm will enjoy large abnormal returns, and the greater the impact on value creation.

The three factors contributing to value creation—spread, growth, and duration—as well as the second-order determinants of these factors are graphically displayed in Figure 15–3. The relationships displayed in the figure have

FIGURE 15–3. Factors Affecting the Market Value of the Firm Under Stationary Growth for a Finite Period

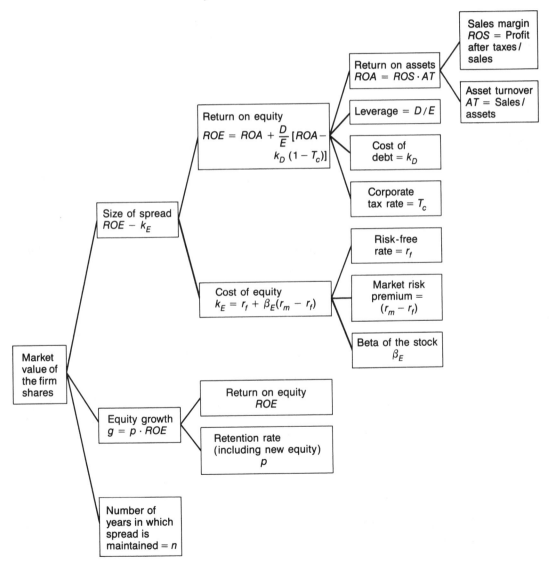

enormous implications for strategic planning and management control. From a planning point of view, we can reflect on the levers that are subject to some degree of control, and could contribute to the increase of the market value of the firm. This relationship allows us to go all the way to some key indicators such as sales margin, assets turnover, leverage, cost of debt, corporate tax rate, and profit reinvestment rate with the purpose of diagnosing where additional opportunities for value creation might reside. Subsequently, having decided on the proper courses of action to take, we can use the targets set for every indicator as an important base for management control.

Throughout this discussion, we have identified the firm as the focus of analysis; however, the same logic can be used to describe the factors that affect value added at the level of the business unit.

Once again, we are confronted with the fundamental question of the options available to the firm to create value based on the development of unique competencies vis-à-vis the firm's competitors. Considering the factors that contribute to value creation that we have recently presented, William Fruhan proposes the following basic options.[5]

- *Increase revenues*, for example by pricing the product higher than what had been possible without the existence of some entry barrier. The barrier could be the existence of patents or some form of successful product differentiation. The barrier might also result from the simple exercise of market forces such as that enjoyed by a monopolist.
- *Reduce costs below that of competitors*, again perhaps as a result of the existence of some barrier that prevents all competitors from achieving equal costs. The barrier in this instance could be, for example, scale economies achievable by only the largest firm in a market, or the ownership of captive sources of low-cost raw materials.
- *Reduce the cost of equity capital*, for example, through the design of an equity security that appeals to a special niche in the capital markets and thereby attracts funds at a cost lower than the free-market rate for equivalent risk investments, or simply by reducing the business risk below the level enjoyed by competitors.
- *Maximize the financial contribution to the market value* of the firm by increasing the tax shield from debt and reducing the cost of debt capital. This can be done by designing a debt security that is suited for a special group of investors in the market.

This message reinforces many of the issues that we have been addressing so far, like barriers to entry, economies of scale, and differentiation. But it adds an additional component of a financial type, which although harder to capture, could still be the foundation of competitive advantages.

THE MARKET-TO-BOOK VALUE
VERSUS SPREAD

One of the important uses of the M/B model is strictly as a diagnostic tool intending to position the firm against its competitors in terms of economic and financial performance. This task is greatly facilitated due to the considerable amount of public information regarding the variables included in the M/B model. The Compustat files, Value Line reports, annual reports, and financial analysts' studies all can be used to produce estimates for the firm's current market value, book value, return on equity, equity growth rate, and cost of equity capital.

A simple way of contrasting the profitability position of various firms is plotting the group of firms under consideration in an M/B-versus-spread diagram. Figures 15-4 and 15-5 on the following pages show this diagram for the firms included in the thirty Dow Jones Industrials, for the years 1980 and 1987, respectively.

A first glance at both figures tends to confirm that there is a positive association between M/B and spread. However, in the upper-right quadrant of Figure 15-4, perhaps the most striking deviation from that perceived association is the position of both Standard Oil of California (SD) and Exxon (XON). Those were companies that in the late 1970s were making extraordinarily high profits, reflected in a large spread. However, the future expectations regarding the ability of these firms to maintain those profit levels were not as high. This was reflected by an M/B ratio which, although greater than 1, did not correspond to the historical values of the spread. The measurement of spread is anchored on past performance, while the M/B ratio contains the future expectations regarding the profitability of the firm on the part of the shareholders.

There is an interesting contrast in the overall comparison of the two figures. In 1980, we had a very depressed economy in the United States, and Figure 15-4 shows it. More than half of the Dow Jones Industrials were having negative spreads and M/B ratios less than 1. Also, the largest levels of spread were about 10, and Merck, the best performer, enjoyed an M/B ratio of 3.5. The 1987 graph, admittedly built with data just before the October Wall Street crash of that year, reflects an extraordinarily bull market. Only five of the Dow Jones Industrials are found in the lower left quadrant. Merck continues to be the leading performer, but this time it exhibits a 22 percent spread and an M/B value of 10. Both market expectations and historical spread were significantly higher for all of the players.

The same kind of analysis can be carried out at different levels, with different focuses of attention. Figure 15-6 on page 174 presents the M/B-versus-spread graph for fourteen United States industries. The drug industry is the leading performer, while the most depressed one is the oil field services. Figure 15-7 on page 175 analyzes the key firms in the United States paper and forest products industry. We observe great differences in spread among those companies, but yet, the M/B ratio is relatively flat and does not necessarily reward the higher performers. Finally, Figure 15-8 on page 176 corresponds to an application of the M/B-versus-spread graph to the portfolio of a business of a given firm. In order to do so, we have to compute directly the market value of each individual business unit by projecting its equity cash flow and then discounting it back using the equity cost of capital as the discount rate. This is not needed in the case of a firm because the market value can be obtained directly from the price of its common shares.

FIGURE 15–4. An M/B-Versus-Spread Graph for the 30 Dow Jones Industrials (1980)

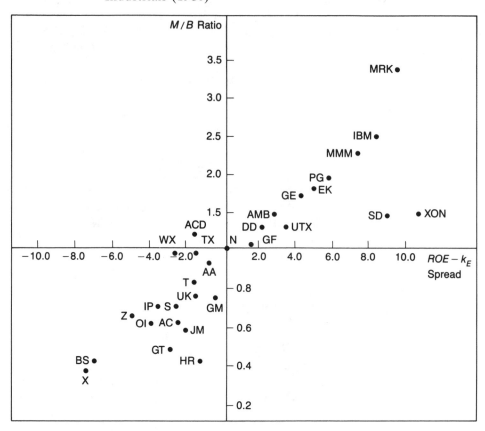

Key for the Figure

AA:	Alcoa	MMM:	Minnesota Mining
AC:	American Can	MRK:	Merck Company
ACD:	Allied Chemical	N:	Inco Limited
AMB:	American Brands	OI:	Owens Illinois
BS:	Bethlehem Steel	PG:	Procter & Gamble
DD:	Du Pont	S:	Sears Roebuck
EK:	Eastman Kodak	SD:	Standard Oil of California
GE:	General Electric	T:	AT&T
GF:	General Foods	TX:	Texaco
GM:	General Motors	UK:	Union Carbide
GT:	Goodyear Tire	UTX:	United Technology
HR:	International Harvester	WX:	Westinghouse
IBM:	IBM	X:	U.S. Steel
IP:	International Paper	XON:	Exxon
JM:	Johns Manville	Z:	Woolworth

SOURCE: Marakon Associates, "Criteria for Determining an Optimum Business Portfolio," 1981. Reprinted by permission of Marakon Associates, San Francisco, CA.

FIGURE 15–5. An M/B-Versus-Spread Graph for the 30 Dow Jones Industrials (1987)

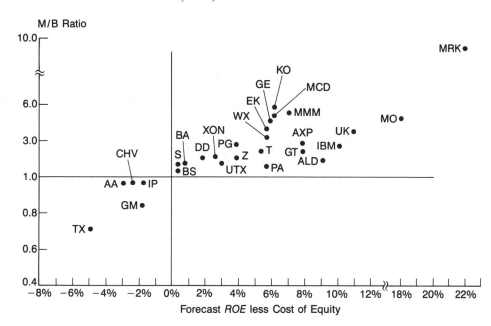

Key for the Figure

ALD:	Allied Signal	MCD:	McDonald's
AA:	Alcoa	MMM:	Minnesota Mining
AXP:	American Express	MRK:	Merck
BS:	Bethlehem Steel	MO:	Philip Morris
BA:	Boeing	PA:	Primerica
CHV:	Chevron Corp.	PG:	Procter & Gamble
DD:	Du Pont	S:	Sears Roebuck
EK:	Eastman Kodak	T:	AT&T
GE:	General Electric	TX:	Texaco
GM:	General Motors	UK:	Union Carbide
GT:	Goodyear Tire	UTX:	United Technologies
IBM:	IBM	WX:	Westinghouse
IP:	International Paper	XON:	Exxon
KO:	Coca Cola	Z:	Woolworth

SOURCE: James M. McTaggart, "The Ultimate Takeover Defense: Closing the Value Gap," *Planning Review,* (January–February 1988), pp. 27–32. Reprinted by permission of *Planning Review,* a publication of The Planning Forum, Oxford, Ohio.

Equity cash flows are determined as follows:

Business profits after tax
- After tax interest payments corresponding to the SBU
- Retained earnings for further investments in the SBU

Equity cash flow contributed by the SBU

CHAPTER 15   Resource Allocation and Portfolio Management   **173**

FIGURE 15-6. Profitability of 15 U.S. Industries (September 1987)

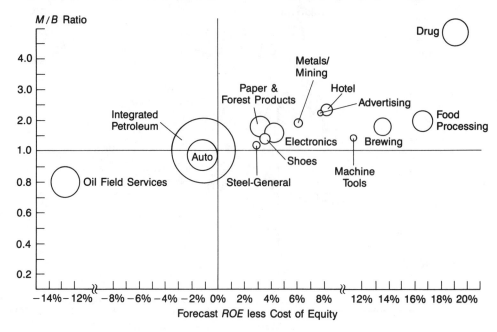

SOURCE: McTaggart, 1988.

Normally the cash flows are projected through a limited time horizon, say five years, at the end of which a terminal value has to be attached. The actual number for the terminal value depends on the assumptions being made with regard to the nature of the cash flows after the planning horizon. If the business unit is going to have an ROE equal to its cost of capital, the terminal value should be the equity book value at the end of the planning horizon. If this results in a fairly conservative assumption, a more realistic estimate of the terminal value should be attached.

Figure 15-8 allows us to distinguish clearly which are the businesses within the company portfolio which are adding value (those placed in the upper-right quadrant) and which are those that are destroying value (those placed in the lower-left quadrant).

THE MARKET-TO-BOOK VALUE RATIO
VERSUS ECONOMIC-TO-BOOK VALUE RATIO
(M/B VS. E/B)

In order to contrast the discrepancy between the market value and the historical performance of the firm, McKinsey and Co. uses a different way of examining the economic performance of a group of firms competing in a given industry. They plot the M/B ratio against an indicator they call economic-to-book value

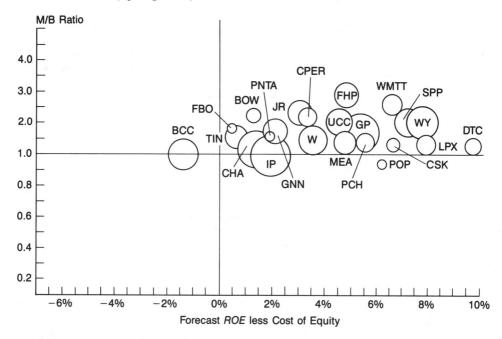

FIGURE 15–7. Profitability of Paper and Forest Products Companies (Spring 1987)

Key for the Figure

BCC	Bolse Cascade			
BOW	Bowater Inc.		LPX	Louisiana Pacific
CHA	Champion International		MEA	Mead Corp.
CPER	Consolidated papers		PCH	Potlach Corp.
CSK	Chesapeake Corp.		PNTA	Pentair Inc.
DTC	Domtar Inc.		POP	Pope & Talbot
FBO	Federal Paperboard		SPP	Scott Paper
FHP	Fort Howard Paper		TIN	Temple Inland
GNN	Great Northern Nekoosa		UCC	Union Camp
GP	Georgia-Pacific		W	Westvaco
IP	International Paper		WMTT	Willamett
JR	James River Corp.		WY	Weyerhauser

SOURCE: McTaggart, 1988.

ratio. The economic value calculation is based on historical performance projected into the future. That is, a company that has earned a positive spread of 3 percentage points, has sustained a 5 percent dividend payout to investors, and has grown its equity base at 10 percent annually, in the recent past, is assumed to do so for the next five years in the economic value calculation. Any significant discrepancy between these two values raises a diagnostic flag which would have to be examined carefully.

Figure 15–9 depicts M/B versus E/B plots for a group of companies in the publishing industry and in the oil industry. Those companies below the diagonal

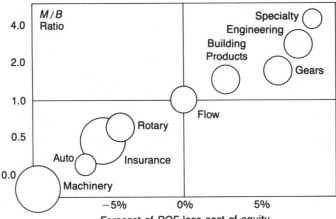

FIGURE 15–8. Profitability of Company Portfolio

SOURCE: McTaggart, 1988.

are assessed by the market as expected to have a poorer performance in the future than they have accomplished in the past. The opposite is true for a firm above the diagonal. Those firms having M/B and E/B ratios below 1 are in a more difficult position. Also, we can observe an industry standard—the regression line in the graph—that attempts to capture average industry performance. In the two examples displayed in the figure, we see the expectations are for industry performance in the future to be above past performance. Therefore, we encounter another yardstick to separate high and low performer firms with regard to the industry standard. Finally, the chart is able to display those firms which have been in a difficult economic position in the past and are expected to stay in that situation in the near future. Those are the firms falling inside the lower-left quadrangle, with both M/B and E/B ratios less than one.

THE PROFITABILITY MATRIX

Marakon Associates developed a very useful scheme to portray the economic contribution of each business unit of a firm in terms of what they refer to as *the profitability matrix.*

There are several ways of constructing such a matrix. The initial form proposed by Marakon is exhibited in Figure 15–10, in which the business ROE is plotted against its corresponding growth. There are two significant cut-off points to separate the status of each business. The ROE axis is divided by the cost of equity capital (k_E) into businesses which are profitable ($ROE > k_E$) versus unprofitable ($ROE < k_E$). The cut-off line for the growth axis corresponds to the total market growth (G) for the industry in which a business is competing. Thus, businesses where growth is greater than G are building market

FIGURE 15–9. The M/B versus E/B Graph

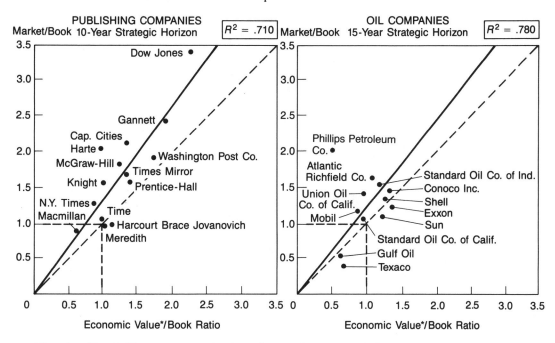

*Based on historic (five-year average) values. Source: Compustat, McKinsey analysis

SOURCE: Lily K. Lai, "Corporate Strategic Planning for a Diversified Company," 1983. Reprinted by permission of Lily K. Lai.

share, and those with a growth lower than G are losing market share, perhaps from being positioned in a harvest strategic mode. Finally, the diagonal separates those businesses which are generating cash from those which are absorbing cash. This can easily be seen by realizing that a business which falls exactly on the diagonal has a profitability equal to its growth rate. Since the business growth is given by

$$g = p \cdot ROE$$

businesses on the diagonal have p equal to 1, which means that they reinvest all their profits. That is, they are cash neutral; they neither require cash from nor deliver cash to the corporation. Businesses which are above the diagonal have a profitability greater than their growth. Therefore, p is less than 1, and they are cash generators. For opposite reasons, businesses below the diagonal are cash users.

An impacting message is derived from this matrix because it has an ability to capture in a simple and clear way the three central strategic objectives

FIGURE 15–10. The Profitability Matrix

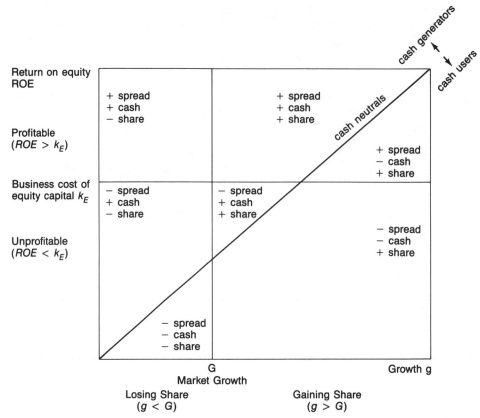

SOURCE: Adapted from Marakon Associates. "The Marakon Profitability Matrix," Commentary No. 7, 1981. Reprinted by permission of Marakon Associates, San Francisco, CA.

constituting the essence of managing the portfolio of businesses from a resource allocation perspective: profitability, market share, and cash flow implications.

Looking at the profitability matrix, it seems that the best of all worlds is to be in a position where one enjoys positive spread, increasing share, and cash generation. But very often the relationship among these variables is more complex than that. If we demand profitability from a business at a too-early stage of development, we may endanger its full potential. If we push for share too aggressively, we might erode our profitability positioning. If we deny the necessary cash to a business by targeting it inappropriately as a cash cow, we might significantly impair its chances of success. Therefore, there is no easy mechanistic way to read the strength of a business in terms of its positioning in the portfolio matrix; but yet the matrix portrays a wealth of relevant information with regard to profitability.

We can think only of three cases where we can tolerate unprofitable businesses. One is when we are dealing with a temporary situation, such as a new start up, where we are investing in the future and have clear expectations of long-run healthy profitability. The second is when the cost of exit far exceeds the cost of staying in business. This often occurs when a business is generating cash and enjoys an accounting profitability below the cost of equity capital, but the nature of its assets is such that their liquidation value is lower than the value that the business is contributing to the firm. The third situation arises when we have a losing business which has a significant strategic importance to the firm. This could happen for a number of reasons. The business could be a subproduct of another dominant activity, or it could add to the product breadth in an essential way for the firm to establish a competitive position, or it could simply have a role as a competitive harrasser, intended to neutralize or diminish the strength of a key adversary.

With regard to market share, the matrix serves to reemphasize the previous comments that profitability and growth are intimately intertwined. You do not grow for growth's sake. Growth is only acceptable when it reinforces a profitable position, in which case it helps to compound the rate of return on investment. Growth is also acceptable because it could be used as a preemptive strategic measure that, however costly as an initial move, will produce significant gains in the long run.

Finally, with regard to cash flow, the matrix states quite clearly that cash generation alone is not a meaningful attribute; it clearly depends on whether the business is profitable or not.

The inherent limitations of the matrix as presented so far reside in the representation of the two cut-off points. Since different businesses have normally different costs of capital as well as total market growth rates, it is not

FIGURE 15–11. An Alternative Profitability Matrix

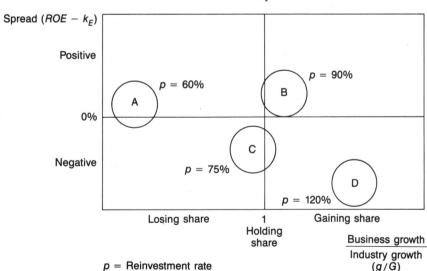

SOURCE: Adapted from Marakon Associates, "The Marakon Profitability Matrix," Commentary No. 7, 1981. Reprinted by permission of Marakon Associates, San Francisco, CA.

possible to identify single cut-off points applicable to all businesses of a corporation. Therefore, a slight modification is needed, as illustrated in Figure 15–11, where spread $(ROE - k_E)$ is used in the vertical axis, and relative growth (business growth/industry growth $= g/G$) in the horizontal axis. Unfortunately, we lose in this characterization the ability to identify what is the cash position of a business; that is, whether it is a cash generator, cash neutral, or cash user. In order to overcome this deficiency, each business unit has attached its corresponding value of the reinvestment rate (p). Obviously, if $p < 100\%$, the business is a cash generator, while if $p > 100\%$, it is a cash user. Finally, the area of each circle is proportional to total sales.

VALUE CREATION AT THE BUSINESS LEVEL

We have addressed previously the question of how to apply some of the value creation methodologies at the level of the business through the M/B-versus-spread graph and the profitability matrix. However, there are additional issues still worth raising. First is the question of contribution of each individual business to the total value of the firm. A compact way of summarizing the value contribution by each individual business of the corporation is presented in Figure 15–12 where market value is plotted against book value. As can be seen from that graph, the company as a whole has a market value lower than its book value, which might suggest that it is an organization in trouble. However, a more careful look indicates that its basic businesses A and B are pretty healthy, and business C is earning its cost of capital. Business D is adding value, but its profitability is below its cost of capital. It should be a candidate for divestment if its liquidation value L exceeds the value contributed by the business. Finally, business E should be divested as soon as possible, since it is subtracting value to the firm. Businesses of this sort are referred to as *cash traps* involving a permanent negative cash flow which is diminishing the contribution of other businesses having positive cash flows. Under such conditions, divestiture might be the most logical decision for a firm to consider. The central question pertaining to that issue is whether or not the liquidation alternative is better than holding onto that unprofitable business.

After all of those rearrangements of the firm's portfolio, the company situation should improve markedly because market value could only increase as a result of the decision to drop unprofitable businesses.

Another issue to be raised at the business level is the proper evaluation of business strategies in terms of their overall contribution to the value of the firm. Certainly, we would like to have a process whereby true options are presented to the top managers of the organization. In practice, this process does not happen. Instead, top managers are confronted with a single monolithic proposal that they either have to accept or reject. It is a typical case of reversed authority. When top managers are asked to cast judgment on the benefits of an investment alternative, the decisions have already been made because the alternatives have already been screened out leaving no real ground for decision making.

FIGURE 15–12. Example of Contribution to Market Value of Each Business of a Hypothetical Firm

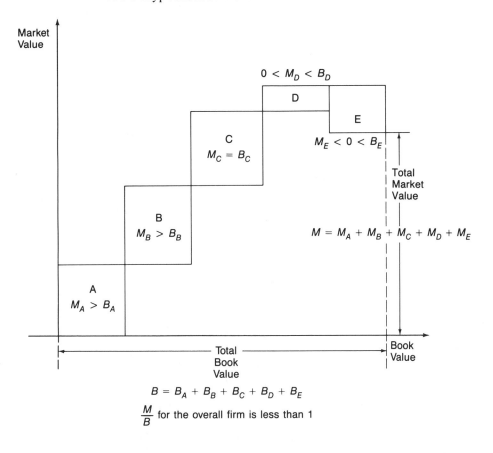

To overcome this limitation, Marakon proposes to require each business unit to submit distinct strategic alternatives based on different sets of competitive strategies. In terms of market share, we could characterize them as build, hold, harvest, and divest. Each one of these central thrusts should generate different scenarios for cash-flow projections that, in turn, produce different market-to-book value results. The collective analysis is then presented to top managers for final consideration, where they can legitimately exercise their decision-making rights. On the surface, this might not seem to be a major deviation of common practice. In reality, it truly enforces a discipline of reflecting on the economic consequences of very different strategic options. The full economic implication of these options are brought into the open with a realistic set of alternatives that otherwise might never arise in a bottom-up resource allocation process. Figure 15–13 attempts to capture the essence of this proposal.

FIGURE 15–13. Selecting the Best Strategy for a Business Unit: Evaluation of Alternative Strategic Thrust Options

For each business unit, characterize the strategic options in terms of market share thrust as:
- Build (aggressively, gradually, or selectively)
- Maintain (aggressively or selectively)
- Harvest
- Divest

Project the equity cash flow associated with each strategic option, and compute the corresponding M/B ratio.
M represents the present value of cash flow and B the existing book value of the equity base.

Summarize the M/B values for the different strategic options, for all of the business units of the firm.

Business Unit	Build	Hold	Harvest	Divest
1	1.0	1.6	1.4	1.2
2	2.1	1.5	0.9	1.8
3	0.8	1.2	1.4	1.1
4	0.3	0.5	0.7	0.8
5	2.2	2.5	1.8	1.9
6	0.5	0.7	0.6	0.5

Shaded values represent the M/B ratios under the optimum strategy for each business unit.

Select, for each business unit, that alternative that takes into account the optimum economic performance, as well as the host of additional impacts that the business positioning might have on the overall competitive standing of the firm.

Portfolio Matrices

During the 1970s and early 1980s, a number of leading consulting firms developed the concept of portfolio matrices to help managers in reaching a better understanding of the competitive position of the overall portfolio of businesses, to suggest strategic alternatives for each of the businesses, and to develop priorities for resource allocation. There has been an undeniable influence of these matrices in the practice of strategic management. Several studies have reported on the widespread use of them among American firms.

There are several elements that portfolio matrices have in common. First, they constitute graphical displays of the overall competitive standing of the portfolio of businesses of the firm. As such, they indeed constitute a powerful communication vehicle because in one single picture we are able to apprehend the overall strength or weakness of the portfolio. In order to avoid visualizing the portfolio as a static snapshot, it is also possible to follow its chronological evolution, including a future projection. In this case, the message has an additional dynamic quality attached to it.

Second, each matrix positions the business unit of the firm according to two dimensions. One is an external dimension which attempts to capture the overall attractiveness of the industry in which the business participates. The other is an internal dimension, relating to the strength of the business within its industry. The factors that describe industry attractiveness are normally uncontrollable by the firm; those that contribute to business strength are largely under the control of the firm.

The most popular portfolio matrices are:

- the growth-share matrix developed by the Boston Consulting Group, which pioneered this concept;
- the industry attractiveness-business strength matrix, conceived jointly by General Electric and McKinsey and Company, which was the first one to introduce multidimensional criteria in the external and internal dimensions;
- the life-cycle matrix developed by Arthur D. Little, Inc., which contains a fairly comprehensive methodology that leads to a wide array of broad action programs to support the desired strategic thrust of each business;
- the alternative Boston Consulting Group matrix that enriches the original BCG matrix, by bringing in broader descriptions of industry structure; and
- the profitability matrix proposed by Marakon, which captures the three most central strategic objectives of each business—profitability, growth, and cash-generation capabilities.

Figure 15–14 briefly summarizes the characteristics of external and internal dimensions used by each one of the portfolio matrices.

Third, the positioning of each business unit in the corresponding portfolio matrix is associated with a strategy that fits the competitive strength enjoyed by the business, and the degree of attractiveness of its industry. This is what has been referred to as generic or natural strategy, which serves as a useful initial reflection in the process of designing the overall strategy for the business unit.

Finally, and most importantly, this methodology contains a suggestion for allocating resources to each business in accordance with the priorities that can be identified by its position in the corresponding matrix. To facilitate this purpose, it might be useful to display not just the position of the business units of the firm within a given matrix, but also to attach some key financial information—such as sales, net income, assets, and return on net assets—in ac-

FIGURE 15–14. The Most Important Portfolio Matrices and Their External and Internal Factors

MATRICES	EXTERNAL FACTORS	INTERNAL FACTORS
Growth-Share Matrix Industry Attractiveness- Business Strength Matrix	Market growth Overall industry attractive- ness • Critical structural factors • Five-forces model	Relative market share Sources of competitive advantage • Critical success factors • Value chain
Life-Cycle Matrix	Industry maturity	Overall measurement of business position
Alternative BCG Matrix	Ways to compete (oppor- tunities for differentia- tion)	Size (sustainability) of competitive advantage
Profitability Matrix	Market growth potential Cost of capital	Profitability Cash generation

cordance to the contribution generated from the businesses in each one of the cells of the matrix. Figure 15–15 provides an example of such a display for the industry attractiveness-business strength matrix. By examining that information, we can analyze the degree of expected performance of a business, due to its position in the matrix, and the actual results. Whenever corrections are needed, the resource allocation process can be instrumental in eliminating the sources of distortion.

Portfolio matrices have received wide attention in the literature.[6] For this reason, we are providing highly compact summaries with only their essential features. Figures 15–16 through 15–19 provide this basic information related to the growth-share matrix, the industry attractiveness-business strength matrix, the life-cycle matrix, and the alternative BCG matrix respectively. The profitability matrix was already discussed in a previous section of this chapter.

CONTRIBUTION OF PORTFOLIO APPROACHES TO STRATEGIC PLANNING

Portfolio approaches have made important contributions to the improvement of strategic planning. Some of the most significant among them follow.

1. They represent simple and effective ways to facilitate the decomposition of the firm's activities into a set of well-defined businesses. Moreover, while conducting the necessary analysis to position the businesses in the two-dimensional matrix, ample opportunities exist to reassess the merits of the proposed segmentation. By permitting a clear differentiation of the nature of each business in terms of industry attractiveness and competitive position, portfolio approaches allow top managers to set appropriate and distinct strategies for each business in accordance to its inherent potential and developmental needs.

2. Portfolio approaches represent a pragmatic way to capture the essence of strategic analysis. By means of a simple visual display of the portfolio of

FIGURE 15–15. Selected Set of Performance Measurements to Describe the Portfolio of Businesses in the Industry Attractiveness-Business Strength Matrix

POSITIONING OF BUSINESSES*
Industry Attractiveness (IA)

		H	M	L	TOTAL
	H	2,9,17 18,19	7,12	16	8
Business Strength (BS)	M	1,3,4,14	8,10,13	11,15	9
	L	5,6	—	—	2
TOTAL		11	5	3	19

DISTRIBUTION OF CORPORATE SALES (%)
IA

		H	M	L	TOTAL
	H	49.2	4.4	6.7	60.3
BS	M	25.5	0.6	1.1	27.2
	L	12.5	—	—	12.5
TOTAL		87.2	5.0	7.8	100

DISTRIBUTION OF CORPORATE NET INCOME (%)
IA

		H	M	L	TOTAL
	H	80.2	6.1	16.3	102.6
BS	M	9.9	(1.2)	1.7	10.4
	L	(13.0)	—	—	(13.0)
TOTAL		77.1	4.9	18.0	100

DISTRIBUTION OF CORPORATE ASSETS (%)
IA

		H	M	L	TOTAL
	H	42.1	3.4	5.7	51.2
BS	M	32.1	0.5	1.1	33.7
	L	15.1	—	—	15.1
TOTAL		89.3	3.9	6.8	100

RETURN ON NET ASSETS (%)
IA

		H	M	L	TOTAL
	H	12.8	12.2	19.1	13.5
BS	M	2.1	(19.5)	12.1	2.0
	L	(5.8)	—	—	(5.8)
TOTAL		5.8	8.7	17.8	6.7

*There are 19 businesses, each one characterized by a number 1 through 19.

businesses, they provide a useful device to understand and communicate important characteristics of the strategic options confronted by the firm.

3. The application of portfolio approaches at the corporate level provides useful guidelines for top managers to address the question of business strategy evaluation and resource allocation.

   a. It allows the establishment of an orderly set of priorities for investment, depending on the business potential for growth and profitability derived from its position in the portfolio matrix.

FIGURE 15–16. The Growth-Share Matrix

Matrix

Relative Market Share

	High	Low
High (Market Growth)	Star	Question Mark
Low (Market Growth)	Cash Cow	Dog

Dimensions of the Matrix

- External: Market growth rate (%) =
  (year 19x1)

$$\frac{\text{Total market}^{19x1} - \text{Total market}^{19x0}}{\text{Total market}^{19x0}} \times 100$$

- Internal: Relative market share =
  (year 19x1)

$$\frac{\text{Business sales}^{19x1}}{\text{Leading competitor's sales}^{19x1}}$$

Cut-off points

- Horizontal: Industry growth rate, or GNP growth rate, or weighted average of industries growth rate, or managerial objective for overall growth

- Vertical: Relative market share equal to 1 for separating leadership from followership, or equal to 1.5 to indicate strong leadership or dominance

Generic Strategies

Business Category	Market Share Thrust	Business Profitability	Investment Required	Net Cash Flow
Stars	Hold/Increase	High	High	Around zero or slightly negative
Cash Cows	Hold	High	Low	Highly positive
Question Marks	Increase *\	None or negative	Very high	Highly negative
	Harvest/ Divest	Low or negative	Disinvest	Positive
Dogs	Harvest/ Divest	Low or negative	Disinvest	Positive

*There is a selective application of the strategy depending on the decision made with regard to the business: either to enter aggressively or withdraw.

FIGURE 15–17. The Industry Attractiveness-Business Strength Matrix

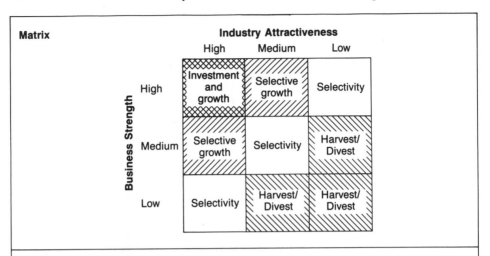

Matrix

Dimensions of the Matrix

- Industry Attractiveness: Subjective assessment based on external factors, noncontrollable by the firm, that are intended to capture the industry and competitive structure in which the business operates

- Business Strength: Subjective assessment based on the critical success factors, largely controllable by the firm, that define the competitive position of a business within its industry

For an illustration of the use of this matrix, see Chapters 7 and 25.

Generic Strategies

	Industry Attractiveness		
Business Strength	High	Medium	Low
High	Grow Seek dominance Maximize investment	Identify growth segments Invest strongly Maintain position elsewhere	Maintain overall position Seek cash flow Invest at maintenance level
Medium	Evaluate potential for leadership via segmentation Identify weaknesses Builds strengths	Identify growth segments Specialize Investment selectively	Prune lines Minimize investment Position to divest
Low	Specialize Seek niches Consider acquisitions	Specialize Seek niches Consider exit	Trust leader's statesmanship Sic on competitor's cash generators Time exit and divest

FIGURE 15–18. The Life-Cycle Portfolio Matrix

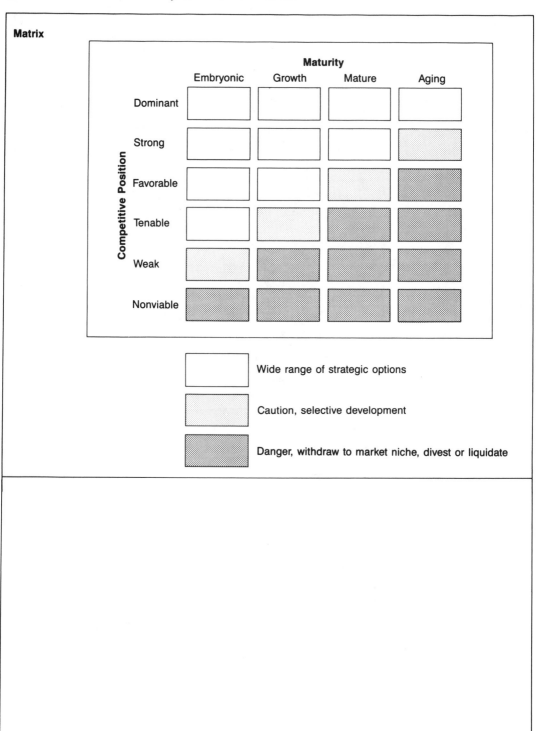

FIGURE 15–18. (continued)

Dimensions of the Matrix

- External: Stages of industry maturity judgmentally assessed based on the following eight external factors and their corresponding description

DESCRIPTORS	DEVELOPMENT STAGE			
	Embryonic	Growth	Mature	Aging
Market Growth Rate	Accelerating; meaningful rate cannot be calculated because the base is too small	Faster than GNP, but constant or decelerating	Equal to or slower than GNP, cyclical	Industry volume cycles but declines over long term
Industry Potential	Usually difficult to determine	Substantially exceeds the industry volume, but is subject to unforeseen developments	Well-known; primary markets approach saturation industry volume	Saturation is reached; no potential remains
Breadth of Product Lines	Basic product line established	Rapid proliferation as product lines are extended	Product turnover, but little or no change in breadth	Shrinking
Number of Competitors	Increasing rapidly	Increasing to peak; followed by shake-out and consolidation	Stable	Declines; but business may break up into many small regional suppliers
Market Share Stability	Volatile	A few firms have major shares; rankings can change, but those with minor shares are unlikely to gain major shares	Firms with major shares are entrenched	Concentration increases as marginal firms drop out; or shares are dispersed among small local firms
Purchasing Patterns	Little or none	Some; buyers are aggressive	Suppliers are well known; buying patterns are established	Strong; number of alternatives decreases
Ease of Entry	Usually easy, but opportunity may not be apparent	Usually easy, the presence of competitors is offset by vigorous growth	Difficult; competitors are entrenched, and growth is slowing	Difficult; little incentive
Technology	Concept development and product engineering	Product line refinement and extension	Process and materials refinement; new product line development to renew growth	Role is minimal

Figure 15–18. The Life-Cycle Portfolio Matrix (continued)

Dimensions of the Matrix (cont.)

- Internal: Competitive position of the business arrived at judgmentally, based on the following six competitive categories:

Criteria for Classification of Competitive Position

1. *Dominant*: Dominant competitors are very rare. Dominance often results from a quasi monopoly or from a strongly protected technological leadership.
2. *Strong*: Not all industries have dominant or strong competitors. Strong competitors can usually follow strategies of their choice, irrespective of their competitors' moves.
3. *Favorable*: When industries are fragmented, with no competitor clearly standing out, the leaders tend to be in a favorable position.
4. *Tenable*: A tenable position can usually be maintained profitably through specialization in a narrow or protected market niche. This can be a geographic specialization or a product specialization.
5. *Weak*: Weak competitors can be intrinsically too small to survive independently and profitably in the long term, given the competitive economics of their industry, or they can be larger and potentially stronger competitors, but suffering from costly past mistakes or from a critical weakness.
6. *Nonviable*: Represents the final recognition that the firm has really no strength whatsoever, now or in the future, in that particular business, and therefore, exiting is the only strategic response.

Generic Strategies

A. *Market share thrust*

	Embryonic	Growth	Mature	Aging
Dominant	All out push for share Hold position	Hold position Hold share	Hold position Grow with industry	Hold position
Strong	Attempt to improve position All out push for share	Attempt to improve position Push for share	Hold position Grow with industry	Hold position or Harvest
Favorable	Selective or all out push for share Selectively attempt to improve position	Attempt to improve position Selective push for share	Custodial or maintenance Find niche and attempt to protect	Harvest or Phased withdrawal
Tenable	Selectively push for position	Find niche and protect it	Find niche and hang on or Phased withdrawal	Phased withdrawal or Abandon
Weak	Up or Out	Turnaround or Abandon	Turnaround or Phased withdrawal	Abandon

FIGURE 15–18. (continued)

B. Investment requirements

	Embryonic	Growth	Mature	Aging
Dominant	Invest slightly faster than market dictates	Invest to sustain growth rate (and preempt new [?] competitors)	Reinvest as necessary	Reinvest as necessary
Strong	Invest as fast as market dictates	Invest to increase growth rate (and improve position)	Reinvest as necessary	Minimum reinvestment or Maintenance
Favorable	Invest selectively	Selective investment to improve position	Minimum and/or Selective reinvestment	Minimum maintenance Investment or Disinvest
Tenable	Invest (very) selectively	Selective investment	Minimum reinvestment or Disinvest	Disinvest or Divest
Weak	Invest or Divest	Invest or Divest	Invest selectively or Disinvest	Divest

The terms invest and divest are used in the broadest sense and are not restricted to property, plant, and equipment.

C. Profitability and cash flow

	Embryonic	Growth	Mature	Aging
Dominant	Probably profitable but not necessary Net cash borrower	Profitable Probably net cash producer (but not necessary)	Profitable Net cash producer	Profitable Net cash producer
Strong	May be unprofitable Net cash borrower	Probably profitable Probably net cash borrower	Profitable Net cash producer	Profitable Net cash producer
Favorable	Probably unprofitable Net cash borrower	Marginally profitable Net cash borrower	Modertely profitable Net cash borrower	Moderately profitable Cash flow balance
Tenable	Unprofitable Net cash borrower	Unprofitable Net cash borrower or Cash flow balance	Minimally profitable Cash flow balance	Minimally profitable Cash flow balance
Weak	Unprofitable Net cash borrower	Unprofitable Net cash borrower or Cash flow balance	Unprofitable Possibly net cash borrower or Net cash producer	Unprofitable (Write-off)

In addition, to cash throw-off or use, each unit may use or throw-off managerial resources. *Note:* In some cases, the tax shield value of a unit should be taken into account in evaluating unit performance.

In addition to the previously prescribed generic strategies, the ADL methodology recommends broad action programs depending on the position of the business unit in its matrix. The strategies of business units are categorized according to four different families: natural development, selective development, prove viability, and out, which are broadly characterized in the following display.

FIGURE 15–18. The Life-Cycle Portfolio Matrix (continued)

Stages of Industry Maturity / Competitive Position	Embryonic	Growth	Mature	Aging
Dominant				
Strong		Natural development		
Favorable			Selective development	
Tenable			Prove viability	
Weak				Out

Source: Arthur D. Little, Inc.

Each family of businesses has the following options regarding the definition of its strategic thrusts:

Natural Development	Selective Development	Prove Viability	Out
Start-up	Find niche	Catch-up	Withdraw
Growth with industry	Exploit niche	Renew	Divest
Gain position gradually	Hold niche	Turnaround	Abandon
Gain position aggressively		Prolong existence	
Defend position			
Harvest			

Once having selected the appropriate strategic thrust from among the ones availabe, for each family, you are offered the following menu of broad action programs:

A	Backward integration	M	Market rationalization
B	Development of overseas business	N	Methods and functions efficiency
C	Development of overseas facilities	O	New products/New markets
D	Distribution rationalization	P	New products/Same market
E	Excess capacity	Q	Production rationalization
F	Export/Same product	R	Product line rationalization
G	Forward integration	S	Pure survival
H	Hesitation	T	Same products/New markets
I	Initial market development	U	Same products/Same markets
J	Licensing abroad	V	Technology efficiency
K	Complete rationalization	W	Traditional cost-cutting efficiency
L	Market penetration	X	Unit abandonment

The ADL methodology suggests the following mapping among families, strategic thrusts, and broad action programs:

Generic Strategies

Strategic Thrust	A	B	C	D	E	F	G	H	I	J	K	L	M	N	O	P	Q	R	S	T	U	V	W	X
NATURAL DEVELOPMENT																								
Start-up					E				I			L												
Growth with industry	A	B	C			F	G			J				N		P				T	U			
Gain position gradually							G					L								T				
Gain position aggressively		B	C		E		G					L		N	O	P				T		V		
Defend position	A		C											N							U	V	W	
Harvest				D				H			K		M				Q	R			U		W	
SELECTIVE DEVELOPMENT																								
Find niche	A						G		I			L	M					R		T				
Exploit niche		B	C		E							L		N		P					U	V		
Hold niche			C	D										N			Q				U			
PROVE VIABILITY																								
Catch-up				D	E							L	M			P	Q	R						
Renew				D									M		O	P	Q	R			U			
Turn around				D								L	M	N			Q	R				V	W	
Prolong existence	A			D		F				J	K		M	N			Q	R	S	T			W	
WITHDRAWAL																								
Withdraw				D									M				Q	R					W	
Divest				D							K						Q	R	S					
Abandon																								X

SOURCE: Arthur D. Little, Inc.

FIGURE 15–19. The Alternative Boston Consulting Group Matrix

Matrix

Size of Competitive Advantage

Ways to Complete (Opportunities for differentiation)	Small	Large
Many	Fragmented	Specialization
Few	Stalemate	Volume

Dimensions of the Matrix

- Ways to Compete: Assess judgmentally whether there are many or few ways to achieve competitive advantage. This is greatly determined by the capabilities of differentiation within the industry.

- Size of Competitive Advantage: Assess judgmentally whether the extent and sustainability of the advantage is small or large. This is largely dependent on the size of barriers to entry into the industry.

Generic Strategy

Category of Business	Generic Strategy
Volume	• Lowest cost position, sales leadership
Specialization	• Either niche in a segment of the market or cover the entire market with differentiated products • Do not get stuck in the middle
Fragmented	• Many ways to compete. Look at your relative strengths and unique competencies
Stalemate	• Survive, reduce costs, maximize productivity

   b. It provides a mechanism to check the consistency between business requests of financial and human resources and their inherent needs obtained from their position in the portfolio matrix.

   c. It facilitates the proper balancing of cash requirements and cash supplies among businesses of the corporation.

   d. It permits the establishment of management control mechanisms suitable for monitoring the performance of each business using key variables consistent with their current and future potential.

4. Portfolio approaches can also be applied in the process of strategy formulation at the business level, but the focus of attention changes from the entire business to the more detailed collection of product-market segments.

5. By representing the complete collection of businesses of the firm, portfolio approaches provide a useful mechanism to consider potential acquisitions and divestitures.

6. Portfolio approaches were most significant in raising the strategic alertness of most managers. To a great extent, the use of portfolio matrices was responsible for accelerating the adoption of formal competitive analyses and for increasing the competitive awareness in American firms. This was accomplished because the implementation of the portfolio approach requires the formal collection and processing of some information regarding competitors. This constitutes a useful first step in improving competitive intelligence. Also, portfolio matrices can be constructed for major competitors, generating valuable insights with regard to their overall strengths and ability to anticipate their potential responses and moves. At the very least, this judgmental call would put in evidence the need to improve the firm's understanding of its major competitors.

In spite of the legitimate contributions attached to the methodology introduced by portfolio matrices, they are not without criticism. In fact, in the recent past, the whole area of strategic planning has been the target of strong attacks, to a great extent due to the legacy that portfolio matrices left to strategic planning in the last decade. The most common complaints have been that matrices tend to trivialize strategic thinking by converting it into simplistic and mechanistic exercises, whose final message is dubious at best. Also, the matrix methodology has tended to take strategic analysis and, subsequently, strategic thinking, away from managers and into the realm of planning departments.

There is a clear element of truth in the explicit criticisms, but what they fail to capture is that matrices are simple tools and not the final output of a properly designed strategic planning process. As with any tool, its final value depends on the craftsmanship of its users. It is our experience that portfolio matrices can assist in bringing intelligent and appropriate communicational opportunities to the hard issue of portfolio management. Every single one of the matrices is a grossly oversimplified model of a complex problem. As is the case with any model, portrolio matrices are simple abstractions that attempt to capture a partial but critical element pertaining to resource allocation in a portfolio setting. Since each one of them adopts a single biased orientation, individually they could be judged as being too narrow in scope, ignoring important additional perspectives. However, collectively, they can produce, from various angles, a combined picture that begins to capture in a much more forceful way the broader complexities of the resource allocation problem. This is the reason why we strongly advise, whenever they are applied, for all of them to be used in conjunction.

The Process of Resource Allocation

From a strict financial theory point of view, one could argue, as we did at the beginning of this chapter, that the only legitimate evaluation tool for resource allocation is the net present value (NPV) of future cash flows to be generated by a business, discounted at a proper cost of capital rate, that includes adjustments for risk and inflation. Without reducing the significance of NPV in judging the quality of investment decisions, we can say that it does not necessarily address all of the central issues present in resource allocation.

First, the decision-making process is not necessarily a cold, analytical, rational activity. Instead, it is loaded with emotions, self-centered interests, and biased positions which are at the heart of a complex bargaining and power game. In a rather humorous way, Brealey and Myers have stated what they have declared to be their "second law" that indicates that the proportion of prepared projects having a positive estimated NPV is independent of top management's estimate of the opportunity cost of capital.[7] It simply means that business managers can actually "prove" to their top counterparts that their investment proposals are acceptable regardless of the hurdle imposed on them.

Second, there is a major difference between project evaluation and project generation. NPV is an important tool to evaluate projects, but by no means does it serve as a stimulus to make business managers generate the right kind of projects to support their businesses according to their strategic positioning. This is probably the most important role that can be played by portfolio matrices because they rank businesses according to the attractiveness of their industry and the intrinsic strength that the firm can achieve. Thus, prior to undertaking numerical calculations that might not add significantly to support the strategic role of a business unit, we might want to communicate to business managers the expectations that corporate officers have with regard to their degree of aggressiveness to be shown by each business in their requests for resource allocation.

The financial theory and the strategic positioning point of view are at the core of an important controversy in resource allocation. We feel that both points of view are legitimate and have important merits on their own. Rather than being alternative procedures for analyzing investment proposals, they truly complement each other.

DIAGNOSING THE VALUE GAP

This chapter has concentrated on describing the concepts and methodologies which allow managers to understand the process of value creation, enhance their diagnostic capabilities on the current status of the business portfolio, and suggest ways in which resources could be allocated to assure a superior competitive advantage for each business. This is in accordance with the effectiveness of the industry and the firm's ability to mobilize unique capabilities. We would expect that, at this stage, both corporate and business managers would have thoroughly prepared all necessary supporting information and analysis that would allow them to have a clear picture of the strength of the overall portfolio. The major question to be asked at this point is whether we could detect a *value gap* between the current standing of the firm and its future potential.

McTaggart offers the following questions to guide an organization in detecting possible opportunities for additional creation of value:[8]

- Are there any businesses in the portfolio that significantly underperform competitors?
- Are there any businesses that are out of their start-up phase and still losing money?
- Are there any businesses that would clearly be worth more to someone else due to synergy or operating economies?
- Are resources allocated to businesses in a way that reflects their profitability potential, or do you tend to overfund losers and underfund winners?
- Is performance measured by using average cost, asset, and debt allocations, and an arbitrary corporate hurdle rate?
- Are any of your long-term incentives tied directly to relative stock performance or indirectly to the drivers of shareholder value?
- Is capital spending driven mostly by capital budgeting rather than the strategic planning process?
- Is the company underleveraged? Could the company be taken private in an LBO at today's stock price?
- If the company did go private in an LBO, which assets would be sold to repay debt? How much overhead could be cut without damaging the long-term health of the company?

We feel that this is an important set of questions that could trigger the recognition of possible opportunities for value creation.

CONSOLIDATION OF BUSINESS AND FUNCTIONAL STRATEGIES AT THE CORPORATE LEVEL

Resource allocation is a crucial step in the planning process that calls for a critical review and sanctioning at the corporate level of the set of broad action programs proposed by business and functional managers. It requires the involvement of all key executives who share the responsibility of shaping the strategic direction of the firm, and it is conducted normally through a one- or two-day meeting, totally dedicated for this purpose. If properly done, it allows for the emergence of a clear consensus and a personal commitment of all participating managers.

We recommend that, at a minimum, the following five issues be addressed at this step.

Resolution of Nonconcurrence Conflicts

Whenever businesses share centralized functional resources, either in a purely functional organization or in a hybrid organization having a strong centralized functional presence, the functional manager might be in the position of analyzing the business strategies and broad action programs proposed by business managers, and cast a concurrence or nonconcurrence vote.

If functional managers decide that a business plan is not acceptable because it is judged to contain inadequate or unrealistic commitments in a functional area, the corresponding functional manager will issue a nonconcurrence statement. Most of the nonconcurrences should be resolved through bilateral discussions between business and functional managers. If this is not the case, the nonconcurrence issue escalates through the organizational hierarchy until it reaches the corporate level. Depending on the nature of the problem as well as the organizational style, we might not want to address publicly and openly this conflict at the managers' meeting. In this case, efforts should be undertaken to resolve the questions prior to the meeting and merely report on the final decision.

Balancing the Business Portfolio of the Firm

This activity spans several dimensions of concern. The most crucial one has to do with short-term profitability versus long-term development. To some extent, that is also linked to the trade-offs between risk and return. An important additional concern has to do with the compounded growth opportunities of the overall portfolio, which are detected by the positioning of the business in the various stages of the industry life cycle. Finally there is a question of cash-flow balance, which does not imply that a balanced portfolio is necessarily optimum, but it serves to address the question of seeking equilibrium between sources and uses of funds in the organization. The portfolio matrices can be very helpful to guide managers in their search for a good compromise resulting in an appropriate balanced portfolio.

Defining the Availability of Strategic Funds, the Debt Policy, and the Maximum Sustainable Growth

Another task which is important at this step is the determination of total strategic funds available at the corporate level to support investment in fixed assets, and in increases in working capital and developmental expenses. A sound way of calculating these funds is first to forecast the sources of funds forthcoming to the firm. The primary components of the sources of funds are:

- earnings
- depreciation
- new debt issuing
- new equity issuing
- divestitures

Notice that earnings contain, as part of the cost of goods sold, the normal levels of developmental expenses which are assigned to the various functions of the organization, in particular R&D.

The second part of the computation requires the forecast of uses of funds, whose most important items are:

- dividends
- debt repayment (principal)

- strategic funds
- new fixed assets and acquisitions
- increases in working capital
- increases in developmental expenses

Therefore, the total strategic funds available can be estimated as:

$$\begin{array}{c}\text{Total strategic funds}\\ \text{availability}\end{array} = \begin{array}{c}\text{Total}\\ \text{sources of funds}\end{array} - \begin{array}{c}\text{Dividend}\\ \text{payments}\end{array} - \begin{array}{c}\text{Debt}\\ \text{repayment}\end{array}$$

It is apparent from this relation that the firm's debt capacity and financial leverage policies have a significant impact on the ability of the firm to increase its growth. Establishing a sound debt policy congruent with the company's financing requirements is another issue to be addressed at this point.

Another useful guide to address the question of corporate growth is the calculation of the *maximum sustainable growth* of the firm, which we have described already in a previous section of this chapter.

Figure 15–20 provides the calculation of strategic funds, debt policy, and maximum sustainable growth for AMAX, Inc.

Once the total strategic funds have been determined, we have to deduct from them the funds appropriated for investments that are required to fulfill legal obligations or correspond to previous commitments to ongoing projects.

Evaluation of Proposed Action Programs and Assignment
of Priorities for Resource Allocation

The previous considerations have allowed us to assess the affordable growth of the corporation and the total funds available for its future development. Having that information in mind, we should now turn our attention to the assignment of priorities to be given to each business unit in terms of resource allocation. This will allow realistic programs to be formulated, which not only respond properly to the desired strategic direction of each business unit, but also are consistent with the financial and human resources in place.

There are various ways to establish those priorities. We recommend using the following categories of strategic growth:[9] build aggressively, build gradually, build selectively, maintain aggressively, maintain selectively, prove viability, divest-liquidate, and competitive harasser. A detailed description of these categories is shown in Figure 15–21.

A form that we have found useful to decide on priorities for resource allocation among existing as well as new business is presented in Figure 15–22. Although resource allocation is clearly a controversial subject, we have found that concentrating on the decisions which are embedded in that figure helps the group of top managers of the organization to open up a thorough discussion of the central issues leading toward the generation of a wide consensus.

There are two major philosophies for the allocation of resources among

FIGURE 15–20. Availability of Strategic Funds, Debt Policy, and Maximum Sustainable Growth for AMAX, Inc.

Availability of Strategic Funds

Sources		Uses	
Earnings	93	Dividends	40
Depreciation	210	Debt repayments	140
New debt issues	–	Strategic funds*	268
New equity issues	40		
Divestitures	75		
Other (deferred taxes)	30		
Total	448	Total	448

*Strategic funds: 448 − 40 − 140 = 268

Debt Policy

Lower the debt-to-total-capital ratio 25% (or a D/E of approximately 35%) from its actual level of 44%.

Maximum Sustainable Growth

$$g = p\left[ROA + \frac{D}{E}(ROA - i)\right]$$

where:

g = maximum sustainable growth
p = fraction of retained earnings   = 0.50
D/E = debt-to-equity ratio   = 0.35
ROA = after-tax return on assets   = 12%
i = after-tax interest on debt   = 6%

$g = 0.50\,[12 + 0.35(12 - 6)]$ = 7%

SOURCE: Adapted from Gray (1984).

the business units of the firm. The first allocates directly the resources to the SBUs, based on the previously identified priorities, leaving up to the SBU managers the assignment of those resources among the individual projects generated at the SBU level. Those who favor this approach argue that this guarantees a strategic fit between the allocation of resources and the strategic positioning of each SBU.

The second philosophy for resource allocation is based on the examination of each project emanating from the business level. This is a totally centralized procedure, where each project is being approved or rejected at the corporate level, based entirely on the assessment of the individual contribution of the project being considered.

It is important, at this point, to warn about resource allocation. We have been stressing throughout only the assignment of financial resources among business units. Often those resources are the easiest to transfer and the most plentiful available with human resources as the most constrained ones. This is the case faced by many high technology firms which find themselves restricted in their growth not because of the availability of financial resources, but rather

FIGURE 15–21. Business Strategic Priorities Emerging from the Portfolio Approach to Strategic Planning

Build aggressively: The business is in a strong position in a highly attractive, fast-growing industry, and management wants to build share as rapidly as possible. This role is usually assigned to an SBU early in the life cycle, especially when there is little doubt as to whether this rapid growth will be sustained.

Build gradually: The business is in a strong position in a very attractive, moderate-growth industry, and management wants to build share, or there is rapid growth but doubt as to whether this rapid growth will be sustained.

Build selectively: The business has good position in a highly attractive industry and wants to build share where it feels it has strength, or can develop strength, to do so.

Maintain aggressively: The business is in a strong position in a currently attractive industry, and management is determined to aggressively maintain that position.

Maintain selectively: Either the business is in a strong position in an industry that is getting less attractive, or the business is in a moderate position in a highly attractive industry. Management wishes to exploit the situation by maximizing the profitability benefits of selectively serving where it best can so so, but with minimum additional resource deployments.

Prove viability: The business is in a less-than-satisfactory position in a less attractive industry. If the business can provide resources for use elsewhere, management may decide to retain it, but without additional resource support. The onus is on the business to justify retention.

Divest-Liquidate: Neither the business nor the industry has any redeeming features. Barring major exit barriers, the business should be divested.

Competitive harasser: This is a business with a poor position in either an attractive or highly attractive industry, and where competitors with a good position in the industry also compete with the company in other industries. The role of competitive harasser is to attack sporadically or continuously the competitor's position, not necessarily with the intention of long-run success. The object is to distract the competition from other areas, deny them from revenue business, or use the business to cross-parry when the competition attacks an important sister business of the strategic aggressor.

SOURCE: Adapted from Ian C. MacMillan, "Seizing Competitive Initiative," Spring 1982. Reprinted by permission of *The Journal of Business Strategy*, Boston, MA.

because of the unavailability of scarce technical talents. Therefore, resources should be interpreted here in its broadest sense.

Resource Allocation and Definition of Performance Measurements for Management Control

Having identified the total funds available for resource allocation and the priorities assigned to each individual business unit, we are faced with the following tasks pertaining to the specific assignment of resources:

- Collection and classification of all the information submitted by SBUs and functional units
- Analysis of the coherence between the strategic role assigned to SBUs and functional units, and the requests for funds
- Analysis of economic indicators and value-creation potentials of proposed programs
- Final allocation of resources for the coming year

FIGURE 15–22. Priorities for Resource Allocation

EXISTING BUSINESSES	BUILD			MAINTAIN			PROVE VIABILITY	DIVEST/ LIQUIDATE
	Aggressively	Gradually	Selectively	Aggressively	Selectively			
1								
2								
3								
4								
5								
6								
7								
8								
9								
10								

NEW BUSINESSES	BUILD			PROVE VIABILITY	HOW TO BUILD		
	Aggressively	Gradually	Selectively		Internal Growth	Acquisition	Joint Venture
1							
2							
3							

- Development of performance measurements to facilitate the controlling and monitoring of the broad and specific action programs supporting business and functional strategies, both in the short run and over an extended planning horizon.

When resources are allocated among SBUs at this stage, we should only be concerned about checking for final consistency between the priorities assigned to each SBU and the final requests for funds.

When resources are allocated on a project-by-project basis, there is a much heavier concentration of responsibilities at the corporate level to evaluate the SBU's proposal, both in terms of conventional financial performance measures, such as net present value, as well as their consistency with the strategic positioning of each business unit.

Notes

1. Alan C. Shapiro, "Corporate Strategy and the Capital Budgeting Decision," *Midland Corporate Finance Journal*, 3, no. 1 (Spring 1985), 22–36.

2. The NPV computation can be expressed as:

$$NPV = -I + \sum_{t=1}^{t=T} \frac{C_t}{(1 + r)^t}$$

where

I = initial investment
T = time horizon
 (the life of the project)
C = expected cash flow in period t
r = cost of capital

For a thorough treatment of the NPV model, the reader is referred to Richard A. Brealey and Stewart C. Myers, *Principles of Corporate Finance*, 3rd ed. (New York: McGraw-Hill Book Co., 1988). For a good discussion of the gap between financial theory and financial strategy, see Stewart C. Myers, "Finance Theory and Financial Strategy," *Interfaces*, 14, no. 1 (January–February 1984), 126–137.

3. For a comprehensive analysis of the M/B model, the reader is referred to Arnoldo C. Hax and Nicolas S. Majluf, *Strategic Management: An Integrative Perspective* (Englewood Cliffs, NJ: Prentice Hall, 1984), Chapter 10; and William E. Fruhan, *Financial Strategy* (Homewood, IL: Richard D. Irwin, Inc., 1979).

4. Alan J. Zakon, "Capital Structure Optimization," in J. F. Weston and M. B. Goudzwaard, eds. *The Treasurer's Handbook* (Homewod, IL: Dow Jones-Irwin, 1976).

5. Fruhan, *Financial Strategy*, 1979.

6. For a comprehensive analysis of portfolio matrices, see Hax and Majluf, *Strategic Management*, (1984), Chapters 6 through 10.

7. Brealey and Myers, *Principles of Corporate Finance*, (1988).

8. James M. McTaggart, "The Ultimate Takeover Defense: Closing the Value Gap," *Planning Review* (January–February 1988), 27–32.

9. The categories of strategic growth were originally proposed by Ian C. Macmillan, "Seizing Competitive Advantage," *The Journal of Business Strategy* (Spring 1982), 43–57.

Appendix: The Relationship Between ROE and ROA

The fundamental managerial objectives are growth and profitability. Therefore, it is appropriate to ask ourselves how to execute a proper measure of these two dimensions. First, with regard to profitability, the most commonly used indicators are return on equity (ROE) and return on assets (ROA). These two indicators are fractions that differ both in the content of the numerator as well as the denominator.

ROE is defined as follows:

$$ROE = \frac{\text{Profit after interest and after taxes}}{\text{Equity}}$$

The numerator is the true bottom line. It represents the net profit of the firm from operations after we pay taxes and interest over the loan. The denominator has also a similar bottom-line characteristic. It measures the equity which belongs to the shareholders of the firm. Therefore, ROE is bottom-line profits as allocated to the owners of the firm. This measure of profitability is commonly used to assess the overall financial performance of the firm.

In contrast, ROA is defined as:

$$ROA = \frac{\text{Profit after taxes but before interest}}{\text{Assets}}$$

Now the distinction between the two measures of profitability is clear. ROA measures profits after taxes but before interest. Since it is normally applied at the level of the business unit, we do not want to make the manager accountable for the means of financing the assets that have been entrusted to him or her. Similarly, the denominator measures total assets as opposed to equity because we are interested in examining the profitability of the business itself without regard to its sources of financing (remember that assets are equal to debt plus equity). There is an important relationship that links ROE and ROA, that can be easily developed:

$$\left\{ \begin{array}{c} \text{Profit after interest} \\ \text{and after taxes} \end{array} \right\} = \left\{ \begin{array}{c} \text{Profit before interest} \\ \text{and after taxes} \end{array} \right\} - \left\{ \begin{array}{c} \text{Interest} \\ \text{after taxes} \end{array} \right\}$$

$$\{E \times ROE\} = \{(D + E) \times ROA\} - \{k_D(1 - T_c) \times D\}$$

$$ROE = ROA + \frac{D}{E} \{ROA - k_D (1 - T_c)\}$$

where

$$D = \text{total debt}$$
$$E = \text{total equity}$$
$$k_D = \text{debt interest rate before tax}$$
$$T_c = \text{corporate tax rate}$$

16

Organization and Managerial Infrastructure: Imprinting the Vision of the Firm

Definition of Strategic Management

Most of what we have discussed so far centers on the planning methodologies needed to support a formulation of the vision of the firm. These planning tasks, although essential for the proper articulation of the overall directions of the enterprise, are insufficient alone to generate the massive mobilization of resources and the deep sense of personal commitment to make the vision a forceful reality that generates the desired changes in an organization. What is needed is to internalize the vision in the organization via a number of formal-analytical approaches (appealing to the rational self to generate calculated reactions), and power-behavioral approaches (appealing to the affective self to generate intuitive reactions) in a way that is congruent with the culture of the firm. The resulting process which we refer to as *imprinting* the vision of the firm is the heart of strategic management.

Strategic management has, as an ultimate objective, the development of corporate values, managerial capabilities, organizational responsibilities, and administrative systems. Such development links strategic and operational decision making at all hierarchical levels and across all businesses and functional lines of authority in a firm. Institutions which have reached this stage of management development have eliminated the conflicts between long-term development and short-term profitability. Strategies and operations are not in conflict with one another, but they are inherently coupled in the definition of the managerial tasks at each level in the organization. This form of conducting a firm is deeply anchored in managerial style, beliefs, values, ethics, and accepted forms of behavior in the organization, which make strategic thinking congruent with the organizational culture.

Figure 16–1 captures the fundamental elements of the framework that we propose to deal with strategic management.

FIGURE 16–1. The Fundamental Elements of Strategic Management: Imprinting the Vision of the Firm Through Formal-Analytical and Power-Behavioral Approaches to Management

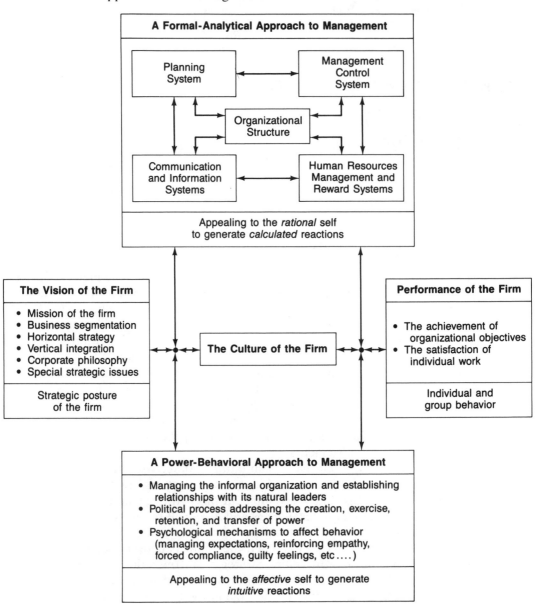

1. The first task to accomplish is the formulation of the vision of the firm, which provides a statement of purpose for the organization as a whole. It is described in terms of the mission of the firm, its business segmentation, the desired horizontal and vertical integration, the corporate philosophy, and whatever other strategic issues are regarded as critical. The strategic

posture of the firm serves as the vehicle to communicate all of the critical action programs that emerge from the vision statement.

2.   Two distinct but highly complementary managerial approaches are invariably needed in order to contribute to the imprinting of the vision in the organization. A formal-analytical approach to management requires the development of the critical administrative processes used by managers to run the firm, particularly planning, management control, human resources management and rewards, and communication and information systems. At the center of the formal-analytical approach to management is the organizational structure which must reflect the vision of the firm in terms of the selection of units represented in it, the assignment of responsibilities throughout the hierarchical network, the extent of formal authority, and the mechanisms of coordination required for the integrated functioning of organizational units.

   The power-behavioral approach to management is geared at those aspects of individual and group behavior which are less amenable to control and overt influence on the part of the firm's executives. It includes managing the informal organization and establishing relationships with its natural leaders, and developing the political process that addresses the creation, exercise, retention, and transfer of power. Also, psychological mechanisms are used to affect behavior, such as managing expectations, reinforcing desirable conduct, empathy, forced compliance, guilty feelings, and so on. In general, all managerial efforts are oriented at affecting motivation and behavior through emotional reactions of individuals.

3.   The strategy of the firm has to be deeply rooted in its corporate culture. The culture is the most pervasive element of the strategic management framework. That is why it is depicted at the very heart of Figure 16–1. It influences every other element of strategic management. At the same time, it is slowly molded by the vision of the firm, the formal-analytical and the power-behavioral approaches to management, and the resulting organizational and individual performance. Culture acts both as an inspiring source of basic strengths and values of the corporation, and as a limiting constraint that prevents the organization from undertaking wild and sudden departures from its current state. Culture preserves a sense of identity of the organization and transmits to future generations the central beliefs for which it stands.

4.   Individuals and groups in the organization react to the stimuli of formal-analytical and power-behavioral approaches to management generating a climate conducive to the achievement of organizational objectives and the satisfaction of their own individual egotistic and altruistic needs. The coherence between organizational and individual goals was already recognized by Doug McGregor who, in his path-breaking book *The Human Side of the Enterprise*,[1] suggested the *principle of integration*. This is derived from his Theory Y, which requires that managers create the conditions that will allow the members of the organization to achieve their own goals *best* by directing their efforts to the success of the enterprise.

Consistent with the overall orientation of this book, we discuss in more detail the formal-analytical approach to management, and the way in which organizational culture impacts the strategy formation process.[2] We start with a presentation of the role of the organizational structure in strategic management. Then we comment briefly on the support that the key administrative systems in planning, control, communication and information, and human resources management and rewards should provide for the appropriate development and implementation of strategy within the firm. Finally, we conclude the chapter with an analysis of corporate culture.

Organizational Structure

WHAT IS AN ORGANIZATION?

Organizations are groups of people seeking the achievement of a common purpose. This is accomplished via division of labor, and integrated through formal-analytical administrative systems and power-behavioral managerial approaches that are congruent with its organizational culture, continuously through time.[3]

Alfred Chandler in his classic historical analysis of the major American industrial enterprises,[4] was the first to draw attention to the significance of strategy in prescribing a sound organizational structure, by enunciating the principle "structure follows strategy." This means that an organization should be designed to facilitate primarily the pursuit of its strategic commitments. It is easy to realize the full implications of this statement by reflecting on the various components of the definition of an organization just given.

First, we start by recognizing that organizations are groups of people sharing a common purpose. Within the framework of strategic management this common purpose is expressed by the vision of the firm, which is central in the articulation of its strategy.

Second, the complexity of the organizational tasks are of such a magnitude that they cannot be performed by a single individual. Therefore, it is necessary to divide those tasks in an orderly way to facilitate their proper execution. This leads to the question of *segmentation* or *differentiation* in the organizational structure. The term *differentiation* stems from the fact that the resulting subunits within the organization tend to create their own unique cultures setting them apart from other subunits. Think, for example, of the significant cultural differences existing among the accounting, R & D, marketing, and manufacturing departments of an organization. The segmentation process creates the organizational hierarchy. We start from a very broad *basic segmentation* at the top, and we proceed by defining finer and more focused tasks as we carry on a *detailed segmentation* of the jobs through the middle and lower echelons of the organizational structure.

Third, the division of labor resulting from the segmentation process forces us to implement a number of *coordination* or *integration* mechanisms to assure that all of the individuals within the organization work harmoniously in seeking the achievement of the organizational vision. This coordination process could be much more complex and subtle than the mere segmentation of the organizational tasks. This should be used as a warning not to judge the quality of an organizational structure exclusively on the organizational chart, because that instrument at best describes the full segmentation of the firm and provides no or little information on its coordination mechanisms. There are two major categories of integration approaches that we have recognized in the strategic management framework. The first one results from the formal-analytical approaches. It is represented by the lateral coordinating mechanisms (mainly the creation of liaison roles, task forces, committees, integrating managers, and matrix relations), and by the central administrative systems of the firm (planning, control, communication and information, and human resources management and reward systems). The character of these formal-analytical mechanisms depends on the kind of strategy they are intended to support. The second one is generated from power-behavioral approaches to management, and they are basically informal, political, and psychological mechanisms intended to affect behavior in the desired strategic direction.

Fourth, the organizational structure should be congruent with its existing culture. The three concepts of culture, strategy, and structure are exceedingly interdependent. To some extent, culture conditions strategy, and in turn, strategy dictates the basic elements of structure.

Finally, the effort of aligning the responsibilities and authorities of the firm, which are ultimately embedded in the organizational structure, is a never-ending process that has to be continuously revisited. Responsibility has to do with the nature of the tasks entrusted to each manager. Authority represents the means available to the manager for the effective execution of the tasks under his or her responsibility. As the operating environment of the firm changes and forces the firm to adopt different competitive strategies, we need to redefine the assignment of responsibilities and authorities. This in turn makes us readdress the firm's vision and the ways to segment and integrate its basic tasks.

ORGANIZATIONAL ARCHETYPES

To gain insight into the question of organizational design, it is useful to reflect on the advantages and disadvantages of the three basic archetypes that represent distinct forms of organizational structure: functional, divisional, and matrix.

Functional and Divisional Organizations

Functional and divisional forms constitute the classical opposite archetypes for organizational design. The functional form is structured around the *inputs* required to perform the tasks of the organization. Typically, these inputs are *functions* or specialties such as finance, marketing, production, engineering, research and development, and personnel.

The divisional form is structured according to the *outputs* generated by the organization. The most common distinction of the outputs is in terms of the *products* delivered. However, other types of outputs could serve as a basis for divisionalization, such as services, programs, and projects. Also, markets, clients, and geographical locations could serve as criteria for divisionalization.

A pervasive character of these organizational structures differentiates the resulting management style. The functional form is more *centralized*, the divisional form is more *decentralized*. A functional organization tends to develop highly qualified technical skills and a climate conducive to technical excellence and high efficiency. It provides a *critical mass* for the career advancement of its professionals and for the realization of economies of scale. But its inherent stress on specialization pushes the decision-making process upwards, because only at the top do we find the confluence of all inputs required for a final decision.

A different situation exists in divisional organizations, where some functional specialization is lost in favor of added autonomy. Many decisions can be resolved at the divisional manager's level, preventing an overburdened top hierarchy. The middle layer of managers created in divisional organizations provides an effective training ground for general management skills. Though in charge of only a fraction of the overall businesses of the firm, divisional managers are exposed to a full range of managerial problems. That experience gives them a decisive advantage over functional managers, who are confronted with situations involving only their narrow fields of specialty.

There is a certain alignment between authority and responsibility in functional organizations that is absent in divisional forms. An illustration may be useful to clarify this point. A manufacturing manager in a functional organization is fully responsible for the operation concerning plant facilities. His or her responsibilities completely match the required authority. Turn now to a divisional organization with two divisional managers responsible for two different product lines. If these product lines are manufactured in a common plant, an unavoidable ambiguity results in the accountability of the plant operations. One or both divisional managers do not have total authority over the output of the plant. In this case, at least one divisional manager has more responsibility than authority.

The resolution of conflicts among managers is also different in functional and divisional organizations. The functional organization has a trouble-free functional line, but conflicts of interest among functional managers are usually handled at the top level. The general manager must act as the final decision maker and arbitrate disputes among specialties, because he or she is the only one fully accountable for the performance of the organization. This situation could be aggravated by a tendency to develop parochial orientations in each functional group. Since in a divisional organization middle managers are accountable for the performance of their individual businesses, there are clear incentives for them to resolve conflicts of interest by direct negotiations among themselves. Normally, ground rules are instituted to facilitate this accommodation process, such as the development of negotiated transfer prices for goods flowing among divisions.

Requirements for a Successful Decentralization

Both functional and divisional forms are extensively used in structuring organizations. Functional forms are more predominant in organizations having single or dominant products, while divisional forms emerge as diversification increases. As complexity begins to grow in the context of the evolution of an organization, decentralization is a must. It becomes impossible for the top manager to retain his or her role as the sole coordinator of all the activities of the organization. Even more important, the top manager is unable to understand intimately the variety of businesses in a diversified setting to provide the necessary strategic guidance. Therefore, in most complex organizations the valid question is not whether to decentralize, but what the degree of decentralization should be. Solomons suggests four thoughtful requirements for successful decentralization.[5]

First, the divisions should be sufficiently independent in terms of production and marketing decision-making capabilities to facilitate separate accountability.

Second, though substantial independence of divisions from each other is necessary for successful divisionalization, if carried to extremes, it would destroy the very idea that such divisions are integral parts of a single firm. This suggests a degree of interdependence among divisions.

Third, no division by seeking its own profit should reduce that of the corporation. This can be accomplished by developing planning, control, information, and reward systems designed to stimulate divisional initiatives, while preventing actions counterproductive to the overall corporate performance.

And fourth, corporate managers should exercise self-constraints in issuing directives to divisional managers. This is not an easy task to do since the final accountability for corporate performance still resides on the chief executive's shoulders. However, no successful decentralization can be accomplished without relinquishing part of the authority to the divisional managers. This creates a definite imbalance of responsibility and authority at that level.

Matrix Organizations

Functional and divisional organizations are structured around *one* central design concept. Inputs (functions or specialties) are the molding principle in functional organizations, and outputs (products, services, programs, markets, geographical locations) are the basic dimensions for divisional forms. This clear identification of a main guideline in the definition of a structure stems from the "unity of command" principle of classical writers, that ordinarily has been interpreted as the *one-boss* rule. Whenever a single focus is selected as the basis for organizational design, a single individual can be assigned responsibility for the management of an organizational unit in charge of performing that task. This leads to the one-boss concept. Matrix organizations are a fundamental departure from this unitary notion. They are structured around *two* or more central design concepts. Thus, under the matrix organizational form a person has *two* (or more) *bosses*.

There is a large amount of inherent ambiguity in a matrix organization that may seem counterproductive under a more traditional perspective. In fact, the implementation of a matrix structure requires properly designed managerial support systems, and people adequately sensitized to the matrix environment.

Davis and Lawrence define three preconditions that have to be met before the organization considers the matrix as a potential structural form.[6] Otherwise, there are alternative managerial systems that can reinforce more traditional organizational forms without having to resort to the full implementation of a matrix. Those preconditions are:

OUTSIDE PRESSURE FOR DUAL FOCUS   As already noted, the first necessary requirement for the development of a matrix organization is the coexistence of more than one fundamental focus of managerial concern, both equally important.

PRESSURES FOR HIGH INFORMATION-PROCESSING CAPACITY   A second necessary requirement for the adoption of a matrix organization is the existence of a need for processing massive amounts of information at key managerial levels. This need could result from changing and unpredictable environmental demands, increased task complexity due to diversification of both products and markets, and strong interdependence among managers for the execution of a given task. The absorption of this voluminous information is facilitated through the intimate coordination assured by the two-boss system.

PRESSURES FOR SHARED RESOURCES   The final necessary condition for developing a matrix organization occurs whenever great pressures for high efficiency force the sharing of critical resources, such as physical facilities, capital and human resources, and professional experience. Matrix organizations guarantee great efficiency in the utilization of these resources by sharing them among all products or projects, while maintaining a functional centralized control.

Furthermore, Davis and Lawrence suggest that a matrix does not result from the mere adoption of a matrix structure, but also requires the establishment of a *matrix system*, a *matrix culture*, and a *matrix behavior*.

The path from a traditional organization to this highly demanding matrix form is facilitated by a gradual implementation of the concept via integrating mechanisms of increased sophistication that enhance lateral relations. Only a gradual approach to the complex and ambiguous operation of a matrix organization gives the people involved the time needed to adapt their behavior to the demands of this organizational form.

The Hybrid Organization

The basic organizational forms presented previously are abstractions of a more complex reality. In general, the structure of organizations stems from more than one of these pure models, though the dominant pattern can be traced back to one of them. In fact, most divisional organizations have a number of functional specialties centralized at the corporate level.

Vancil sampled around 300 divisionalized corporations and reported the following percentages of firms having decentralized functions:[7]

Administration	54%
R&D	65%
Manufacturing	70%
Distribution	79%
Sales	82%

He concluded from these empirical results that there is a stronger tendency to decentralization for functions closer to the final consumer.

Consequently, an organizational structure in a real case is usually a *hybrid* of the basic archetypes. The challenge of organizational design is to seek a proper balance among these three alternatives to respond more effectively to the performance of the organizational tasks.

We have observed that most divisional organizations retain some centralized functions. Likewise, most large functional organizations tend to create an independent subsidiary or a divisional business operation to add autonomy to secondary segments of its business. Similarly, organizations often adopt partial matrix structures to link selected products with related functions.

STEPS IN THE DESIGN OF THE ORGANIZATIONAL STRUCTURE

We have found that two distinct steps should be recognized in the organizational design process. The first step is the definition of a *basic organizational structure*. This basic structure represents the major segmentation of the businesses the firm is engaged in through a hierarchical order which reveals the priorities managers assign to the firm's central activities. Only the primary echelons of the organizational chart that are intimately linked to the strategic positioning of the firm are recognized in this step.

A second step in the organizational design process is the definition of a *detailed organizational structure*. At this stage, the basic organizational structure is fleshed out with the numerous specific details pertaining to the operational domain of the firm.

Normally, a number of basic alternatives might emerge as competitors for a final design, each one originating different combinations at the detail level. The process of selecting a final structure implies a soul-searching effort of a fairly subjective nature. Here key top executives engage in a time-consuming activity of proposing, defining, testing, and selecting alternative configurations.

The design of an organizational structure is completed with the specification of a *balance* between the organizational structure chosen and the managerial processes that go with it: planning, management control, communication and information, and human resources management and reward systems.

The steps in the organizational design process are now more extensively discussed.

Design of a Basic Organizational Structure

The fundamental objective of this step is to translate the strategic positioning of the firm in terms of a set of distinctive units ordered in the highest hierarchical levels of the organizational structure. Since the focus of strategy is business development, this step requires the full recognition of the businesses the firm is engaged in with its further segmentation into manageable units.

FIRST: IDENTIFY AND LIST YOUR CRITICAL DIMENSIONS   A simple way to begin the search for business segmentation is to prepare a list of the *critical dimensions* for the business activities. Normally, this list includes:

- Products
- Markets: industrial, commercial, government, original equipment manufacturing (OEM), and so on
- Functions: production, sales, marketing, finance, administration, personnel, R&D, engineering, and so on
- Technologies
- Geographic locations: markets, production, distribution, and R&D facilities

A business segment is composed of an orderly assignment of some or all of the preceding dimensions. At the bare minimum, a business encompasses a combination of products, markets, and some autonomous capacity for product change.

SECOND: FOCUS ALTERNATIVELY ON DIFFERENT CRITICAL DIMENSIONS   Some companies decide to organize their basic structure in accordance with their primary business segmentation. This is normally the case in divisionalized firms, where each division has production and marketing responsibilities, as well as some decentralized functional support. Under these conditions, there is a clear alignment between the strategic and operational objectives of the organization.

However, a basic segmentation following business categories is not always desirable or possible. A company might choose a functional focus as the primary dimension for its basic structure. This selection reflects operational efficiency and technical excellence as its fundamental concern for organizational design. Similarly, market location as a primary dimension stresses the importance of good customer service. And the choice of clients or markets attempts to emphasize the need for a special coverage of a market segment.

THIRD: RANK CRITICAL DIMENSIONS IN ORDER OF DECREASING IMPORTANCE   In any event, this step of the organizational design process calls for a hierarchical recognition of the critical dimensions identified previously with the purpose of obtaining a focus for the basic segmentation. Unfortunately, it is rarely the case that the basic structure can be simply expressed in terms of a unique dimension. In the process of designing this structure, managers are confronted with a complex choice among competing foci that must be subjected to a thoughtful trade-off.

Fourth: Define One or More Primary Structures   A careful weighing of the advantages and disadvantages will most likely lead to a primary structure which is not homogeneous. For example, in Figure 16–2, some primary units correspond to products, some to functions, some to clients, and some to geographical regions (international versus domestic focus).

The absence of a homogeneous criterion of segmentation and the lack of symmetry are not the exception but the rule in the formulation of a basic organizational structure. More than one organizational level is usually required to capture the implications of the choice made by managers. One could say that it is possible "to read" the strategic priorities of the organization from the arrangement of its basic structure.

When a corporation decides not to organize according to its business segments, a special effort should be made to provide a managerial focus superimposed on the basic organizational structure.

Detailed Organizational Design
The objective sought in the detailed organizational design phase is twofold: to identify all the major operational tasks the organization should undertake in the pursuit of its daily activities, and to assign those tasks to the organizational segments identified in the basic structure previously defined. The basic structure brings the selected strategy into the design process, while the detailed analysis comes to recognize the operational functional activities.

Simulate the Operation of the Firm with the New Structure: Ask "What if" Questions   Many questions surge naturally from people familiar with the organization to test the responsiveness of its structure against a multitude of vital situations. For example, one might ask how a request from an individual customer located in a remote area for a specific product or service would be handled under the proposed structure. When answering the question, if one detects ambiguities, lack of efficiency, or undesirable splitting of responsibilities, some structural overhauling must be performed.

Figure 16–2.   Example of the Multiplicity of Criteria Used in the Definition of a Strategic Focus

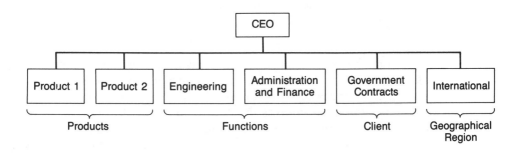

MORE SPECIFIC QUESTIONS TO BE ADDRESSED

    (a) If the organization is mainly functional,

- How to insure that products are given their share of attention? Are integrating managers necessary in the role of product directors?
- Should the marketing function be subdivided by product? By client? By region? Should sales be centralized or regionalized?
- How should the production function be subdivided? By plants? By production stages? By products? By geographical regions?
- How is the R&D function going to interact with engineering, production, and marketing functions?
- How would distribution be responsive to local requests for delivery of products manufactured in several plants?
- How to provide an effective training ground for general managers? How to evaluate managerial performance in a strategic mode?
- If the firm engages in a strategy of growth via acquisition, how to integrate the newly acquired firms into the functional structure?
- If the firm expands its business to cover international markets, how to deal with the different business needs in each country?
- What integrative mechanisms should be in place to coordinate functional activities at a level other than that of the chief executive officer (CEO)?
- How to prevent an overloaded CEO principally concerned with operational matters?
- How to prevent excessive "parochialism" among functional managers?

    (b) If the organization is mainly divisionalized around product lines,

- Which functions should be centralized and which decentralized?
- For centralized functions, should they report to the CEO or to a lower hierarchical level?
- If plants, distribution facilities, warehouses, and resources in general are shared by more than one product line, who is in charge of them? How to insure that each division obtains fair treatment?
- How to deal with regional affairs?
- Are there special clients that require preferential attention? How to handle these situations?
- For decentralized functions, how to assure the preservation of economies of scale and operational efficiency?
- Should divisionalization be conducted by major product lines, by geographical areas, by type of technologies?
- How to deal with international activities?
- How much autonomy should each division have, both in operational and strategic modes? What coordination mechanisms should be enforced among divisions?

    Along the more detailed analysis performed for each alternative structural design, some of the options will be discarded from further consideration because of undesirable characteristics surfaced by this more careful inquiry. At the end, only two or three alternatives should be competing. For the final selection, the detailed analysis performed in this step provides a visceral understanding of the strategic and operational implications for each design under scrutiny.

Balance Between Organizational Structure and Managerial Processes

The positioning of units and subunits of the organization in an ordered hierarchical network must be completed with the definition of all complementary managerial systems. The full-fledged operation of these systems provides a background of integrative relationships that the simple organizational structure fails to represent. Moreover, these systems must be designed both to reinforce the primary focus chosen by the organization, and to support those activities relegated to a secondary level in the definition of the organizational structure. For example, a planning system in a functional organization must be especially sharp in the definition of strategic business units. This is because the primary structure does not give sufficient weight to the identification of businesses the firm is engaged in, and this may weaken the long-term strategic positioning of the firm. On the other hand, the segments defined in divisional organizations are more long-term oriented, but the operational efficiency is enhanced by giving ample autonomy to the divisional manager and by linking his or her rewards with the divisional performance. In this way, balance and alignment are established between the long- and short-term concepts.

BALANCED PROFILES FOR AN ORGANIZATION   A comprehensive conceptual scheme identifying the major design and managerial variables to consider when analyzing the degree of fitness between strategy and organizational structure is presented in Figure 16–3. Three broad strategic options—single or dominant business, related diversified, and unrelated diversified—are used to identify the changes in the organizational structure and administrative processes congruent with the respective strategic options.[8]

Alternatively, Figure 16–4 provides a compact description of the primary characteristics of the managerial systems and organizational climate within each stage of industry maturity—embryonic, growth, maturity, aging. The chart reflects Arthur D. Little's strategic planning approach. This approach could serve as a consistency check between the nature of the managerial systems used by the firm against the stages of the life cycles of the industries in which the businesses operate.

This last stage in the organizational design process seeks to establish the congruency of the formal-analytical managerial systems in the strategic management framework.

Symptoms of an Inadequate Organizational Structure

The organizational structure has two primary roles: support the full implementation of strategic programs, and permit the normal conduct of the firm's operating activities.

External and internal changes call for a continuous adjustment of the organizational structure in order to insure an optimum handling of strategic and operating activities. However, practice has shown that despite these adjustments, organizations need, from time to time, a more comprehensive overhaul. As a structure grows older, it usually lacks the flexibility to accommodate new strategic and operational demands. The managerial team should maintain an eye on signs of stress that evidence an inadequate structure, because keeping

FIGURE 16-3. Strategy-Organization Fit

	FUNCTIONAL ORGANIZATION	MULTIDIVISONAL ORGANIZATION	CONGLOMERATE FIRM
STRATEGY	• Dominant business • Vertically integrated	• Related diversified • Growth through internal development, some acquisition	• Unrelated diversified • Growth through acquisition
STRATEGIC FOCUS AND TASK FOCUS	• Degree of integration • Market share • Product line breadth	• Realization of synergy from related products, process, technologies, markets • Resource allocation • Diversification opportunities	• Degree of diversity • Types of business • Resource allocation across discrete businesses • Entry and exit businesses
STRUCTURE AND DECISION-MAKING STYLE	• Centralized functional • Top control of strategic decisions • Delegation of operations through plans and procedures	• Multidivisional/profit centers • Grouping of highly related business with some centralized functions within groups • Delegated responsibility for operations • Shared responsibility for strategy	• Highly decentralized product divisions/profit centers • Small corporate office • No centralized line functions • Almost complete delegation of operations and strategy within existing businesses • Control through results, selection of management, and capital allocation
INFORMATION AND DECISION PROCESS	• Coordination and integration through structure, rules, planning, and budgeting • Use of integrating roles for project activity across functions	• Coordinate and integrate across businesses and between levels with planning, integrating roles, integrating departments	• No integration across businesses • Coordination and information flows between corporate and division levels around management information systems and budgets
REWARDS	• Performance against functional objectives • Mix of objective and subjective performance measures	• Bonus based on divisional and corporate profit performance • Mix of objective and subjective performance measures	• Formula-based bonus on ROI or profitability of divisions • Equity rewards • Strict objective, impersonal evaluation
PEOPLE AND CAREERS	• Primarily functional specialists • Some interfunctional movement to develop some general managers	• Broad requirements for general managers and integrators • Career developments cross-functional, interdivisional, and corporate-divisional	• Aggressive, independent general managers of divisions • Career development opportunities are primarily intradivisional.

SOURCE: Jay Galbraith and Robert K. Kanzanjian, *Strategy Implementation: Structure, Systems, and Process,* 2nd Ed., (St. Paul, MN: West Publishing and Co., © 1986), pp. 116–117. Reprinted by permission; all rights reserved.

218

FIGURE 16–4. Consistency of Management Systems and Industry Maturity

DESCRIPTORS / CHARACTERISTICS	EMBRYONIC	GROWTH	MATURE	AGING
GENERAL THRUST	Entrepreneurship • Start-up • Flexibility • Survival	Sophisticated management of markets • Growth • Develop advantageous competitive position	Critical administration • Maximize efficiency • Optimize profits	Opportunistic milking • Prolongation • Maximize profits • Survival
PLANNING SYSTEM				
• Time Frame	Long enough to encompass life cycle (10 yrs.)	Long-term investment payout (7 yrs.)	Intermediate (3 yrs.)	Short term (1 yr.)
• Content	By product/customer	By product and program	By product/market/function	By plant
• Approach	Flexible	Less flexible	Formalized	Formalized
ORGANIZATION				
• Size	Small; rapidly growing	Moderate; moderate growth	Large	Large; moderate shrinkage
• Stability	Fluctuating	Less Fluctuating	Stable	Less stable
• Structure	Loose/informal; authorities/responsibilities not clearly defined, with some overlapping	Becoming more formal	Tight/formal; authorities/responsibilities clearly defined and described	Formal/pared down
• Complexity	Simple; few functions and hierarchical levels	Becoming complex; increasing number and variety of functions, divisions and hierarchical levels	Complex; multifunctional, multidivisional and multilevel	Simplified functions, divisions, levels
• Flexibility	High flexibility	Becoming more rigid	Rigid	Less rigid
MANAGERIAL MODE				
• Orientation	Task/growth/financing	Task/performance/people	People/performance	Performance/survival

Figure 16–4. Consistency of Management Systems and Industry Maturity (continued)

DESCRIPTORS / CHARACTERISTICS	EMBRYONIC	GROWTH	MATURE	AGING
• Style	Open; ad hoc; consultative, fire-fighting	Participative; becoming more formal; delegation	Formal; leadership; delegation; control	Autocratic; tight control; expedient
• Skills	Generalist	More specialized	Specialist	More generalist
• Risk	High	Moderately high	Moderate	Low
• Time Span/Concern	Short	Long	Intermediate	Short
• Key Activity	Innovation	Planning	Systems	Control
REWARD SYSTEM				
• Main purpose	Incentive	Incentive/equity	Equity	Equity/incentive
• Structure of Pay Package	High variable/low fixed	Balanced variable and fixed	Low variable/high fixed	Fixed only
• Character	Loose/informal	Becoming formal	Formal/rigid	Formal/rigid
• Basis	Functional worth and individual performance	Functional worth and individual and group performance	Functional worth and group performance	Functional worth and individual and group performance
• Timing	Quarterly	Semi-annually—annually	Annually; some deferred for succeeding 2–3 years	Annually
• Fringe Emphasis	Shares	Time off from work	Time off/retirement	Retirement

FIGURE 16-4. Continued

	Rapid responsiveness	Planning	Coordination/control	Control
COMMUNICATIONS AND INFORMATION SYSTEM				
• Main Purpose	Rapid responsiveness	Planning	Coordination/control	Control
• Character	Informal/tailored	Formal/tailored	Formal/uniform	Little or none by direction
• Content of Reporting	Qualitative; market-oriented; unsystematic	Qualitative and quantitative; early warning system, all functions	Quantitative; production-oriented; systematic	Quantitative; oriented to balance sheet; systematic
• Policies	Few	More	Many	Many
• Procedures	None	Few	Many	Many
CONTROL AND MEASURING SYSTEM				
• Main Purpose	Identify significant need for rapid response	Early warning	Improved quality of management decisions	Control
• Principal Focus	Market/marketing/product development	Marketing/manufacturing	Manufacturing/financial performance	Financial performance
• Measures Used	Few fixed	Multiple/adjustable	Multiple/adjustable	Few/fixed
• Frequency of Measurement	Often	Relative often	Traditionally periodic	Less often
Detail of measurement	Less	More	Great	Less
SUMMARY CHARACTERIZATION				

SOURCE: This figure reflects the strategic planning approach of Arthur D. Little, Inc.

it longer than necessary may impair the normal growth and development of a firm.

Some of the most common symptoms that can be traced back to an inadequate organizational structure are:

1. **Lack of opportunities for general manager development.** This is usually the case of functionally-oriented organizations.
2. **Insufficient time devoted to strategic thinking** due to too much concentration on operational issues, excessive decision making at the top, or overworked key personnel.
3. **Intensively antagonistic working climate.** The motivational and reward system should be in tune with the given structure. An antagonistic climate may be signaling a problem of balance between structure and processes.
4. **Lack of definition in portfolio business planning, neglect of special markets, and inappropriate setting for maximizing growth and profit.** These are among the clearest evidence of an organizational structure which cannot accommodate the new strategic positioning of the firm.
5. **Lack of coordination among divisions.** This points to a failure of integrating mechanisms.
6. **Excessive duplication of functions in different units of the firm.** The differentiation among units is not well established. Redefinition of tasks or the fusion of some units might be advantageous.
7. **Excessive dispersion of functions in one unit of the firm.** Determine if the differentiation of tasks warrants the segmentation of this unit.
8. **Poor profit performance and low return expectations.** The organizational structure cannot escape a major revision in a situation like this. The firm should examine its strategy and adopt an organizational structure suitable for the implementation of the agreed strategy.

ORGANIZATIONAL STRUCTURE IN THE STRATEGIC MODE

The segmentation issue should centrally consider the questions of how the various SBUs are going to receive proper managerial attention. When the organizational structure is segmented according to SBUs, we find no real conflict between strategic and operational performance. A given manager simply has to "wear two hats" and becomes accountable in these two modes. When this is not the case, significant coordinational pressures are exercised on the organization to maintain a degree of alertness in both strategic and operational responsibilities.

Some business firms face a fairly complex dilemma. On the one hand, they find themselves competing in a variety of markets which forces them to identify several SBUs in order to conduct an appropriate strategic process. However, because of pressures to share resources and seek economies of scale to achieve operational efficiencies, the organization cannot be structured according to independent SBUs. Rather, the SBUs become simply a planning focus, which cuts across several organizational units, insofar as the development and implementation of its corresponding strategic programs is concerned. Some of the coordinating mechanisms that can be used to provide due attention to the SBUs are:

ASSIGN TO THE SBU MANAGER A PERMANENT COORDINATING ROLE   This is a solution often adopted in professional organizations such as engineering and consulting firms, and universities, where the segmentation structure is according to major disciplines, and coordinating managers are in charge of developing the firm's position in its primary programs, markets, or businesses. It is essential in those cases to maintain a high level of disciplinary excellence, which is the basic resource of those institutions. Therefore, it would be unacceptable to fragment disciplinary groups, giving away the benefits to be derived from a large professional critical mass. If a concerted effort, however, is not made to respond effectively to the requirements of the external businesses of the firm, the organization will significantly lack strategic alertness. That role is assumed by the SBU coordinating manager. It is a difficult role because the manager's responsibility by far exceeds his or her authority. As a minimum, there are two conditions that should coexist for the SBU manager to have a meaningful chance for success. First, there should be a full understanding and complete support on the part of the CEO and top operating managers, on the significance of the SBU coordinating manager's tasks. Second, the SBU manager should have full authority over the strategic component of the SBU budget, which constitutes the only meaningful mechanism for exercising some leverage over operating managers.

We have found some misconceptions with regard to how these organizational solutions are perceived in practice. Many people tend to associate a matrix form with this organizational structure. This is clearly not the case. Under this scheme, the SBU manager does not have direct authority over the individuals working in various organizational units. Therefore, there is no duality of bosses, which is an essential attribute of a matrix organization. The SBU manager is strictly a *coordinating* manager. This alternative can also be used in functional organizations, which participate in a plurality of businesses.

ASSIGN TO A TOP MANAGEMENT COMMITTEE THE RESPONSIBILITIES FOR SBUs' MANAGEMENT   This second coordinating mechanism consists of assigning a committee, normally composed of the CEO and top operational managers, the task of developing and implementing the necessary SBUs' strategic programs. This organizational form is prevalent in many European nations, foremost in England. The committee meets normally once a week to discuss questions of operational and strategic significance. It is central for the success of this organizational solution that managers distinguish very clearly their duality of roles. As heads of their corresponding operational units, they have the normal profit and loss, or expense accountability which emanates from their routine operational activities. However, as members of the SBU management committee, they are supposed to act on behalf of the ultimate corporate interests, and not as parochial defenders of their own areas of operational responsibilities. In this capacity their role is essentially strategic in character.

ADOPT A MATRIX FORM OF ORGANIZATION FOR DEALING WITH OPERATIONAL AND STRATEGIC RESPONSIBILITIES   The most extreme form that can be adopted in seeking integration between operational and strategic responsibilities, when these responsibilities cannot be squarely assigned to a single individual, is the matrix structure. This organizational structure institutionalizes the dual responsibilities and accountabilities in both strategic and operational modes.

Normally the operational side of the matrix is represented by functional managers, who are responsible for expense centers, while the strategic dimensions correspond to SBU managers responsible for profit centers. This is indicated in Figure 16–5.

For the matrix to operate effectively, it is important that each functional unit is segmented according to SBU lines. Under those conditions, the SBU managers would have clear access to functional resources, thus avoiding some of the inherent ambiguity of the matrix form. Moreover, it is necessary to establish a coordinating committee, chaired by the SBU manager, and composed by one representative from each functional specialty linked to the SBU, thus institutionalizing the necessary coordination among the various functional units from a business dimension. Finally, every administrative system (planning, control, information, and reward systems) should be designed to support the matrix structure. If all of these recommendations are properly implemented, the matrix can become an effective organizational form.

Organizational design is an art, not a science. We adhere to concepts expressed by the contingency theory approach. This suggests that there is no single way to establish the best organizational structure of the firm. This does not mean, however, that any organizational alternative is equally acceptable.

FIGURE 16–5.   Matrix Form of Organization to Deal with Strategic and Operational Responsibilities

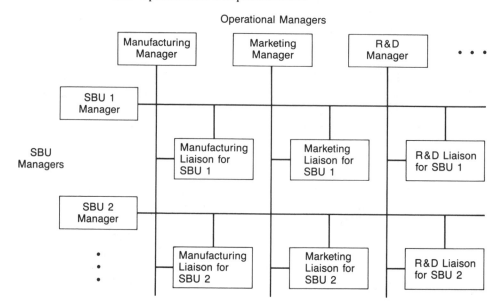

The effectiveness of a given organizational structure depends on situational characteristics such as the environment that the firm faces, the nature of the tasks the organization is to undertake, and the people involved in the performance of those tasks.[9] In the appendix to this chapter we discuss a case study on matching strategy and structure.

The Planning System

This is a book on planning; so there is no point in repeating here the basic components of a planning system. But it is worth stressing that though in important ways the vision of the firm or modifications to it are expected to emerge from the planning process, this is also a fundamental management system that must be imprinted with this same vision. All corporate efforts and formal documents are intended to be concrete guidelines for acquiring and sharing a common vision. Tasks developed at all levels of the organization, formal meetings, and the multiple negotiations conducted under the umbrella of the planning process are powerful integrating mechanisms. Demands made by corporate managers to business and functional managers, the need to present and defend requests for capital appropriation, and other mechanisms embedded in a planning process are clear opportunities to advance in building a common vision of the firm.

A BRIEF COMMENT ON THE ROLE
OF THE PLANNING DEPARTMENTS

Parenthetically, a relatively common pitfall in some organizations is to rely on a centralized planning department as the major force behind the development of a balanced system. This is normally a serious pitfall on two accounts. First, planners should not plan. Planning, as we have stressed throughout, is an inherent managerial responsibility that cannot be delegated to staff units. A legitimate role for planners is the gathering of information, primarily external to the firm, to enlighten managerial decision making. Also, they should act as catalysts, inquirers, educators, and synthesizers to guide the planning process in an effective manner. But planners should not plan, this should be done by the line executives.

It is probably better to have a lean planning department composed of intelligent and energetic young individuals who could benefit from a brief stay there, a location with a remarkable vantage point in the organization, and be moved later to a more permanent line or staff position.

The second potential pitfall of having a centralized planning department is that it tends to isolate the planning activity from the remaining administrative systems. This is the sure way of transforming planning into a largely irrelevant activity. No wonder then that, in many instances, planning becomes a yearly ritual, conducted by staff members. This culminates in a thick book that gathers dust on the shelves of those managers who were not involved in the preparations, but whose tasks the book intended to define. Most of the benefits of the planning process, if properly done, accrue in the realization of the process itself. Planning is a decision-making activity, and the planning books are simply subproducts for refreshing our memory and documenting the decisions made. They are certainly not the final aims of the planning process.

The Management Control System

The management control system is one of the major devices used by executives to judge the performance of the overall corporation and all its key organizational units. Management control is a structured process, quantitatively oriented, that is based on the definition of performance standards for the entire firm and each one of its units, and on the comparison of planned with actual results obtained from operations. In this way, top managers can derive an opinion on the effectiveness obtained in the implementation of strategic directions and the efficiency achieved in the use of its primary resources. Managers may then act accordingly, taking corrective actions whenever needed. Management control is a system for managing day-to-day operational and strategic activities, with a unitary sense of direction imprinted in the quantitative benchmarks selected as standards of comparison. Finally, management control, mainly when coupled with the compensation and reward systems, becomes a driver of individual behavior in the organizational setting.

We recognize the following steps in the design of a management control system which captures the interactions existing among management control, organizational structure, and the other administrative systems.

1. Determining the unit of analysis: the linkage between management control and the segmentation of the central activities of the firm.
2. Selecting performance standards: integration between planning and management control.
3. Developing monitoring capabilities (analysis, performance evaluation, diagnosis, and corrective action): integration between information systems and management control.
4. Influencing intended behavior: the linkage between management control and the human resources management and reward system.

DETERMINING THE UNIT OF ANALYSIS:
THE LINKAGE BETWEEN MANAGEMENT
CONTROL AND THE SEGMENTATION
OF THE CENTRAL ACTIVITIES OF THE FIRM

As we have previously seen, the first key step in designing any formal administrative system is to identify the central focus of attention of the corresponding process. Therefore, it is appropriate for us to reflect first on the entities which are going to be the subject of management control. To respond to this question, it is useful to segment the activities of the firm into two modes: strategic and operational.

The strategic segmentation of the firm was already captured when analyzing the various hierarchical levels in which the planning process is conducted. At the corporate level, the firm as a whole is the central focus of analysis. At the business level we define the concept of a strategic business unit (SBU) as the key element of concern. Finally, at the functional level exists a similar kind of organizational entity which we refer to as strategic functional unit (SFU). The SFUs classify the functional activities into six major strategic foci: finance, human resources, technology, procurement, manufacturing, and marketing.[10]

The congruency between planning and control has to start by recognizing the same units of analysis. Therefore, strategic planning as well as strategic control recognize three primary levels of segmentation: the firm, the strategic business units, and the strategic functional units.

This segmentation, although able to capture the central strategic dimensions of the firm, is not enough to permit a comprehensive control of the complete set of the firm's activities. We have seen that the process of defining the organizational structure of the firm forces us to conduct a much deeper segmentation that carries through the full allocation of responsibilities and authorities all the way from the CEO to the lowest echelons within the firm. The resulting organizational units should encompass the key strategic tasks, but expanding into much more detailed levels of operational issues. All of the resulting entities contribute in various degrees to the fulfillment of the overall objectives of the firm, and their performance should also be subjected to careful planning and control attention.

An important concept that contributes to facilitate these operational control functions is the *responsibility center*. This concept was initially developed within the framework of managerial accounting,[11] and therefore has a strong financial and accounting bias in terms of the performance criteria used to control each of the resulting activities. This does not need to be so, and in fact it is easy to incorporate into the accounting parameters whatever measurements are needed to capture the overall strategic as well as operational performance requirements. We begin the presentation of responsibility center with the conventional definition prevailing in the managerial accounting literature. Later in this chapter, we add a strategic dimension to this concept.

A *responsibility center* is an organizational unit with a clearly identified scope of activities that has been entrusted to a responsible manager. It may be pictured in terms of three main factors: (1) its inputs; such as materials, parts, components, and labor, (2) its outputs; as the different kinds of products and services generated by the unit, and (3) the fixed resources assigned to the manager; such as total assets or net investment. Depending on the nature of managerial control, the responsibility center may be defined as: (1) *cost centers* where managers are accountable for expenses generated from the input streams, (2) *revenue centers* where accountability stems from revenues generated from the output streams as well as expenses from the input streams, (3) *profit centers* where accountability is judged by ability to generate profits (revenues minus expenses), or (4) *investment centers* where accountability is measured in terms of profits as percentage of the total investment base. The subtle difference between revenue and profit centers' managers is that the latter are given the authority to set up their own prices, while the former are given fixed prices from the corporate level. Investment centers are normally measured in terms of return on investment (ROI).

Cost centers can be further classified into standard cost centers and discretionary cost centers. *Standard cost centers* are characterized by having well-defined output measures, and clean relationships between the required inputs and the resulting outputs. Such is the case with manufacturing operations where standards can be computed to the amount of inputs (labor, raw materials, supplies, and additional supporting services) needed to produce a unit of a specific product. On the contrary, *discretionary cost centers* deliver outputs that cannot be measured in a strict financial way, or where there is no clear association between inputs and outputs. Such is the case with most of the administrative activities of a firm, for example, legal, human resources, accounting departments, the research and development function, and marketing activities such as promotion and advertising.

The key for the identification of responsibility centers is to adjust their definition to their intended strategic positioning. If for a given unit a business orientation has been decided, it could be appropriate to treat it as a profit or investment center. In this way the divisional manager is granted the necessary leeway to operate with the required degree of autonomy. If, on the contrary, the unit is mainly a support for the development of a business, it could be preferable to define it as a cost or revenue center, oriented to the efficient use of internal resources and the proper execution of programs that are externally imposed to a great extent. Once responsibility centers have been defined, we need to identify the interrelationship among units, the internal transfer of materials, products, and services, the degree of freedom to obtain them from sources external to the firm, the way in which prices are going to be set, and the procedures to conduct negotiations among units and solve conflicts as they arise.

The most common criteria to establish *transfer prices* are market prices; cost measured either as a total cost, marginal cost, or standard cost; cost plus a profit margin, where cost is measured according to the same alternatives just stated; and negotiated prices, either directly by the parties involved, via a mediator designated by both parties, or determined by top managers.[12]

The preferred transfer price mechanism is market prices whenever available, with an additional freedom on the part of the responsibility center manager to go outside to satisfy the required needs if the internal organization is unable to provide them effectively. This mode of operation guarantees incentives for maintaining a sharp competitive alertness. The worst alternative seems to be total cost plus a profit margin. This type of transfer price makes the responsibility center captive to all the potential inefficiencies of the providing center where not only total cost is absorbed, but a profit margin is guaranteed. When market prices are not available, it is preferable to establish a base for negotiating prices among the involved parties or simply to adopt a standard cost, which demands a reasonable level of efficiency.

SELECTING PERFORMANCE STANDARDS: INTEGRATION BETWEEN PLANNING AND MANAGEMENT CONTROL

The management process used to define the benchmarks for each unit of the organization is the natural conclusion or extension of the planning effort. In fact, one could argue that planning and control are indivisible activities, two sides of the same coin. The process of planning and formulating objectives, programs, and budgets cannot be terminated properly without defining appropriate procedures for monitoring, analyzing, and controlling the planning activities. Otherwise planning simply becomes an abstract expression of too general and broad commitments, with little if any implementation qualities. Consequently, a well-designed planning process should include the definition of performance measurements which are the basis of management control.

Figure 16–6 represents the essence of integration between planning and control processes. This figure emphasizes the role of budgeting as a bridge between planning and control. From this perspective, budgeting can be viewed as a part of both the planning process and the management control process.

From a planning standpoint, the budget produces a set of financial statements identical to those used in financial accounting: balance sheet, income statement, and statement of changes in the financial position. The basic difference is that budget figures are estimates of the intended future results based on broad and specific action programs derived from the planning process rather than historical data of what has happened in the past.

From a management control standpoint, the budget and the definition of strategic programs provide all necessary information for monitoring, analyzing, and scheduling the development of strategic and operational tasks. The figure also illustrates that an important element of the management control process is to incorporate revisions in either budgets, strategic programs, or the strategic objectives whenever the deviations between proposed plans and actual results are so significant as to warrant the incorporation of these changes prior to beginning a new planning cycle.

The strategic planning process flows naturally into the management control process through the definition of strategic objectives, and broad and specific action programs. To make them controllable, all objectives and programs must be translated into quantitative indicators at the level of the overall firm, business unit, functional areas, and of each particular responsibility center. In this way, they become measurable, allowing for the achievement of an objective to be ascertained and the advancement of a program to be monitored.

The management control process requires a quantitative model expressed in the form of indicators that can be readily followed up. The question is how to select a set of indices that is representative of the vision of the firm.

FIGURE 16–6. Integration of the Planning and Management Control Process

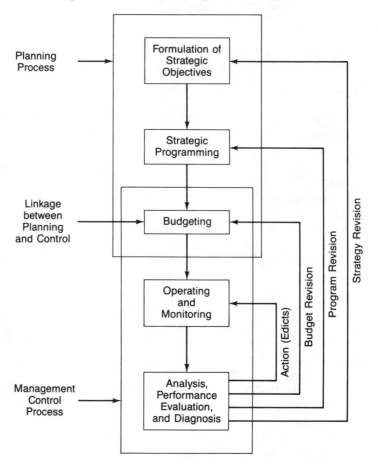

In Chapter 7 we suggest performance measurements to be used at the level of a business unit. Chapter 14 offers indicators as corporate performance objectives. Chapter 19 discusses performance measurements for each of the key managerial functions, that is, finance, human resources, technology, procurement, manufacturing, and marketing. The reader should refer to those chapters for recommendations for specific control indices at the three hierarchical levels of the firm. We now discuss broader issues relevant to the design of an effective management control system.

Financial Performance: The Heart of Management Control
Financial performance is at the heart of every business firm. Although profit making is not the only objective to be pursued, it cannot be ignored. Lack of profitability will affect adversely all other objectives of the firm. Managers, particularly the CEO, consider profitability as one of the central concerns.

Well-designed and implemented management control systems are powerful tools for the definition, monitoring, and attainment of profit targets. The major issue, however, is to prevent excessive myopia and undue concern for short-term profitability at the expense of the long-term development of the firm. Much has been said on the pitfalls of depending too strongly on achieving good profitability performance in the short term. Many organizations have found themselves inadvertently weakening their asset base and discouraging necessary investments by compromising the long-term competitive standing of the firm in exchange for a hefty next-year return on investment (ROI).

The conceptual answer to this dilemma is relatively straightforward: budgeted ROI figures should stem from the strategic direction selected by the firm rather than becoming goals unto themselves. In other words, strategic commitments should condition financial performance in the short and long run. We should keep in mind that a good financial performance is originated by the proper management and development of all physical, technological, and human resources. Consequently, rather than manipulating the ROI index, we should act over the determinants of that index.

Firms which depend entirely on budgetary and financial control measurements for their planning systems quite often are exceedingly vulnerable to fall into near-sighted ROI traps. Unless there is a clear articulation of the business competitive strategy, properly understood at all organizational levels, a pure budgeting and financial control system will prove inadequate to avoid undesirable consequences.

Thus, the proper development and communication of the business strategy and the translation of the resulting strategic commitments into meaningful financial indicators are essential requirements to prevent the misuse of budgeting and financial control. One way of assuring this quality of strategy articulation is to adopt a formal strategic planning system. Companies which do not adopt a formal planning system have to rely on other mechanisms to develop and communicate their strategies, like implicit rather than explicit avenues for strategy formulation, entrepreneurial strategic thinking on the part of the CEO and his top team, and opportunistic decision making. But this planning approach could become increasingly dysfunctional when the complexity of businesses grows. The excessive financial bias would prevent a proper diagnosis of the underlying causes of short- and long-term profitability and would cloud the sense of priorities. Financial targets for a given year can probably be achieved. The main question is, at what price?

Other Indicators for Management Control

Accounting measures are considered today insufficient to properly characterize the operational and strategic requirements of a management control system. Kaplan and Johnson point to the lost relevance of management accounting, and the need to complement this information with data that are not required by the strictly legal obligations imposed by financial accounting.[13]

When going beyond the purely accounting measurements, several approaches have been designed to provide managers at all levels with relevant information, both of a strategic and operational nature. Rockart offers a good classification of those approaches.[14] We will comment briefly on two of the leading contenders to satisfy executive information needs: the key performance indicator method, and the critical success factor method.

The key performance indicator method requires the selection of a set of key variables, meaning a stable set of indicators that allow managers to detect and monitor the competitive position of all businesses the firm is engaged in. Obviously, information has to be collected to report the performance of each indicator, and the results are made available to the pertinent managers at all levels, possibly on an exception basis.

One of the first companies to institutionalize this process was General Electric, which more than twenty-five years ago began to measure performance in all its departments according to the eight key result areas listed in Figure 16–7.

The critical success factor method (CSF) was first proposed by Daniel.[15] However, it has been Rockart who has championed this idea as central for the design of top-management information systems. Daniel defines CSFs as

> the limited number of areas in which results, if they are satisfactory, will ensure successful competitive performance for the organization. They are the few key areas where "things must go right" for the business to flourish. If results in these areas are not adequate, the organization's efforts for the period will be less than desired.

FIGURE 16–7. Key Result Areas and Performance Measurements Originally Defined by General Electric

AREA	PERFORMANCE MEASUREMENT
1. Profitability	Residual income
2. Market position	Market share
3. Productivity	Output (value added)/Input (payroll + depreciation)
4. Product leadership	—Competitive standing
	—R&D and innovation in engineering, manufacturing, and marketing
5. Personnel development	—Development programs
	—Inventory of promotable people
	—Effectiveness of program implementation
6. Employee attitudes	—Statistical indicators
	—Periodic employees surveys
7. Public responsibility	Surveys
8. Balance between short- and long-range goals	All previous factors have short- and long-term dimensions

SOURCE: Adapted from Robert N. Anthony and Robert H. Kaplan, General Electric Company. Boston: Harvard Business School; Case 6-113-121 in Robert N. Anthony and John Dearden, *Management Control Systems.* (Homewood, IL: Richard D. Irwin, 1980), pp. 101–9. Copyright © 1964 by the President and Fellows of Harvard College. Used with permission of the Harvard Business School.

Figure 16–8 provides an example of the critical success factors identified for Microwave Associates, Inc., as reported by Rockart. Rockart considers that there are four primary sources of CSFs:

- the structure of the particular industry
- the company's competitive strategy, its industry position, and its geographical location
- environmental factors
- temporal factors, which refer to areas of activities that become significant for an organization for a limited period of time

The primary differences between the key performance indicator method and the CSF method is that the former tends to be more permanent and uniformly applied to all organizational units of the firm, as stated in the GE example; while the latter is tailor-made to fit each manager and the characteristics of the corresponding business units. The CSF method must be constantly adapted to reflect changes taking place in the organization or its environment.

Operational and Strategic Accountability

There are several ways of expressing in the reporting system the dichotomy between operational and strategic accountability. One of the first firms to adopt this separation of funds was Texas Instruments (TI) which simplified the profit and loss statement for a given PCC (product-customer center) as presented in Figure 16–9.

FIGURE 16–8. Critical Success Factors Developed to Meet Microwave Associates' Organizational Goals

CRITICAL SUCCESS FACTORS	PRIME MEASURES
1. Image in financial markets	Price/Earnings ratio
2. Technological reputation with customers	Orders/Bid ratio
	Customer "perception" interview review
3. Market success	Change in market share (each product)
	Growth rates of company markets
4. Risk recognition in bids and contracts	Company's years of experience with similar products
	"New" or "old" customer
	Prior customer relationship
5. Profit margin on jobs	Bid profit margin as ratio of profit on similar jobs in this product line
6. Company morale	Turnover, absenteeism, etc.
	Informal feedback
7. Performance to budget on major jobs	Job cost budgeted/actual

SOURCE: Reprinted by permission of *Harvard Business Review*. An exhibit and excerpt from "Chief Executives Define Their Own Data Needs," by J.F. Rockart (March–April 1979). Copyright © 1979 by the President and Fellows of Harvard College; all rights reserved.

FIGURE 16–9. Simplified Profit and Loss Statement Used by Texas Instruments

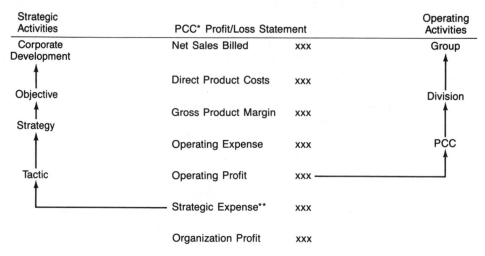

Strategic Activities	PCC* Profit/Loss Statement		Operating Activities
Corporate Development	Net Sales Billed	xxx	Group
↑ Objective	Direct Product Costs	xxx	↑ Division
↑ Strategy	Gross Product Margin	xxx	↑
↑	Operating Expense	xxx	PCC
Tactic	Operating Profit	xxx	↑
↑	Strategic Expense**	xxx	
	Organization Profit	xxx	

*PCC = (Product-Customer Center Center).
**Also called Developmental Expense.

Source: Richard F. Vancil and Ronald Hall, Texas Instruments, Inc.: Management Systems, 1972. Boston: Harvard Business School, Case 9-172-054, p. 11. Reprinted by permission.

Normally, a PCC manager is expected to wear "two hats," the first as an operating manager concerned with today's operating results, and the second as a strategic manager concerned with longer-range results. As Figure 16–9 shows, operating results are being measured through operating profits; strategic results are measured by how effectively a manager utilizes the strategic expenses at his or her disposal. In TI, those strategic expenses are centrally assigned through the OST (objectives-strategies-tactics) system. It is interesting to notice that the allocation of strategic expenses results from allocating resources to specific projects which finally become the responsibility of the PCC manager.

Figure 16–10 shows a seemingly similar reporting document for the decentralized departmental manager at GE, who is also a profit center manager. The three categories of expenses listed beneath the contribution margin are collectively called "base costs." Readiness-to-serve costs are the fixed expenses of the operating component stemming from its current capacity. It includes depreciation, other manufacturing costs, and sales and administrative overhead. Program expenses are discretionary expenses intended to increase future profits through specific strategic programs (for example, developing new products, entering new markets, or improving productivity). Assessment from corporate headquarters and allocation of corporate overhead are based on the department's cost of operations and are expressed as a proportion of such costs in all departments, roughly 1 percent of sales.[16]

There are two basic differences between the TI and GE reporting systems.

FIGURE 16–10. Simplified Profit and Loss Statement Used by General Electric Co.

Net Sales billed	xxx
Less: Materials in cost of goods sold	(xxx)
Contributed value from operations	xxx
Less: Direct labor	(xxx)
Other variable costs	(xxx)
LIFO revaluation provision	(xxx)
Contribution margin	xxx
Less: Readiness-to-serve costs	(xxx)
Program expenses	(xxx)
Assessments from corporate,	
sector, group, and division	(xxx)
Operating profit	xxx
Less: Interest expense/income	(xxx)
Income taxes	(xxx)
Net income	xxx

SOURCE: Richard F. Vancil and Paul Browne, General Electric Company, Background Note on Management Systems. Boston: Harvard Business School, Case 9-181-111, p. 8, Table A. Copyright © 1981 by the President and Fellows of Harvard College; all rights reserved.

At GE the department manager proposes what he or she considers a desirable amount for operating and strategic expenses. This amount is modified or accepted at the corporate level in accordance with the position of the business within the corporate portfolio. This represents an allocation of resources in terms of overall strategic attractiveness, rather than an assignment on a project-by-project basis conducted at the corporate level, as is done by TI. The second difference resides in the bottom-line accountability used by GE, forcing managers to absorb their share of interest and taxes prior to determining the net income generated by each department. This seems to contradict some basic principles of accountability that require a manager to be made responsible only for expenses which are truly under his or her control. However, by making managers responsible for the true bottom line, one begins to instill the utmost sense of managerial accountability, and this provides a genuine ground for general managers' development.

A third form of splitting operational and strategic expense reporting is illustrated in Figure 16–11. The conventional statement column shows the profit and loss statement generated by applying the generally accepted financial accounting principles. The two additional columns break every expense category into operational expenses (efforts supporting the ongoing business), and strategic expenses (efforts applied to the future development of the business). Notice the remarkable difference in terms of managerial accountability when comparing the conventional statement to the revised breakdown, in terms of operational and strategic expenses. In the conventional statement, a division manager is supposed to generate 10 units of profit. When the business conditions get rough, it is entirely possible for the manager to deliver those 10 units by

FIGURE 16–11. Splitting the Profit and Loss Statement of a Division in Terms of Operational and Strategic Expenses

	CONVENTIONAL STATEMENT	OPERATIONAL EXPENSES	STRATEGIC* EXPENSES
Net sales	100	100	—
Less: Variable manufacturing			—
costs	30	30	
Depreciation	20	20	—
Other fixed	10	5	5
manufacturing costs			
Gross margin	40	45	—
Less: Marketing expenses	15	5	10
Administrative expenses	10	5	5
Research expenses	5	0	5
Division margin	10		
Operating margin		35	
Total strategic expenses			25

*Also called Developmental Expenses.

curtailing severely strategic expenses, and thus jeopardizing the future development of this unit. However, in the breakdown statement, the manager is entrusted with a much more difficult task. He or she is expected to deliver 35 units of divisional profit from its existing business base, and to wisely use 25 units in strategic expenses intended to strengthen the future development of this unit. Each entry in the strategic expense column identifies strategic action programs, whose purpose is to reinforce the competitive position of the firm in the long term, as opposed to simply delivering short-term profitability.

To support this kind of strategic control system, the cost-accounting method must be specially designed to permit the breaking down of expenses into strategic and operational concerns. Some companies, like TI, have chosen to classify every expense as either operational or strategic, and charge the corresponding account accordingly. This requires an extraordinary effort to adjust the overall cost-accounting system of a firm. To avoid that, some firms simply treat strategic programs as independent projects, and report them within the framework of the existing management control system without necessarily changing the accounting procedures of the firm as a whole.

INTEGRATION BETWEEN INFORMATION SYSTEMS AND MANAGEMENT CONTROL

Information and communication are ubiquitous in a firm. After all, every administrative system is information based and managers are coordinated primarily via information-driven mechanisms. Most of the managerial time and energy are spent processing massive amounts of very dissimilar information and establishing significant communication with interested parties, external and internal to the firm. This makes clear that an effective information and communication system cannot be independent of planning, management control, rewards, and the organizational structure. One more time, there should be a clear balance and integration among all of them.

We attach the label *information system* to the more formal process of gathering, digesting, filtering, and distributing the information relevant to managers at all hierarchical levels. The term *communication* is reserved to mean a more sophisticated and elaborate managerial activity. This implies the ability to transmit at all organizational levels, as well as to the relevant external stakeholders, the messages that managers think should be given to interested parties related to the organization.

The development of an effective communication and information system is an order of magnitude more difficult, in our opinion, than the development of a planning system. First, it has to gather, process, and evaluate large volumes of data, coming both from internal and external sources. Second, it has to filter, diagnose, and discriminate relevant information to be made available to the different levels of the managerial hierarchy. Rather than submitting large volumes of unprocessed data, which tend to saturate manager's ability to digest a large number of trivia, a proper information system should be intelligent enough to discriminate the essential from the secondary at each level, and to provide supporting detail only by means of exceptional reporting. And third, managers should have the ability to translate that information into meaningful messages to relevant audiences, by developing clear and well-defined communicational actions.

Information and Communication Systems in the Strategic Mode

When analyzing the information and communication system of a firm, searching for their strategic quality, one often observes serious deficiencies. A most common one is the excessive reliance on internal sources, mainly the accounting base, as the primary vehicle for supplying information to managers. Needless to say, accounting-driven sources have little relevance for guiding strategic decision making and strategic performance. From a strategic point of view, it is not enough to know our own cost structure; rather, it is the industry cost structure and our relative position in it that is relevant. The same can be said about every other financial measure of performance that could be originated from internally-driven data.

Rockart and Treacy have proposed a framework for the development of an executive information system (EIS). This system is supported by a common core of data, identified as the *data cube* (Figure 16–12), which contains important business indicators (dimension 1), through time (dimension 2) for all businesses of the firm, competitors, customers, and industries (dimension 3). These data can be used in two modes: *status access* providing simple displays of the data in the cube; and *personalized analysis* which permits a more advanced manipulation of data through special statistical programs and other kinds of models.

Let us now turn our attention to the requirements for a strategic communication system. We define the articulation of the central objectives and programs the organization is intending to pursue as the primary thrust of the

FIGURE 16-12. The Data Cube

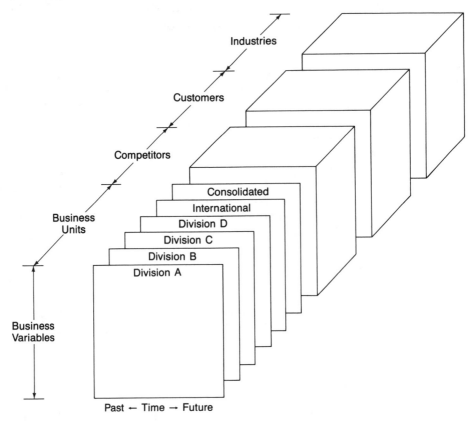

communication process. This is to be done in a way which is amenable to key external and internal audiences, with the purpose of increasing the level of understanding and the degree of commitments of the firm to its stakeholders.

When viewed from this perspective, the central role of the CEO appears to be that of generating and communicating the basic strategic goals of the organization. Every publicly-owned firm needs to keep external groups informed of the main strategic direction the organization is following. Particularly, providing sound information to the financial community is a most relevant task, since the market value of the stock of the firm develops from the expectation of future cash flows derived not only from assets the firm has already in place, but also from those it intends to deploy in the future. Appropriate external communications, therefore, are essential to achieve the warranted market value of the firm. Likewise, internal communications fraught with strategic content are essential to mobilize all the individuals working in the firm in the same desired direction. Everybody, even the most modest workers, has a role to play in shaping the future of the organization. If strategy is treated as if it were a top secret and a highly confidential matter that can be trusted only to a select few, it will never become a real driving force. It is a central role of the CEO, not only to serve as the key architect for shaping the strategy of the firm, but equally important to communicate it effectively to all levels in the organization.

INTEGRATION BETWEEN REWARD SYSTEMS AND MANAGEMENT CONTROL

To a great extent, the motivational and reward systems are responsible for shaping behavior in the organization and assuring, if properly done, congruency between individual and corporate objectives. People tend to behave according to the explicit or implicit mechanisms which regulate their rewards. Therefore, if we want the commitments identified in the planning process to become vivid realities, certainly we have to assure the establishment of a well-designed management control system. This must be consistent with the assignment of responsibilities and authorities reflected in the organizational structure, and able to provide the right clues for problem solving and managerial decision making. But this is not enough. We have to make sure that the motivational and reward systems reinforce the implementation of those planned commitments. Otherwise, planning will become a worthless exercise.

Motivational and Reward Systems in the Strategic Mode

People tend to act in a way consistent with the performance measures exercised upon them, and which in turn determine future career paths in the organization. Therefore, if we are seeking a strong organizational commitment in the pursuit of an agreed-upon strategy, there is not a more central administrative system to seek congruency with than establishing individual rewards and motivations. Yet, it is the lack of congruency that is perhaps the most appalling when one performs a strategic audit at many American corporations. Most U.S. firms suffer significantly from the use of short-term, accounting-driven measures of performance to establish the reward mechanisms for high-level managers, who are mainly responsible for implementing strategic actions. Particularly, the exceeding reliance on return on investment (ROI) has been singled out as a primary cause for discouraging investments in industrial firms, and as a strong determinant for the continuous erosion of the U.S. presence in world markets. There have been organizations which have used ROI as the sole performance measurement for assigning bonuses to their top managers. This is a dangerous practice. In an inflationary economy, total investment inaction could be translated into a short-term increase in ROI. Profits would tend to increase numerically, simply because of the inflationary effects. Moreover, the lack of investment commitments would reduce the investment base significantly since its replacement value would not be updated, according to the existing accounting practices in the United States, and depreciation would further decrease it. A manager who is forced to match an ROI target might temporarily reach it while contributing to the destruction of the long-term development of the firm.

Another common faulty design in the reward system of some American firms resides in creating internal competition by rewarding different divisions within a firm according to the relevant ROI performance. In this case, a percentage of the total profits of the organization is reported to be distributed as bonuses, the amount to be given to each divisional manager depending on its ROI performance vis-à-vis the other divisions of the firm. Not only does this procedure have the disadvantages of short-term responses to which we already alluded, but it creates a parochial attitude of divisiveness, aggressiveness, and conflict among units that might benefit from working together against their real competitors, which are the other firms participating in the industry.

These two limitations lead us to propose a different way of looking at the implications of a reward system. This is characterized by the simple 2×2 matrix depicted in Figure 16–13, modified from the compensation scheme of Corning Glass Works. The future shows the two critical dimensions for establishing a well-balanced reward system: the observed results, as measured by individual and group performance, and the period of observation, defined as short or long term.

In our previous comments, we have addressed situations where almost all the weight resides on observed individual performance in the short term, defined by the ROI, which tends to create myopic and aggressively dysfunctional behavior in the organization. The great challenge is how to expand the performance measurement and reward system into the other three cells of the matrix. The basic idea behind this scheme is to align the compensation of a given manager with the overall performance of the organization, so as to make the final monetary compensation increase whenever the entire firm shows a sustained profit-generating capability. Let us discuss briefly the other three cells in the matrix.

It seems obvious that an individual should benefit from the performance of the group to which he or she belongs. The major question is ascertaining the relevant group that should be used as a reference point. Corning Glass Works has opted for what we consider a rather novel solution. In this case, the reference group is always one step above the hierarchical level of the manager. For example, a department manager will have as a relevant unit the division in which the department belongs. In turn, the divisional manager will

FIGURE 16–13. Determinants of Managerial Compensation

	Period of Observation	
	Short-term	Long-term
Observed individual performance	Salary increases	Incentive plan
Observed group performance	Bonus	Stock options

have the group in which the division fits. Finally, the group manager will have the corporation as a whole as a reference level.

What kind of behavioral responses does such a system generate? It is an attempt to create a reasonably broad attitude; thus, when a good manager is confronted with a decision that could favorably affect his or her own group, but could be dysfunctional to the overall corporation, the manager has the proper kind of influencing forces, so that a decision could be made more objectively considering all the relevant trade-offs. In any event, it is important to identify which is the relevant group, and what percentage of the individual reward will be determined by the group performance in the short term.

Regarding the long term, it is relatively easy to measure group performance in that mode. What is normally done is to take the corporation as the relevant group and to use mechanisms such as stock options to reward executives for the improvements of corporate performance at a future date. Stock options is a financial arrangement by which managers are offered the right to purchase corporate stock at a future date, and at a price agreed upon when the option is granted (normally the current market price or a slightly lower figure).

The most difficult task involves measuring individual performance in the long term. People normally do not stay indefinitely in a given job, inherit conditions shaped by others, and leave conditions to their successors for which they should receive full credit or blame. Keeping track of individual achievements through time requires a great deal of skill. Many different schema to compensate managers for the long-term impact of their decisions have been instituted.

Regardless of the allocation of weights used on individual versus group, and short- versus long-term performance, it is imperative to find mechanisms for obtaining a better integration of management incentives and strategic plans. Rappaport proposes three approaches addressing that issue: (1) the extended performance evaluation approach, (2) the strategic factors approach, and (3) the management accounting approach.[17]

In the *extended performance evaluation approach*, the firm rewards managers for achieving certain performance levels over a multiyear period, by awarding the manager with deferred stock or stock options according to his or her ability to fulfill various strategic goals over the agreed-upon planning horizon. This method also allows for a more appropriate use of accounting measurements. For example, ROI is used as a target, based on expected profit and the investment deployments the manager is committed to make over an extended time horizon.

The *strategic factors approach* involves the identification of the critical success factors governing the future profitability of the business, and the assignment of proper weights depending on the inherent characteristics of the business unit, and its agreed-upon strategy. This approach allows for establishing congruency in terms of the performance measurements to be used, and the position of the business within the corporate portfolio. Stonich proposes the use of four measurements of performance—return on assets (ROA), cash

FIGURE 16–14. An Illustration of the Strategic Factors Approach for the Reward of Managers

SBU CATEGORY	WEIGHTS TO BE ASSIGNED TO STRATEGIC FACTORS (%)			
	ROA	Cash Flow	Strategic Funds	Market Share Increase
High Growth	10	0	45	45
Medium Growth	25	25	25	25
Low Growth	50	50	0	0

flow, strategic funds programs, and market share increase—receiving different weights depending on the expected growth of the corresponding business unit.[18] Figure 16–14 illustrates his suggestion. In different situations and according to the nature of the SBU, many other factors could be used, such as productivity levels, product-quality measures, product-development measures, and personnel-development measures.

The *management accounting approach* considers the motivation and implications of accounting measurements, and therefore adjusts rather than adopts the financial account model for the company's internal usage. The primary mechanism to seek congruency between strategic objectives and managerial measures of performance is to resort to a break down of expenses into operational and strategic categories (see Figure 16–11 already presented). At the risk of being redundant, we should emphasize the unusual aspects of strategic funds accountability. Developmental expenses, such as R&D, are conventionally included as overhead in the Sales, General, and Administrative Expenses (SG&A), as shown in the conventional statement of Figure 16–15. Under the strategic funds accountability, however, it will be taken out of SG&A, which now will include only operating expenses, transferring all other expenses into the strategic expense item.

Rappaport also recommends capitalizing certain R&D expenses, and expensing them gradually in subsequent years to encourage executives to take reasonable business risks without affecting their operating margins too severely.

FIGURE 16–15. Conventional versus Strategic Funds Accountability

CONVENTIONAL STATEMENT		STRATEGIC EXPENSES STATEMENT	
Sales	100	Sales	100
Cost of Goods Sold	60	Operating Cost of Goods Sold	55
Gross margin	40	Gross Operating Margin	45
Sales, General and Ad. Exp.	30	Operating SG&A	10
Division Margin	10	Operating Margin	35
		Strategic Expenses	25
		Division Margin	10

Note: Same numbers as in Figure 16.11.

Likewise, if companies were to use accelerated depreciation for tax purposes, it might be desirable in the management accounting approach to have less rather than more depreciation during the initial years of investment.

All of these comments amount to one single lesson: financial accounting, which intends to provide objective information to external parties to the firm, might tend to discourage sound managerial actions, particularly if the reward system stresses short-term operational performance. Managers could benefit from changing some of these rules if necessary to create conditions supporting the desired strategic directions of the firm.

Integration Between the Managerial Infrastructure and the Corporate Culture

So far, we have dealt entirely with administrative processes and structure. This might lead one to believe that strategic management is a rather mechanistic and abstract activity. Obviously, this is far from true. There are no quick recipes and universal rules of thumb on how to plan, control, organize, inform, and set rewards for a business firm. What makes these tasks immensely challenging is people and the culture prevailing in the organization. We have purposely left to the very end of these reflections on the requirements for strategic management the most subtle of all integration demands. Strategy does not need only to be congruent with the organizational structure and the key administrative processes, but most centrally it has to be integrated within the corporate culture. This last section attempts to shed light on this issue.

TOWARDS A DEFINITION OF ORGANIZATIONAL CULTURE

Drawing mainly from the work of Schein, we propose a definition of corporate culture which elicits some of the main characteristics of this rather difficult concept:[19]

1. Organizational culture is a complex set of basic underlying assumptions and deeply held beliefs shared by all members of the group, that operate at a preconscious level and drive their behavior in important ways.
2. We can observe manifestations of the organizational culture in the form of a pattern of behavioral regularities at two levels: artifacts and creations, and values (see Figure 16–16). But the cultural ethos corresponds to the deeper level of assumptions, perceptions, thoughts, and feelings that are patterned.
3. These basic behavior drivers allow an individual to identify, in an automatic leap of thought, the right way to perceive, think, and feel in most of the situations he or she must confront, intuitively separating what is considered normal from the exceptional, right from wrong, real from illusion, true from false, and acceptable from unacceptable. Then, attention should be paid just to those cases which are not considered to be customary or common, thus avoiding or reducing the anxiety and cognitive overload that would otherwise

FIGURE 16–16. The Levels of Organizational Culture

LEVEL 1	Manifestation of culture in the form of behavioral regularities in the artifacts and creations (easy to observe, but often undecipherable) • Technology • Art • Language, speech • Rituals, social forms, overt behavior, actions • Status, stratification
LEVEL 2	Expression of culture in the form of espoused values: what "ought" to be (great level of awareness) • Expression of corporate philosophy (relationship with stakeholders) • Norms of behavior in working groups • Leitmotif or slogans espoused by an organization • Rules for getting along in the organization • In general: explicitly declared values, and socially sanctioned values (by virtue of tradition or custom)
LEVEL 3	Cultural ethos (taken for granted, invisible, preconscious) • "The distinguishing character, sentiment, moral nature, or guiding beliefs of a person, group, or institution" (Webster Dictionary for *ethos*)

arise if required to improvise answers whenever facing a dilemma demanding attention.

4. Provided that these basic underlying assumptions are shared by all members of a group, they are like a "blueprint of conducts" that produces a coordinated behavior among them, and provides coherence to something that, otherwise, would be just a disconnected, independent, autonomous behavior.

5. These deeply held beliefs are the result of a learning process set in motion by the group's experience acquired when dealing with difficult situations that jeopardize its survival (because of threats from the external environment), and stability (due to deficiencies in the internal integration among the group's members). These risks force them to develop, uncover, or invent unusual answers in each new situation. If they happen to be satisfactory, they are socially validated and adopted as solutions, gradually producing a cognitive transformation in all members of the group, as long as the initial success of the answer is reiterated in each new instance. In the end, the answer becomes automatic and falls out from conscience, thus being elevated to the higher category of principle, value, or dogma that might be transmitted to succeeding generations.

6. Finally, we should recognize that culture is defined in reference to a group of people; so, we refer to western culture, country culture, professional culture, ethnic culture, and so on. In an organization we might well identify a number of subcultures for each one of the relevant groups we decide to focus on, for example, the engineering culture, the sales culture, and the manufacturing culture. But we may also refer to the overall organization culture as corresponding to the common principles shared by all members.

CULTURAL AUDIT

In order to uncover the basic underlying principles at the core of an organizational culture, we need to perform a cultural audit. This is a very difficult task because there is no agreement on the conceptual categories that we should be using to address it. We limit ourselves to offering a number of different alternative approaches presented in the literature.

Cultural Audit I: Schein's Basic Underlying Assumptions and State of Internal Integration
Schein suggests that a cultural analysis should have as its central objective the unveiling of the basic assumptions behind the cultural values of a firm. And we can structure our observations around the question of how the organization relates to its environment, how it manages, how it deals with space, and what can be observed about people's relationships to each other. He indicates that these basic assumptions fall into five major categories: the organization's relationship to its environment, the nature of reality and truth, the nature of human nature, the nature of human activity, and the nature of human relationships. Figure 16–17 presents Schein's summarized descriptions of these categories.

First, Schein suggests looking for units with a reasonably long history and stable membership. For analytical purposes, he distinguishes sharply between artifacts which are "the visible creations of the culture," values which are "the stated operating principles of the culture," and basic assumptions which are "the essence of the culture, a pattern which permits us to decipher the significance of values and artifacts." He also suggests that the best model for studying organizational culture is a combination of anthropology and clinical psychology.

FIGURE 16–17. Basic Underlying Assumptions around Which Cultural Paradigms Form

---

1. ***The Organization's Relationship to Its Environment.*** Reflecting even more basic assumptions around the relationship of humanity to nature, one can assess whether the key members of the organization view the relationship as one of dominance, submission, harmonizing, finding an appropriate niche, and so on.
2. ***The Nature of Reality and Truth.*** Here are the linguistic and behavioral rules that define what is real and what is not, what is "fact," how truth is ultimately to be determined, and whether truth is "revealed" or "discovered"; basic concepts of time as linear or cyclical, monochronic, or polychronic; basic concepts such as space as limited or infinite and property as communal or individual; and so forth.
3. ***The Nature of Human Nature.*** What does it mean to be "human," and what attributes are considered intrinsic or ultimate? Is human nature good, evil, or neutral? Are human beings perfectible or not? What is better, Theory X or Theory Y?
4. ***The Nature of Human Activity.*** What is the "right" thing for human beings to do, on the basis of the above assumptions about reality, the environment, and human nature: to be active, passive, self-developmental, fatalistic, or what? What is work and what is play?
5. ***The Nature of Human Relationships.*** What is considered to be the "right" way for people to relate to each other, to distribute power and love? Is life cooperative or competitive; individualistic, group collaborative, or communal; based on traditional lineal authority, law, or charisma; or what?

SOURCE: Reprinted from "Coming to a New Awareness of Organizational Culture," by Edgar Schein *Sloan Management Review,* 26 (Winter 1984), p. 6, by permission of the publisher. Copyright © 1984 by the Sloan Management Review Association. All rights reserved.

The clinical method implies that each cultural analysis is essentially a case study. Even if one finds common elements across cultures, one must know how to pull data from many informants into the patterns which make up the unique culture of a particular organization. For an excellent case analysis following this approach, the reader is referred to Dyer.[20]

To assist further the cultural audit process, Schein proposes the six categories described in Figure 16–18 to profile the state of internal integration: language, boundaries, power and status, intimacy, reward and punishment, and ideology. This is a good set of variables to uncover the way in which culture emerges in the human side of the organization, thus producing a valuable proxy of the deeper characteristics of culture.

Cultural Audit II: Likert's Profile of the Process of Internal Interactions

Likert proposes an approach to describe an organization from the perspective of its human side, and the quality of interaction affecting its members.[21] He argues that an organization can be described through eight basic processes: (1) leadership, (2) motivation, (3) communication, (4) interpersonal interactions and influence, (5) decision making, (6) goal setting or ordering, (7) control, and (8) performance goals and training. The nature of each of these characteristics can be located in a continuum spanning four general types of organizational management systems:

- System 1, Exploitative Authoritative, provides an environment where there is low motivation, little interpersonal support and participation, only downward communication, and authoritarian control.

FIGURE 16–18. Problems of Internal Integration

Language:	Common language and conceptual categories. If members cannot communicate with and understand each other, a group is impossible by definition.
Boundaries:	Consensus on group boundaries and criteria for inclusion and exclusion. One of the most important areas of culture is the shared consensus on who is in, who is out, and by what criteria one determines membership.
Power and Status:	Consensus on criteria for the allocation of power and status. Every organization must work out its pecking order and its rules for how one gets, maintains, and loses power. This area of consensus is crucial in helping members manage their own feelings of aggression.
Intimacy:	Consensus on criteria for intimacy, friendship, and love. Every organization must work out its rules of the game for peer relationships, for relationships between the sexes, and for the manner in which openness and intimacy are to be handled in the context of managing the organization's task.
Rewards and Punishments:	Consensus on criteria for allocation of rewards and punishments. Every group must know what its heroic and sinful behaviors are; what gets rewarded with property, status, and power; and what gets punished through the withdrawal of rewards and, ultimately, excommunication.
Ideology:	Consensus on ideology and "religion." Every organization, like every society, faces unexplainable events that must be given meaning so that members can respond to them and avoid the anxiety of dealing with the unexplainable and uncontrollable.

SOURCE: Schein (1984).

- System 2, Benevolent Authoritative, is similar to system 1 but it is more paternalistic.
- System 3, Consultative, provides an environment having upward and downward communication, supporting leadership, a certain degree of self-regulation, and consultative goal setting.
- System 4, Participative, provides an environment with more emphasis on self-regulation and mutual support, openness and trust, high performance goals, and more involved participation at all levels.

Likert provides a well-structured process, supported with detailed questionnaires, to categorize an organization within the continuum from system 1 to system 4. Those questionnaires, which are reproduced in Likert's book, can greatly facilitate what otherwise would be a highly judgmental and subjective process.

Figure 16–19 presents an illustration of what a profile might look like after applying Likert's methodology. There are two major benefits to be derived from assessing such a profile. One is the value of having a description of important cultural components of the organization, and second its conclusions might lead to undertaking normative efforts intended to correct perceived in-

FIGURE 16–19. Likert's Profile of the Process of Internal Interactions

ORGANIZATIONAL VARIABLES	SYSTEM OF ORGANIZATION			
	Exploitative Authoritative	Benevolent Authoritative	Consultative	Participative Group
Leadership process used				
Character of motivational forces				
Character of communication process				
Character of interaction–influence process				
Character of decision-making process				
Character of goal setting or ordering				
Character of control process				
Performance goals and training				

consistencies among the managerial processes. Most organizations find themselves in system 2 or 3.

Cultural Audit III: Ouchi's Intertemporal Profile of Culture

A framework we consider useful when performing a cultural audit is the Rockwell International Culture Analysis described in the appendix of Ouchi's book
Theory Z.[22] Rockwell uses five categories to describe the cultural profile: short-
versus long-term environment, communication, information sharing, individual
orientation, and job security. Each of these categories is represented in terms
of past, present, and future characteristics, according to the form illustrated in
Figure 16–20.

Cultural Audit IV: Schwartz and Davis' Corporate Culture Matrix

Schwartz and Davis suggest an approach for cultural audit, based on an assessment of the managerial tasks and their key relationships in the organization.[23] They define six managerial tasks, somewhat reminiscent of Likert's,
which they believe are central for performing a cultural assessment: innovating,
decision making, communicating, organizing, monitoring, and appraising and
rewarding. Each task should be described in terms of how it is handled within
the context of four types of relationships: company-wide, boss-subordinate,
peer, and interdepartmental. This results in a matrix, such as the one presented
in Figure 16–21. This serves both as a checklist to conduct a cultural analysis
and as a framework interpreting the meaning of the artifacts in which much of
the data about organizational culture are reflected. For an example of how to
use the matrix, the reader is referred to Schwartz and Davis' original paper.

FIGURE 16–20. Rockwell International Culture Analysis

CULTURE CATEGORY	WHERE WE WERE	WHAT WE'VE DONE	WHERE WE ARE	FUTURE DIRECTION
Short- vs. Long-Term Environment				
Organization Communication				
Information Sharing				
Individual Orientation				
Job Security				

SOURCE: Adapted from William G. Ouchi, *Theory Z,* © 1981, Addison-Wesley Publishing Co., Inc., Reading, MA. Reprinted with permission of the publisher.

FIGURE 16–21. Corporate Culture Matrix

TASKS	RELATIONSHIPS			
	Company-Wide	Boss-Subordinate	Peer	Interdepartmental
Innovating				
Decision Making				
Communicating				
Organizing				
Monitoring				
Appraising and Rewarding				

SOURCE: Howard Schwartz and Stanley M. Davis, "Matching Corporate Culture and Business Strategy," 1981, p. 36. Reprinted by permission of Organizational Dynamics, New York, NY.

CONGRUENCY BETWEEN STRATEGY AND CORPORATE CULTURE

From the perspective of strategy formulation and implementation, we cannot be satisfied by a mere description of the cultural characteristics of the firm. Having done that, the major question still remaining is whether or not the proposed strategies are congruent with the culture, and if not, what to do about it.

In order to address the first part of this question, we should decompose the overall strategy into its major tasks, which is what we have referred to as broad strategic action programs. Having those tasks as a central focus of analysis, we can address the importance of each task to the success of the strategy and the degree of compatibility that exists between the strategy and the organizational culture. Schwartz and Davis propose a matrix to portray these two dimensions of cultural risk assessment, as illustrated in Figure 16–22. Their approach requires positioning each task in the matrix by exercising crude managerial judgment. The result of this effort should serve as a guide to start reflecting on what ought to be done when serious incompatibilities arise. Actions taken to make the implementation of the strategy more compatible with culture will tend to decrease the cultural risk and, consequently, enhance the chances of a successful implementation.

Schwartz and Davis offer four generic alternatives to deal with this question of strategy and cultural compatibility.

1. Ignore the culture, which is a dangerous and unacceptable alternative when significant inconsistencies still remain.

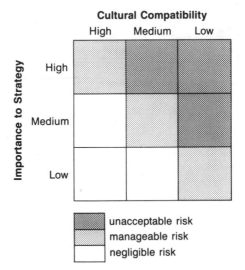

FIGURE 16–22. Cultural Risk Assessment

Cultural Compatibility

SOURCE: Howard Schwartz and Stanley M. Davis (1981).

2. Manage around the culture by changing the implementation plan. This alternative is based on recognizing the cultural barriers which represent serious obstacles for the implementation of the desirable strategy. Alternative approaches must be offered to bypass the cultural obstacles but not change the intended strategic focus. Figure 16–23 reproduces a list of examples suggested by Schwartz and Davis on how to accomplish this task.

3. Attempt to change the culture to fit the strategy. This is an extremely difficult task to accomplish, requiring a lengthy process and significant resources. There are, however, situations where this could be a central determinant for the long-term success of a firm. One of the clearest illustrations of this case is represented by AT&T after its restructuring. Due to the dramatic change in AT&T's external and internal environment, it will be hard to conceive that a successful strategy will not call for a deep and permanent change in its culture. When a cultural change is explicitly intended, it should be coordinated with all the necessary internal changes in management systems and organizational structure to seek a mutual and positive reinforcement of overall strategic management infrastructure.

4. Change the strategy to fit the culture, perhaps by reducing performance expectations.

The lesson to be derived from these brief comments on cultural and strategic compatibility is that every effort should be made to minimize the cultural risk inherent in a proposed strategy. When this cannot be avoided, either because of structural changes in the industry in which the firm is located, or because of critical and serious lack of performance, a combination of the last three alternatives (managing around the culture, changing the culture, and modifying the strategy) should be used to bring cultural risk to an acceptable level.

FIGURE 16–23. How to Manage Around the Company Culture

	STRATEGY	"RIGHT" APPROACH	CULTURAL BARRIERS	ALTERNATIVE APPROACHES
COMPANY A	Product/market diversification	Divisionalization	Centralized power One-man rule Functional Hierarchical	Business teams Explicit strategic planning Business measurement
COMPANY B	Focus marketing on most profitable segments	Fine tune reward system Adjust MIS	Diffused power Highly individualized Relationship oriented	Dedicated full-time personnel to each key market
COMPANY C	Extend technology to new markets	Matrix organization	Multiple power centers Functional focus	Program coordinators Planning committees Greater top management involvement

SOURCE: Adapted from Howard Schwartz and Stanley M. Davis, "Matching Corporate Culture and Business Strategy," 1981, p. 44. Reprinted by permission of Organizational Dynamics, New York, NY.

Merits and Limitations of Strategic Management

Strategic management represents the most advanced and coherent form of strategic thinking. Not only does it attempt to extend the strategic vision throughout all the operational and functional units of the firm, but it also encompasses every administrative system, recognizing the central role to be played by the individual and groups within an organization and its resulting culture. Stated in this form, it is hard to argue against strategic management. In itself, it is a mature and overall-encompassing concept which embraces most of what we know about the practice, art, and science of management.

The first overwhelming fact that one encounters when analyzing a large number of organizations is that very few have reached the quality of excellence that would naturally result from a fully implemented strategic management approach. Occasionally, one wonders why such an obviously desirable managerial state, so easily describable in conceptual terms, is so hard to accomplish. The answer to this question can be argued in many different ways.

First and foremost, management is a very complex social activity which cannot be comprehended by a simple set of rules and normative processes. We may never have a sufficiently well-developed body of knowledge to provide the scientific foundation for a managerial methodology to facilitate the implementation of strategic management. We are left with broad concepts and pragmatic responses based on experiential perceptions, rather than undisputable principles. We are forced to admit, therefore, that strategy is an ad-hoc process and that there is no single way to guide us into the realizations of this ultimate goal as represented by the strategic management ideal.

If we admit this concept of strategic management as ideal, it is not hard to explain that we only see it, at best, partially realized in most organizations. Therefore, we will be forced to strive permanently and endlessly toward the pursuit of this form of management. Implicit in this search is the constant development and learning which provide an enrichment and maturity for all members in an organization. That is why it is hard, if not impossible, to skip stages or greatly accelerate this process. Time is of the essence to consolidate the goal for integration, which is so basic in strategic management. Integration brings in the more methodological dimension—the quality of congruency of all the administrative processes with the organizational structure in strategic and operational mode. But most significantly, integration consolidates a common strategic vision among all the members of the organization, supported by rich and highly shared values and beliefs creating a top quality of cultural support.

Appendix: A Case Study on Matching Strategy and Structure

INTRODUCTION

The structure of an organization is no longer viewed as a rigid definition of hierarchical levels and interrelationships among different groups. Managers use the organizational design process as a fundamental tool for implementing and communicating the strategic direction selected for the firm.

This appendix discusses a case study concerned with the identification of alternative structures for a business firm and the recommendation of one of those alternatives to be adopted. Throughout this appendix, the central scheme relies on matching strategy and structure. However, in the actual process of evaluating the various organizational designs, proper weight was given to the behavioral dimensions of the problem. Personalities, individual competencies, cultural traditions, and managerial styles dominated our discussions. The utmost concern in the minds of those involved in the study was the question regarding their personal positions and spheres of influence that would result under each alternative. Many concessions and departures from an "optimal alternative" had to be made to accommodate these personal trade-offs. We have purposely omitted all comments in this regard for the sake of brevity as well as for the preservation of the legitimate confidentiality of those issues.

Since Chandler's historical analysis of a selected group of American firms,[24] it has been strongly advocated that "structure follows strategy"; that is to say, that the organizational structure should be designed to facilitate the strategic pursuits of a firm. Our work is strongly influenced by this axiom. However, it should be recognized that strategy and structure is a two-way street, in which strategy is certainly influencing the resulting organizational design, but also the existing structure somehow constrains the strategic alternatives of the firm.

The objective of this appendix is to illustrate the application of this methodology to the design of an organizational structure for a company wholly-owned by a U.S. corporation. The Company, as we will refer to it, has been engaged primarily in the sales, service, and distribution of large and small equipment, which in turn were manufactured and developed by another company belonging to the same corporation. That equipment is sold to a variety of commercial, industrial, and government markets. The equipment needs special types of chemical products as primary inputs for its operation and specialized computer systems support.

To maintain the confidentiality of the information pertaining to this case, all the specific characteristics of the Company businesses have been altered.

BRIEF DISCUSSION OF THE EXISTING ORGANIZATION

The primary organizational structure of the Company is presented in Figure 16–24. Initially the Company was organized according to a pure functional form, where the managerial functions represented were Distribution, Sales, Services (all of them included under the Regional Centers), Marketing, and Financial Control. Manufacturing, and Research and Development were not part of the Company's activities. Those functions were represented in other sister companies of the corporation.

However, as time passed, new responsibilities were added to the Company primarily through the acquisition of Computer Systems, Inc., a firm involved in data management. This new unit constituted an autonomous business, managed in a completely decentralized way, with self-sufficient functional support which included Research, Development, and Manufacturing.

Moreover, the Company acquired a small firm, Chemicals, Inc., with Manufacturing, Research, and Development capabilities for the chemical products needed to operate the major equipment.

FIGURE 16–24. Existing Organization

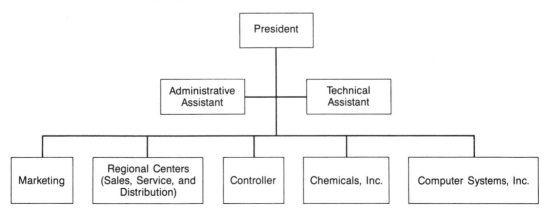

These two acquisitions provided an integrated capability of the Company's businesses. Now, the Company was not only able to distribute, sell, and service major equipment, but also manufacture, develop, and market the chemicals and computer systems to support the equipment's operation. Finally, the Company began to expand its international operations into Canada and Mexico. This introduced an international concern that did not exist previously.

These new responsibilities seriously affected the organizational structure of the Company, changing it from a functional organization into a hybrid organization with functions, products, and international dimensions.

Even more important, new developments were expected for the immediate future. Among them we can cite the possible expansion of activities in Central and South America, the absorption of two new business concerns, and a significant projected growth in almost all product lines. Furthermore, potential new acquisitions were under consideration. All of these events triggered a serious concern on the part of the top management of the Company to critically review the present organizational structure and to propose more effective organizational alternatives.

Figures 16–25 and 16–26 provide the organizational charts describing the existing structure of the Regional Centers and Computer Systems, Inc., respectively. It is worth noting that the Regional Centers are the fundamental operational core of the Company, including a regionalized Sales, Service, and Distribution coverage. Moreover, the Regional Center vice president had a centralized responsibility for Sales, Training and Implementation, National Distribution, Materials Control, Government Accounts, and the overall management of customers' orders. This is clearly evident in the organigram of the Regional Centers of Figure 16–25. Also important to reemphasize is the self-standing nature of the Computer Systems, Inc. organization given in Figure 16–26. Computer Systems, Inc. operated as an independent business unit with all the necessary managerial functions reporting to the Computer Systems Vice President.

CRITIQUE OF THE EXISTING ORGANIZATION

The first task undertaken in our attempt to provide organizational alternatives for the Company was to reflect on the most pressing problem of a general nature that could be traced back to the current structure. A consensus emerged in identifying the following issues as the most important to address in a new proposal for the organizational structure:

1. lack of opportunities for general management development;
2. too much concentration on operational issues;
3. lack of a portfolio-management vision;
4. lack of coordination with other Companies within the Corporation;
5. intensive antagonistic environment;
6. neglect of special markets (such as government accounts and international business accounts);

FIGURE 16–25. Existing Organization of Regional Centers

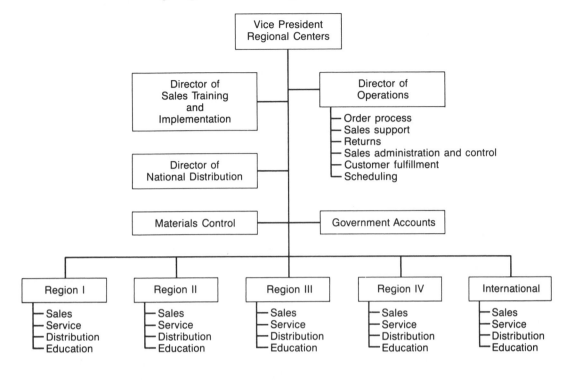

7. excessive concentration of decision making at the top;
8. organization not appropriate for maximizing growth and profit;
9. overworked key personnel.

All of the issues just listed not only reveal problems that result from an inappropriate organizational structure, but also eloquently point to the need for an organizational structure that better permits the development of a formal

FIGURE 16–26. Existing Organization: Computer Systems, Inc.

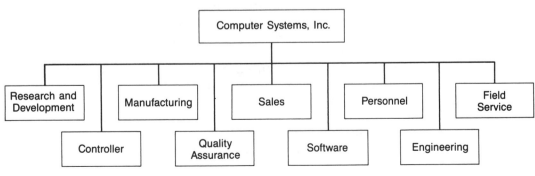

strategic and operational planning system. Such a system should balance the long-term concerns of the Company with the proper pressure for short-term performance.

PRIMARY CRITERIA FOR THE DESIGN OF A NEW ORGANIZATION

In order to determine the basic segmentation of responsibilities of an organization, one dimension perceived to be the dominant force of organizational activities must be selected. In this case, there are three primary dimensions that could be candidates for this focus of attention. They are (1) functions, (2) business segments, and (3) geographical areas.

Functions

The functional form of organization is structured around the inputs required to perform the organizational task. Typically, these inputs are centered around professional specialities or disciplines such as finance, marketing, production, sales, engineering, research and development, and personnel. The functional form leads to a centralization of management activities, since only at the highest level does the responsibility of coordinating all functional tasks reside. A functional organization tends to develop highly qualified technical skills and a climate conducive to technical excellence and high efficiency. It provides a "critical mass" for the career advancement of its professionals. But its inherent strength on specialization pushes the decision-making process upward, because only at the top do we find the confluence of all inputs required for the final decision.

Business Segments

The selection of business segments as the dominant dimension for organizational design allows for an effective exploitation of the opportunities which might be available in each individual business segment. A business-focused organization leads to a divisionalized segmentation, in which every division is relatively autonomous in an operational sense. The division then becomes a self-sustaining business in its own right, having a legitimate business climate which allows for the identification of genuine profit centers. Each individual business unit cannot only operate efficiently in the day-to-day operations, but can carry on effectively long-term strategic actions pertaining to their development. Thus, each business division provides an excellent training ground for the development of general managers. The top manager of the organization is significantly relieved from the routine operational tasks and can therefore exercise a much more meaningful role in planning the business portfolio and overall divisional growth.

This form of organization allows for the strategic development of each major business of the firm, either by internal growth or by the consolidation of new acquisitions into the appropriate business segments.

Geographical Areas

For organizations covering wide geographical territories with a strong need for maintaining a high level of services responsive to the individual idiosyncrasies of each area, a geographical divisionalized organization could be appropriate. Thus, the basic segmentation results in regional managers who can ultimately be in total control of all the functions and businesses in their own region.

As is apparent from this brief discussion, an organizational structure in a complex situation normally does not have a single dominant dimension, but rather becomes a hybrid structure. In such a structure, some centralized functions can report directly to the president, some regionalization focus can emerge either at the first or second organizational level, and some business divisions can also report to the president.

IDENTIFICATION OF THE CRITICAL DIMENSIONS FOR THE COMPANY'S ORGANIZATION

As a first attempt to single out the organizational dimensions relevant to the Company, we constructed a list of the major products, markets, locations, and functions represented in the current Company's activities. That list is given in Figure 16–27.

Furthermore, in order to define the major business segments of the Company, we constructed a matrix of products and markets, as shown in Figure 16–28. From that product-market segmentation it became clear that the primary businesses could be characterized as presented in the figure.

Notice that a business is not necessarily a product line. In the case of Equipment, it is important to distinguish both Large and Small Equipment, as well as Commercial, Industrial, and Government Markets, each of them split into Small and Large Accounts. This segmentation allows managers to detect the different opportunities that each business offers.

FIGURE 16–27. Identification of Major Products, Markets, Locations, and Functions

PRODUCTS	MARKETS	LOCATIONS	FUNCTIONS
Major Equipment Large and Small Equipment A Large and Small Equipment B Large and Small Equipment C Computer Systems Chemicals	Commercial Clients Large and Small Industrial Clients Large and Small Government Clients	Markets USA Canada Mexico Central America South America Plants Detroit Los Angeles Boston New Orleans	Marketing Sales Distribution Manufacturing Research and Development Finance Service Education and Training Project Engineering

FIGURE 16–28. Identification of Product-Market Segments

MARKET / PRODUCTS	COMMERCIAL CLIENTS		INDUSTRIAL CLIENTS		GOVERNMENT CLIENTS
	Large	Small	Large	Small	
Large Equipment A	X		X		X
Large Equipment B	X		X		X
Large Equipment C	X		X		X
Small Equipment A	X	X	X	X	X
Small Equipment B	X	X	X	X	X
Small Equipment C	X	X	X	X	X
Computer Systems	X	X	X	X	X
Chemicals	X	X	X	X	X

Finally, the Company's president provided his own personal objectives for the design of an alternative organizational form. His instructions were as follows:

1. permit a shift of the president's time from routine day-to-day decisions to actions pertaining to business development and strategic management;
2. organize to facilitate absorption of new acquisitions;
3. do not break new businesses;
4. allow for the development of general managers.

Statements 1 and 4 clearly eliminate the pure functional form as an organizational alternative. Moreover, statements 2 and 3 can be interpreted as favoring a business divisionalized form.

DESIGN OF A BASIC ORGANIZATIONAL STRUCTURE: THE SELECTION OF LEADING ALTERNATIVES

As we had indicated before, the first step in the organizational design process is the recognition of competing forms for the basic organizational structure. This basic structure identifies the primary echelons of the organizational chart which are linked to the strategic positioning of the firm.

We recognized four major alternatives for the basic organizational structure of the Company. These alternatives are:

1. alternative organization based on primary businesses
2. alternative organization based on a centralized sales, service, and distribution function

FIGURE 16–29. Alternative Organization Based on Primary Businesses

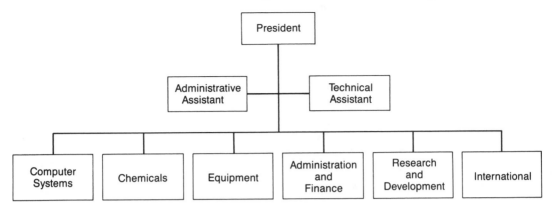

3. alternative organization with geographical regions and business segments
4. alternative organization with geographical regions and centralized manufacturing

These basic organizational alternatives are presented in Figures 16–29 through 16–32, respectively.

Obviously many other alternatives were discussed in the first stage of our study. However, they were discarded after a more in-depth analysis because

FIGURE 16–30. Alternative Organization Based on a Centralized Sales, Service, and Distribution Function

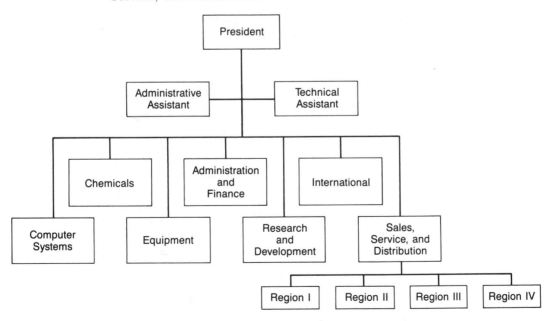

FIGURE 16–31. Alternative Organization with Geographical Regions
and Business Segments

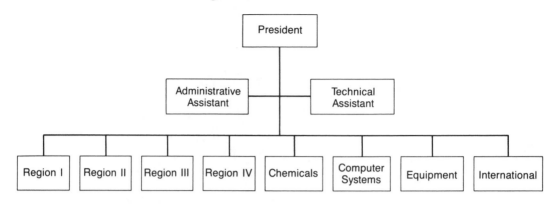

they were clearly dominated by either one or more of the four basic alternatives
indicated previously. We now comment briefly on the salient characteristics of
each of the leading basic structure alternatives.

ALTERNATIVE ORGANIZATION BASED ON PRIMARY BUSINESSES

The heart of this alternative (see Figure 16–29) is the identification of three
primary autonomous businesses: Computer Systems, Chemicals, and Equip-

FIGURE 16–32. Alternative Organization with Geographical Regions
and Centralized Manufacturing

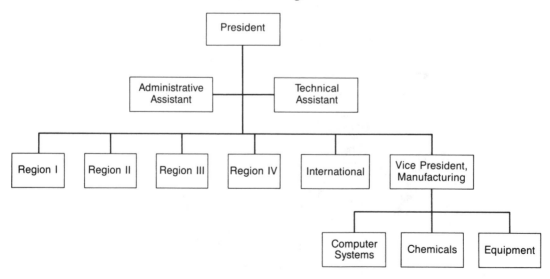

ment. Although these businesses are closely related to one another, the adoption of this organizational form might contribute to the realization of opportunities unique to each individual segment. That is to say, that Chemicals and Computer Systems not only will be developed to satisfy the important role they should play in supporting the Equipment operation, but they can also seek penetration in other markets not necessarily tied to the Equipment business environment. The strategic implications of adopting this organizational form are enormous. It means that the Company will no longer view itself as being solely in the business of Equipment, but as being in three autonomous, although related, business segments.

Other characteristics worth noting in this basic structure are:

- There is a centralized Administration and Finance function to provide the normal controller's duties for the whole Company, as well as handling centralized personnel, and business development and planning functions. The Controller's responsibilities include the development of a financial system that allows for the effective monitoring of the long- and short-term performance of each business unit. It is important to recognize that this organizational structure permits a new business-oriented management control system to be implemented.
- There is a centralized Research and Development function for the whole Company to facilitate a coordinated Research and Development activity for all its business segments.
- The staff offices of Technical Affairs and Administrative Assistant are kept unmodified from their current status.
- This organization permits appropriate emphasis on the emerging international responsibilities by ultimately identifying and appointing a manager for an International segment.

ALTERNATIVE ORGANIZATION BASED ON A CENTRALIZED SALES, SERVICE, AND DISTRIBUTION FUNCTION

Given the predominant role played by the Regional Centers in the existing organization of the Company, a primary contender for an alternative basic organization should be a regional geographical segmentation as the dominant dimension.

However, such an alternative is not easy to develop if one wants to respect the four objectives for the design of an organization form given by the Company's president outlined earlier in this appendix. His concern to facilitate absorption of new acquisitions without breaking new businesses and his determination to adopt a structure to facilitate the strategic development of the Company's major businesses make it desirable to maintain a segmentation focus having Computer Systems, Chemicals, and Equipment as primary units. A geographical focus can be brought in by establishing a centralized Sales, Service, and Distribution function which is further segmented by geographical regions.

That function would serve a purpose quite similar to the existing Regional Centers, but under a business-oriented organizational structure.

Figure 16–30 describes the first two hierarchical levels of such an organization. The comparisons of Figure 16–30 with the organizational alternative based on primary businesses, depicted in Figure 16–29, simply shows the addition of a new centralized function, while preserving all the other organizational units. However, there are fundamental differences in the way in which the Company will operate, both in the short and the long run, under these two organizational forms.

The organizational alternative that has a centralized Sales, Service, and Distribution function (Figure 16–30) allows for a comprehensive geographical regionalization, which generates the following major advantages:

- It provides a single company image to all customers.
- It permits better coordination among the various businesses of the Company in the interface with customers.
- It assures efficiency at the operational level.
- It is consistent with the current Regional Center concept, and therefore, would encounter less resistance in its implementation.

However, the major disadvantages of the geographical regionalization alternative relative to the business-oriented organization (Figure 16–29) are:

- It divides managerial accountability between Sales, Service, and Distribution on the one hand, and the business segments on the other. This makes sound management control principles very hard to apply.
- There is a loss of strategic focus for specific business development, since the business units do not possess complete autonomy in Sales, Service, and Distribution.
- It forces newly acquired, self-standing businesses to be broken.
- The Company president would have to play a very strong integrating role to coordinate the operational activities of the business units with the centralized function of Sales, Service, and Distribution. This will prevent a major concentration of the president's time to the strategic directions of the Company.

It should be clear from the preceding remarks that the business-oriented segmentation alternative responds more effectively to the criteria proposed as the basis for a new organization, particularly with respect to allowing for a strong strategic focus for business development.

ALTERNATIVE ORGANIZATION WITH GEOGRAPHICAL REGIONS AND BUSINESS SEGMENTS

Figure 16–31 shows a segmentation based on four major geographical regions and the three basic business units: Computer Systems, Chemicals, and Equipment. This alternative is dominated by the alternative just discussed—the Centralized Sales, Service, and Distribution function. This reduces the span of control of the Company president and separates him from the operational routines of running the day-to-day activities of the Regional Centers.

Since our previous analysis suggested a strong preference for the alternative based on a business-oriented segmentation over the alternative based on Centralized Sales, Service, and Distribution function, we can abandon from further consideration the organization with Geographical Regions and Business Segments.

ALTERNATIVE ORGANIZATION WITH GEOGRAPHICAL REGIONS AND CENTRALIZED MANUFACTURING

Figure 16–32 shows an organizational alternative that preserves the four Regional Center managers, but has the three basic business units reporting to a Vice President of Manufacturing. This alternative would make the Computer Systems, Chemicals, and Equipment businesses simply cost centers in charge of providing the goods to be required by the Regional Center managers. We discarded this alternative since it would have unduly emphasized the operational concerns of the Company, sacrificing its strategic business focus.

We have provided only a synoptic description of the arguments supporting our final recommendation to adopt the business-oriented organization for the Company. In the actual study we examined in detail all the four basic alternatives discussed previously.

DETAILED DESIGN: DESCRIPTION OF EACH ORGANIZATIONAL UNIT OF THE BUSINESS-ORIENTED ALTERNATIVE

Having selected a preferred basic alternative, the second step in the design process is the definition of the associated detailed organizational structure.

We limit ourselves to some brief comments characterizing the nature of each of the units reporting to the President of the Company under the alternative organization based on primary businesses (see Figure 16–29).

Computer Systems
Figure 16–33 shows the proposed organizational chart for the Computer Systems business. Since Computer Systems has been operating as a self-sustaining unit, its organization does not change significantly. It is proposed that in the future, Sales and Marketing would be combined in a single subunit, which would both improve the necessary coordination of these functions, as well as reduce the span of control of the Computer Systems Vice President.

Figure 16–33. Proposed Organization for Computer Systems

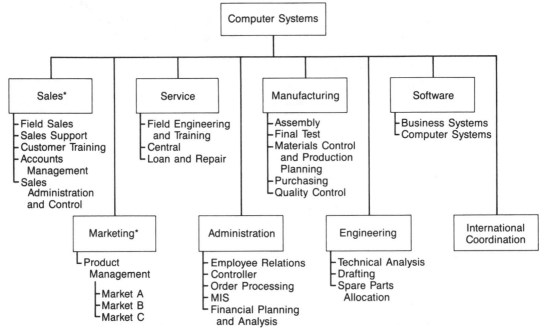

*Sales and Marketing could be combined, which will reduce the span of control of the Computer Systems Vice President.

Chemicals

Figure 16–34 presents the organizational chart for the Chemicals segment. The most important element to bear in mind is that the Advertising and Distribution Management functions reporting to the Vice President of Chemicals not only serve those functional needs for the Chemicals business, but also are centralized functions for Computer Systems and Equipment. We could have opted for a centralized functional structure reporting directly to the president. We rejected that alternative because it would have loaded the president with operational responsibilities. Since Chemicals is the business that most heavily needs Distribution and Advertising support, it was an obvious choice to assign those centralized functions to Chemicals.

Equipment

The Equipment organizational chart (see Figure 16–35) singles out a unit responsible primarily for manufacturing Small Equipment. The remaining functions (Sales and Services, Marketing, Management Development and Training, and Administration) are common for both Small and Large Equipment. At least for the time being, Large Equipment will still be produced and developed by a sister company. This explains the absence of Manufacturing and Research and Development for Equipment.

FIGURE 16–34. Proposed Organization for Chemicals

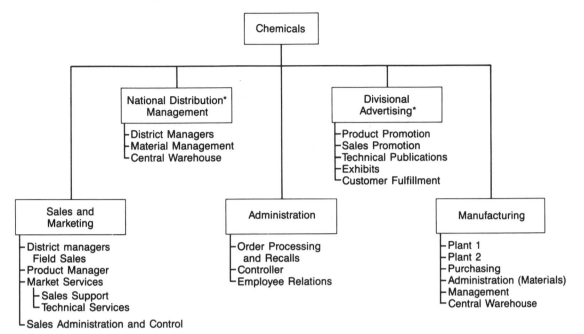

*Denotes centralized divisional functions.

An important issue to be recognized in the Equipment organization is the presence of regional managers reporting to the Sales and Services unit. Naturally, given the broad geographical area coverage of the Company's activities, it is essential to have Sales and Services regional managers' offices. The question is to whom those regional managers should report and how Sales and Services forces from different businesses should be coordinated. The answer to those questions is to maintain regional managers subordinated to the Equipment business, given the very strong importance of Sales and Services functions for that group. However, the Sales forces from Chemicals and Computer Systems would also be using those regional physical facilities, as is currently done between Equipment and Computer Systems Sales forces. The coordination of the Sales activities between different businesses will be assured by continuing the current practice of giving commissions to sales people for all types of sales. This allows for the payment of double commissions for a single sale as necessary, and so preserves a strong supporting effort of the Sales force. In addition, monthly meetings will be conducted among all sales people in a given regional office to coordinate sales efforts across the board in that region.

It should also be recognized that the Marketing function of Equipment has centralized Company responsibilities for activities concerning governmental accounts, legislative affairs, and divisional market research. This means that in those activities the Marketing group is not only overseeing the interests of

FIGURE 16–35. Proposed Organization for Equipment

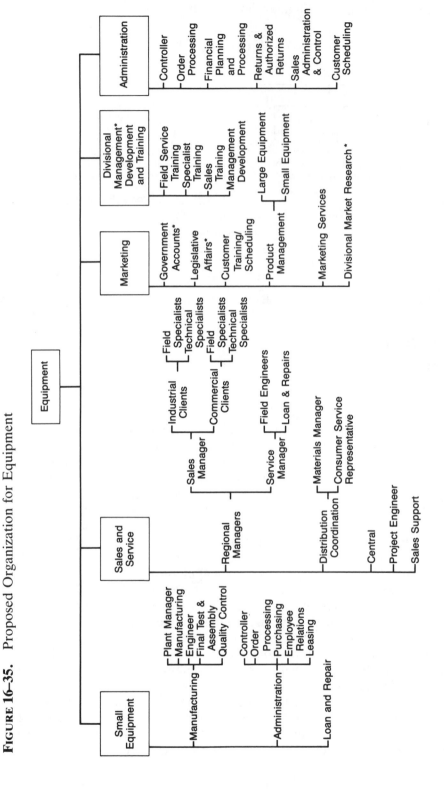

*Denotes centralized divisional functions.

the Equipment business, but also the interests of Computer Systems and Chemicals. Similarly, the Management Development and Training group has equally centralized Company responsibilities for that particular function.

Administration and Finance

Figure 16–36 describes the proposed organizational chart for Administration and Finance. It is important to recognize that this function has been expanded beyond the traditional Controller's responsibility, by adding an Office of Business Development and Planning for the whole Company. This office will play an essential role in establishing the processes, practices, and tools to facilitate the implementation of the strategic and operational planning system of the Company.

Research and Development

The proposed organizational chart for the Research and Development function is presented in Figure 16–37. Notice that we have opted for a centralized Research and Development function. We decided on this alternative because we consider it essential to allow for a strong Research and Development group with a significant critical mass. Decentralizing that function would have resulted in the proliferation of small Research and Development efforts under each business, preventing cross-fertilization and allowing for separate and uncoordinated programs to take place. Although a centralized Research and Development function creates some problem for the coordination of Research and Development with a specific Manufacturing and Marketing function of each business, we believe this is a bearable price to pay to implement coordinated Research and Development programs among the businesses.

FIGURE 16–36. Proposed Organization for Administration and Finance

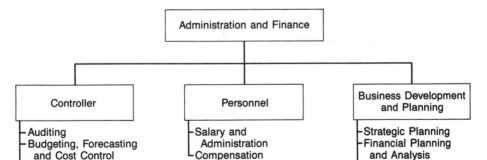

FIGURE 16–37. Proposed Organization for Research and Development

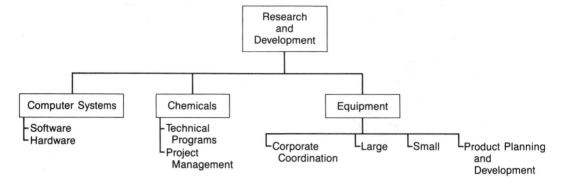

International

The Company had recently accepted new business responsibilities in Mexico. It is contemplating in the future to expand those responsibilities to Central America, and eventually to South America and the Caribbean. Those commitments create a need for a concentrated focus of activities with an international concern. It is mandatory to achieve a deep understanding of the business, social, and political climates in those international areas. Furthermore, special instruments might have to be developed to serve those special markets and tailor-made prices and marketing policies would have to be adopted.

At this time, when the Company has an embryonic presence in the international market, the international unit is merely composed of a single manager. The fact that he reports directly to the president of the Company is a clear indication of the high priority that the development of an international scope has for the Company. As these activities grow, we envision a further segmentation of the international unit into three potential territories: Mexico and Central America, Canada, and South America. At the time this study was conducted, these were the targets for international penetration.

TESTING THE PROPOSED ORGANIZATIONAL STRUCTURE AGAINST THE CURRENT ORGANIZATION

Numerous questions were raised to test the effectiveness of the proposed structure. To achieve this goal we conducted several tests aimed at contrasting the performance of the proposed organization against the existing one, under a variety of critical decisions. As an illustration of how this methodology was applied, we comment on a particularly challenging project requiring important inputs from several businesses and managerial functions. The project identified for these purposes was the development of a Small Equipment that would use a specific type of chemical material (Equipment-Alpha). This project required the performance of the following major planning tasks:

- business plan
- product marketing
- advertising program
- sales
- service
- distribution
- training
- servicing
- acquisition plans
- budgeting and finance
- interfacing with other divisions of the company
- chemicals and equipment delivery schedule
- manufacturing, quality control, and shipment
- check-up
- profit and loss statements
- manufacturing of chemicals
- methods approval
- regulation and quality assurance
- financial approval and final approval.

Figure 16–38 illustrates the participation of each of the major line and functional managers in the development of the Equipment-Alpha project. This figure should be contrasted with Figure 16–39, which shows similar involvement under the proposed organization.

The following conclusions emerge from that comparison. The number of executive involvements have been reduced from 95 in the current organization to 48 in the proposed organization. The depth of involvement has been reduced from 11 to 9. The president's participation has been greatly reduced. His involvement is mostly in critical decisions that have long-term impact, as he has been removed from the more operational issues. The proposed organization shows a much clearer assignment of responsibilities concentrated in the Small

FIGURE 16–38. Involvement of Various Managerial Levels in the Execution of Tasks for the Development of Equipment-Alpha and Current Organization

MANAGEMENT LEVEL \ TASKS	1	2	3	4	5	6	7	8	9	10	11	12	13	14	15	16	17	18	19
President	X	X	X	X	X	X		X	X	X		X	X		X	X	X		X
Marketing	X	X	X	X		X	X		X	X	X	X	X	X	X	X	X	X	
Regional Centers	X	X		X	X	X	X	X		X		X	X	X		X		X	
Service	X	X			X		X	X		X	X			X					
Controller	X	X		X					X	X	X	X	X	X	X	X			X
Corporate Officer 1												X							
Chemicals, Inc.	X		X	X			X	X	X		X	X	X	X	X	X		X	
Corporate Officer 2				X		X						X	X			X			
Corporate Officer 3															X	X			
Corporate Officer 4				X									X		X	X	X	X	
Corporate Officer 5								X	X					X					X

FIGURE 16–39. Involvement of Various Managerial Levels in the Execution of Tasks for the Development of Equipment-Alpha and Proposed Organization

MANAGE-MENT LEVEL \ TASKS	1	2	3	4	5	6	7	8	9	10	11	12	13	14	15	16	17	18	19
President	X								X	X									X
Chemicals, Inc.	X	X	X	X		X			X	X		X	X			X	X	X	
Small Equipment	X	X	X	X	X	X	X	X	X	X	X	X	X	X	X	X	X		X
Large Equipment						X													
R&D																	X		
Administration and Finance	X	X		X					X	X					X				X
Data Management												X							
Corporate Officer 4															X		X	X	
Corporate Officer 5									X	X									X

Equipment and Chemicals businesses. This is a highly desirable outcome, given the nature of the project. To summarize, the proposed organization shows a better concentration of responsibilities at the important managerial levels. This prevents a dispersion of responsibilities throughout the organization that would necessarily call for the president's direct coordination in a multitude of issues.

CONCLUSION

The case study just described represents an illustration of how to implement the two-stage approach for organizational design that we outline at the beginning of this chapter. Although any case study has the inherent limitation of being restricted to a particular situation, we believe our experience can be useful in guiding a manager confronted with the task of redesigning his or her organization. We found the available literature to be lacking on specific examples of this sort.

A disciplined approach for organizational design can facilitate the task of developing a new organizational structure by bringing in all important information related to the strategic posture of the firm. This is essentially the first step in identifying basic organizational alternatives as well as the definition of operational tasks which are handled at the detailed segmentation stage.

Notes

1. Douglas McGregor, *The Human Side of the Enterprise* (Cambridge, MA: The MIT Press, 1960).

2. For analyzing in more detail the question of power in the firm, the following books are recommended: John P. Kotter, *Power and Influence—Beyond Formal Authority* (New York: Free Press, 1985); Henry Mintzberg, *Power In and Around Organizations*, (Englewood Cliffs, NJ: Prentice Hall, 1983). For reviewing the issue of leadership, the reader is referred to: B. M. Bass, *Leadership and Performance Beyond Expectations* (New York: Free Press, 1985); Warren Bennis and Bert Nanus, *Leaders: The Strategies of Taking Charge* (New York: Harper and Row, 1985); James B. Burns, *Leadership* (New York: Harper and Row, 1968); R. M. Kanter, *The Change Masters: Innovation and Entrepreneurship in the American Corporations* (New York: Simon and Schuster, 1983); Edgar H. Schein, *Organizational Culture and Leadership: A Dynamic View*, (San Francisco: Jossey-Bass, 1985); Noel M. Tichy and Mary Anne Devanna, *The Transformational Leadership* (New York: John Wiley and Sons, 1986).

3. For a further analysis of organizational structure and the issue of strategy-structure fit see: Jay Galbraith, *Organization Design*, (Reading, MA: Addison Wesley, 1977); Jay Galbraith and Robert K. Kanzanjian, *Strategy Implementation: Structure, Systems, and Process* (St. Paul, MN: West Publishing Co., 1986); Henry Mintzberg, *The Structuring of Organizations* (Englewood Cliffs, NJ: Prentice Hall, 1979). Our presentation follows closely Arnoldo C. Hax and Nicolas S. Majluf, "Organizational Design: A Survey and an Approach," *Operations Research*, 29, no. 3 (May–June 1981) 417–447.

4. Alfred D. Chandler, Jr., *Strategy and Structure: Chapters in the History of the American Industrial Enterprise* (Cambridge, MA: The MIT Press, 1962).

5. David Solomons, *Divisional Performance: Measurement and Control* (Homewood, IL: Richard D. Irwin, 1965).

6. Stanley M. Davis and Paul L. Lawrence, *Matrix* (Reading, MA: Addison Wesley, 1977).

7. Richard F. Vancil, *Decentralization: Managerial Ambiguity by Design*, (Homewood, IL: Dow Jones-Irwin, 1978).

8. Galbraith and Kanzanjian, *Strategy Implementation*, (1986), op. cit.

9. For a description of the contingency theory approach to organizational design, see Paul R. Lawrence and Jay W. Lorsch, *Organizations and Environment: Managing Differentiation and Integration* (Homewood, IL: Richard D. Irwin, 1967).

10. A full coverage of the concept of strategic functional unit (SFU) and its implication for the development of functional strategy is presented in Chapters 18, 19, and 20.

11. For further references on managerial accounting, the reader is referred to: Charles T. Horngren and George Foster. *Cost Accounting: A Managerial Emphasis*, 6th ed. (Englewood Cliffs, NJ: Prentice Hall, 1987); Robert S.

Kaplan and Anthony A. Atkinson, *Advanced Management Accounting* (Englewood Cliffs, NJ: Prentice Hall, 1989).

12. For a good discussion of transfer prices, see Vancil, *Decentralization*, (1978), op. cit., and Kaplan and Atkinson, *Advanced Management Accounting*, (1989), op. cit.

13. For a coverage on the new accounting practices needed to improve management control see Kaplan and Atkinson, *Advanced Management Accounting* (1989); Robert S. Kaplan and H. Thomas Johnson, *Relevance Lost: The Rise and Fall of Management Accounting*, (Boston, MA: Harvard Business School Press, 1987); Robert S. Kaplan, "One Cost System Isn't Enough," *Harvard Business Review*, 66, no. 1 (January–February 1988), 61–66; Robin Cooper and Robert S. Kaplan, "Measure Costs Right: Make the Right Decisions," *Harvard Business Review*, 66, no. 5 (September–October 1988), 96–103.

14. Good references for Rockart's work are John F. Rockart, "Chief Executives Define Their Own Data Needs," *Harvard Business Review*, 57, no. 2 (March–April 1979), 81–92; John F. Rockart and Christine V. Bullen, eds., *The Rise of Managerial Computing* (Cambridge, MA: MIT, 1986); John F. Rockart and David W. DeLong, *Executive Support Systems: The Emergence of Top Management Computer Use* (Homewood, IL: Dow Jones-Irwin, 1988); John F. Rockart and Michael E. Treacy, "The CEO Goes On-Line," *Harvard Business Review*, 60, no. 1 (January–February 1982), 82–88.

15. D. Ronald Daniel, "Management Information Crisis," *Harvard Business Review*, 39, no. 5 (September–October 1961), 111–121.

16. General Electric Company, "Background Note on Management Systems," Case No. 181-111, (Boston, MA: Harvard Business School, 1981).

17. Alfred Rappaport, "Executive Incentives vs. Corporate Growth," *Harvard Business Review*, 56, no. 4 (July–August 1978), 81–88; Alfred Rappaport, *Creating Shareholder Value: The New Standard for Business Performance*, (New York: The Free Press, 1986).

18. Paul J. Stonich, "Using Rewards in Implementing Strategy," *Strategic Management Journal*, 2, no. 4 (October–December 1981), 345–352.

19. Edgar S. Schein, "Does Japanese Management Style Have a Message for American Managers?" *Sloan Management Review*, 23, no. 1 (Fall 1981), 55–67; Edgar S. Schein, "Coming to a New Awareness of Organizational Culture," *Sloan Management Review*, 25, no. 2 (Winter 1984), 3–16; Edgar S. Schein, *Organizational Culture and Leadership* (San Francisco, CA: Jossey-Bass, 1985).

20. Gibb W. Dyer, Jr., "Culture in Organizations: A Case Study and Analysis," unpublished master thesis, Alfred P. Sloan School of Management, MIT, (1982).

21. Rensis Likert, *The Human Organization: Its Management and Value* (New York: McGraw-Hill, 1967).

22. William G. Ouchi, *Theory Z*, (Reading, MA: Addison Wesley, 1981).

23. Howard Schwartz and Stanley M. Davis, "Matching Corporate Culture and Business Strategy," *Organizational Dynamics*, 10 (Summer 1981), 30–48.

24. Chandler, A. D., Jr., *Strategy and Structure: Chapters in the History of the American Industrial Enterprise* (Cambridge, MA: M.I.T. Press, 1962).

CHAPTER 17

Human Resources Management of Key Personnel

The central priority of most managers requiring the greatest amount of time and attention is the proper identification, development, promotion, and reward of key personnel. According to General Electric's chairman Jack Welsch, if you define the right tasks, put the appropriate persons in charge of them, and back them up with the right kind of reward system, you do not need to be a good manager to obtain excellent results.[1]

The undeniable importance of human resources for every organization has been intensified in American firms due to the presence of a number of forces requiring a broader, strategy-oriented treatment of this subject. Recent pressures that have raised the level of concern on human resources management can be summarized as follows:[2]

- increasing international competition, particularly from the Far East
- increasing complexity and size of organizations
- slower growth or declining markets in a great many industries
- greater government involvement in human resources practices
- increasing education of the work force
- changing values of the work force
- more concern with career and life satisfaction
- changes in work-force demographics.

These concerns have drawn attention to the problem of managing human resources in a strategic manner, that is, in a way that allows firms to establish and sustain a long-term advantage over their competitors. However, in spite of growing interest, the strategic management of human resources is far from a reality in most American enterprises. The formulation of corporate and business strategies is becoming commonplace, but the issue of human resources is not being addressed with a proper sense of priorities. Rather, the personnel requirements embedded in those strategies are identified after the fact and passed only to personnel managers so they can supply the necessary managers, workers, and administrative staff at the various skill levels demanded by the strategic plans.

This practice not only diminishes the strategic role of human resources, but also fails to recognize that the effective use and development of human resources involve *every* line manager in the organization. It is not a staff activity to be relegated exclusively to the personnel function.

Strategic Decision Categories Linked to Human Resources Management

We recognize that any methodology to support the development of a human resources strategy should be tailor-made to accommodate for the idiosyncrasies of a given firm, the characteristics of its industry and its competitive environment, and the managerial style and culture of the organization. However, we find that there are enough common issues in the formulation of a human resources strategy to allow us to generate a useful, general-purpose process to guide managerial thinking in this area.

A human resources strategy must be comprehensive, in the sense of addressing all of the diverse personnel and human resource activities central to the long-term development of the businesses of the firm. Its foundation lies in the proper recognition of the major categories of human resource strategic decision making:[3]

- selection, promotion, and placement managing the flow of people in, through, and out of the organization
- appraisal to evaluate the performance of people within the organization
- rewards providing adequate compensation, fringe benefits, and motivational support to employees at all levels
- management development creating mechanisms to enhance skills, promotional opportunities, and career paths
- labor/employee relations and voice to establish a cooperative climate among managers and employees

These categories of decisions are further defined in Figure 17–1. That figure also describes the central strategic issues related to each category, as well as the corresponding strategic choices. The alternatives available as strategic options for each category are responsible for defining the human resources policy and the resulting quality of the organization as a working place. It is, therefore, useful to reflect briefly on the nature of these options.

FIGURE 17-1. The Major Strategic Decision-Making Categories Linked to Human Resources Management

	SELECTION, PROMOTION, AND PLACEMENT	APPRAISAL	REWARDS	MANAGEMENT DEVELOPMENT	LABOR/EMPLOYEE RELATIONS AND VOICE
DEFINITION	Includes all those activities related to the internal movement of people across positions and to the external hiring into the organization. The essential process is one of matching available human resources to jobs in the organization.	Perhaps the least liked managerial activity. It contributes to three essential processes: • Rewards can be allocated in relation to performance. • Human resources planning and development of current inventory of talent. • Development process.	Pays in various forms: promotion, management praise, career opportunities, appreciation from customers and clients, personal sense of well-being, opportunities to learn, security, responsibility, respect from coworkers, friendship with coworkers.	Activities designed to insure that individuals are properly equipped with skills and knowledge to carry out their jobs.	Activities oriented toward establishing a degree of collaboration between management and labor/employee forces.
STRATEGIC ISSUES	• Devising an organization-wide selection and promotion system to support corporate and business strategies. • Creating internal flows of people that match the business strategies. • Matching key executives to the business strategies.	Designing an appraisal system supportive of the corporate and business strategies.	Designing a reward system to reverse the tendency of short-sighted management, providing balanced support to short-term and long-term strategic goals.	• Job improvement: the development of specific job skills. • Career planning: a longitudinal form of individual growth. • Succession planning: insuring an adequate supply of human resource talent by projected needs.	Developing a policy regarding the amount of influence employees have with regard to matters such as business goals, pay, working conditions, career progression, employment security, etc.
STRATEGIC CHOICES	• Make vs. buy. • Little recruiting above entry level vs. sophisticated recruiting at all levels. • Selection based on weeding out undesirable employees vs. careful initial screening.	• Process-oriented vs. result-oriented system. • Identification of training needs vs. staffing needs. • Individual/group vs. division/corporate performance evaluation. • Time-series vs. cross-section comparisons.	• Compensation oriented toward position in the organizational hierarchy vs. toward performance. • Internal consistency vs. external competitiveness. • Total compensation driven by cash vs. non-cash incentives.	• Formal vs. informal development programs. • Extensive vs. limited development programs. • Skills building vs. skills identification and acquisition.	• Unionization vs. non-unionization. • Minimize vs. share power and influence of labor force. • Autocratic vs. participatory management systems. • Development of employee-influence mechanisms such as self-management groups, task forces, quality of work life committees, ombudsmen, etc.

SELECTION, PROMOTION, AND PLACEMENT: STRATEGIC CHOICES

Make versus Buy

A pure make human resources strategy only allows hiring at the entry level, counting on promotion, placement, and development processes for building necessary skills for individuals to do their job effectively. On the contrary, a pure buy strategy permits acquiring human resources as needed at any level in the organizational hierarchy. In practice, business firms may locate themselves anywhere in the spectrum between these two extremes.

Little Recruiting Above Entry Level versus Sophisticated Recruiting at All Levels

Firms which embrace the pure make strategic option in human resources tend to concentrate on recruiting exclusively at the entry level; and only in the most exceptional circumstances will they recruit at higher levels in the organization. The converse also follows with a pure buy strategy.

Selection Based on Weeding Out Undesirable Employees versus Careful Initial Screening

Firms engaged in a practice of adhering to life-long employment would be required to exercise a great amount of care in the initial screening process. Some financial institutions regard the hiring decision of key personnel to carry with them a life-long $5 million price tag. This clearly conveys the economic significance of such a decision.

APPRAISAL: STRATEGIC CHOICES

Process-Oriented versus Result-Oriented System

In a pure result-oriented appraisal system, we are only concerned about the ability of the individual to meet a prearranged set of performance indicators, without paying much attention to the conditions that facilitate or deter the realization of those indicators. On the contrary, a pure process-oriented appraisal system tries to penetrate into the circumstances that are part of the process of achieving the desired results, both of internal and external nature.

Identification of Training Needs versus Staffing Needs

In a pure make system, identification of training needs is mandatory, so that we develop the necessary skills and knowledge of our existing working force. In a purely buy system, identification of staffing needs replaces the training requirement.

Individual-Group versus Division-Corporate Performance Evaluation

This taxonomy serves to discriminate the scope within which performance is evaluated. On one end of the spectrum, only individual performance matters; on the other extreme, the individual disappears, and only corporate goals are measured. A critical choice to be made in most appraisal and reward systems is what weight to give to individual, group, and corporate performance, in such a way as to stimulate both the recognition of employee efforts and the development of a constructive group attitude.

Time-Series versus Cross-Section Comparisons

A time-series appraisal system has memory. It judges how performance has evolved through a relevant historical time frame. On the contrary, a cross-section comparison appraises performance at a single point in time. The only relative meaningful comparison could be against peers in the organization or in other institutions.

REWARDS: STRATEGIC CHOICES

Compensation Oriented Toward Position in the Organizational Hierarchy versus Toward Performance

At the one extreme of this dichotomy, we have a system where compensation is dictated by the nature of the work itself. Jobs tend to have a specific rank depending on where they are in the organizational hierarchy, which carry with them a compensation figure. At the other extreme, we encounter firms that pay almost no attention to structure but compensate entirely on performance.

Internal Consistency versus External Competitiveness

This choice points to the degree to which compensation is driven by a sense of internal fairness or by responses generated from the external labor market.

Total Compensation Driven by Cash versus Noncash Incentives

Pay could come in various forms, one of which is monetary. The question posed by this taxonomy is the extent to which compensation includes other forms of incentives, such as employment stability, career development, appreciation, respect from the various constituencies of the enterprise, and an overall sense of well-being. Particularly in the higher echelons of the firm, the development, retention, and exercise of power could be an important noncash incentive.

MANAGEMENT DEVELOPMENT: STRATEGIC CHOICES

Formal versus Informal Development Programs; Extensive versus limited development programs; and skills building versus skills identification and acquisitions

These three types of choices signal the degree of commitment that the firm has to management development. Companies which regard management development as the core activity in human resources management opt for formal and extensive development programs aimed at building and constantly updating the skills and knowledge required for managers to perform their jobs effectively. To the contrary, companies which resort to buying human resources tend to have informal and sporadic development programs and use them to identify the skills which should be acquired from the external marketplace.

LABOR/EMPLOYEE RELATIONS AND VOICE:
STRATEGIC OPTIONS

Unionization versus Nonunionization; Minimize versus share power and influence of labor force; autocratic versus participatory management system; development of employee-influence mechanisms, such as self-management groups, task forces, quality of work-life committees, ombudsmen, and so on
All of these strategic choices finally determine the degree, quality, and collaboration prevailing among management, employees, and the labor force.

Congruency of the Human Resources Management Strategy

The strategic choices we have just commented on define the character and quality of the human resources environment. The strategic choices of each of the five decision categories have to be consistent with one another; otherwise, the human resources strategy lacks coherence, and it may fail to operate as intended. The significance of this deficiency could be overwhelming. It is unthinkable that the firm will successfully deploy and sustain a winning strategy without having an effective human resources strategy, particularly with regard to its key personnel. We present this as the last strategic task residing at the corporate level, because it indeed provides the glue that allows all of the previous activities to be properly executed.

It is easy to see how the five human resources strategic categories of decision are linked. Selection, promotion, and placement identify the best available talent to perform the critical job of the enterprise. These alone will not be enough in a world where knowledge and skills have to be continuously updated in order for the human resources to remain competent. Thus, management development is a key strategic activity. Furthermore, a skillful and properly developed work force must be wholeheartedly committed to the organization. This brings into focus the importance of the rewards and motivational activities, as well as a careful management of the labor/employee relations and voice. And finally, none of these tasks could be properly done if an effective appraisal system is not in place, which allows for the proper matching of the available human resources to the necessary jobs in the organization, the planning and execution of management development efforts, the design and operation of an intelligent rewards system, and the detection of the necessary activities to establish the kind of participatory environment needed for the success of the enterprise.

FIGURE 17-2. The Major Human Resources Strategic Categories and the Business Life Cycle

Business Life Cycle

Human Resource Strategic Decision Category	EMBRYONIC	GROWTH	MATURITY	DECLINE
SELECTION, PROMOTION, AND PLACEMENT	Recruit best technical/professional talent Entrepreneurial style	Recruit adequate mix of qualified workers Management succession planning Manage rapid internal labor market movements	Encourage sufficient turnover to minimize layoffs and provide new openings Encourage mobility as reorganizations shift jobs around	Plan and implement work force reductions and reallocations Transfers to different businesses Early retirement
APPRAISAL	Appraise milestones linked to plans for the business, flexible	Linked to growth criteria, e.g., market share, volume unit cost reduction	Evaluate efficiency and profit margin performance	Evaluate cost savings
REWARDS	Salary plus large equity position	Salary plus bonus for growth targets, plus equity for key people	Incentive plan linked to efficiency and high-profit margins	Incentive plan linked to cost savings
MANAGEMENT DEVELOPMENT	Minimum until a critical mass of people in business, then job related	Good orientation programs for fast start-ups Job skills Middle-management development	Emphasis on job training Good supervisory and management development programs	Career planning and support services for transferring people
LABOR/EMPLOYEE RELATIONS AND VOICE	Set basic employee relation philosophy and organization	Maintain labor peace, employee motivation and morale	Control labor costs and maintain labor peace Improve productivity	Improve productivity Achieve flexibility in work rules Negotiate job security and employment adjustment policies

279

Besides the need of the five decision categories to be consistent with one another, the resulting human resources strategy has to be congruent with the corporate and business strategies it intends to support. A common way of recognizing this fact is to reflect on the necessary changes to be made in the human resources strategy as a business travels through the various stages of its business life cycle. Figure 17–2 tries to capture how the management of human resources is modified through the four major life-cycle stages of embryonic, growth, maturity, and decline.

A Framework for Strategic Decision Making in Human Resources Management: An Illustration

We propose a simple conceptual framework to organize the thought process regarding strategic decision making for the management of key personnel. Using the five major categories of decisions linked to human resources management as the focus of primary attention, we suggest a three-step approach involving:

1. Diagnosis to characterize the state of present policies regarding the major strategic decision categories in human resources management, and define the performance measurements to describe the existing quality of human resources management in the organization.
2. Profile of strategic choices to represent current policies and select the desired options to define the future policies of human resources management.
3. Definition of strategic broad action program to specify the key tasks to be undertaken by the major strategic decision categories in human resources management.

We illustrate the framework with a hypothetical case adapted from a real application to a major firm.

DIAGNOSIS OF EXISTING HUMAN RESOURCES MANAGEMENT PRACTICES

We have found it useful to start the process of defining human resources strategies of key personnel by requesting the top management team to provide a brief description of the current policies by each of the five strategic decision categories. Also included should be an evaluation of their current strengths and weaknesses. Figure 17–3 summarizes the outcome of such a task. In spite of its brevity, the figure eloquently portrays the enormous complexity of human resources management. It is clear that this organization has a strong character and well-defined human resources policies which result in impressive strengths; however, invariably the achievement of some strengths tends to generate a counterpart of weaknesses. The resulting trade-offs are hard to resolve, and

DECISION CATEGORY	DESCRIPTION OF POLICY	STRENGTHS	WEAKNESSES
Selection, Promotion, and Placement	Strongly promote from within, and purely on merits Heavy recruiting at entry level, through highly selected screening	High retention rate Thorough knowledge of business Continuity with regard to customer Development of strong culture	Stagnation Some lack of objectivity Short-term focus on business goals conflict with human resource development needs
Appraisal	Appraise individuals in a very objective manner using specific MBOs (for both officers and clerks) Narrative appraisal format vs. check-off list Connection of appraisal directly to development needs via negotiated and signed commitments between supervisors	Clarity and objectivity No surprises Benchmark oriented Direct connection between weaknesses and development	Too rigid goals Not focused on coaching but appraisal Friction Overly competitive environment Short-term orientation
Rewards	Merits driven with differentiation based on performance ranking MBO oriented	Clarity Bottom-line oriented Motivates aggressive people Discriminates outstanding, average, and below average performers	Creates an elitist environment Short-term oriented Demotivates the average performer
Development	To supply managers with both pragmatic and conceptual skills, to enable them to manage both people and businesses	Evolution of a well-rounded manager Development of a sense of ownership and professionalism	Creation of conflict between financial goals and people development goals Too many activities competing for people's time
Labor/Employee Relations, Voice	The full and complete participation of all staff based upon the belief that those closest to the work and/or customer are best equipped to come out with the best solutions	Obtain the best information Create a sense of ownership down to the lowest levels Reduction of cost and increase service	Weakening the authority of the manager Lengthening of the decision-making process

often it is impossible to correct the weaknesses without losing substantial advantage.

It is also a helpful diagnostic instrument to measure the overall quality of human resources by a set of properly designed performance indicators. A set of such indicators and relevant measurements are presented in Figure 17–4. As it shows, some indicators are highly qualitative and need to be measured by personal communications, management by objectives, and different types of surveys. Altogether, they could give us a good description of the existing quality of human resources management, as well as providing goals for improving performance in that area.

PROFILE OF STRATEGIC CHOICES IN HUMAN RESOURCES MANAGEMENT

We have already discussed the available strategic choices in each of the major categories in human resources management. At this stage of the process, it is recommended to prepare a profile of those choices as illustrated in Figure 17–5. The case presented in the figure denotes an organization which tends to favor extreme positions: a pure make strategy as far as selection, promotion, and placement; an appraisal system characterized by a purely result orientation, individual and cross-sectional performance; a reward system seeking internal consistency with compensation depending on performance; a management de-

FIGURE 17–4. Strategic Performance Measurements for Human Resources Management

INDICATORS	ASSOCIATED MEASUREMENTS
Job Satisfaction	Personal communications Employees retention rate Continuous employee reaction survey (CERS)
Job Performance	Management by objectives (MBO)
Turnover	Statistics
Absenteeism	Statistics
Motivation	CERS Job diagnostic service (JDS)
Job Security	CERS
Career Projects	JDS
Physchological Stress	JDS
Safety/Health	JDS
Income	Comparison with external surveys

FIGURE 17-5. Profile of Strategic Choices Linked to Human Resources Management

Selection, Promotion, and Placement

Left	1	2	3	4	5	6	Right
Make	X						Buy
Little recruiting above entry level	X						Sophisticated recruiting at all levels
Selection based on weeding out undesirable employees						X	Careful initial screening

Appraisal

Left	1	2	3	4	5	6	Right
Process-oriented system						X	Result-oriented system
Identification of training needs	X						Identification of staffing needs
Individual performance evaluation	X						Corporate performance evaluation
Time-series comparisons						X	Cross-section comparisons

Rewards

Left	1	2	3	4	5	6	Right
Compensation depending on position in hierarchy						X	Compensation depending on performance
Internal consistency	X						External competitiveness
Total compensation driven by cash				X			Total compensation driven by noncash incentives

Management Development

Left	1	2	3	4	5	6	Right
Formal development programs	X						Informal development programs
Extensive development programs	X						Limited development programs
Skills building	X						Skills identification and acquisition

Labor-Employee Relations and Voice

Left	1	2	3	4	5	6	Right
Unionization						X	Nonunionization
Minimize power and influence of labor force				X			Share power and influence of labor force
Autocratic management systems					X		Participatory management systems
High use of employee-influence mechanisms				X			Low use of employee-influence mechanisms

FIGURE 17–6. Definition of Broad Action Programs for Each Strategic Decision-Making Category

DECISION CATEGORY	OBJECTIVES		BROAD ACTION PROGRAMS
	Long Range	Short Range	
Selection, Promotion, and Placement	Develop the present staff via cross-training and re-training to occupy future positions	Development of individual manpower plan for all staff	Manpower plan Massive training Analysis of future required skills Management trainee program at entry level
Appraisal	Change appraisal into a coaching system	To get managers more comfortable with the appraisal system	Performance appraisal career awareness workshop with joint participation of supervisors and subordinates Corrective action workshop (how to deal with poor performance) Staff relations workshop Develop management skills workshop
Rewards	To continue differentiating without alienating the average performer	To reinforce the differentiation among performers	Compensation workshop for supervisors, connecting appraisal and rewards Ongoing coaching to managers by compensation unit of human resources Quality service award Trying smarter awards Perfect attendance awards Global account management/global account profitability awards Bonus programs and stock options
Development	To increase market share, service quality and productivity	To prepare managers for the changing environment of the industry	Executive development program Management resource planning reviews at corporate level Managing people series Organizational growth project Zero defect process
Labor/Employee Relations, Voice	Nonunionization Increase profits and market share	Motivation of staff at all levels	Weekly breakfast and lunch programs with staff and supervisors Variety of formal communication programs at all levels with great frequency (all monitored and tracked)

284

velopment activity based on extensive and formal development programs aimed at skills building; and a labor/employee relation marked by strong nonunionization policies with an intermediate participatory climate. The overall pattern of decision tends to be quite consistent, and it also serves to reaffirm the recognition of strengths and weaknesses described in the previous step.

DEFINITION OF STRATEGIC BROAD ACTION PROGRAMS

Based on the information collected in the diagnostic stages and the profiling of the strategic choices previously performed, we can now establish long- and short-range objectives and broad action programs for each of the human resources strategic decision-making categories. This step is illustrated in Figure 17–6. The programs proposed in the figure are intended to correct the weaknesses uncovered in the diagnostic phase. Notice the overabundance of training and development activities to overcome limitations present in all the decision categories. This is not necessarily a general trend in human resources management, but it is one which is widely adopted by the institution in this case study.

The emphasis of this task has been the human resources management issues of key personnel. We revisit this subject when dealing with the overall question of human resources management strategy, as part of the methodology to address functional strategies in Chapters 18, 19, and 20.

Notes

1. For further references on the subject of human resources management, see Thomas A. Barocci and Thomas A. Kochan, *Human Resources Management and Industrial Relations* (Boston, MA: Little Brown and Company, 1985); Michael Beer, Bert Spector, Paul R. Lawrence, D. Quinn Mills, and Richard E. Walton, *Managing Human Assets* (New York: The Free Press, 1984); Charles J. Fombrum, Noel M. Tichy, and Mary Ann Devanna, *Strategic Human Resources Management* (New York: John Wiley, 1984); Arnoldo C. Hax, "A New Competitive Weapon: The Human Resources Strategy," *Training and Development Journal*, 39, no. 5 (May 1985), 76–82; Edgar H. Schein, *Career Dynamics*, (New York: Addison Wesley, 1976).

2. Beer, et al., *Managing Human Assets*, (1984), op. cit.

3. See Barocci and Kochan, *Human Resources Management and Industrial Relations*, (1984); Beer, et al., *Managing Human Assets*, (1984); Fombrum, et al., *Strategic Human Resources Management*, (1984), op. cit.

CHAPTER 18

Functional Strategy: The Core Concepts

Of the three levels of corporate, business, and functional strategy formulation, the functional dimension has been probably the most neglected in America. We believe that this neglect has been one of the central sources of the decline of global competitiveness in this country.

Dealing with functions strategically means to be aware of what competitors are doing in terms of developing unique capabilities, and being able to match or exceed their competencies. Think of manufacturing as a key managerial function; unarguably, in many industries, manufacturing represents a key competitive weapon. However, if treated entirely as an operational activity, inwardly oriented, without any understanding of the external forces that are fundamentally changing the production environment, we are liable to commit a most central mistake. From a strategic point of view, we are not interested in simply knowing our cost base, or our productivity rate, or the rate of product innovation, or the advances we are making in adopting new technologies and refining our manufacturing processes. We are not interested only in the state of utilization or modernization of our physical facilities, or the degree in which information technology is changing our operational and administrative skills. None of that is relevant unless we position it in full contrast with similar kinds of skills being developed by competitors. It is not our cost that matters, but it is our cost relative to our key competitors. It is not our productivity, but our ability to match our competitors' productivity, and so on.

This simply means that we really have to treat the managerial functions strategically; in other words, we need to utilize the same core concepts that we apply at the level of the business in reflecting how to treat the managerial function as a central means to achieving sustainable competitive advantage.

Functional Segmentation: The Concept of Strategic Functional Unit

Prior to beginning the process of analyzing and formulating a business strategy, we need to generate a special segmentation of the overall activities of a firm, which originates the concept of SBU. Pragmatically, an SBU simply constitutes the focus of attention of the business strategic planning process, which means that an SBU is composed of a set of products and services sharing the same strategic concerns and objectives. This is exactly the same question that we have to pose prior to analyzing and developing the functional strategy.

In order to be more specific in our analysis, let us consider the value chain as a conceptual framework to define the key managerial functions of the firm. In Figure 18–1 we have grouped the firm's activities in a way that generates six major areas for strategic functional analysis:

- financial strategy
- human resources strategy
- technology strategy
- procurement strategy
- manufacturing strategy
- marketing strategy

These are the central areas of functional strategic concern treated in this part of the book. We have purposely left aside the ones that we refer to as central administrative functions, not because they lack strategic significance,

FIGURE 18–1. The Central Areas of Functional Strategy as Derived from the Value Chain

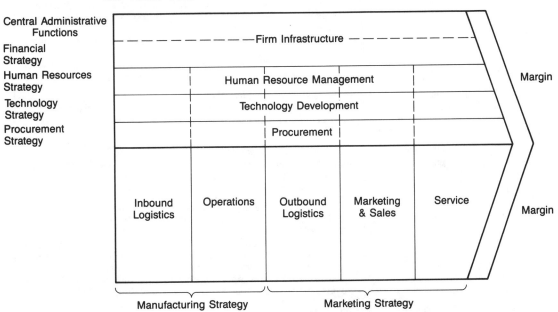

SOURCE: Michael E. Porter, *Competitive Advantage: Creating and Sustaining Superior Performance* (New York: The Free Press, 1985).

but because of our inability to deal with them effectively within the scope of this book.

As it is well known, a central concept to formulate business strategy is the SBU (strategic business unit). An SBU is a distinct group of products or services which is sold to a uniform set of customers facing a well-defined set of competitors. The SBU is the central focus of analysis of business strategies. Similarly, every function has associated its corresponding SFU (strategic functional unit) which represents the focus of attention that drives the particular functional analysis. Figure 18–2 summarizes the definition of SFUs for each of the six functional strategies.

FIGURE 18–2. Definition of Strategic Functional Units

AREAS OF FUNCTIONAL STRATEGY	STRATEGIC FUNCTIONAL UNITS (SFUs)
1. Financial Strategy	*The entire business firm* Finance is the most centralized function of the firm simply because its final accountability resides with the CEO. Decisions pertaining to obtaining and allocating financial resources have to be made from the perspective of the firm as a whole. Although balancing the portfolio of businesses is key for a sound financial strategy, the overall perspective still resides at the level of the firm.
2. Human Resources Strategy	Two dimensions of strategic attention: *The segmentation of labor markets* and *the Strategic Business Unit (SBU)* One level of attention of human resources strategy is the categories represented in the labor market: managers, professionals, clerical workers, and hourly-paid workers. Recognition of more specialized segments of the market may be desirable for some firms. The other level is the SBU to distinguish among the needs of distinct business units in terms of their strategic human resources support.
3. Technology Strategy	*Strategic Technology Unit* (STU) An STU is a unit of analysis which includes the skills or disciplines that are applied to a particular product or service addressing a specific market need.
4. Manufacturing Strategy	*Strategic Manufacturing Unit* (SMU) An SMU is a group of products sharing the same manufacturing strategic objectives expressed in terms of cost, quality, dependability, flexibility, and innovativeness.
5. Procurement Strategy	Two dimensions of strategic attention: The *Strategic Manufacturing Unit* (SMU), and the *Strategic Business Unit* (SBU) The SMU, as defined above, is the focus of attention when concentrating on make-vs.-buy decisions, a central strategic procurement issue which defines the degree of vertical integration of the firm. The SBU becomes the central concern when looking at procurement as a basic function to support the strategic development of the businesses.
6. Marketing Strategy	*The Strategic Business Unit* (SBU) The SBU is defined as having an external marketing and competitors orientation; therefore, there is a clear congruency between the focus of attention of business and marketing strategies.

The Fundamental Elements in the Definition
of a Functional Strategy

Having defined the concept of an SFU, we are now in a position to propose an overall framework for the definition of a functional strategy, whose basic elements are portrayed in Figure 18–3. Not surprisingly, the central tasks required in the development of a functional strategy follow a close parallel to those indicated at the business level. However, there are differences worth noticing, as follow.

First, the corporate strategy provides a most important initial input. It defines basic requirements that the functional strategy has to attend; it specifies targets and scope for the functional strategy. At the corporate level, the major inputs emerge from the statement of the mission of the firm and, particularly, that portion that addresses the central ways to compete.

It is often in that statement where top managers identify the critical roles played by each function in developing a unique competitive advantage. Moreover, the full set of strategic thrusts carries implications for functional challenges which are passed on from the corporate level.

Likewise, the businesses strategies carry an enormous functional impact. The statement of business mission has a similar relevance as the mission of the firm, except that the functional implications tend now to be sharper and more detailed, having as a central objective to support the desired competitive position of the business unit. The implications of the business challenges for each individual function are also clearly spelled out in the full set of broad and specific action programs developed at the business level.

Next, as discussed in the previous section, the strategic functional units constitute the focus of attention for the realization of the functional environmental scan and internal scrutiny tasks. As is the case with business strategy, the environmental scanning process is aimed at obtaining an understanding of the critical industrial trends, and the present and future standings of key competitors. But in this case of the functional environmental scan, we stress a new dimension which we have labeled *functional intelligence*. Its purpose is to generate all the relevant information concerning the current and future state of development of each individual function. It is not only the existing managerial practice and state of technological progress that are important to detect. Even more critical is the recognition of future trends, state-of-the-art developments, and their embodiment in actions by competitors.

With regard to the functional internal scrutiny, besides the recognition of overall strengths and weaknesses typical of the analysis at the business level, we need to determine the specific skills that we could build for each individual function in order to gain competitive advantage. We group these as *strategic categories of decisions* linked to functional strategies.

Finally, we have the remaining tasks of defining broad and specific action programs, budgets, and performance measurements. These tasks are central not only because they spell out in concrete terms the functional strategic commitments, but also because they merge all of the relevant inputs into a coherent

FIGURE 18–3. The Fundamental Elements in the Definition of a Functional Strategy

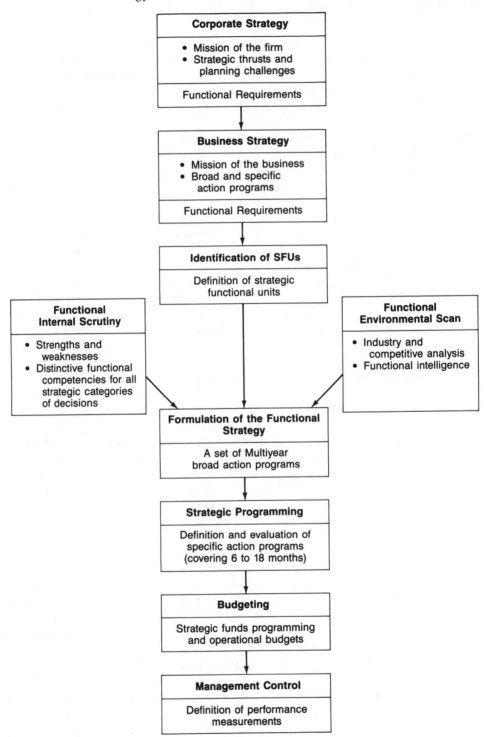

expression of functional strategy consistent with corporate and business long-term objectives.

It is also particularly important to do justice to the final step indicated in Figure 18–3, which calls for the identification of strategic performance measurements for each function. This is, by no means, a trivial task; if properly done, it raises the level of strategic awareness at the functional level and provides meaningful yardsticks for functional effectiveness.

Some Comments on the Process of Functional Strategy Formation

It is clear from our previous comments that the formation of a functional strategy takes place at all of the key hierarchical levels of the firm. Corporate managers have to define, as part of the firm's mission statement, the strategic significance of the development of functional capabilities. In recent years, this has been particularly important to human resources management, technology, and manufacturing. The first two represent fundamental resources that cut across businesses and functions, and are playing more and more critical competitive roles. We have also singled out manufacturing (or, more broadly, the line activities in charge of generating the products and services that constitute the key outputs of the firm) because of the imperative need of raising the strategic awareness of that function. As we have indicated at the outset, dealing with manufacturing merely as a short-term operational activity inevitably produces a fatal deterioration in the ability to compete effectively, particularly in a global setting.

Next, functional strategies are also formulated at the business level. We have defined a business strategy as containing primarily a set of well coordinated multifunctional programs aimed at creating or reinforcing the competitive standing of the business. Therefore, during the process of business strategy formation, we need to identify all of the necessary functional support, thus producing the most critical set of functional requirements. From this perspective, it can be clearly ascertained that a functional strategy cannot be generated independently of the businesses it is intending to support.

Finally, at the functional level resides the task of interpreting all of the requirements emerging not only from corporate and business demands, but also from the inherent external and internal characteristics of the function itself. Even when the SBUs of the firms are completely autonomous and decentralized, the functional managers should participate actively and directly in the formulation of the business strategies, because it is at this level where the functional competitive position is defined. On the other hand, whenever a given function is shared by two or more SBUs, the functional managers have the additional task of consolidating a *horizontal strategy*. This consists of identifying and properly exploiting the synergisms present in the functional strategy formation in those cases.

In some instances, particularly when centralized functions are required to support a variety of businesses in the organization, legitimate conflicts may arise between business and functional managers on the nature of their corresponding strategic roles. Different firms use distinct mechanisms to address these potential disagreements, where direct negotiations do not lead to a solution. One such mechanism is the formation of an executive committee—for example, to deal with technological matters—which has a final say in dictating policy and sanctioning conflicts related to a critical functional capability involving technology. A second mechanism is the so-called *issue escalation*, which simply means that whenever critical disagreements cannot be resolved by the immediate parties involved, the issue is moved to the next higher level in the managerial hierarchy for final sanctioning. It is conceivable that issues of enormous significance would have to be dealt with at the highest level of decision making within the firm.

CHAPTER 19

Developing Functional Strategies

In the previous chapter, we have provided a common framework for the development of functional strategies. Now, we comment briefly on the nature of the specific decisions which constitute the core of each of the six major managerial functions previously indicated. These are the areas of finance, human resources management, technology, procurement, manufacturing, and marketing. We comment as well on the measurement to be used in evaluating the performance of functional strategies.

Functional Interactions

It is important to point out some elements of commonality in the development of functional strategies. First, as we have emphasized many times already, functional strategy formulation depends heavily on the guidelines provided at the corporate and business levels. There is a shared set of characteristics from the firm and each one of the businesses that provides a pattern and a common substratum to all functions. As a result of this coincident basis, all of the functions interact greatly with one another.

Second, a number of central strategic decisions cut across several of the functions. For example, a decision such as the degree of vertical integration has ingredients that affect all functions: manufacturing (to analyze the capabilities of the firm to make rather than buy a given product), procurement (to explore the detailed purchasing alternatives and cost), technology (to examine the design capabilities and the resulting manufacturability of the product), finance (to consider the economic and financial consequences of the decision), marketing (to assess the demand implications), and human resources (to assure the availability of the necessary labor and managerial skills). It is not surprising, therefore, that several strategic decision categories attributed primarily to one function are also considered an important matter of concern for another function.

Third, as it is the case with strategic objectives at every level, functional strategies attempt to capture the challenges generated from the external environment in a way that contributes to competitive advantage. Therefore, we need to understand how each function has to deal with all the major external markets—financial, labor, technology, products, and other factors of production—in order to improve the strategic functional position. It is worth noticing that all of these external markets are naturally lined up with a given functional area. One could argue that financial markets are the province of the finance function, labor markets of human resources management, technology markets of the technology function, product markets of the marketing function, and other factors of production of the procurement function. Curiously, the only function that does not seem "to own" any specific external market is manufacturing; perhaps this can explain why manufacturing tends to have an inward orientation, unless this is purposely avoided. Figure 19–1 depicts this situation. We can observe that to deal with an external market, we must line up the mediation of the specific function. This is another important reason for heavy interdependence among functions.

FIGURE 19–1. Main Functional Relations with External Markets

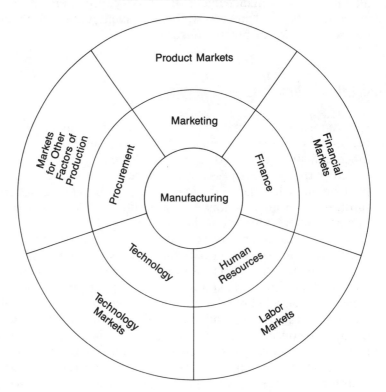

The Urgent Need for Better Coordination Across Functions

These observations have two important practical implications for the development and implementation of functional strategies. First, a proper formulation of each functional strategy has to be done through a careful interaction among key functional managers. This allows for the adequate recognition of the impact that the external markets have on each function, and the formulation of broad and specific action programs with the needed interfunctional flavor. Second, in order to facilitate the functional interactions, the firm has to put in place the necessary coordinating mechanisms such as committees, task forces, integrating managers, and the like for attaining the proper alignment of all functions when formulating and executing the key strategic tasks.

Functional interactions have an enormous importance in the quality of strategic decision making. When contrasting Japanese and American managerial styles, a major difference that is readily apparent is the excessive functional specialization of American managers. This practice is purposely avoided by their Japanese counterparts, who assign great value to a rich multidisciplinary background in their cadres and favor widely spread job rotations. Moreover, American firms tend to isolate the major functions, as it is typically the case in the development of new products, with technology (responsible exclusively for product design), manufacturing (for its production, after the termination of the design), and marketing (for its sale after production). This is not the case in most Japanese industries, which, on average, take only one third the time of their American counterparts for developing a new product from the design board to the market introduction. This difference seems to be explained by the ability of all of the key managers in the three functions just indicated to work together as a team with a much clearer integrative capability.

Functional Strategic Decisions and Performance Measurements

Although there are a number of common elements in the development of a functional strategy which we have been emphasizing throughout this part, there are also specific knowledge, skills, and capabilities which apply to each individual function. The thorough understanding of that know-how constitutes the substance of a given functional strategy. Obviously, it is outside the scope of this book to examine in depth the host of methodological frameworks that apply to each managerial function. However, it is meaningful to address two seemingly straightforward central issues in developing a functional strategy. One is the identification of the key *strategic decision-making categories* that are linked to each one of the major functions, and that lead to the identification of the sources of competitive advantages that reside at the functional level. No attempt is made here to perform a detailed description of the endless tasks associated with the operations of a function. The second issue is the definition of *strategic measures of functional performance*. By that we mean an attempt to capture the quality of the final outputs of a functional strategy, in terms of their ability to achieve competitive advantage.

For reasons of conciseness, we are presenting the key strategic decision categories and performance measures of the six central functions in a figure format. We urge the readers to reflect on the lists we are putting forward and to expand and modify them according to the circumstances of their own particular settings. The proposed lists must be continuously adjusted to reflect different times, circumstances, country, and firm idiosyncracies. The figures that we present should be taken merely as an initial suggestion in a complex and formidable task.

Figures 19–2 through 19–13 (all included at the end of this section) provide the information on major strategic decision categories and strategic performance measures for each one of the six functions. There are just two common categories of strategic decisions for all functions: the capturing of external intelligence, and the development of the appropriate managerial infrastructure. The first deals with the understanding of the external environment, and the second with the mechanisms to be put in place for the proper implementation of selected strategies. Also, horizontal strategy is an option that should be kept in mind for all functions because there is always the possibility of special economies of scale or scope, or of a unique form of interrelationship among functions (Chapter 11). We have chosen to stress horizontal strategy only within the realm of technology, but there are additional horizontal opportunities in all of the other functions. Now, we comment briefly on each one of the six functions.

Finance is the most centralized of functions, and this is reflected in strategic categories that are mostly in the sphere of corporate decision making, and performance measures that are closely watched by external audiences that embody the economic results of the firm as a whole.

Human resources management is the most decentralized and pervasive of functions. The strategic decisions cannot be realized without the full participation and responsibility of managers and supervisors at all hierarchical levels. Think, for example, of selection or appraisal; only at the working place resides all the information necessary for a proper assessment of an individual. The measures of performance are oriented at detecting the attitudes and behavior of individuals in the firm through a broad array of approaches, in order to produce an indication of the healthiness of the organizational climate.

Technology is also everywhere, and it is currently considered to be one of the central functions in achieving competitive advantage because we are living through a period of fast-paced technological transformation. Technology intelligence is essential to gather information on the dynamics of technological markets; but also the laborious and delicate process of internal management of technology must be carefully addressed. This is reflected in the major categories of decisions listed in Figure 19–6, and in the measures of performance in Figure 19–7.

Procurement participates, as expected, in supplying all the needs of raw materials, goods, and services for a smooth operation of the firm's businesses, at minimum cost, and with a high level of service and quality. Procurement management also requires creating a special base of suppliers, developing relationships with them, participating in the design of process and products, and contributing to the resolution of the make-versus-buy decisions. This last subject is at the heart of the vertical integration issue.

Manufacturing is a very peculiar function due to the fact that all relationships with external markets are mediated through other functions. This requires a certain reiteration of issues that may well be considered in the realm of other functions, but they are also central for manufacturing. Therefore, it is worthwhile to include them in the major categories of strategic decisions in Figure 19–10. The issues that are most clearly interfaced with other functions are: (1) vertical integration with procurement for backward integration, and with marketing for forward integration; (2) process technologies with the technology function; (3) product scope and introduction of new products with marketing; (4) human resources with the human resources management function; (5) and suppliers relation with the procurement function. This subject is further expanded in Chapter 20, which is fully devoted to the development of the manufacturing strategy.

Marketing is oriented toward the satisfaction of consumer needs, and includes all the logistics of distribution and the after-sales services. This function is characterized by being preferentially decentralized at the level of the SBU, and by the largely external nature of its main ares of attention. The key is the understanding of consumers' needs, the inducement of new necessities, and the triggering of purchasing behavior. The main categories of decisions, reflected in Figures 19–12 and 19–13, are related to product strategy, distribution strategy, price strategy, and promotion and advertising strategy.

Let us close this section with a caveat. The categories of decision making represent our own biases in the selection of central areas of strategic attention in each function. We have borrowed heavily from the sources identified at the bottom of each figure. Likewise, the performance measurements are intended to possess only a strategic orientation. The ability to follow up the quality of execution of action programs supporting each strategic category is not relevant, since that is the domain of conventional management control systems design. What is relevant is the capturing of the competitive strength resulting from the overall functional strategy. These are not easy tasks, so every effort must be made to complete them in a comprehensive and consistent way.

FIGURE 19–2. Major Categories of Strategic Decisions Linked to Finance

---

1. FINANCIAL INTELLIGENCE

It is a primary effort oriented at understanding the current characteristics of financial and capital markets around the world, and the most important trends observed in them. Important areas of attention are the enormous array of financing opportunities being offered by financial intermediaries in search of new and creative financing alternatives, the changes in legislation that may open or close attractive opportunities, the fluctuations in exchange rates, and the alternatives for risk reduction through financial transactions.

2. CAPITAL BUDGETING

Although the final authority in capital budgeting decisions corresponds to the top managers of the firm, the finance function provides a variety of fundamental supports; the most important ones being: defining the criteria to be used for deciding on the goodness of an investment; managing the request for capital appropriations by type of investment—legal requirements, cost reductions and productivity improvements, maintenance of existing businesses, expansion of existing business, new business development in related products and markets, and unrelated diversification; and setting up the levels for total capital expenditures.

3. MERGERS, ACQUISITIONS, AND DIVESTMENTS

Again, the final authority for deciding on mergers, acquisitions, and divestments strategy resides with the top managers of the firm. The role of finance is: to assist in providing guidelines for making those decisions; to identify opportunities for mergers and acquisitions, and for evaluating them; to recommend alternatives for ownership—including joint ventures, and minority position of ownership; and to identify alternatives for international investments, and considerations with regard to the forms of entry in other countries.

4. EQUITY MANAGEMENT AND DIVIDENDS POLICY

This includes decisions affecting: dividends policy and retained earnings; share repurchasing; new equity issues and preferred stocks; stocks splits and stocks consolidations; and policies concerning leveraged buyouts (LBOs).

5. LONG-TERM DEBT FINANCING

These decisions are central for determining the capital structure of the firm and the debt rating. They include: selecting sources and magnitudes of long-term debt, among a wide variety of instruments—bonds, debentures, syndicated loans, international loans, warrants, convertible debt, junk bonds, project financing, venture capital funds, and leasing; and establishing debt terms through a wide variety of mechanisms—type of interest (fixed vs. floating), maturity conditions, repayment provisions, coupon payments, collaterals, mortgage, debentures, and debt subordination (seniority).

6. WORKING CAPITAL MANAGEMENT

These decisions clearly affect the short-term financing of the firm. They include: cash management—in terms of short-term borrowing and investment policies, float management, the degree of cash centralization, and cash budgeting, credit management—through credit evaluation, collection practices, and accounts payable policy; and inventory management.

7. PENSION FUND MANAGEMENT

This includes decisions on investments related to the portfolio management of funds contributed by the firm and its employees for retirement purposes.

FIGURE 19–2. Continued

8. TAX MANAGEMENT

It involves a number of financial and legal issues that determines the total tax payments of the corporation to a variety of governmental institutions (domestic and abroad). They include, among others, interactions with: investment, acquisitions, and divestment decisions; financing and dividend policies; and international ventures.

9. RISK MANAGEMENT

The overall risk of firms contributes significantly to its cost of capital, including the risk of financial hardship or default in extreme situations. This set of decisions addresses the variety of mechanisms that are available to the firm in order to manage its risk exposures through: hedging by means of options, futures, forwards, swaps, or other alternatives, to protect the firm from risks originated in inflation, interest and exchange rates, commodity prices, and stock market instability, among others; investment strategy by trading off fixed vs. current assets, long- vs. short-lived assets, and business, industry, and international diversification practices; alliances and partnerships; financing stategies, mainly project financing and leases; tax management; governmental protection and concessions; and a variety of additional means, which include trade-offs along dimensions such as: make vs. buy, long- vs. short-term contracts with suppliers and buyers, fixed vs. variable salaries, and fixed vs. variable cost alternatives.

10. MANAGING THE RELATIONSHIP WITH THE FINANCIAL COMMUNITY

This includes establishing and cultivating relationships with a host of financial institutions, such as commercial, and investment banks, international organizations, industry analysts, and rating agencies.

11. FINANCIAL ORGANIZATION AND MANAGERIAL INFRASTRUCTURE

The finance function requires its adequate definition in the organization structure, and the proper design of managerial systems in consonance with the organizational culture. Important decisions are the definition of: accounting procedures, responsibility centers, measures of financial performance, the scope of the treasury function, and the information systems support.

SOURCES: Harold Bierman, Jr., *Strategic Financial Planning,* (New York: The Free Press, 1980) and Richard A. Brealey and Stewart C. Myers, *Principles of Corporate Finance,* 3rd ed. (New York: McGraw Hill Book Co., 1988).

FIGURE 19–3. Measures of Performance Related to the Financial Strategy

---

1. CAPITAL MARKET INDICES

These are measures which attempt to capture the capital market assessment of the economic performance of the firm. They are sound strategic measures because they permit an easy comparison between the position of the firm and its key competitors. They include indices such as: dividend yield (dividend-price ratio), total return (including capital gains or losses), price-earnings ratio (P/E), market-to-book value ratio (M/B), and Tobin's q (market value of assets/replacement cost of assets). Other popular indicators are: earnings per share (EPS), dividends per share, price per share, and book value per share.

2. PROFITABILITY MEASURES

These are the standard measures that relate to the ability of the firm to generate profits. The most widely used are return on assets (ROA), return on equity (ROE) and sales margin. A superior measure of profitability is the firm's spread, which is equal to return of equity minus cost of equity capital ($ROE - k_E$), since it records the capability of the firm to earn a profitability above its cost of capital, which is a true measure of economic-value-creation abilities. They can also be contrasted with similar measures of the firm's competitors to judge the firm's performance against its industry.

3. RISK, COST OF CAPITAL, AND GROWTH MEASURES

These constitute another set of important dimensions of financial performance. Several indicators can be used to measure: *risk*—such as unlevered beta (operating risk), levered beta (financial and operating risk), leverage (D/E), and bond rating; *cost of capital*—cost of equity capital, cost of debt capital, weighted average cost of capital, and cost of capital of the unlevered firm; and *growth*—asset growth, earnings growth, and market value of growth opportunities.

SOURCES: Bierman (1980), Brealey and Myers (1988).

1. HUMAN RESOURCES MANAGEMENT INTELLIGENCE

Understanding the practices of management prevailing in human resources markets, and the expected changes in them. Important issues are: reward structures, levels or compensations for different positions and jobs, alternatives for training and capacities development, changes in legislation related to human resources management, trends in unionization, external focuses of attraction of key specialists, obsolescence of skills in lower level personnel, and retraining tendencies.

2. SELECTION, PROMOTION AND PLACEMENT

Managing the flow of people in, through, and out of the organization. The essential process is one of matching available human resources to jobs in the organization.

3. APPRAISAL

Evaluations of the performance of people within the organization. It contributes to the proper allocation of rewards, the design of effective management development programs, the maintenance of current inventory of talent, and the proper promotion and placement of personnel.

4. REWARDS

Providing compensations in various forms: monetary, promotion, management praise, career opportunities, appreciation from customers, personal sense of well-being, opportunities to learn, security, responsibility, respect for and friendship with coworkers.

5. MANAGEMENT DEVELOPMENT

Creating mechanisms to enhance skills, promotional opportunities, and career paths.

6. LABOR/EMPLOYEE RELATIONS AND VOICE

Establishing a cooperative climate between managers and employees.

7. HUMAN RESOURCES MANAGEMENT ORGANIZATION AND MANAGERIAL INFRASTRUCTURE

Defining the location of human resources management in the organizational structure, and the procedures and systems required for its smooth administration. It is essential to address the issue of centralization vs. decentralization, by defining the responsibilities that fall in a centralized human resources unit, and the participation required from other units of the firm in each one of the major categories of decision related to personnel management.

SOURCES: For useful references in human resources management see Thomas A. Barocci, and Thomas A. Kochan, (Boston, MA: *Human Resources Management and Industrial Relations,* Little Brown and Company 1985); M. Beer, B. Spector, P.R. Lawrence, D.Q. Mills, and R.E. Walton, *Managing Human Assets,* (New York: The Free Press, 1984); C.J., Fombrum, N.M. Tichy, and M.A. Devanna, *Strategic Human Resource Management,* (New York: John Wiley, 1984); Arnoldo C. Hax, "A New Competitive Weapon: The Human Resources Strategy," *Training and Development Journal,* 39, no. 5 (May 1985), pp. 76–82, and Edgar S. Schein, *Career Dynamics* (Part 3), (New York: Addison Wesley, 1978), 189–256.

FIGURE 19–5. Measures of Performance Related to a Human Resources Strategy

---

The following dimensions are critical for assessing the overall quality of human resources management in an organization:

- Job satisfaction
- Job performance
- Turnover
- Absenteeism
- Motivation
- Job security
- Career prospects
- Psychological stress
- Safety/Health conditions
- Income

These attributes are subject to measure through the collection of statistics, personal communication between supervisors and supervisees, commitments generated by management-by-objectives type systems, employee reaction services, and job diagnostic services.

In essence, we have to mobilize a wide array of mechanisms to detect the degree of health of the human resources climate. Moreover, the proposed list can be easily expanded or modified to fit more closely the strategic position of the firm and its individual circumstances.

SOURCES: Barocci and Kochan (1985); Beer, Spector, Lawrence, Mills, and Walton (1984); Fombrum, Tichy, and Devanna (1984); Hax (1985); Schein (1978).

FIGURE 19–6. Major Categories of Strategic Decisions Linked to Technology

---

1. TECHNOLOGY INTELLIGENCE

An effort oriented at gathering information concerning the current and future state of technology development. Some of the tasks associated with it are: identification of strategic technical units (STUs), evaluation of competitive technical strengths by STU, detection of the focus of innovation by key product areas (users, manufacturers, suppliers, others), collection and comparison of expenditures in technology by key competitive firms.

2. TECHNOLOGY SELECTION

It addresses the issue of selecting the technologies in which the firm will specialize, and the ways in which they will be embodied in the firm's products and processes. Some of the issues to be recognized are: selection of the technologies needed for product and process innovation, assuring the congruency of technology development with the business life cycle and with the desired business strategy, and assigning the appropriate priorities to resulting technological efforts.

3. TIMING OF NEW TECHNOLOGY INTRODUCTION

It involves the decision as to whether to lead or to lag behind competitors in process and product innovations. Issues to be addressed are: identifying the benefits and risks associated with a leadership and followership strategy, and assuring the congruency of the selected technology strategy with the generic business strategy.

FIGURE 19–6. Continued

4. MODES OF TECHNOLOGY ACQUISITION

The extent to which the firm will rely on its own internal efforts in developing internal capabilities, versus resorting to external sources. The options available for the modes of technology acquisition of products and processes are: internal development, acquisition, licensing, internal ventures, joint ventures or alliances, venture capital, and education acquisition.

5. HORIZONTAL STRATEGY OF TECHNOLOGY

It consists of identifying and exploiting technological interrelationships that exist across distinct but related businesses. It is a mechanism by which a diversified firm enhances the competitive advantage of its business units. Sources of technological interrelationships are: common product technologies, common process technologies, common technologies in other value-added activities, one product incorporated into another, and interface among products.

6. PROJECT SELECTION, EVALUATION, RESOURCE ALLOCATION, AND CONTROL

The principal concern in this case is the appropriate allocation of resources to support the desired technological strategy. Issues to be addressed are: criteria for resource allocation, project-oriented resources versus loosely controlled funds to support and plan projects, the degree of fluctuation in technology funding, and the magnitude in the profit gap to be filled by new products.

7. TECHNOLOGY ORGANIZATION AND MANAGERIAL INFRASTRUCTURE

It is oriented toward the definition of the organizational structure of the technology function. It includes the identification of the horizontal coordinating mechanisms needed to exploit the technological interrelationships existing among the various business units and the activities of the value chain. Issues to be considered are: centralization versus decentralization of the technology function, development of career paths for scientists and technical professionals, use of project team, use of lateral mechanisms to facilitate sharing technological resources, design of motivational and reward systems for scientists and technical professionals, degree of involvement of top managers in technological decisions, decision-making process for resource allocation to technological projects, protection of technological know-how, patents policies, and publication policies.

SOURCES: For useful references in technology see Robert A. Burgelman, and Modesto A. Maidique, *Strategic Management of Technology and Innovation,* (Homewood, IL: Richard D. Irwin Press, 1988); Mel Horwitch, (ed.) *Technology in the Modern Corporation: A Strategic Perspective,* (New York: Pergamon Press, 1986); Michael E. Porter, *Competitive Advantage: Creating and Sustaining Superior Performance,* (New York: The Free Press, 1985), Chapter 5; Edward B. Roberts, (ed.), *Generating Technological Innovation,* (New York: Oxford University Press, 1987); David J. Teece, (ed.), *The Competitive Challenge: Strategies for Industrial Innovation and Renewal,* (Cambridge, MA: Ballinger Publishing Co., 1987); Brian Twiss, *Managing Technological Innovation,* (London: Longman Group, 1982), and Eric von Hippel, *The Sources of Innovation,* (New York: Oxford University Press, 1988).

FIGURE 19–7. Measures of Performance Related to Technology Strategy

1. RATE OF TECHNOLOGICAL INNOVATION

This implies selecting one or more measures of technological performance for key products and processes, and tracking their progress through time. The S-curve is a good graphical portrayal of the rate of technological innovation.

2. R&D PRODUCTIVITY

As any measure of productivity, it can be defined as the ratio of the change in output to the change in input, i.e., the improvement in the performance of the product or process divided by the incremental investment in R&D.

3. RATE OF RETURN IN R&D INVESTMENT

This, also referred to as R&D yield, measures the profit generated by the amount of R&D investment.

4. RESOURCES ALLOCATED TO R&D

This measurement monitors the level of expenditures being allocated to the various projects and businesses and at the level of the firm as a whole.

5. RATE OF NEW PRODUCT INTRODUCTION

This can be measured by the number of new products introduced per year, the number of patents obtained, or the percentage of sales derived from new products.

6. TECHNOLOGY-BASED DIVERSIFICATION

Whenever the technology strategy is at least partly oriented toward a diversification objective, it is important to measure the degree of success in achieving this goal via, for example, the percentage of sales resulting from related or unrelated diversification efforts.

7. OTHER APPROPRIATE MEASUREMENTS

Depending on the nature of the firm other measurements can be used, such as: royalties or sales of technology, training time of people on new technology, cycle time of product development, developmental cost per stage, and level of technological competence.

SOURCES: Burgelman and Maidique (1988); Horwitch (1986); Porter (1985); Roberts (1987); Teece (1987); Twiss (1982); von Hippel (1988).

FIGURE 19–8. Major Categories of Strategic Decisions Linked
to Procurement

1. PROCUREMENT INTELLIGENCE

It requires understanding the common practices prevailing in markets which are factors of production for the firm, and trying to anticipate transformations that may affect the performance of the procurement function. Important issues are: alternative sources of supply from around the world, legislative changes, cartelization of suppliers, general health and competitive standing of key suppliers, technological changes that may affect procurement, distribution patterns, and material management practices and innovations.

FIGURE 19–8. Continued

2. SELECTION, EVALUATION, AND DEVELOPMENT OF SUPPLIERS

This category of decisions has as an objective finding, selecting, developing, administering, and motivating suppliers able and willing to provide consistent quality, service, and competitive prices. Decisions included are: survey of possible sources, inquiring the qualifications and relative advantages of potential sources; negotiation and selection, and maintaining a healthy relationship with suppliers. Other related decisions in which the procurement function could play a significant role are: subcontracting, buying inside the company, and make-vs.-buy decisions.

3. QUALITY MANAGEMENT OF PURCHASED GOODS

The procurement function has the responsibility of meeting the quality objectives of the firm, since the materials and component parts being purchased have a direct effect on the quality and cost of the end products. The responsibility for quality of purchased goods includes: defining the proper quality specifications of the procured goods—in terms of the eight dimensions of quality: performance, features, reliability, conformance, durability, serviceability, aesthetics, and perceived quality; inspection of the purchased items to ensure conformance with the stated specification; and even establishing a quality control process at the suppliers plant.

4. MATERIALS MANAGEMENT OF PURCHASED GOODS

It deals with the flow of all of the purchased goods into the organization. Specific decisions are: materials planning and control, order processing, incoming traffic, inventory control, receiving, management, in-plant materials movement and surplus disposal.

5. VALUE ANALYSIS, PRICE/COST ANALYSIS, AND STANDARDIZATION

Value is a concept that cut across several functional areas, and leads to a new procurement activity referred to as value analysis. The Department of Defense defines value analysis as a systematic effort directed at analyzing the functional requirements of a product for the purpose of achieving the essential functions at a lowest total cost, consistent with the needed performance, reliability, quality and maintainability. At the essence of value analysis are the trade-offs to be made among price, quality, design, manufacturability, standardization, and cost.

6. PROCUREMENT ORGANIZATION AND MANAGERIAL INFRASTRUCTURE

A. ORGANIZATION The decisions regarding the way to structure the procurement function should address two central issues: the degree of centralization vs. decentralization of purchasing, and the need to coordinate the procurement activities with the other managerial functions—most importantly manufacturing, technology, marketing, distribution, quality control, and finance. Four prerogatives should reside with the procurement function; selection of the supplies sources, contact with suppliers, auditing the purchase request against the need, and managing the commercial aspects of the function—including the manner of purchase, price, terms and conditions of the order, packaging and shipping instructions, etc.

B. PROCUREMENT SYSTEM A key element of the managerial infrastructure support is the development of a comprehensive procurement logistic systems including, among others, the following elements: checking requisitions, securing quotations, analyzing quotations, choosing between contracts and open-market purchases, scheduling purchases and deliveries, issuing purchase orders, checking legal conditions of contracts, following up for delivery, checking receipt of materials, and verifying invoices. Moreover, the system should be capable of maintaining and updating, among others, the following records: purchase, price, stock and consumption, suppliers, specification files, salespersons' performance, and catalog files.

SOURCES: Stuart F. Heinritz, Paul V. Farrell, and Clifton L. Smith, *Purchasing: Principles and Applications,* 7th ed. (Englewood Cliffs, NJ: Prentice Hall, 1986).

FIGURE 19–9. Measures of Performance Related to Procurement Strategy

An effective measurement for procurement performance is hard to define because of the many factors that have to be traded off to provide a steady flow of materials as needed, at lowest ultimate cost. The desired objectives for procurement are to obtain: optimum quality, minimum final cost, effective supplier service, continuity of supply, solid supplier know-how, and good and permanent supplier relations.

1. INDICATORS FOR COST PERFORMANCE

Costs of procured goods vs. standard costs
Administrative cost of the purchasing department as a fraction of total purchases
Total value added of purchased goods, as a fraction of total cost
Inventory turnover ratios
Cost savings

2. INDICATORS FOR SERVICES PERFORMANCE

Percentage of on-time orders
Average delay on delinquent orders

3. INDICATORS FOR QUALITY PERFORMANCE

Percentage of orders meeting intended specifications
Reliability of purchased goods
Vendor quality

4. INDICATORS FOR VENDOR RELATIONSHIPS

SOURCE: Heinritz, Farrell, and Smith (1986).

FIGURE 19–10. Major Categories of Strategic Decisions Linked to Manufacturing

1. MANUFACTURING INTELLIGENCE

The practices and trends of manufacturing in the industry are important issues to watch. Changes in competitors' facilities, technological developments in process technologies, new raw materials or components, standardization, capital investment practices, and environmental legislation are among the subjects that may affect the smooth evolvement of the manufacturing function.

2. FACILITIES

It addresses the issue of the number of plants, their sites and locations, and, most importantly, how specialized or focused facilities are.

3. CAPACITY

Capacity and facilities decisions are highly interconnected. Capacity is determined by: the plant equipment and human resources available, the slack in the use of capacity with regard to demand, the ability of handling demand peaks, and the decisions pertaining to the sequences of capacity expansion.

4. VERTICAL INTEGRATION

Important issues are: the definitions of the boundaries of the firm with regard to its value chain—the questions of make vs. buy, the management of the relationship among the firm and its external constituencies—primarily suppliers, distributors, and customers, and the conditions under which those characteristics should be altered to gain competitive advantage and to increase the appropriation of value by the firm.

5. PROCESS TECHNOLOGIES

It involves decisions as to: the degree of specificity of the technology and process equipment used—from general to specific purposes, the labor skills required, the degree of automation, and the flexibility of scope and volume, as well as the rate of new product introductions.

6. PRODUCT SCOPE AND INTRODUCTION OF NEW PRODUCTS

It includes issues such as: the definitions of the breadth of product lines, the rate and mode of new products introductions, and the desirable length of the product life-cycle.

7. HUMAN RESOURCES

It addresses questions like: recruitment, selection, promotion, and placement; appraisal; rewards, incentives, and job security; skills development and adjustment to changing technological demands; and labor/employee relations and innovations.

8. QUALITY MANAGEMENT

There are eight basic elements of product quality: performance, features, reliability, conformance, durability, serviceability, aesthetics and perceived quality. The management of quality deals with: the definition of the desirable product quality in tune with those eight dimensions, quality improvement program, assignment of responsibilities for quality, training, quality control, prevention, and testing.

9. SUPPLIERS RELATIONS

It includes issues such as: suppliers selection, qualification, degree of partnership, manufacturer/supplier strategies, list of competitive biddings, and suppliers controls. This has been another area receiving close attention because of the different kinds of practices existing in Japan among manufacturers and suppliers, based primarily on close partnership and trust as opposed to the arm-length attitudes prevailing until recently among American firms.

10. MANUFACTURING ORGANIZATION AND MANAGERIAL INFRASTRUCTURE

Important matters of decision are: the design of the proper organizational structure—including the degree of centralization of responsibilities, the design of planning and scheduling systems, control and information systems and forecasting and inventory management. This area has attracted significant attention due to the revolutionary innovation of Japanese manufacturing management, represented particularly by Just-in-Time (JIT) and Total-Quality-Control (TQC) systems.

SOURCES: For useful references in manufacturing see Elwood S. Buffa, *Meeting the Competitive Challenge: Manufacturing Strategy for U.S. Companies,* (Homewood, Il: Richard D. Irwin, 1984); Charles Fine, and Arnoldo C. Hax, "Manufacturing Strategy: A Methodology and an Illustration," *Interfaces,* 15, no. 6 (November–December 1985), 28–46; David A. Garvin, *Managing Quality: The Strategic and Competitive Edge,* (New York: The Free Press, 1988); Thomas G. Gunn, *Manufacturing for Competitive Advantage: Becoming a World Class Manufacturer,* (Cambridge, MA: Ballinger Publishing Co., 1987); Kathryn Rudie Harrigan, *Strategic Flexibility: A Management Guide for Changing Times,* (Lexington, MA: Lexington Books, 1985); Robert H. Hayes and Steven C. Wheelwright, *Restoring Our Competitive Edge: Competing Through Manufacturing,* (New York: John Wiley, 1984); Robert H. Hayes, Steven C. Wheelwright, and Kim B. Clark, *Creating the Learning Organization,* (New York: The Free Press, 1988); Richard J. Schonberger, *Japanese Manufacturing Techniques,* (New York: The Free Press, 1982); Richard J. Schonberger, *World Class Manufacturing: The Lessons of Simplicity Applied,* (New York: The Free Press, 1986); Wickham Skinner, *Manufacturing: The Formidable Competitive Weapon,* (New York: John Wiley & Sons, 1985); and Kiyoshi Suzaki, *The Manufacturing Challenge: Techniques for Continuous Improvements,* (New York: The Free Press, 1987).

FIGURE 19–11. Measures of Performance Related to Manufacturing Strategy

---

1. COST

It can be measured in a variety of ways; the most relevant ones being: variable unit cost and total unit cost from the point of view of the manufacturer; and total life-cycle cost from the point of view of the user.

2. DELIVERY

It is measured in terms of: percentage of on-time shipments, predictability of delivery dates, and response time to demand changes.

3. QUALITY

It is measured in terms of the adherence of products to the various dimensions of quality—performance, features, reliability, conformance, durability, serviceability, aesthetics, and perceived quality—rejection rates, return rates, cost and rates of field repair, and cost of quality.

4. FLEXIBILITY TO VOLUME CHANGES AND NEW PRODUCT INTRODUCTION

It is measured as: response to product or volume changes, product substitutability, and product options or variants.

Normally, cost and delivery represent a different way to compete from quality and flexibility. If a firm wants to establish itself as a low-cost producer, it might adopt a strategy that prevents delivering highly customized products and simultaneously being able to absorb significant changes both in volume and in product innovation.

SOURCES: Buffa (1984); Fine and Hax (1985); Gunn (1987); Garvin (1988); Harrigan (1985); Hayes and Wheelwright (1984); Schonberger (1982, 1986); Skinner (1985); Suzaki (1987).

FIGURE 19–12. Major Categories of Strategic Decisions Linked to Marketing

1. MARKETING INTELLIGENCE

It corresponds to the effort conducted by the firm to decipher competitors' standing and try to anticipate their future moves. Important issues are product introductions, marketing approaches, changes in segmentation practices, price policies, product liabilities, new distribution channels, and improved services approaches.

2. DEFINING AND ANALYZING MARKETS

These decisions are concerned with generating marketing intelligence for the firm. It starts with an appropriate market segmentation, and a finer definition of product-market segments so as to capture the different preferences and needs of customers. In each of those segments, an analysis of the behavior of consumers and organizational buyers is conducted, as well as of the overall strategic competitive situation.

3. PRODUCT STRATEGY

It refers to decisions on how to position a business unit product offering—including the specific products, breadth of product lines, mix, and bundling—to serve its target markets, establishing strategic objectives for products—market share, profit contribution, and selecting a branding strategy.

4. NEW PRODUCTS DEVELOPMENT AND INTRODUCTION

Issues included are: idea generation, screening and evaluation of ideas, business analysis, development and testing of a prototype, formulation of a marketing approach, market testing in pilot regions, adjustment of administrative and support systems, and new product introduction.

5. DISTRIBUTION STRATEGY

Decisions involved: selection of a distribution channel—whether direct or via retailers, wholesalers, or agents; design and management of the physical distribution system—including customer service, demand forecasting, inventory control, materials handling, order processing, parts and service support, warehousing and storage, procurement, packaging, returned goods handling, and traffic and transportation; and push vs. pull mode of operation of the distribution and sales systems.

6. PRICE STRATEGY

The central factors that affect price strategy are product competitive positioning, product mix, brand strategy, and product quality and features. The distribution strategy also influences how the price decision will be affected by the advertising and sales force strategy.

7. PROMOTION AND ADVERTISING STRATEGIES

An integrated promotion strategy has four components: advertising—presentation and promotion of ideas, goods, or services by an identified sponsor; personal selling—oral presentation to one or more prospective purchasers; sales promotion—includes trade shows, contests, samples, point-of-purchase displays, and coupons; and publicity—exhibition in mass media not paid for directly by sponsor.

FIGURE 19–12.   **Continued.**

---

8. MARKETING ORGANIZATION AND MANAGERIAL INFRASTRUCTURE

It includes the development of an organizational structure; planning, control, and information systems; and rewards and incentives systems in accordance with the culture of the firm and the marketing strategy.

SOURCES: David W. Cravens, *Strategic Marketing* (Homewood, IL: Richard D. Irwin, 1987); George S. Day, *Strategic Market Planning* (St. Paul, MN: West Publishing, 1984).

A Methodology for the Development of Functional Strategies

In this section we make explicit some of the steps that may be followed to develop a functional strategy in accordance with the general framework presented in Figure 18–3. We limit ourselves to presenting the content of some forms that we have used to help practicing managers in the construction of functional strategies. These forms should not be interpreted as a set of structured and mechanistic instructions, but rather as conceptual frameworks to lead

FIGURE 19–13.   Measures of Performance Related to Marketing Strategy

---

At the heart of marketing strategy there are four major strategic positionings that, taken as a whole, can serve as the primary criteria for marketing strategic performance:

1. PRODUCT STRATEGY

Sales growth rate
Market share
Relative market share
Breadth of product line, market coverage, degree of differentiation
Rate of successful new product introductions
Product bundling

2. DISTRIBUTION STRATEGY

Efficiency of distribution channels
Customer service levels
Distribution costs per channel
Distribution and sales force productivity

3. PRICE STRATEGY

Price sensitivity
Pricing of marketing mix

4. PROMOTION AND ADVERTISING STRATEGY

Product segmentation
Brand acceptance
Marketing intelligence: ability to anticipate customer needs and to detect changes in marketing trends

---

SOURCES: Cravens (1987), Day (1984).

us in a more systematic way toward the analysis of the central issues that affect the formulation of functional strategies. In the next chapter we provide a full illustration of this procedure for the case of the manufacturing function. A summary of the methodology is shown in Figure 19–14.

FIGURE 19–14. A Methodological Approach for the Development of a Functional Strategy

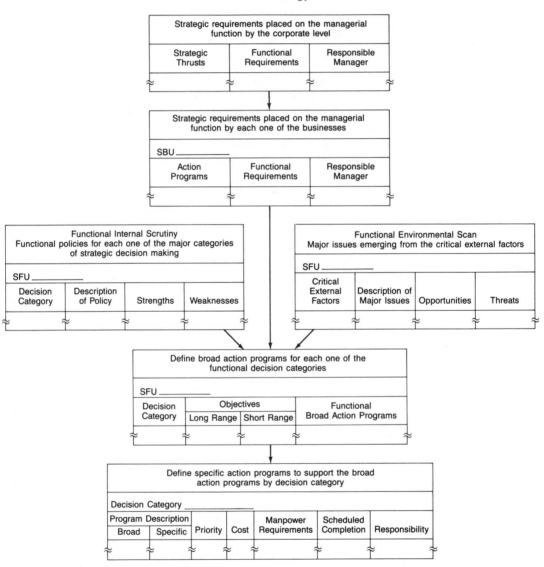

CHAPTER 20

The Development of a Functional
Strategy: The Case of Manufacturing

In the previous chapters, we have presented a framework for the formulation of functional strategies, and we have commented on the key strategic decision categories and performance measures of the basic managerial functions. We provide now an example of the more detailed aspects emerging when dealing with a functional strategy, using manufacturing as the illustrative case.[1]

For most industrial companies, the manufacturing operation is the largest, the most complex, and the most difficult to manage component of the firm. The formation of a comprehensive manufacturing strategy affects and is affected by many organizational groups inside and outside the firm. These are mainly business units, other functions, competitors, and the various external markets represented in Figure 20–1. It can be observed that in developing the strategy, manufacturing has to interact with all the remaining managerial functions of the firm: finance, marketing, technology, human resources management, and procurement. Cooperation and consistency of overall objectives is the key to success in these interactions. Also, the definition of the manufacturing strategy must be based on careful monitoring by manufacturing specialists of the firm's basic external markets, along with the other functional groups. For example, manufacturing managers in conjunction with the technology group may monitor developments in the electronics industry to be aware of new applications to process technology. Similarly, manufacturing in conjunction with marketing monitors the product markets in which they compete to maintain alertness with regard to their competitors' improvements and new product introductions.

Manufacturing Strategic Performance Measures

Normally, manufacturing objectives are expressed in terms of the four major dimensions of performance measurement used in formulating manufacturing strategy: cost, quality, delivery, and flexibility. Important trade-offs must be

313

FIGURE 20–1. Interaction of Manufacturing with Basic External Markets Through the Mediation of Other Functions

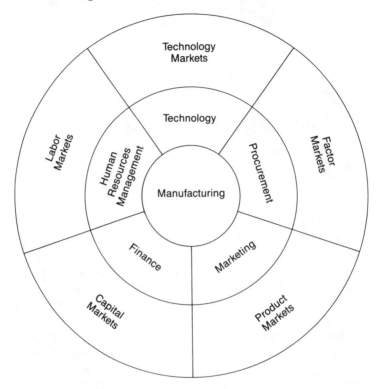

made among these objectives; it is impossible to excel in all of them simultaneously. Defining the central manufacturing competitive thrusts, the tasks to accomplish these goals, and a performance measurement system are central to designing manufacturing strategy.[2]

Cost objectives are frequently measured using labor, materials, and capital productivity, inventory turnover, and unit costs. *Quality* measures include percent defective or rejected, the frequency of failure in the field, cost of quality, and mean time between failures. To measure *delivery* performance, percentage of on time shipments, average delay, and expediting response time may be used. *Flexibility* may be measured with respect to product mix, volume, and lead time for new products. Matching performance measures to corporate and business objectives can be difficult because changed short-term operating policies often have uncertain long-term effects.

Strategic Decision Categories in Manufacturing

A manufacturing strategy must be comprehensive, but at the same time the complex web of decisions required must be broken down into analyzable pieces.

We use nine strategic decision categories: facilities, capacity, vertical integration, process technologies, product scope and introduction of new products, human resources, quality management, manufacturing organization and managerial infrastructure, and supplier relations. This is shown in Figure 20–2. The outer ring displays the basic strategic manufacturing decision categories. The figure further suggests which other functional departments in the firm are the main contributors of each decision category. For instance, manufacturing has to interact with both marketing and sales, and finance in making capacity decisions. However, in human resources decisions it is enough for manufacturing to interact solely with personnel. Vertical integration deals with make-versus-buy decisions and, therefore, requires a joint manufacturing and procurement involvement.

We now comment on the nine categories of strategic decisions.

Facilities

Facilities decisions are classic long-term, "cast-in-concrete" manufacturing decisions. A key step in devising policies for a multifacility organization is choosing

FIGURE 20–2. Major Categories of Strategic Decisions Linked to Manufacturing and Their Relationship with Basic External Markets

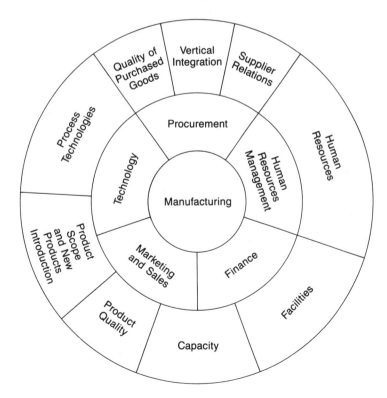

how to specialize or focus each facility.[3] Facilities may be focused by geography, product group, process type, volume, or stage in the product life cycle.

In any industry, decisions on the focus of facilities usually depend on the economics of production and distribution. For example, because of the economies of scale in refining and the high cost of transportation, oil companies tend to locate process-focused plants near crude oil sources (oil wells or ports). Consumer-product companies have large, centralized plants where they can achieve significant economies of scale in manufacturing and delivery time is not critical (for example, nonperishable food manufacturers). Firms have small plants focused on a product or location if scale economies are not significant or closeness to the customers is important (for example, furniture manufacturers). Firms in rapidly changing industries, such as semiconductor firms, often focus plants by stages in the product life cycle. They may have low-volume, high-flexibility facilities for manufacturing prototypes and high-volume, dedicated plants for maturing products in high demand.

Developing a well-thought-out strategy for facility focus automatically guides the firm in determining the size, location, and capabilities of each facility.

Capacity

Capacity decisions are highly interconnected with facility decisions. Capacity is determined by the plant, equipment, and human capital of the firm. Important decisions include how to deal with cyclical demand (for example, by holding "excess" capacity, by holding seasonal inventories, by peak-load pricing, or by subcontracting), whether to add capacity in anticipation of future demand (aggressive, flexible approach) or in response to existing demand (conservative, low-cost approach), and how to use capacity decisions to affect the capacity decisions of competitors.

Vertical Integration

Operations managers are directly affected by decisions to integrate vertically because they are responsible for coordinating the larger and more complex system that usually results. Such decisions involve replacing a market mechanism, over which the operations managers have limited control, with an internal mechanism, which is their sole responsibility. Before making such a decision, a firm must be sure that it can design and control an internal mechanism that will be more efficient than the market it replaces.

Important issues related to vertical integration include the cost of the business to be acquired or entered, the degree of supplier reliability, whether the product or process to be brought in house is proprietary to the firm, and the transaction costs of contracting through market compared to nonmarket mechanism.[4] Other important issues are the impact of integration on the risk, product quality, cost structure, and degree of focus of the firm.

Legal ownership of the series of productive processes may not itself produce the benefits of integration. Toyota Motor Company in Japan plays a large role in directing the operations of its legally independent suppliers. Toyota benefits from lower transaction costs because they coordinate the production of independently-owned suppliers with the just-in-time system. The success of this system points out that the crucial element for success of integrated operations is not *ownership* but *management and coordination* of the series of processes.

Process Technologies

The traditional approach has been to choose among the principal generic process types (project, job shop, batch, assembly line, continuous flow) by matching product characteristics with process characteristics.[5] Although crude, this framework is quite useful for conceptualizing important trade-offs in process choice. Compared to assembly lines, job shops use more general purpose machines and more highly skilled labor, provide more product flexibility, and yield higher unit production costs.

Recent innovations in computer-aided design (CAD), computer-aided manufacturing (CAM), robotics, and flexible manufacturing systems have made decisions on technology more complex. New highly automated factories can be extremely expensive. In many cases, such advanced technology can drastically change the manufacturing cost structure, capital intensity, unskilled labor usage, and ability to deliver high-quality products rapidly at low cost.

Many firms decide to invest in these new technologies because they believe their survival depends on it. Traditional financial and accounting evaluation tools are often unable to capture all of the benefits that can be derived from these systems. Therefore, thorough strategic analysis is necessary to properly evaluate them.

Product Scope and Introduction of New Products

The degree of difficulty of the manufacturing management task is strongly influenced by the range of products and processes, and the rate of new product introductions. In well-run organizations, manufacturing management has significant input in decisions about product scope and new products. Firms with rapid and frequent product introductions or broad product lines must design flexible, responsive, efficient manufacturing organizations. Its product designers must understand what demands product design will place on manufacturing. Design, marketing, and manufacturing must be in close communication to prevent excessive diversification and lack of focus in the products manufactured in a given plant.

Human Resources Management

The principal issues in human resources management are selection, promotion, and placement of personnel, appraisal of employee performance, rewards and motivational support, management development, and employee relations. Human resources managers must design policies to motivate employees to work as a team to achieve the firm's goals.[6]

Designing such policies can be quite complex. For example, a firm must decide whether to compensate its people as a function of hours worked, quantity or quality of output, seniority, skill levels, effort expended, or loyalty. Asymmetries in information about skill levels or effort levels complicate the matter because the firm can base compensation only on observable measures. Aside from pecuniary compensation, employees are often rewarded with perquisites (such as cars or loans), training (human capital investments by the firm), employment guarantee, recognition for achievement, promotions to better jobs, and so forth. A well-thought-out incentive system will combine these elements to promote quality, efficiency, and employee satisfaction.

Quality Management

Managing quality improvement is a crucial and extremely challenging task in most U.S. firms today. A strategy for quality improvement requires zealous support from top management, a well-articulated philosophy, and concrete objectives. It must specify how responsibilities are to be allocated, what decision tools and measurement systems are to be used, and what training programs will be instituted. To be successful, a quality improvement program must be a permanent and ongoing process applied throughout the organization, and its chief objective must be the constant quest for improvement.

Quality can be categorized as design quality and conformance quality. Although manufacturing managers should be somewhat involved with design quality (especially regarding manufacturability), their most crucial role is with conformance quality.

Three important issues related to conformance quality are quality measurement, economic justification of quality improvements, and allocation of responsibility for quality. The principal tool of quality measurement is statistical quality control.

Economic justification of quality improvements is difficult and controversial. Cost of quality accounting (COQ), the only economic tool widely used to evaluate quality projects and programs, has two severe drawbacks. First, COQ ignores revenue effects of quality such as market-share benefits and price premiums for high-quality products. Second, it emphasizes short-term cost effects without considering long-term consequences. A system that measures the revenue effects of quality as well as the cost effects is needed for sound decision making. We know of no instances where measurement of the revenue effects of conformance quality has been attempted.

Responsibility for product quality has traditionally resided in the quality assurance or quality control unit in the firm. Recently, the viewpoint has been advanced that each worker should be responsible for the quality of his or her work. Implementing this proposal would require a significant change in many companies where hourly workers are not expected to exercise judgment. Where implemented successfully, this corporate cultural regime has proven to be very efficient.[7]

Manufacturing Organization and Managerial Infrastructure

A solid organizational infrastructure is essential to support decision making and implementation and requires planning and control systems, operating policies, and well-understood lines of authority and responsibility. A corporate culture that reinforces the manufacturing strategy is also crucial.

Manufacturing management must also make decisions on materials management, production planning, scheduling, and control. In managing materials, firms should consider the relative merits of classical production and inventory systems, materials requirements planning (MRP), and just-in-time (JIT) systems.

Production planning and scheduling decisions are typically thought of as tactical rather than strategic. However, aggregate production planning and delivery system design include strategic considerations. In aggregate planning, the firm must decide how to match productive capacity to variable demand over the medium-term planning horizon (12 to 18 months). The choices are usually to hire or lay off workers, schedule overtime or undertime, increase or reduce the number of work shifts, or build up or run down seasonal inventories.

In designing the delivery system, the principal decision is whether the system should produce to stock or to order. In a make-to-order shop where flexibility is crucial, scheduling is difficult, but the system responds readily to varying customer requirements. Make-to-stock shops are generally "under the gun" less often because they have finished goods inventories to buffer the production operation from customer demand; however, they have significant holding costs. In many machine shops, where the number of possible products is extremely high, a make-to-stock system is not feasible.

Supplier Relations

There are two popular but diametrically opposed views on purchasing and supplier-relations strategy—the competitive approach and the cooperative or Japanese approach. The competitive approach recommends developing multiple sources for materials inputs, so that a number of firms compete to retain supply contracts. Buyer-supplier relationships resemble spot contracting more than long-term contracting because suppliers can be dropped on short or no notice. Tapered integration is recommended as an additional threat to take business away from errant suppliers. Tapered integration is used by some major automobile producers (such as General Motors and Ford). They produce some components in house and purchase the rest; this makes a threat of backward integration credible and also gives them detailed knowledge of costs. All contracts formally account for many contingencies. Dependence on a supplier is to be avoided.

The cooperative approach recommends developing long-term relationships based on mutual dependence and trust. Suppliers are given advice and training if their performance is unsatisfactory. Contracts are informal and contingencies are dealt with as they occur. Single sourcing is common.

The contrast between these two views is quite sharp. Each approach is practiced by successful firms. However, the recent trend in the United States seems to be toward the cooperative approach.[8]

Developing Manufacturing Strategy

Although we recognize that a methodology should be tailor-made to a given firm, we find enough common issues in the formulation of a manufacturing strategy to recommend the following useful general-purpose process to guide managerial thinking:

1. Provide a framework for strategic decision making in manufacturing.
2. Assure that business strategies and manufacturing strategy are linked.
3. Conduct an initial manufacturing strategic audit to detect strengths and weaknesses in the current manufacturing strategy by each decision category and to assess the relative standing of each product line against those of the most relevant competitors.
4. Address the issue of product grouping by positioning the product lines in the product or process life cycle and by assessing commonality of performance objectives and product family missions.
5. Examine the degree of focus existing at each plant or manufacturing unit.
6. Develop manufacturing strategies and suggest allocation of product lines to plants or manufacturing units.

We review now each step in the process, occasionally presenting the forms we use for reporting results. To illustrate the process, we describe an application of the methodology to Packard Electric, a component division of General Motors. We concentrate on Packard's wire and cable SBU, which had four plants: three near division headquarters in Warren, Ohio, and one in Clinton, Mississippi. A vast majority of Packard's sales is to General Motors. Recently Packard has been pressured to reduce costs, improve quality, and improve product development.[9]

A Framework for Strategic Decision Making in Manufacturing

The framework we present in this chapter identifies the nine major categories of manufacturing strategic decision making just discussed and the four performance measures presented at the outset to address the objectives of the manufacturing strategy:

- Cost (unit cost, total cost, life-cycle cost)
- Delivery (percentage of on-time shipments, predictability of delivery dates, response time to demand changes)
- Quality (return rate, product reliability, cost and rate of field repairs, cost of quality)
- Flexibility (product substitutability, product options or variants, response to product or volume changes)

Linking Manufacturing Strategy to Business Strategies

The strategic planning process is hierarchical. First, the corporate level articulates the vision of the firm and its strategic posture; next, the business managers develop business strategies in consonance with the corporate thrusts and challenges; and finally the functional managers provide the necessary functional strategic support.

It is important, therefore, to assure that the business strategies and the resulting manufacturing strategy are properly linked. To accomplish this, we start by identifying the manufacturing requirements imposed by the broad action programs of each strategic business unit (SBU). Figure 20–3 shows the requirements placed on manufacturing by the wire and cable business unit's broad action programs at Packard Electric Division of General Motors. Out of all the action programs which are part of the wire and cable business strategy, we have identified the three which involve the manufacturing function. For these three programs, we have identified more specifically the manufacturing requirements.

Occasionally, business and manufacturing managers may disagree as to the effectiveness or feasibility of some of these manufacturing requirements. If they cannot agree through direct negotiation on some issues, those issues may be referred to higher levels of the organization for resolution.

Initial Manufacturing Strategic Audit

Early in the planning process, a strategic audit should be performed on the current manufacturing strategy. Although later analysis provides a more thorough diagnosis, it is useful at the outset to extract the participating managers' feelings about the status of their manufacturing function.

This initial audit has two objectives: to assess the strengths and weaknesses of existing policies in each of the nine manufacturing categories, and to establish

FIGURE 20–3. Linking Manufacturing Strategy to Business Strategy

SMU Wire and Cable SBU, Packard Electric

SBU	BROAD ACTION PROGRAMS	MANUFACTURING REQUIREMENTS
Wire and Cable	Identify GM requirements not being supplied Study impact of silicon chips on cable substitution Design packaging for new customers	Assure capacity and technology for new demand Plan for eventual electronics change-over Develop new packaging capability

the competitive standing of each major product line according to the four measures of manufacturing performance. Figure 20–4 presents an analysis of existing manufacturing policies at the wire and cable business unit of Packard Electric. The major policies pertaining to each manufacturing strategic decision category are broadly described, and the corresponding strengths and weaknesses against the leading competitor are assessed. Figure 20–5 provides an evaluation of the relative importance and performance of the product lines of the wire and cable business unit of Packard Electric.

FIGURE 20–4. Strategic Audit of Manufacturing: Assessment of Strengths and Weaknesses of Existing Policies in Each of the Nine Categories of Strategic Decision Making

SMU Wire and Cable SBU, Packard Electric

DECISION CATEGORY	DESCRIPTION OF PAST POLICY	STRENGTHS	WEAKNESSES
Facilities	Process focus	Economies of scale	Long physical supply distances
Capacity	Use overtime, third shift, and inventories to respond to cyclicalities	Flexibility	Layoffs and overtime are costly
Vertical Integration	Significant backward integration— all the way to wire rod	Good control over cost and quality	Less focus, transfer pricing complications
Process Technologies	Cable and copper in automated, continuous processes Printed circuits in job shop process	State-of-the-art in cable and copper	Automation in printed circuits could reduce costs
Product Scope and Introduction of New Products	Respond to GM in principal lines	Low risk	Reactive rather than anticipatory Focus concept ignored
Human Resources Management	Strong quality of work life programs	Employee participation in decisions, good communications	Compensation system does not consider quality of output
Quality Management	Heavy use of statistical process Control and cost of quality tools	Integrated approach Top management support	Quality lags relative to Japanese competition
Manufacturing Organization and Managerial Infrastructure	Control system with short-term, tactical orientation	Good control orientation	Short-sighted system
Supplier Relations	Cost-oriented competitive bidding Multiple sources	Keeps costs down	Hurts quality, and cooperative ventures

FIGURE 20–5. Strategic Audit of Manufacturing: Establishing the Competitive Standing of Each Product Line by Each of the Four Measures of Manufacturing Performance

SMU Wire and Cable SBU, Packard Electric

PRODUCT LINE	EXTERNAL PERFORMANCE MEASURES							
	Cost		Quality		Delivery		Flexibility	
	Import.	*Perfor.*	*Import.*	*Perfor.*	*Import.*	*Perfor.*	*Import.*	*Perfor.*
1. Cable	30	+ +	40	–	20	E	10	–
2. Printed Circuits	20	–	50	E	20	+	10	+
3. Copper	20	+	40	+	30	+ +	10	–

Note: One hundred points are distributed among the four external performance measurements (cost, quality, delivery, and flexibility) to identify their relative importance in each product line. Furthermore, a subjective assessment is made of the competitive performance of each product against its most relevant competitor in each of the performance criteria. We use the following convention to classify performance levels: — (very high weakness), – (mild weakness), E (even), + (mild strength), + + (very high strength).

Addressing the Issue of Product Grouping

One of the most difficult problems in manufacturing planning revolves around the product grouping. Even in small firms, manufactured items proliferate. Since it is impossible to deal with each item separately, they must be aggregated into sensible product groups sharing common attributes.

Two analytical devices are helpful. The first is the product-process life-cycle matrix.[10] This matrix positions each product line in a two-dimensional grid (Figure 20–6). The horizontal axis represents the stages in the product life cycle, which has long been recognized as a valuable tool for analyzing the dynamic evolution of products and industries. This evolution is a four-phase process initiated by low-volume, one-of-a-kind products and culminating in highly standardized commodity products. Similarly, the vertical axis captures the production processes, which evolve from highly flexible but costly job-shop processes to special-purpose, highly automated manufacturing processes.

The matrix captures the interaction between product and process life cycles. For our analysis it provides two useful insights. First, it can show which of the firm's product lines are similarly positioned within their product-process cycles and are therefore candidates for homogeneous strategic groups. Second, and more important, it is useful for detecting the degree of congruency between a product structure and its "natural" process structure. The natural congruency exists when product lines fall in the diagonal of the product-process matrix. A product line outside the diagonal could either be explained by inadequate managerial attention or by concerted strategic actions seeking to depart from conventional competitive moves. Figure 20–7 provides a sharp description of

FIGURE 20-6. The Product-Process Life-Cycle Matrix

PRODUCT STRUCTURE
PRODUCT LIFE-CYCLE STAGE

PROCESS STRUCTURE / PROCESS LIFE-CYCLE STAGE	I LOW VOLUME—LOW STANDARDIZATION, ONE OF A KIND	II MULTIPLE PRODUCTS, LOW VOLUME	III FEW MAJOR PRODUCTS, HIGHER VOLUME	IV HIGH VOLUME—HIGH STANDARDIZATION, COMMODITY PRODUCTS	Key management tasks:
I JUMBLED FLOW (Job Shop)					Flexibility—quality
II DISCONNECTED LINE FLOW (Batch)					Fast reaction / Loading plant, estimating capacity / Estimating costs and delivery times / Breaking bottlenecks / Order tracking and expediting
III CONNECTED LINE FLOW (Assembly Line)					Systematizing diverse elements / Developing standards and methods, improvement / Balancing process stages / Managing large, specialized, and complex operations
IV CONTINUOUS FLOW					Meeting material requirements / Running equipment at peak efficiency / Timing expansion and technological change / Raising required capital
					Dependability—cost

Flexibility—quality

Dependability—cost

Dominant competitive mode:

Flexibility—quality

Custom design / General purpose / High margins	Custom design / Quality control / Service / High margins	Standardized design / Volume manufacturing / Finished goods inventory / Distribution / Backup suppliers	Vertical integration / Long runs / Specialized equipment and processes / Economies of scale / Standardized material

Dependability—cost

Note: The margin of the matrix indicate the trade-offs to be made among the four external performance measurements (flexibility, quality, dependability, and cost), and the changing nature of the managerial tasks and competitive modes in different stages of the product-process life-cycle matrix.

SOURCE: Hayes and Wheelwright (1979).

FIGURE 20-7. The Relationship of Product Innovation and Production Process Characteristics

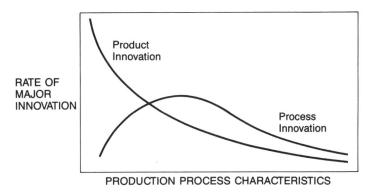

RATE OF MAJOR INNOVATION

Product Innovation

Process Innovation

PRODUCTION PROCESS CHARACTERISTICS

Fluid Pattern	**Transitional Pattern**	**Specific Pattern**
Product Innovation • Emphasis on maximizing product performance • Stimulated by information on user needs • Novelty or radicalness high • Frequency of product innovation is rapid • Predominant type is product rather than process	Product Innovation • Emphasis on product variation • Increasingly stimulated by opportunities created through an expanding technical capability • Predominant type is process required by rising volume • Demands placed on suppliers for specialized components, materials and equipment	Product Innovation • Emphasizes cost reduction • Predominant mode is incremental for product and process • Effect is cumulative • Novel or radical innovations occur infrequently and originate outside productive unit • Stimulation arises from disruptive external forces
Production Process • Flexible and inefficient • Small size or scale • General purpose equipment used • Available materials used as inputs • Product is frequently changed or custom designed	Production Process • Some sub-processes are automated creating "islands of automation" • Production tasks and control become more specialized • Process changes tend to be major and discontinuous involving new methods of organization and changed product design • At least one product design is stable enough to have significant production volume	Production Process • Efficient, system-like, capital-intensive • Cost of change is high • Scale and facility market share is large • Special purpose process equipment used • Specialized input materials or extensive vertical integration • Products are commodity-like and largely undifferentiated

SOURCE: James Utterback, "Management of Technology," in *Studies in Operations Management,* ed. Arnoldo C. Hax (New York: North Holland Publishing, 1978).

the matching characteristics of product and process as they evolve from a "fluid" to a more "specific" state.

Special forms are used to collect data to establish product-line grouping by product and market characteristics, and to map these groupings onto the product-process life-cycle matrix. Figure 20–8 shows the assessment of the stage

FIGURE 20–8. Assessment of the Stage of Product Life Cycle

SMU Wire and Cable SBU, Packard Electric

PRODUCT LINE	PRODUCT/MARKET CHARACTERISTICS					PRODUCT LIFE-CYCLE STAGE(*)
	Breadth of Product Line	*Market Volume*	*Market Growth*	*Product Standardization*	*Pace of Product Introduction*	
1. Cable	High	High	Medium	Low	Medium	III
2. Copper Rod	Medium	Low	Medium	High	Low	I
3. Printed Circuits	Medium	High	High	Low	High	II

(*) Key:
   I: Low volume, low standardization, one of a kind
   II: Multiple products, low volume
   III: Few major products, higher volume
   IV: High volume, high standardization, commodity products

of the product life cycle for the product lines of the wire and cable business unit of Packard Electric. Breadth of product line, market volume, market growth rate, product standardization, and pace of product introduction are used to determine the product life-cycle stage of each product line. Figure 20–9 portrays the positioning of each product line of the wire and cable business unit of Packard Electric in the product-process life-cycle matrix. The location of copper rod manufacturing appears anomolous in this matrix because low-volume products are being manufactured on a continuous-flow process. Historically, this came about because the copper rod is produced in the cable factory, which has always been solely a continuous-flow operation.

Another way to arrive at product groupings is to identify families of product lines sharing similar competitive success requirements and product family missions. Carrying out this task after the product-process life-cycle matrix exercise tends to produce additional insights for grouping products.

Assessing the Degree of Focus at Each Plant

Ever since Wickham Skinner wrote his classic paper on the focused factory, manufacturing managers in the United States have paid attention to this important but simple concept: A plant cannot do a large variety of very different tasks exceptionally well. A factory with a clear competitive objective that focuses on a narrow product mix for a well-defined market will outperform a conventional plant with an inconsistent set of manufacturing policies that attempts to do too many conflicting tasks.

FIGURE 20–9. Positioning of Each Product Line in the Product-Process Life-Cycle Matrix

SMU Wire and Cable SBU, Packard Electric

PROCESS STRUCTURE PROCESS LIFE-CYCLE STAGE	PRODUCT STRUCTURE PRODUCT LIFE-CYCLE STAGE			
	I LOW VOLUME–LOW STANDARDIZATION, ONE OF A KIND	II MULTIPLE PRODUCTS, LOW VOLUME	III FEW MAJOR PRODUCTS, HIGHER VOLUME	IV HIGH VOLUME–HIGH STANDARDIZATION COMMODITY PRODUCTS
JOB SHOP		Printed Circuits		
BATCH				
ASSEMBLY LINE				
CONTINUOUS FLOW	Copper Rod		Cable	

To detect the degree of focus at each plant of a firm, we once again use the product-process matrix. This time we prepare one matrix for each plant, positioning within the matrix every product line manufactured at that plant. The resulting plot allows us to judge the plant's degree of focus and to examine the degree of consistency between the products and the processes employed to manufacture them.

The final diagnosis can be summarized in a form like that exhibited in Figure 20–10. This form is used to diagnose the degree of focus of each of the plants making the product lines of the wire and cable business unit of Packard Electric. Plant 10 is the most focused of the three plants. Plant 3 has the highest degree of diversity.

Development of Manufacturing Strategies

After this analysis, the next step is to state strategic objectives to be articulated through broad action programs for each of the nine manufacturing strategic decision categories. Action programs may be targeted at one or more product groups. Figure 20–11 establishes the definition of broad action programs pertaining to the wire and cable business of Packard Electric for each manufacturing decision category. Each broad action program has to be more thoroughly defined by a set of specific action programs that can be monitored easily, and whose contributions are measurable. We spell out the specific action programs corresponding to the quality management decision category in Figure 20–12.

Finally, we consider the reallocation of products to plants, if the previous analysis of products and plants suggests such a change.

FIGURE 20–10.   Assessing the Degree of Focus at Each Plant

SMU Wire and Cable SBU, Packard Electric

PLANT	EXISTING LINES MANUFACTURED IN EACH PLANT OR OPERATING UNIT	STRATEGY FOR PRODUCT LINE	STAGE OF PRODUCT-LIFE CYCLE	PROCESS TECHNOLOGY CURRENTLY USED
10	Cable Copper rod	Grow with industry Grow with industry	Mature Mature	Continuous flow Continuous flow
22	Cable Metal stamping Molding	Grow with industry Hold position Hold position	Mature Aging Aging	Continuous flow Job shop Job shop
3	Printed circuits Plastic molding Ignition cable Neoprene	Up or out Hold position Improve position Fine niche and protect	Embryonic Aging Mature Mature	Job shop Job shop Assembly line Job shop

FIGURE 20–11. Definition of Broad Action Programs

SMU Wire and Cable SBU, Packard Electric

DECISION CATEGORY	OBJECTIVES		BROAD ACTION PROGRAMS
	Long-Range	Short-Range	
Facilities	Rationalize plant focus	Study focus issue	Consider separating stamping and molding operations
Capacity	Respond better to fluctuations	Meet recent demand upturn	Design a model to simulate the impact of product substitution in cable capacity
Vertical integration	Integrate only when strategically justified	Standardize make-or-buy decision process	Reduce backward integration for increased flexibility
Process technologies	Maintain state-of-the-art	Install more automation	Increase automation where possible
Product scope and introduction of new products	Anticipate customer needs	Upgrade customer contact	Become involved in GM decision process
Human resources management	Utilize fully employee resources	Upgrade personnel function	Improve compensation system
Quality Management	Institutionalize improvement	Improve training	Increase self-inspection by operators
Manufacturing Organization and Managerial Infrastructure	Develop central system to support new automated manufacturing technologies	Improve performance measurement system	Design new performance measures
Supplier Relations	Develop closer ties	Propose joint projects	Identify supplier candidates for joint projects

329

FIGURE 20–12. Definition of Specific Action Programs

DECISION CATEGORY <u>Quality Management</u>   **SMU** <u>Wire and Cable SBU, Packard Electric</u>

PROGRAM DESCRIPTION	PRIORITY	COST	MANPOWER REQUIREMENTS	SCHEDULED COMPLETION	RESPONSIBILITY
Improve quality training	A	$150K	2 man-yrs	August '86	Quality VP
Develop cost-of-quality system	B	$700K	10 man-yrs	1987	Controller and Quality VP
Implement experimental design concepts	C	$25K	1/2 man-yr	1986	SQC experts and design engineers
Fit quality into incentive scheme	B	$75K	1 man-yr	1986	Personnel and Quality VP

Categorize as follows:
A = Absolute first priority: Postponement will significantly hurt our position
B = Highly desirable: Postponement will adversely affect our position in the market
C = Desirable: If funds were to be available to enhance our position

Conclusion

The manufacturing function can be a formidable weapon to achieve competitive superiority. After painful experiences in a wide range of industries, most American managers today clearly understand this. We have attempted to provide a conceptual framework and a set of pragmatic guidelines for designing a manufacturing strategy.

We recognize that different companies will pursue different paths to manufacturing strategy design. However, we have tried to capture in the proposed framework and methodology the essential elements that must be considered by any firm attempting to design a manufacturing strategy.

Notes

1. The presentation follows Charles Fine and Arnoldo Hax, "Manufacturing Strategy: A Methodology and an Illustration," *Interfaces*, 15, no. 6 (November–December 1985), 28–46.

2. On manufacturing performance measures see Steven C. Wheelwright, "Japan, Where Operations Really Are Strategic," *Harvard Business Re-*

view, 59, no. 4 (July–August 1981), 67–74; and on matching performance measures with business objectives, see Robert S. Kaplan, "Measuring Manufacturing Performance: A New Challenge for Managerial Accounting Research," *The Accounting Review*, 58, no. 4 (October 1983), 686–705.

3. For deciding on the organization of

facilities and the degree of focus of a factory, see Wickham Skinner, "The Focused Factory," *Harvard Business Review*, 52, no. 3 (May–June 1974), 113–121.

4. Oliver E. Williamson has worked extensively on the costs and benefits of internalizing in the firm the transaction costs incurred by the operation of market mechanisms. See Oliver E. Williamson, *Market and Hierarchies* (New York: The Free Press, 1975).

5. The framework for matching product and process characteristics has been proposed among others by Paul W. Marshall, et al., *Operations Management: Text and Cases* (Homewood, IL: Richard D. Irwin, 1975); and Robert H. Hayes and Steven C. Wheelwright, "Link Manufacturing Process and Product Life Cycles," *Harvard Business Review*, 57, no. 2 (January–February 1979), 133–140.

6. We have dealt with the issue of human resources management in Chapters 17 and 19. See also Arnoldo C. Hax, "A New Competitive Weapon: The Human Resource Strategy," *Training and Development Journal*, 39, no. 5 (May 1985), 76–82.

7. The issue of quality management is treated by Charles H. Fine, "Quality Control and Learning in Productive Systems," Sloan School of Management Working Paper, #1494-83 (Cambridge, MA: MIT, 1983); Charles H. Fine and David M. Bridge, "Managing Quality Improvement," Sloan School of Management Working Paper, # 1607-84 (Cambridge, MA: MIT, November 1984). Statistical quality control has a long history, and it is well covered in Eugene L. Grant and Richard S. Leavenworth, *Statistical Quality Control* (San Francisco, CA: McGraw-Hill, 1980).

The economic impact of quality on costs is presented in the classical work by Joseph M. Juran, ed., *Quality Control Handbook*, 3rd ed. (New York: McGraw-Hill, 1974). Also, Joseph M. Juran and Frank M. Gryna, *Quality Planning and Analysis* (New York: McGraw-Hill, 1980) provide a good treatment of this subject.

Quality as a direct responsibility of involved workers is a new and very successful approach to quality control. Many works have been presented in this area including buzzwords like "quality circles." The interested reader is referred William E. Deming, *Quality, Productivity, and Competitive Position* (Cambridge, MA: MIT CAES, 1983); and Richard J. Schonberger, *Japanese Manufacturing Techniques* (New York: The Free Press, 1982).

8. Michael E. Porter had championed the competitive approach in his very successful book *Competitive Strategy* (New York: The Free Press, 1980). The five-forces model conceptualizes the industry as a power game among rival firms, suppliers, clients, and other potential participants. The co-operative approach is linked to Japanese management practices; see, for example, Schonberger, (1982), op. cit.

9. This illustration has been adapted from Luis A. Ortega, "Analysis of the Development of a Strategic Planning System," unpublished master thesis, Sloan School of Management, (Cambridge, MA: MIT, 1985).

10. The product-process life-cycle matrix was originally proposed by Robert H. Hayes and Steven C. Wheelwright, "Link Manufacturing Process and Product Life Cycles," (1979), op. cit.

CHAPTER 21

Methodology for the Development of a Strategic Plan: Introduction

In previous parts we discussed the basic concepts associated with corporate, business, and functional strategy. This part is intended to illustrate how those concepts could be translated into a comprehensive strategic plan. To attain that objective, we propose a methodology which is general enough to fit reasonably well a wide variety of business conditions. We have tried this methodology in a number of different settings with very encouraging results. However, as we have indicated many times already, planning is a managerial activity that should be deeply rooted in the unique characteristics of a firm, its culture, people, organizational structure, administrative systems, the nature of its businesses, and their environment. Therefore, we offer this methodology as a broad general framework, which follows the twelve steps outlined in Chapter 2. We urge those who might consider using this approach for the development of their own corporate strategy to view it as a simple guideline, to be modified and adapted in order to better capture the specific idiosyncrasies of their own firms.

The methodology covered in this part represents an attempt to structure as much as possible the strategic planning process. We have done that purposely, so as to guide in a very pragmatic way the implementation of concepts and ideas pertaining to corporate strategy. When we tested this implementation in a variety of academic and consulting activities, this high degree of pragmatism was helpful and warmly received by its users. This methodology does not end with abstract concepts about the quality of strategic thinking, but it serves to guide a group of key managers into an orderly sequence of logical steps, intended to address all the key strategic issues of the organization.

Having said that about the intended objective of the methodology, we have to raise a word of caution. Planning is not a mechanistic activity. It cannot be interpreted simply as filling in forms. The planning documents are just subproducts of the process. When they begin to get in the way of effective strategic thinking, it is time to put all forms away and provide complete freedom in the way of documenting the basic strategic issues. A firm which is in an embryonic stage in the development of strategy formulation might benefit from

FIGURE 21–1.   General Electric: Topics to be Covered in Strategic Plans

1. The identification and formulation of environmental assumptions of strategic importance
2. The identification and in-depth analysis of competitors, including assumptions about their probable strategies
3. The analysis of the SBU's own resources
4. The development and evaluation of Strategic Alternatives
5. The preparation of the SBU Strategic Plan, including an estimate of capital spending for the next five years
6. The preparation of the SBU Operating Plan, which details the next year of the SBU Strategic Plan

SOURCE: Francis J. Aguilar and Richard G. Hamermesh, "General Electric: Strategic Position—1981," Case 9-381-174, (Boston, MA: Harvard Business School, revised March 1982), p. 5. Reprinted by permission.

a more structured process, to assure some degree of uniformity in the planning effort across all organizational units. However, firms which already have acquired a high degree of sophistication in this area could become much less dependent on a rigid format. For example, General Electric simply listed a set of topics to be covered by each SBU manager (see Figure 21–1).

The ensuing chapters cover the twelve steps in the strategic planning process. Although they represent a sequence in which every outcome of a given step conditions and enlightens the subsequent ones, it should not be interpreted as a rigid linear process. More often than not, in the middle of the process, one discovers that a given issue did not receive the proper attention and is forced to go back and resolve that question prior to continuing with the planning process.

We have chosen the case of Citibank Taipei, which we have adapted from a master thesis conducted by a Sloan Fellow at MIT,[1] to illustrate most of the steps in the implementation of this methodology. Sloan Fellows are experienced business managers who spent twelve months in a general management program leading to a master's degree at the Sloan School of Management. The strategic analysis reported should not be interpreted as the official strategic commitments of those organizations. They represent an academic effort to apply our strategic planning framework by MIT students under the supervision of Arnoldo Hax.

To avoid unnecessary repetitions, we are not going to cover the descriptive material already presented for each step in Chapter 2 and expanded in Parts II, III, and IV. The reader should keep in mind that content for a more fruitful reading of the material in this part.

Figure 21–2 reproduces the sequence of twelve steps which we have adopted for the strategic planning process; and Figure 21–3 provides background information on Citibank Taipei, a branch of Citibank in the capital city of Taiwan.

FIGURE 21–2. The Twelve Steps of Strategic Planning

Hierarchical Levels of Planning	Structural Conditioners	Planning Cycle		
		Strategy Formulation	Strategic Programming	Strategic and Operational Planning
Corporate	①– – –▶②	⑥	⑨	⑫
Business	③– – –▶④	⑦	⑩	
Functional		⑤	⑧	⑪

① (a) Vision of the firm: mission of the firm, business segmentation, horizontal and vertical integration, corporate philosophy, special strategic issues
   (b) Managerial infrastructure, corporate culture, and management of key personnel

② Strategic posture and planning guidelines: corporate strategic thrusts, planning challenges at corporate, business, and functional levels, and corporate performance objectives

③ The mission of the business: business scope, ways to compete, and identification of product-market segments

④ Formulation of business strategy and broad action programs

⑤ Formulation of functional strategy: participation of business planning, concurrence or nonconcurrence to business strategy proposals, broad action programs

⑥ Consolidation of business and functional strategies, portfolio management, and assignment of resource allocation priorities

⑦ Definition and evaluation of specific action programs at the business level

⑧ Definition and evaluation of specific action programs at the functional level

⑨ Resource allocation and definition of performance measurements for management control

⑩ Budgeting at the business level

⑪ Budgeting at the functional level

⑫ Budgeting consolidations, and approval of strategic and operational funds

FIGURE 21-3. Background Information on Citibank Taipei (1986)

Citibank is a major corporation with subsidiaries all over the world. The illustration presented is based on Citibank Taipei, the largest foreign bank in the country, and is referred specifically to the lending strategy to be applied by the corporate Banking Group to motorcycle manufacturers, a mature industry in Taiwan, with some basic weaknesses from the point of view of the bank.

This section presents some of the characteristics of commercial banking in Taiwan, highlighting the need for an effective lending strategy in mature industries. Also a description of the motorcycle industry in Taiwan is included.

COMMERCIAL BANKING IN TAIWAN

Banking was strictly regulated in Taiwan in the past. It is generally agreed that the banking and finance sectors in Taiwan were previously unable to meet the growing demands for credits spurred by rapid industrialization and economic growth. Rigid collateral requirements of local banks restrained business growth and led to a flourishing unofficial money market where funds were offered at very high rates to borrowers. To fit the financial needs of local industries, foreign banks provided these industries with a wide range of financial services.

DOMESTIC COMMERCIAL BANKS

Taiwan's 24 domestic commercial banks extend similar interest rates and follow the same basic lending procedures. The government controls 12 major local banks, the rest being privately owned. The total net assets of all domestic banks were NT$1,813.6 billion (U.S. $45.3 billion equivalent) as of Janaury 1, 1985, representing 60% of the total net assets held by Taiwan's Financial institutions.

Except for the Export-Import Bank of China, domestic banks are restricted from extending more than 25% of their net worth to a single customer. Most banks provide mainly short-term credit, export financing services, and guarantees for commercial paper issuance. Although the personal relationship between the banker and borrower carries much weight in obtaining a credit line, they are usually granted on security considerations and the borrower's credit standing. Therefore, most loans extended by local banks are well secured.

FOREIGN COMMERCIAL BANKS

The number of foreign banks in Taipei as of June 30, 1985, was 32, including 14 American, 10 European, and 2 Canadian, 2 from Singapore, and the rest from Hong Kong, Japan, and other countries. Foreign banks provide basically the same services as do the local banks. However, there are several restrictions on foreign bank operations:

- The local currency demand and time deposits of foreign banks cannot exceed 12.5 times their paid-in capital, or NT$2 billion, whichever is lower.

- Foreign banks may not lend to an individual customer more than 7% of their total credit extended to customers.

- The extension of all foreign currency loans is subject to the approval of the Central Bank of China.

- Export promotion loans (pre-export financing) extended by a foreign bank cannot exceed $6 million U.S. dollars within one week.

- Guaranty of commercial paper issuance is limited to 5 times a foreign bank branch's net worth.

All foreign banks have some problems in local currency funding because of limited sources. Also, the rapid increase in the number of foreign bank branches, including the introduction of Citibank Taipei, in 1981, has intensified the competition in the banking industry.

FIGURE 21–3. Background Information on Citibank Taipei (1986) (continued)

PREVAILING SITUATION (1986): THE NEED FOR AN EFFECTIVE LENDING STRATEGY IN MATURE INDUSTRIES

Banks are currently in the midst of what is probably the worst credit environment in Taiwan's history, with an unprecedented series of bankruptcies of both large and medium-sized companies. Reasons include the prolonged recession, vulnerable industry structure, and, in most individual cases, poor management. A significant contributing factor in the over-extension of many companies has been the availability of cheap and easy (unsecured) credit from the 15 new foreign banks which have opened branches in Taiwan over the past three years. The foreign banking community, with its many new banks, has been especially hard hit. It is estimated that foreign banks in Taiwan as a whole wrote off their aggregate capital in 1983, and 75% of them suffered operating losses in 1984. Accumulated problem loans among foreign banks as of early 1985 reached a record high of half a billion U.S. dollars. Wells Fargo Bank withdrew its representative office from Taipei in May 1985, partly because of its internal policy to reduce international business, and partly because of the unsatisfactory credit environment in Taiwan.

Under this scenario, it is crucial to develop an effective lending strategy to better fit long-term outlooks and the bank's current positioning, a key component being to manage effectively the loan portolio to an industry throughout its life cycle. It is especially important for a bank to set up target market strategy and credit acceptance criteria for a mature industry. This will give the account officers a more controlled prospect identification system and qualification screen for present clients.

Note

Chin-Tain Chiu, "Commercial Lending Strategy for Mature Industry: The Case of the Motorcycle Industry in Taiwan," unpublished master thesis, Sloan School of Management (Cambridge, MA: MIT, May 1986).

CHAPTER 22

Step 1: The Vision of the Firm

The vision of the firm is a permanent statement to communicate the nature of the existence of the organization in terms of corporate purpose, business scope, and competitive leadership; to provide the framework that regulates the relationships among the firm and its primary stakeholders; and to state the broad objectives of the firm's performance.

The primary components of the vision of the firm are:

- the mission of the firm
- business segmentation (identification of SBUs)
- horizontal strategy and vertical integration (SBUs' interactions)
- corporate philosophy
- special strategic issues

Also, as part of this first step in the strategic planning process, we have to consider the managerial infrastructure, the corporate culture, and the management of key personnel.

The Mission of the Firm

This is a statement of current and future expected product, market, and geographical scope, as well as a way to attain competitive leadership.

Figure 22–1 provides the mission statement for Citibank Taipei. The premise of the branch's mission is to offer an array of products and services to all of its market segments where a customer need has been established. Corporate banking has been a highly profitable segment and continues to serve as a major market for the branch. The bank will also continue its active participation in legislative reform, since many of the laws and regulations in existence today preclude foreign banks' activities in various product-market and geographical segments within Taiwan.

FIGURE 22–1. Mission Statement of Citibank Taipei

	CURRENT	FUTURE
PRODUCT SCOPE	Provide corporate customers with financial services including electronic cash management, trade services, foreign exchange investment advisory service, and project finance Build products and services generating fee-based revenue	Expand product scope by delivering a broader range of integrated financial services Continue to develop fee and commission-based products Emphasize product differentiation through expertise and innovation
MARKET SCOPE	Provide products and services to government, private corporations, and financial institutions through integrated services and global communications network	Limit to large customers and selected middle market names only Participate in capital market at home and abroad
GEOGRAPHICAL SCOPE	Major parts of Taiwan	Expand geographic boundaries of banking within Taiwan, including additional branches outside Taipei
WAYS TO ACHIEVE COMPETITIVE LEADERSHIP	Hire and keep talented people	Increase efficiency, market share, and product service expertise Continue new product development Active participation in legislative reform

Identification of SBUs

The cornerstone of the strategic planning process is the segmentation of the firm's activities in terms of business units (SBUs). An SBU can be defined as an operating unit or a planning focus that sells a distinct set of products or services to an identifiable group of customers in competition with a well-defined set of competitors. The SBU represents the level of analysis where most of the strategic planning effort is centered.

Citibank Taipei's core business lies in three areas:

1. *Commercial Banking:* Corporate Banking Group (CBG) offers a wide range of corporate financial services to government and corporations. CBG is the most important segment in the Taipei branch, contributing 70 percent of the branch's total earning. CBG is divided into multinational and local groups according to the ownership of corporate customers and is segmented by industries.

2. *Travelers' Check (TC):* Citibank is the largest bank in Taiwan issuing travelers' checks. Its market share is around 70 percent. Due to local regulations, foreign banks in Taiwan cannot sell travelers' checks directly to the Taiwanese. Therefore, distribution is made through local banks' branch offices throughout the island. The travelers' check business has grown rapidly since touring abroad was opened to the public in 1973. The profit of the TC department accounts for 20 percent of total earnings of the branch. In 1984, the department's turnover reached U.S. $25 million on travelers' checks.

3. *Financial Institution and Treasury:* Financial institution (FI) is responsible for interbank relations. It deals with the subject of correspondent banking and provides other banks with collection and remittance services, takes care of foreign transactions, supplies credit information, and assistance on loans.

The treasury function is to match the sources and uses of funds. Its objectives are designed to enable the bank to maintain solvency and to meet liquidity requirements without exposing itself to unusual pressure. It also takes position through buying and selling foreign exchanges.

Although FI and Treasury are support departments, they are treated as profit centers and each has external competitors and services an external market. Therefore, they are also classified as SBUs.

Horizontal Strategy and Vertical Integration

Horizontal strategy is a coordinated set of goals and policies across distinct but interrelated business units. Defining horizontal strategy requires searching for and exploiting potential interrelationships among the various businesses of the firm. There are three types of possible interrelationships:

1. *Tangible interrelationships,* arising from opportunities to share activities in the value chain.
2. *Intangible interrelationships,* involving the transference of management know-how among separate value chains. Similarities among two or more businesses should be sought after, either in type of buyer, or type of purchase by buyer, or type of manufacturing process, and so on.
3. *Competitor interrelationships,* stemming from the existence of rivals that actually or potentially compete with a firm in more than one industry.

Vertical integration involves a set of decisions addressing:

1. The boundaries a firm should establish over its generic activities on the value chain (the question of make versus buy).
2. The relationship of the firm with constituents outside its boundaries, particularly suppliers, distributors, and customers.
3. The identification of circumstances under which those boundaries and relationships should be changed to enhance the firm's competitive position.

For Citibank Taipei, vertical integration is not an issue. With regard to horizontal strategy, this is represented in the form of shared resources (tangible

RESOURCE	SBU NAME		
	CBG	TC	FI/ Treasury
Potential sharing of the same markets generates overall interdependence	X	X	X
Capital base	X	X	X
Transferrable human resources	X	X	X
Account relationship officer	X	X	X
Global communication network	X	X	X
Treasury funding activity and exchange transaction	X		X

X = Indicates sharing of resources.

interrelationships) and shared concerns (intangible interrelationships). Competitor interrelationships are not relevant for this case.

The resources in the banking industry are people, capital, and systems. The potential for sharing them among the three businesses of Citibank Taipei is indicated in Figure 22–2. The interrelationships which exist for the branch suggest a critical need for cooperation among different businesses, especially where customer needs are served and where the effective placement of human resources becomes important. The dependance of Treasury on the account relationship team within CBG in order to position its services exemplifies further the need to consider these dimensions in developing a strategy.

The potential for sharing concerns is presented in Figure 22–3. It stresses further the need for ample coordination among business units to provide adequate satisfaction to customers' needs, mainly under a strict regulatory environment.

FIGURE 22–3. Citibank Taipei: Intangible Interrelationships
Identification of Shared Concerns

CONCERN	SBU NAME		
	CBG	TC	FI/ Treasury
Servicing major client's needs	X	X	X
Domestic market	X	X	X
Industries	X		
Foreign bank entry	X		X
Market segmentation	X	X	X
Product/service packing and delivery	X	X	X
Funding cost	X		
Interest/credit/liquidity risk assessment	X	X	X

X = Indicates sharing of concerns.

Corporate Philosophy

Corporate philosophy is a subtle but fundamental part of the corporate vision of the firm. A well-formulated corporate philosophy contains:

1. An articulation of the relationship between the firm and its primary stakeholders, employees, customers, shareholders, debtholders, suppliers, communities and government.
2. A definition of broad objectives of the firm's expected performance, primarily in terms of growth and profitability
3. A formulation of corporate policies based on management style, organizational policies, human resources management, financial policies, marketing, and technology
4. A statement of corporate values—ethics, beliefs, and rules of personal and corporate behavior.

In Figure 22–4 we present the corporate philosophy of Citibank Taipei.

Special Strategic Issues

The vision of the firm held by executives is profoundly affected by major environmental shifts that put certain trends or new practices of management in the limelight of attention. Since the late 1980s, there are three issues that should be given special consideration: the unstoppable tendency toward global markets, the ubiquitousness and acceleration of technological change, and the need for new and more agile forms of leadership and organization to confront successfully new challenges.

Citibank Taipei is a national branch of a global giant. The international game is being played in headquarters, but the branch is well aware of its position in this endeavor. On the other hand, Citibank has been a prime innovator in technology and management practices in the banking industry, and this drive is clearly captured in the statement of philosophy by Citibank Taipei.

Managerial Infrastructure, Corporate Culture, and Management of Key Personnel

The managerial infrastructure is the organizational structure and the set of formal administrative systems of a firm, mainly the planning, management control, human resources management and rewards, and communication and information systems.

The corporate culture is the underlying set of values, ideas, beliefs, rules of conduct, and basic assumptions shared by all members of the organization that powerfully shape personal behavior and interactions among individuals in a firm.

FIGURE 22–4. Citibank Taipei: Corporate Philosophy

RELATIONSHIP WITH PRIMARY STAKEHOLDERS

EMPLOYEES

The relationship with its employees can be described as tough but fair, where one's intelligence, wit, and energy, without regard to sex or creed, can become the driving force in predicting how far one can move within the corporation. Its objectives are to offer employees a challenging and stable working environment, above-average compensations, and to build mutual respect, confidence, and trust in personal relationships based upon commitments to integrity, honesty, openness, and competence.

CUSTOMERS

Satisfying the needs of our customers is fundamental to our survival and prosperity. These needs can best be understood in terms of support we lend in helping our customers meet their financial objectives. Our goal is to provide superior products and services which offer innovative solutions to our customers' problems. We must understand the business of our customers and establish long-term relationships based on performance and integrity.

BROAD CORPORATE OBJECTIVES

As the branch looks ahead toward the future by moving through the coming decade, its efforts will be guided by the following corporate goals:

Continue the development and implementation of products available to the local market which will quickly benefit from Citibank's position, distribution, and resource leadership in Taiwan.

Maintain steady business growth and sustained profitability. Achieve 8 to 10% annual profit center earning (PCE) growth rate, ROE in excess of 25% and ROA in excess of 1.20%.

Maintain a preeminent position as a cross-border bank

Maintain reputation in marketplace for being aggressive, innovative, and supportive

CORPORATE POLICIES

TECHNOLOGICAL POLICY

Citibank has a strong commitment to technology development, because information about money is becoming almost as important as money itself. The branch recognizes that its customers will be looking for information-based services on a global scale, and in order to respond to that technology will become a major force.

The branch will continue to dedicate itself to developing its ability to deliver prompt, accurate information electronically to the corporate treasurer's desk. The branch is also aimed at achieving efficient, low-cost electronic delivery of its key products, and maintaining its market leadership in processing, delivery technology, and communication technology.

MANAGEMENT STYLE

Managerial resources are vital to Citibank's achievement of financial leadership and therefore it is committed to a system where talented and capable people are recognized, tracked, and given opportunities to develop their skills and assume greater responsibilities. This system involves consistent line management review of performance and career development plans of each officer from every organizational level. Generally speaking, Citibank is an open society that encourages people to speak their mind. Two-way communication is emphasized while participation in decision-making processes is highly encouraged.

CREDIT POLICY

Lending is the essence of commercial banking, consequently, a well-conceived credit policy and careful lending practices are essential if a bank is to perform its credit-creating function effectively and minimize the risk inherent in any extension of credit. Credit policy

FIGURE 22–4. Continued

should, in every case, be reduced to writing, since only then will they be clearly and uniformly understood. The policy needs periodic review in the light of ever-changing conditions in the market.

The purpose of the credit policy is to guide officers in balancing the quality and quantity of the loan portfolio to achieve earning objectives while also meeting appropriate credit needs, maintaining proper credit standards, holding risk to reasonable limits, minimizing losses, evaluating new business opportunities, adjusting to changes in the regulatory environment, and providing adequate liquidity.

A sound credit policy should consider dedicating some time and effort to:

Assess the needs of the credit market the bank serves or intends to serve

Determine the size of the loan portfolio and search out opportunities to make sound loans

Justify if a loan is made for a sound purpose and if the repayments are realistically scheduled to flow from the liquidation of the transaction being financed

Outline the criteria in evaluating a credit package and gain collaterals if necessary

Specify the lending limit of the bank and of the individual client. Specify also the size of loan-loss reserve and composition of the asset portfolio

CORPORATE VALUES

Citicorp's global network results in a highly decentralized structure. Citibankers are expected to make decisions and solve problems whenever they are assigned without a central decision-making authority. It is through its decentralization that Citibank ensures diversification in risk taking and enhances efficiency in business development.

Innovativeness is another characteristic of Citiculture. The ability of creativity, uniqueness, and a dauntless approach to problem solving have been emphasized in the organization. Citibankers share a passion to excel with an energetic commitment to be first in whatever needs to be done.

The management of key personnel is a major responsibility of top executives who must identify, develop, promote, compensate, and motivate talented executives to prepare them for the highest ranks of managerial cadres.

The vision of the firm is intimately related to these three managerial concerns. In fact, if the vision is to become a basic driver of activities in the company, it has to be:

1. Represented in the organizational structure in the form of strategic and operational units, and in proper coordinating mechanisms
2. Aligned with all formal management processes, mainly the management control and reward systems
3. Fitted with the corporate culture and cogent with expectations of individuals in the firm
4. Translated into the management policies of key personnel.

At Citibank Taipei, the organization, management systems, and culture are patterned after the mold imposed by Citicorp all over the world. The organizational structure is defined around decentralized business-oriented divisions (derived from Corporate Banking, Personal Banking, and Investment Banking), and the management control and reward systems stress competitive and aggressive profit-seeking behavior throughout management ranks. To develop fully this illustration would require inordinate amounts of detail about intimate aspects of the firm, so the example is not further expanded.

CHAPTER 23

Step 2: The Development of the Strategic Posture of the Firm

The strategic posture is a pragmatic and concrete set of guidelines which serves as an immediate challenge for the development of strategic proposals at the business and major functional levels of the firm. It is expressed primarily by (1) corporate strategic thrusts, (2) corporate, business, and functional planning challenges, and (3) corporate performance objectives.

As shown in Figure 23–1, for its derivation it is important to have completed the vision of the firm, because it provides the broad framework for strategy formulation. Two additional steps are also required: (1) environmental scan at the corporate level, and (2) internal scrutiny at the corporate level.

Environmental Scan at the Corporate Level

The environmental scan attempts to diagnose the general health of the industrial sectors relevant to the corporation's business. It concentrates on assessing the overall economic, political, technological, social, and legal climates that affect the corporation as a whole. This assessment should be conducted first, from a historical perspective; and second, from the perspective of future trends in the environment.

The output of the environmental scan normally starts with the statement of an economic overview which exhibits the most likely trends affecting the next planning cycle. Possibly, the development of contingency plans addressing either optimistic or pessimistic departures from this most likely trend are included. Other topics in this economic overview are:

- economic growth—GNP and major influencing factors
- inflation rate
- prime interest rate

FIGURE 23–1. The Vision of the Firm and Its Strategic Posture

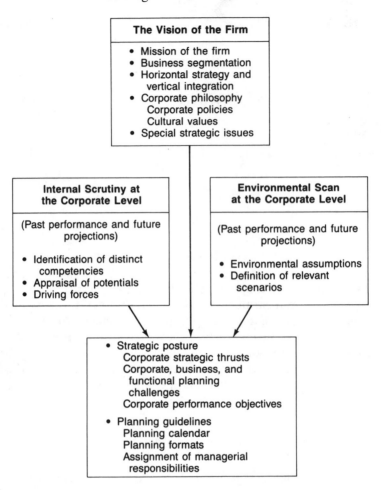

The Vision of the Firm

- Mission of the firm
- Business segmentation
- Horizontal strategy and vertical integration
- Corporate philosophy Corporate policies Cultural values
- Special strategic issues

Internal Scrutiny at the Corporate Level

(Past performance and future projections)

- Identification of distinct competencies
- Appraisal of potentials
- Driving forces

Environmental Scan at the Corporate Level

(Past performance and future projections)

- Environmental assumptions
- Definition of relevant scenarios

- Strategic posture Corporate strategic thrusts Corporate, business, and functional planning challenges Corporate performance objectives
- Planning guidelines Planning calendar Planning formats Assignment of managerial responsibilities

- unemployment
- overview of foreign markets, and foreign exchange rate considerations
- population growth in critical geographical areas
- disposable income
- growth of critical industrial sectors, such as housing, defense, health, and so forth

A second component of the environmental scan is a broad assessment of basic external factors which includes a summary of the economic overview and of global trends in primary markets. It considers also a brief analysis of technological trends, supply of human resources, political events, and social and legal issues, among other factors which might be deemed relevant. This effort is oriented toward the identification of important developments expected in the future and major opportunities and threats, in each one of the preceding dimensions.

The environmental scanning is completed with the definition of pessimistic and optimistic planning scenarios, which give insights into the kinds of contingencies that can be met in the future, and that the organization should be prepared to deal with.

Citibank Taipei: Environmental Scan at the Corporate Level—Economic Overview

The overview for the Taiwanese economy is presented in Figure 23–2. A moderate growth of the country and a positive trend of disposable personal income are forecasted. Prices have been stable for the past three years, and inflation is expected to remain low. Interest rates have remained extremely low during the past years and no changes are expected in this matter. Population growth rate is around 1.5 percent per annum, and unemployment rate has been tending upward in recent years mainly because of the stagnant economic condition and low incentives of private investments.

The economy of Taiwan has been highly dependent on trades with exports making up over 50 percent of GNP in 1984. In recent years, there has been a serious trend toward increased protectionism in the world markets and toward retaliation for serious and chronic trade imbalances. This could weaken Taiwan's economic growth rate for the coming years. Besides, it is essential to

FIGURE 23–2. Citibank Taipei: Environmental scan at the Corporate Level

Taiwan Economic Overview*

	PAST YEARS						CURRENT	PROJECTIONS		
	78	*79*	*80*	*81*	*82*	*83*	*84*	*85*	*86*	*87*
GNP (at constant price of 1976)	12.0	8.6	4.2	5.4	4.0	8.6	11.4	12.1	12.8	13.7
INFLATION (consumer price 1981 = 100)	5.8	9.7	19.0	16.3	3.4	1.8	1.7	2.0	2.3	2.6
UNEMPLOYMENT**	1.0	0.7	0.7	0.8	1.2	1.6	1.4	1.8	2.5	2.3
POPULATION GROWTH	1.9	2.0	1.9	1.9	1.8	1.5	1.5	1.4	1.4	1.3
DISPOSABLE PERSONAL INCOME	16.1	19.4	24.8	19.9	8.3	10.4	12.0	12.6	13.2	13.9

* Annual Growth Rates
** Refers to civilian labor force only

SOURCE: "1985 Taiwan Statistical Data Book" Council for Economic Planning and Development, ROC.

upgrade Taiwan's industrial base toward a more capital- and technology-intensive industrial sector to overcome the problems of rising real wages and the loss of comparative advantage in cheap abundant labor to other developing countries in Asia. An Economic Reform Committee (ERC) was formed in 1985 to respond to these problems and to evaluate the country's economic and financial structure, and to recommend the government appropriate strategies.

BROAD ASSESSMENT OF BASIC EXTERNAL FACTORS

Figure 23–3 presents a summary of the main considerations with regard to the economic overview, primary market overview, technological trends, political and social events, legal issues, and supply of human resources.

A moderate economic recovery is expected to stimulate credit demand. However, because of banks' large unsatisfactory portfolio, a transition period of tighter credit is forecasted, to permit banks a reduction of their potential losses. Banking strategies of financial institutions will be modified. Cost reduction will continue playing a major role in the future and regulatory freedom is anticipated to allow foreign banks to expand their business in Taiwan. Therefore, enhancing their competitive edge will be the major task of financial institutions in the future.

DEFINITION OF ALTERNATIVE PLANNING SCENARIOS

Figure 23–4 presents the basic optimistic and pessimistic scenarios, which are defined basically in terms of economic growth perspectives for Taiwan.

Internal Scrutiny at the Corporate Level

The internal scrutiny is concerned with a broad evaluation of the human, financial, productive, physical, and technological resources of the corporation, with the purpose of identifying the firm's distinct competitive strengths. The basic purpose of this task is to assist in the identification of the distinct competencies of the firm as a whole (strengths), as well as the required competencies which are not yet present, but need to be developed (weaknesses). The tool suggested to guide this effort is the value chain, which permits focusing sequentially in each one of the major functions with a corporate perspective.

The main strengths (distinct competencies) and weaknesses (required competencies) for Citibank Taipei are:

Strengths:
1. large and well-diversified customer base

FIGURE 23–3. Citibank Taipei: Environmental Scan at the Corporate Level

Broad Assessment of Basic External Factors

	PAST	FUTURE	MAJOR OPPORTUNITIES AND THREATS
ECONOMIC OVERVIEW	*1978–1981* • Moderate growth, high inflation, low employment *1982–1984* • Growth rate slowdown, low inflation, low interest rates • World recession	• Moderate economic growth, with inflation under control • Moderate world economic recovery but incentives of private investment could be low in spite of continuing low interest rates • Moderate U.S. recovery anticipated	• Sustained economic recovery will improve credit demand • Provide opportunity in trade financing
PRIMARY MARKET	• Growth opportunity narrowed due to slowdown of economy and intensifying competition among banks • Weak industry structure and below-average financial standing • Unsatisfactory credit environment forces banks to take conservative loan policy	• Increasing competition among banks • Specific growth markets: multinational companies, exporter/importer • Industry reshuffle or shakeout • Tightening liquidity in middle market, resulting from bank's pulling back and company's weak capital structure	• Emphasize foreign exchange transactions, fee-based/non-credit services • Loan loss provision increased
TECHNOLOGICAL TRENDS	• Computer technology increased efficiency • Little customer automation	• Integration of financial services • Rapid customer automation	• Reduction in cost due to computerization
POLITICAL AND SOCIAL EVENTS	• Recent political movement toward open door policy of foreign bank entry • Political stability	• Political concerns over deregulation of banking system • Pursue stability in the financial system	• Lobbying effort will play an important role • Opportunity for improved competitive position
LEGAL ISSUES	• Current regulation restricting product diversification and geographic expansion • Constraints on providing comprehensive financial services to all market segments	• Changes in legislation including a lowering of product and place restrictions • Complete regulatory freedom expected	• Time allowed for strategic positioning in preparation for deregulation
SUPPLY OF HUMAN RESOURCES	• Good performance and well-developed corporate image attracted talented people	• Competition in attracting best people • Continuing emphasis on training and development of employees	• Efforts to hire, keep and develop best people

349

FIGURE 23–4. Citibank Taipei: Environmental Scan at the Corporate Level

Definition of Alternative Planning Scenarios

	OPTIMISTIC	PESSIMISTIC
GENERAL DESCRIPTION	• Brisk world economic recovery • Sharp increase in domestic GNP growth • High demand for credit	• Long period of sluggish economic growth • Increased protectionism • Reduction in credit demand
PRIMARY MARKET OVERVIEW	• Favorable credit environment	• Cut-throat competition, mainly among foreign banks
TECHNOLOGICAL TRENDS	• Rapid adoption of information technologies	• Uneven pace in the adoption of information technologies makes competition sharper
POLITICAL AND LEGAL ISSUES	• Regulatory freedom	• Tighten regulation

2. global communication network connecting major operations within 92 countries
3. high-caliber staff with professional expertise
4. market leadership in technology
5. innovativeness in financial services delivery and favorable corporate image provides for customer attraction
6. good management system with high decentralization
7. risk-taking ability and willingness.

Weaknesses:
1. lack of complete understanding of the cost dynamics of the business
2. regulatory constraints on the scope of business
3. increasing customer complains about bureaucracy, tedious procedures, and tight security requirement
4. increasing personnel bottleneck with middle management and high turnover of junior account officers
5. uncompetitive pricing leads the bank to lose market share
6. weak motivation and reward system
7. loan portfolio quality needs to be improved

Corporate Strategic Thrusts and Planning Challenges

Corporate strategic thrusts are the primary issues the firm has to address in the next three to five years to establish a healthy competitive position. The strategic thrusts should contain specific and meaningful planning challenges

FIGURE 23-5. Citibank Taipei: Statement of Strategic Thrusts and Assignment of Planning Challenges

STRATEGIC THRUSTS	CORPORATE LEVEL	BUSINESS			FUNCTIONS	
		CBG	TC	FI/Treasury	Human Resources	Operations
1. Significantly improve the motivation and reward system and provide more emphasis on strategic and long-term performance	2	1	1	1	1	1
2. Maintain leading position as most profitable bank by becoming a low-cost, high-efficiency producer of financial services	1	1	1	1	3	3
3. Maintain a good credit portfolio and reduce potential credit loss	2	1	–	–	3	3
4. Establish a means whereby new earnings streams can be generated through innovation and product development	3	1	1	1	–	–
5. Increase market share selectively and eliminate unprofitable or risky accounts	3	1	1	–	–	–
6. Expand business by establishing additional branches geographically and by tapping investment banking business	1	1	2	2	3	3
7. Continue lobbying efforts to ease banking regulation	1	2	2	3	–	3
8. Improve customer service quality by enhancing efficiency	2	1	1	1	–	1

Code: 1   Vital
2   Important
3   Secondary
–   Not applicable

351

FIGURE 23–6. Citibank Taipei: Derivation of Corporate Strategic Thrusts

---

Formulation of Corporate Strategic Thrusts

Changes in Mission

- Expansion of product scope and emphasis on product differentiation
- Concentration on upper-end market plus selected middle market names
- Establishment of additional branches
- Efficiency improvement, effective cost control, and new product development

---

Strengths and Weaknesses

Strengths

- Large customer base, global network
- Risk-taking ability and willingness
- High-caliber staff
- Leadership in technology and good innovation capability
- Good management system with high decentralization

Weaknesses

- Limitation on business scope
- Increasing customer complaints about efficiency
- Increasing turnover of junior account officers
- Weak motivation and reward system
- Unsatisfactory loan portfolio quality

Opportunities and Threats

Opportunities

- Gradual economy recovery provides business opportunity
- Cost reduction through automation
- Anticipated deregulation of banking system provides business potential

Threats

- Tightening liquidity of middle market names would increase loan loss
- Increasing competition and rivalry among banks
- Ability to keep and develop high potential staff

Strategic Thrusts

1. Improve motivation and reward system, training and development program, and provide more emphasis on strategic and long-term performance
2. Maintain leading position as most profitable bank by becoming a low-cost, high-efficiency producer of financial services
3. Maintain good credit portfolio and reduce potential credit loss
4. Establish a means whereby new earning streams can be generated through innovation and new product development
5. Grow market share selectively and eliminate unprofitable/shaky accounts
6. Expand business by establishing additional branches geographically and by tapping investment banking business
7. Continue lobbying efforts to ease banking regulation
8. Improve customer service quality by enhancing efficiency

FIGURE 23–7. Citibank Taipei: Corporate Performance Objectives

PERFORMANCE INDICATORS	PAST YEARS			CURRENT YEAR	OBJECTIVES
	1982	*1983*	*1984*	*1985*	
Return on equity*	29	29	24	25	25
Return on assets*	1.10	1.13	0.94	0.98	1.20

* Shown as a percentage.

addressed at the corporate level, each business unit of the firm, and some key centralized functions.

The strategic thrusts are the recipients of all the analysis conducted so far, and they should be articulated in such a way as to convey a sense of the critical tasks that every unit in the organization has to deal with, in order to develop an effective strategic position.

For Citibank Taipei, the definition of strategic thrusts and the assignment of planning challenges at all levels in the firm is presented in Figure 23–5. As observed, each thrust requires a different kind of commitment from corporate, business, and functional units. Figure 23–6 illustrates the interrelationship among the various phases discussed so far, which leads to the identification of strategic thrusts.

Corporate Performance Objectives

Corporate performance objectives are quantitative indicators related to the overall performance of the firm. Typically, they are financial objectives related to total revenue, profit performance, and growth rate.

By articulating broad financial expectations, the corporation adds to the challenges implicit in the strategic thrusts but, at the same time, provides a more realistic framework to guide the desirability of proposed action programs that will emerge from the subsequent steps in the strategic planning process.

This task requires first the selection of a few key indicators, which are essential proxies of the successful performance of the corporation, and then the assignment of historical as well as target values for each one of them.

The performance indicators for Citibank Taipei are expressed solely in terms of profitability, as shown in Figure 23–7. Citibank is not interested in being the largest financial institution, but in being the most profitable one. Therefore, the asset size is not listed as a performance indicator. It is the returns which count.

CHAPTER 24

Step 3: The Mission of the Business

The mission of the business follows exactly the same characterization as the mission of the firm, except that it is conducted at a more detailed level to get a sharper understanding of each SBU. The mission of a business is a statement of the current and future expected product, market, and geographical scopes, and a definition of the way to attain competitive leadership.

The statement of mission is particularly informative of the changes that are being considered by top management.

Citibank Taipei: The Motorcycle Industry Unit
Statement of Mission

The motorcycle industry business is a unit in the Corporate Banking Group of Citibank Taipei. The main thrust of this unit is to provide banking services to companies in the motorcycle industry, particularly loans, complying with the bank's portfolio management objectives and generating profitable levels of fee income. The credit risk involved with weak accounts should be minimized through reducing unsatisfactory loan portfolio previously extended to the customers.

Figure 24–1 presents the mission statement of the motorcycle industry business. The changes point unmistakably toward a selective pruning of loans, and a reduction of the bank's commitments in the industry.

FIGURE 24–1. Citibank Taipei: The Motorcycle Industry Unit Statement of Mission

	CURRENT	FUTURE
PRODUCT SCOPE	Core products to provide • working capital • trade financing • project financing	Products to finance working capital needs and trade transactions only
MARKET SCOPE	Target market is set at middle/high segments	Focus on top industry names only
GOEGRAPHICAL SCOPE	Only Taiwan	Maintain geographical scope
WAYS TO ACHIEVE COMPETITIVE LEADERSHIP	Innovative structuring in package deal Investment in back office technology and position the business against industry segments Tighten security requirement to improve bank's position	Develop broader base of skilled relationship manager and establish product packaging technique Liquidate loan outstandings of unjustified accounts and only retain acceptable credit portfolio

CHAPTER 25

Step 4: Formulation of Business Strategy and Broad Action Programs

A business strategy is a set of objectives supported by well-coordinated action programs aimed at establishing a long-term sustainable advantage over competitors. At this stage, we are interested in addressing the general direction the business should follow, expressed in terms of broad action programs defined over a multiyear planning horizon. In subsequent steps, each of these broad action programs will have to be defined by means of a set of specific action programs with a clear implementation purpose.

The business strategy is derived from (see Figure 25–1):

- the corporate strategic thrusts and planning challenges which are relevant to the business unit
- the mission of the business
- environmental scan at the business level
- internal scrutiny at the business level

The first two tasks from the preceding list have already been accomplished; therefore, we proceed now by commenting on the last two tasks prior to the development of a business strategy.

Environmental Scan at the Business Level

The environmental scan at the business level attempts to identify the degree of attractiveness of the industry in which the business belongs. We discuss two ways of performing this task.

ASSESSMENT OF INDUSTRY ATTRACTIVENESS

The first methodology is based on the identification of noncontrollable external factors, through the following steps indicated in Chapter 6:

FIGURE 25–1. Formulation of Business Strategy and Broad Action Programs

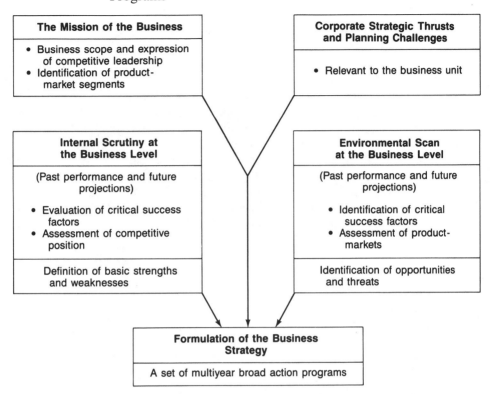

- Identify the external factors, outside the control of business managers, which impact each SBU.
- Measure the degree of attractiveness of each of these factors in relation to the firm's "average business base," both for current state and future projections.
- Determine the opportunities and threats associated with each SBU.

PORTER'S FRAMEWORK FOR INDUSTRY ANALYSIS

An alternative methodology to conduct the environmental scan at the business level is the model proposed by Porter, as discussed in Chapter 5. The forces that determine the profitability of an industry are:

- barriers to entry
- barriers to exit
- rivalry among competitors
- power of buyers
- power of suppliers
- availability of substitutes
- government actions

The task to be performed is to assess how these forces are affecting the SBU in order to determine the degree of attractiveness of its industry.

SELECTING BETWEEN THE TWO FRAMEWORKS

Our experience with the use of these two different frameworks to deal with environmental scan leads us to give a slight preference to the first method of analyzing the ongoing businesses of the firm. The mere process of extracting from managers the relevant factors for the analysis forces a useful and creative probing on their part, leading toward a more pragmatic diagnosis of the industry. Certainly, Porter's framework is quite enlightening and could be used in addition to the first method to further enrich the understanding of the environment. However, we have found Porter's framework, which deals with deeper structural factors of the industry rather than with more mundane managerial concerns, better in guiding the analysis of industries in which the firm does not operate but is considering a possible entry.

IDENTIFICATION OF OPPORTUNITIES
AND THREATS

The environmental scan should lead to the clear identification of the major forces affecting the industry attractiveness in the form of a short list of opportunities and threats faced by the business.

Citibank Taipei: The Motorcycle Unit
Environmental Scan at the Business Level

The essence of the problem being illustrated through the example of the Motorcycle Unit in Citibank Taipei is the formulation of a lending strategy for firms in the motorcycle industry. There is an added complication in the environmental analysis in a case like this, because Citibank's industry is certainly banking and its competitors are other banks and financial institutions. But the manager in charge of the Motorcycle Unit in Citibank Taipei also needs full awareness of developments and characteristics of the motorcycle industry. Consequently, the task is twice as hard in this case, and the environmental scan is presented for both the motorcycle and the banking industries.

AN ASSESSMENT OF THE MOTORCYCLE
INDUSTRY MATURITY AND PROFIT POTENTIAL

The analysis of the basic factors suggested by the Arthur D. Little methodology (Chapter 15) to determine the maturity of an industry indicates very clearly that the motorcycle industry is in the mature stage, as observed in Figure 25–2. Also, the industry analysis prepared with Porter's model shown in Figure

25–3 suggests that the potential for profit making is below average. This is due to its saturated demand, intense rivalry among existing competitors, increasing pressure from substitute products, and relatively high bargaining power of key parts suppliers.

ATTRACTIVENESS OF THE MARKET FOR BANK CREDIT TO THE MOTORCYCLE INDUSTRY

The methodology used for assessing the market attractiveness is based on the identification of key external factors and their evaluation relative to the average portfolio of business opportunities faced by Citibank Taipei. Figure 25–4 sum-

FIGURE 25–2. Determination of the Motorcycle Industry Maturity in Taiwan

DESCRIPTION	DEVELOPMENT STAGE			
	Embryonic	Growth	Mature	Aging
Market Growth Rate • slow growth rate since 1980			X	
Industry Potential • saturated market • no growth potential for domestic sales				X
Breadth of Product Lines • lines unchanged since late 1970 • fast product turnover			X	
Number of Competitors • stable • likely shake-out of marginal produc- ers			X ———→	
Market Share Stability • high stability despite a tendency to- ward concentration in Honda motor- cycles in later years			X ———→	
Purchasing Patterns • stable patterns based on status and income • well-known suppliers • established brand names			X	
Ease of Entry • low incentives for new entry • moderate economies of scale • high barriers to entry in a large scale operation (barriers are low for small producers)			X	
Technology • no significant change in 30 years			X	
Overall Assessment of Industry Matu- rity			X Mature	

FIGURE 25–3. Industry Analysis for the Motorcycle Industry in Taiwan

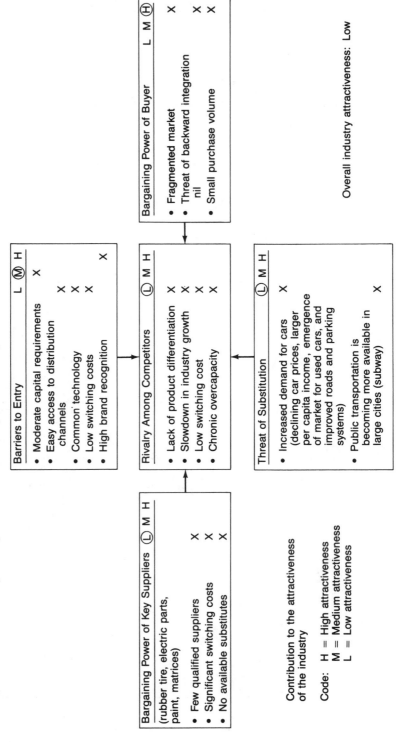

Barriers to Entry	L	Ⓜ	H
• Moderate capital requirements			X
• Easy access to distribution channels	X		
• Common technology	X		
• Low switching costs	X		
• High brand recognition			X

Bargaining Power of Key Suppliers	Ⓛ	M	H
(rubber tire, electric parts, paint, matrices)			
• Few qualified suppliers			X
• Significant switching costs			X
• No available substitutes			X

Rivalry Among Competitors	Ⓛ	M	H
• Lack of product differentiation	X		
• Slowdown in industry growth	X		
• Low switching cost	X		
• Chronic overcapacity	X		

Bargaining Power of Buyer	L	M	Ⓗ
• Fragmented market			X
• Threat of backward integration nil			X
• Small purchase volume			X

Threat of Substitution	Ⓛ	M	H
• Increased demand for cars (declining car prices, larger per capita income, emergence of market for used cars, and improved roads and parking systems)	X		
• Public transportation is becoming more available in large cities (subway)		X	

Contribution to the attractiveness of the industry

Code: H = High attractiveness
       M = Medium attractiveness
       L = Low attractiveness

Overall industry attractiveness: Low

360

FIGURE 25-4. Citibank Taipei: The Motorcycle Unit
Environmental Scan at the Business Level

Factors	Current State $- / - \quad - \quad E \quad + \quad + / +$	Comments
1. Market Factor • Market size • Market growth potential	fc	• Medium market size (US $120 million in 1984) • Limited growth potential due to stagnant economy and saturated demand for motorcycles
2. Account Profitability	f c	• Good accounts profit and return because of higher pricing • Concern with downsize credit risks
3. Credit Risk	f c	• Whole industry in poor condition due to chronic overcapacity, market saturation, eroding profitability, and weak financial structure • Unstable management • Tightening liquidity problem may lead to a shake-out
4. Industry Competitiveness • Competitive intensity • Barrier to entry • Barrier to exit • Availability of substitutes	f c f c f c f c	• Below average attractiveness because of saturated demand, high exit barrier, intense rivalry among existing competitors, increasing pressure from substitute products, and relatively high bargaining power of key parts suppliers
5. Industry Maturity	f c	• Mature industry with symptoms of moving toward an aging stage
6. Economic & Environmental • Structural change of Taiwan economy • Regulation • Overall credit environment	fc fc	• Increased protectionism in prolonging recessionary cycle in Taiwan • Air pollution regulation required for motorcycle retarded growth and increased costs • Poor credit environment with flourishing of economic crime

c = Current State
f = Future Projection

Key
−/−   Extremely unattractive industry
−   Mildly unattractive industry
E   Even or neutral
+   Mildly attractive industry
+/+   Extremely attractive industry

FIGURE 25–5. Citibank Taipei: The Motorcycle Unit
Summary of the Environmental Scan

	OVERALL ASSESSMENT OF INDUSTRY ATTRACTIVENESS		
	Low	*Medium*	*High*
CURRENT		C	
FUTURE	F		

marizes the considerations done in this respect. They lead to the categorization of the industry as *medium* in the overall assessment of attractiveness, shown in Figure 25–5, with an expected deterioration in the future due to the worsening of conditions in the motorcycle industry.

IDENTIFICATION OF OPPORTUNITIES
AND THREATS

An overall summary of those forces which represent opportunities and threats for the Motorcycle Unit is given in Figure 25–6.

Internal Scrutiny at the Business Level

The internal scrutiny at the business level attempts to identify the major strengths and weaknesses of the firm against its most relevant competitors.

FIGURE 25–6. Citibank Taipei: The Motorcycle Unit
Identification of Environmental Opportunities and Threats

OPPORTUNITIES

1. Significant profits contributed to the business unit
2. Business potential for top industry names

THREATS

1. Gloomy industry outlook with falling sales and profitability, chronic overcapacity, and saturated market demand; an industry shake-out is expected
2. Increasing credit risk because of poor financial structure and tightening liquidity problems
3. Frequent change in ownership of several companies represents a strong signal of management problems inside the organization
4. Unfavorable regulation regarding the ban on manufacturing large motorcycles and the restriction on air pollution issues hinder the industry growth and export potential
5. Overall unsatisfactory credit environment with economic crimes prevalent in the business circle

IDENTIFICATION OF THE MOST RELEVANT COMPETITORS

A relevant competitor is one who fulfills one or more of the following conditions:

From a market point of view

- It has a high market share.
- It has experienced a sustained market growth.
- It earns high levels of profitability with regard to the industry average.
- It has demonstrated an aggressive competitive attitude against your entire business or important segments.
- It has a highly vulnerable position against your own competitive actions.

From a functional point of view

- It has the lowest cost structure.
- It has the strongest technical base.
- It has the strongest marketing.
- It offers the best product quality.
- It shows the highest level of vertical integration.
- It exhibits the highest level of capacity utilization.

ASSESSMENT OF THE BUSINESS'S STRENGTHS AND WEAKNESSES

This assessment follows the methodology presented in Chapter 6.

- Determination of critical success factors, that is, those capabilities controllable by the firm, in which it has to excel in order to secure a long-term success over its competitors.
- Assessment of the business's strengths and weaknesses against each of the most relevant competitors.
- Identification of the overall strengths and weaknesses associated with the SBU.

One should realize that there is a major difference between the future projections in the environmental scan and in the internal scrutiny process. When we are dealing with uncontrollable processes, as is the case in the environmental scan process, we are making forecasts of the future. However, in the internal scrutiny phase, the future profiles represent not a forecast, but rather a desirable position that we would like to achieve against our leading competitors. This will have to be translated into a consistent set of action programs and resource deployment that would allow us to fulfill the desirable competitive profile.

IDENTIFICATION OF THE MOST RELEVANT COMPETITORS

The most relevant competitors of Citibank Taipei are foreign banks in Taiwan because local banks are large government-owned institutions with rigid security requirements, a more conservative lending policy, and are less sensitive to customer needs and market fluctuations. Figure 25–7 provides a profile of Bank of America, Chase Manhattan, and Bankers Trust, the three most important competitors.

ASSESSMENT OF CITIBANK TAIPEI'S STRENGTHS AND WEAKNESSES

The selection of key internal factors, mostly controllable by the firm, is the primary step for contrasting Citibank Taipei with its main competitors. The factors chosen are defined in Figure 25–8.

FIGURE 25–7. Citibank Taipei: The Motorcycle Unit
Internal Scrutiny at the Business Level—
Identification of the Most Relevant Competitors

BANK OF AMERICA (BOA)

BOA has been in the market as long as Citibank has in Taiwan (20 years). BOA also has a large customer base with expertise inside the bank. BOA's competitive edge against Citibank lies in its flexible pricing policy which gives it leverage to capture business in a competitive environment. BOA has changed its credit policy to be more conservative since three years ago, when several public-listed companies went bankrupt. BOA's performance in terms of profitability and ROE is just second to Citibank.

CHASE MANHATTAN

Chase is the third largest foreign bank in Taiwan. Its history in Taipei (12 years) is shorter than Citibank and BOA, but its performance is good. Chase has been very aggressive in pushing electronic banking projects. Its INFOCASH is widely regarded as a strong competitor of Citibanking for electronic cash management services. INFOCASH provides a full array of cash reporting and transaction processing services, including cash account balances, real-time transaction flows, and instantaneous funds transfers. This system will put Chase's global network at the customer's fingertips through their own computer terminals.

BANKERS TRUST (BT)

Bankers Trust (BT) is very young (5 years) in Taiwan's financial market. But it has a strong driving force in expanding its business. With a group of young and aggressive account officers, BT has efficiently penetrated the middle market. BT is emphasizing the creation of a unique package of services that attract customers to depend on them. This causes high switching costs for the customer, if the client chooses to use a competitor's products. This is one "barrier" BT seeks to establish from relationship management.

FIGURE 25–8. Citibank Taipei: The Motorcycle Unit
Internal Scrutiny at the Business Level—
Factors for Assessing Strengths and Weaknesses

1. PORTFOLIO MANAGEMENT

Objectives for managing portfolios can be classified as achieving desired profitability, contributing to the overall funds management goals of the bank, and accomplishing business development results on both sides of the balance sheet. The following items are included in this category.

RELATIONSHIP MANAGEMENT

Relationship management is the process of monitoring the desires and needs of corporate customers to ensure that the optimum level of bank services are rendered. The role is ever changing, particularly in these highly competitive times, and requires commercial lenders to increase continually their knowledge and personal development. The quality and professionalism of the management team (including loan officer), specialized industry know-how, and lending skills are major indicators for management competence.

PORTFOLIO QUALITY

To ensure good portfolio quality, the bank should make a thorough review of the existing commercial loan portfolio by analyzing geographical area, size of borrower, industry, type and size of loan, etc. This portfolio analysis may very well disclose that certain industries are not being penetrated at all by the commercial lending activities of the bank, or that there is an undue concentration of risk in one particular industry. The aim of this portfolio analysis is to obtain the maximum amount of income with the minimum exposure to risk.

SECURITY POSITION

Although collateral (security support) in itself is not necessarily the determining factor in commercial lending, it is important to the lenders in an unsatisfactory credit environment. Security coverage (value of collateral against loans outstanding) is an indicator showing how well the bank can get its second way out. So, analysis of collateral values is an important step in the credit extension. Lenders do not want to proceed against collateral because it is seldom cost effective. However, bankers recognize that things do not always work out as planned. Therefore, strengthening security position is important in the process of portfolio management.

CREDIT INITIATION

The process of credit initiation includes the following categories:
 (i) *Origin:* The initial contacts may come from client request, prospect discovery, and outside referral.
 (ii) *Evaluation:* The credit evaluation should be based on its purpose, business outlook, management competence, as well as financial performance. The character of the borrower, financial capacities as revealed in the past record and future prospects, and capital position are the principal factors determining the desirability of the loan to a bank.
 (iii) *Negotiation:* This includes the tenor of the loan, the terms, covenants, pricing, and in some case, the repayment schedules.
 (iv) *Approvals:* Credit proposal is initiated by the responsible account officer and then approved by senior credit officers at appropriate levels, according to their providing authority.

The whole credit initiation process is aimed at evaluating the client's credit standing and providing a suitable credit package to meet the client's financial objectives. It also provides a base for marketing strategy formulation. The risk evaluation and early problem recognition pave the way for taking remedial actions to protect the bank's interest.

FIGURE 25-8. Citibank Taipei: The Motorcycle Unit
Internal Scrutiny at the Business Level—
Factors for Assessing Strengths and Weaknesses
(continued)

2. MARKETING

The marketing concept is a philosophy that advocates a customer-oriented organization and views customers as the lifeblood of a business. Marketing can be defined as both the creation and delivery of customer-satisfying products at a profit to the banks.

Human resources are the driving force of marketing activities. The multifaceted position of relationship managers involves numerous functions that fall into five categories: 1) account management; 2) credit management; 3) product management; 4) profitability management; and 5) sales management.

Marketing forces in Citibank Taipei are more sophisticated and well-trained when compared with those in other banks. The branch has a good system for in-house and offshore training. The breadth of product line is similar among banks. However, Citibankers are more skillful in product management and development. Its sales force is more creative in providing structured products and new financing mechanisms to satisfy customers' needs. The branch also has favorable corporate image as a supportive, aggressive, and innovative bank.

3. OPERATIONS

The Operating Group performs the physical work of processing the bank's business transactions, auditing and controlling, designing its computer systems, as well as managing the bank's internal building services.

LEGAL DOCUMENTATION

Every lending institution continuously uses standardized forms and legal documents in connection with its lending activities.

All loan forms should be reviewed and updated periodically. Any change in laws or regulations which affect a commercial lending operation should result in review and revision of the pertinent lending documents. Any deficiency in loan provisions discovered during legal proceedings to collect a loan should result in a review and revision. At the very least, even if these problems do not occur, the lending institution's legal counsel should review all loan forms and documents at least every three years, and any suggested changes should be considered and implemented by management.

COST EFFECTIVENESS

Earning power has proved to be the first line of defense against the risks inherent in the banking business. Only out of ample earnings can banks afford to bid in today's highly competitive market for the best of prospective talent. Bank's earnings have been rising in recent years but increasing expenses have nearly kept pace with earnings. Therefore, cost effectiveness will have a direct impact on the bank's earnings. How to enhance cost effectiveness through holding expenses flat or cutting them down is an important issue to the Bank.

CONTROL AND AUDIT

Control is a mechanical or procedural device introduced into a process or chain of events that will automatically require that something be done in a specified and predetermined manner. The function of auditing, on the other hand, is to make certain that controls are maintained and that proofs are accurate.

AUTOMATION

In bank accounting, automation is usually by means of electronic data processing which would result in a smaller number of employees in the Operations Department of a bank. The great advantage in a bank automation system is the capacity of such a system to handle a greatly increased volume of items with a marginal increase in cost.

Figure 25–8. (continued)

> ### 4. FINANCIAL POLICY
>
> #### Risk Taking Ability and Willingness
> In the commercial lending area, there are constraints from the risks of credit, liquidity, interest sensitivity, and economic conditions. These risks must be recognized, quantified to the extent possible, and managed. Risk-taking ability and willingness reflect a bank's capacity to be an aggressive and supportive one.
>
> For *credit risk*, management must decide how much it is willing to take and what rewards it expects in return. Increased risk demands strong and experienced loan officers, good systems and procedures, and an ability to react rapidly to adversity. Management must also determine how much appetite it has for risk.
>
> For *liquidity risk*, a bank must maintain a reasonable liquidity level to avoid severe consequences. On the asset side of the balance sheet, liquidity can be maintained through unpledged short-term investments, loan run-off, and the ability to sell or participate in loans because of their credit quality and appropriate pricing. On the liability side, liquidity can be raised through deposits or borrowing. Raising liquidity through liabilities depends on confidence in the bank. This, in turn, can be related to asset quality and earnings.
>
> *Interest sensitivity risk* concerns the yield on interest-earning assets. The risk is that they will not respond appropriately to changes in rates of the liabilities that fund them. Interest risk can be alleviated through funds management.
>
> As for *economic risks*, loan officers attempt to limit the effect economic swings have on their portfolios although they can do nothing to control general economic conditions. Business cycles affect a loan portfolio in three ways: 1) concentration by industry or country; 2) concentration by financial structure; and 3) concentration by products.
>
> After isolating exposures in these areas, the loan officer must set limitations which are subject to periodic review and discussion.
>
> #### Asset and Liability Management
> The bank usually has an ALCO (Asset and Liability Committee) which is responsible for managing the bank's mismatched position between the duration and composition of assets and liabilities. The ALCO basically determines the loan/investment portfolio and essentially assumes profit center responsibility for the management of interest rates, foreign exchange, and liquidity risk for the balance of strategic assets and liabilities.

Citibank Taipei is compared against its most relevant competitor among foreign participants in the market—Bank of America—across all factors just stated. The result of this analysis and some comments are displayed in Figure 25–9.

Summary of the Internal Scrutiny

Figure 25–10 on page 369 shows that Citibank Taipei is considered to be on an even standing with Bank of America, and that the situation is expected to prevail in the near future, though there are a few relative changes in some of the competitive factors displayed. In fact, Citibank Taipei was in slight advantage to BOA, but this was a momentary situation resulting from Citibank's strong marketing team and operations group. The major threat comes from the portfolio management because of Citibank's deeper penetration into the motorcycle market with a less attractive portfolio quality. How to effectively

FIGURE 25-9. Citibank Taipei: The Motorcycle Unit
Internal Scrutiny at the Business Level

Competitive Profile Between Citibank Taipei and Bank of America

Factors	Current State − / − − E + + / +	Comments
1. Portfolio Management • Relationship management • Portfolio quality • Security position • Credit initiation	(profile plotted)	• Possesses high degree of management integrity, quick to recognize market opportunity and respond to threats • High penetration into motorcycle market with below-average portfolio quality • Fair security position • Have strict credit initiation process and better ability for problem recognition
2. Marketing • Human resources • Breadth of product line • Sales force innovation/ complexity of structure • Business image	(profile plotted)	• Ability to attract qualified personnel • High creativity in developing new financing techniques • Favorable corporate image
3. Operations • Legal documentation • Cost effectiveness • Control and audit • Automation • Legal staff support	(profile plotted)	• Requirements on documentation are more strict • Highly automated with high caliber staff • Ability to understand and circumvent restrictive regulations
4. Financial Policy • Risk taking willingness and ability • Asset/liability management	(profile plotted)	• Branch's policy is to be supportive and willing to take risks • Matching of asset and liability maturities reduces risk of interest rate volatility

KEY:
− / −   Severe competitive disadvantage
−   Mild competitive disadvantage
E   Equal competitive standing
+   Mild competitive advantage
+ / +   Severe competitive advantage

FIGURE 25–10. Citibank Taipei: The Motorcycle Unit
Internal Scrutiny at the Business Level

Overall Assessment of Citibank's Business Strength Compared to Bank of America

	CURRENT			FUTURE		
	Low	*Medium*	*High*	*Low*	*Medium*	*High*
PORTFOLIO MANAGEMENT		X				X
MARKETING			X		X	
OPERATIONS			X			X
FINANCIAL POLICY		X			X	
OVERALL ASSESSMENT		X			X	

manage this portfolio and to liquidate/reduce loan outstandings in time are critical issues to the bank.

Summing up, the major strengths and weaknesses of Citibank Taipei with regard to competitors are shown in Figure 25–11.

Formulation of the Business Strategy

The business strategy is expressed as a collection of broad action programs derived from:

- corporate strategic thrusts and planning challenges addressed specifically to the business
- changes in the business mission
- opportunities or potentially adverse impacts found in the environmental scan
- basic strengths or major weaknesses identified in the internal scrutiny and competitive analysis

FIGURE 25–11. Citibank Taipei: The Motorcycle Unit
Internal Scrutiny at the Business Level

Summary Assessment of Major Strengths and Weaknesses

MAJOR STRENGTHS
High integrity of management system
Sound credit process/initiation system
Strong marketing team with innovative capability and favorable business image
Well-developed supportive system

MAJOR WEAKNESSES
Below-average credit portfolio quality
Weak motivation and reward system
Inferior security position to local banks

POSITION OF THE SBU IN THE INDUSTRY ATTRACTIVENESS-BUSINESS STRENGTH MATRIX

The environmental and internal analyses can be summarized by positioning the SBU in the industry attractiveness-business strength matrix. This might not seem to be a very helpful representation at the SBU level, but it is extremely valuable when the information collected for all the SBUs of the firm is gathered together for purposes of representing the portfolio of businesses. We take this issue up again in step 6 of the planning process.

DEVELOPMENT OF BROAD ACTION PROGRAMS FOR EACH BUSINESS UNIT

This is the key task of this step. All previous analyses should lead to an intelligent definition of broad action programs intended to exploit the inherent capabilities of the firm, and position the business toward a long-term advantage with regard to its competitors. For each action program defined, a priority for resource allocation should be indicated, according to the following categories, expressed in terms of market-share positioning:

- build aggressively
- build gradually
- build selectively
- maintain aggressively
- maintain selectively
- prove viability
- divest/liquidate
- competitive harasser

Citibank Taipei: The Motorcycle Unit Formulation of the Business Strategy

POSITION OF THE MOTORCYCLE UNIT IN THE INDUSTRY ATTRACTIVENESS-BUSINESS STRENGTH MATRIX

Essentially, the message portrayed in Figure 25–12 is that the competitive position can be maintained, despite shaky loans to the motorcycle industry and falling attractiveness, by selectivity of the clientele and the efficient liquidation of unacceptable portfolios.

FIGURE 25–12. Citibank Taipei: The Motorcycle Unit
Formulation of Business Strategy

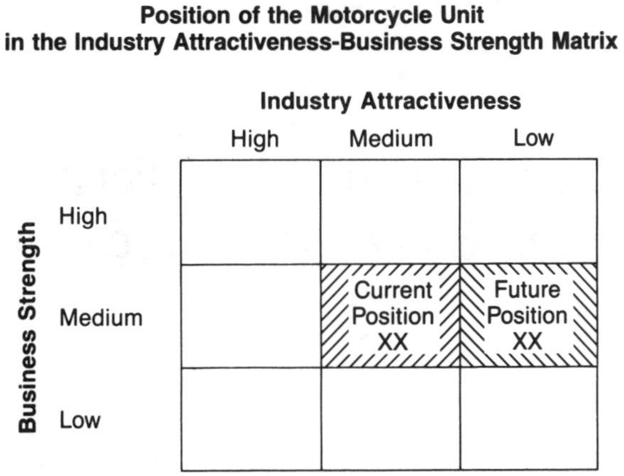

**Position of the Motorcycle Unit
in the Industry Attractiveness-Business Strength Matrix**

Industry Attractiveness

	High	Medium	Low
High			
Medium		Current Position XX	Future Position XX
Low			

Business Strength

DEVELOPMENT OF BROAD ACTION PROGRAMS
FOR THE MOTORCYCLE UNIT
SUGGESTED PRIORITY FOR RESOURCE
ALLOCATION: MAINTAIN SELECTIVITY

Broad Action Programs:
1. Refine the lending policy.
2. Manage selectively outstanding loans.
3. Look for opportunities to increase revenues and reduce costs.

The first two of these programs are geared at improving the risk-return profile of the current portfolio of loans to motorcycle manufacturers. The last one responds to more general requisitions from the corporate level. A brief description of these programs comes next.

1. Refine the lending strategy through a redefinition of the target market criteria, a careful selection of operations to be funded, the proper assessment of risk, and selectivity in market requirements.
2. Manage selectively outstanding loans through sorting out of accounts, increased liquidity coverage, close monitoring of classified loans, and preparation to call the loan if things do not improve.
3. Look broadly for all opportunities to increase revenues and improve the productivity through technology support.

CHAPTER 26

Step 5: Formulation of Functional Strategy and Broad Action Programs

The business strategy materializes the long-term development of a business through the articulation of well-coordinated programs, many of them having a functional content. Therefore, the functional strategies should be an integral part of the business strategy. Whenever there is complete functional autonomy at the business level, most of the functional strategies are indeed embedded in the business broad action programs. There is only one important exception to that, arising when there are specific strategic thrusts related exclusively to the functional management, whose resolution does not reside at the business level.

When businesses share centralized functional resources, there is still another level of concern regarding functional strategies. Although, as we do recommend, functional managers might have been strongly involved in the development of the corresponding functional strategies supporting each business, there might still be some inconsistencies in search of reconciliation. These are presented when the central functional managers analyze all the functional requirements originated by the totality of businesses. At the time of adding up all these requirements, there could emerge legitimate reasons for disagreement between businesses and functional managers. These disagreements could generate a nonconcurrent vote on the part of the functional manager, which could either be resolved through direct discussions between the affected parties, or could escalate at the corporate level in the next step of the planning process.

The functional programs at this step should be broadly stated and provide a time frame for accomplishing various milestones, and a first estimate of the strategic resource requirements, that is, labor, dollars, and so on. In subsequent steps, these programs, once developed, are consolidated with all the firm's programs at the corporate level. Upon approval, the functional managers develop detailed budgets, rate of return, net present value, and labor requirement projections.

To summarize, functional strategies are formulated first at the business level, where functional managers actively participate in their formulation; second, at the functional level, where they have to respond to the corporate thrusts involving directly the specific function, and not contained in any proposed business plan. These functional broad action programs should be supported by an environmental scan and an internal scrutiny process, similar to those discussed at the business level, except that now the focus of attention is the actual standing and proper development of functional capabilities. Finally, at the intersection of business and functional levels, functional managers cast a concurrence or a nonconcurrence vote, after the business strategies have been developed. If agreement cannot be reached among them whenever a nonconcurrence exists, the issue would escalate at the corporate level.

This issue of functional strategy is treated in Part IV of the book and illustrated for the specific case of manufacturing in Chapter 20.

CHAPTER **27**

Step 6: Consolidation of Business and Functional Strategies at the Corporate Level

This step in the planning process calls for a critical review and sanctioning at the corporate level of the set of broad action programs proposed by business and functional managers. It requires the involvement of all key executives who share responsibility for shaping the strategic direction of the firm.

In this step, the following issues have to be addressed:

- resolution of nonconcurrence conflicts
- balancing the business portfolio of the firm
- defining the availability of strategic funds, the debt policy, and maximum sustainable growth
- preliminary evaluation of proposed action programs and assignment of priorities for resource allocation to each business.

The resolution of nonconcurrence conflicts requires reaching a consensus among interested parties. We will not give any further consideration to this matter, since its treatment heavily depends on the specific circumstances surrounding each individual issue.

Balancing the Business Portfolio of the Firm

Having developed individual assessments and proposals for broad action programs at the business and functional levels, it is time to look at them from the overall perspective of the corporate level. The different portfolio matrices, discussed in Chapter 15, constitute valuable tools to accomplish this task. The popularity enjoyed by these tools results primarily from their effectiveness in providing a compact and graphical method portraying the strengths of the portfolio of businesses in a firm.

Balancing the business portfolio requires looking at issues like: short-term profitability versus long-term development, and risk versus return.

The case of Citibank Taipei cannot be used as an example of this task because only one business has been fully analyzed, and the entire set of businesses is required to determine the portfolio balance.

As an illustration of this task, the business portfolio of Martin Marietta (MM) in 1982 is used. The SBUs considered are the following six:

- Aerospace, providing full development, design, manufacturing, field support, and logistics services for sophisticated weapons systems.
- Aluminum, which includes primary products (ingots), fabricated products (sheets, forgings, extrusions), titanium products (extrusions, bar, seamless pipe), and calcined coke (carbon) for consumer and industrial markets.
- Aggregates, representing construction aggregates (such as crushed stone, sand, and gravels primarily for highway and general construction), and high-grade silica sands (used mainly in the glass and foundry industry).
- Cement, primarily Portland and masonry cement sold for use in the construction industry.
- Specialty chemicals, including concrete admixtures, refractories, and dyestuffs.
- Data systems, offering a wide range of data processing services (such as remote computer power, computer systems, and facilities management), for both private industry and government.

To assess the portfolio balance, various matrices should be used because their messages are often complementary, thus providing a deeper comprehension of the quality of the portfolio of businesses, and of the characteristics of each one of the SBUs. In the case of MM, three matrices are used: the growth-share matrix, the industry attractiveness-business strength matrix, and the profitability matrix (Figure 27–1).

The three matrices tend to convey consistent information about the strategic positioning of all of Martin Marietta's business. Perhaps the only discrepancy arises from the status of the Aggregates SBU, which is portrayed in a very unattractive category in the growth-share matrix, while appearing stronger in the other two matrices. Also, notice that the Aluminum SBU is squarely depicted as a loser in all three matrices, while Aerospace is a clear winner.

With regard to the portfolio balance, it is a major plus for the Aerospace business because it is the largest and most profitable; also Chemicals looks promising. Aluminum and Cement, on the other hand, are draining resources. This portfolio seems to be somewhat loaded toward riskier businesses. A large and stable cash generator is missed.

FIGURE 27–1. Matrix Display of the Overall Portfolio of Martin Marietta

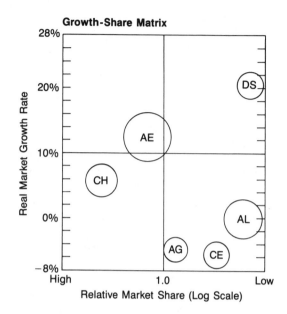

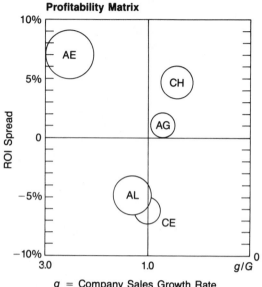

g = Company Sales Growth Rate
G = Industry Sales Growth Rate

- The scale in the horizontal axis has been reversed with regard to the normal Marakon matrix, to facilitate comparison with the other portfolio matrices
- DS not portrayed in this matrix

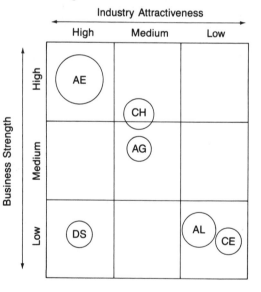

Keys:
Size of circle indicates size of sales revenue in 1981
AE = Aerospace   CE = Cement
AG = Aggregates   CH = Chemicals
AL = Aluminum   DS = Data Systems

SOURCE: Lily K. Lai, "Corporate Strategic Planning for a Diversified Company," © 1983. Reprinted by permission of Lily K. Lai.

Defining the Availability of Strategic Funds, the Debt Policy, and the Maximum Sustainable Growth

Strategic funds are expense items required for the implementation of strategic action programs whose benefits are expected to be accrued in the long term, beyond the current budget period. There are three major components of strategic funds:

- Investments in tangible assets, such as new production capacity, new tools, new space, and new acquisitions.
- Increases or decreases in working capital resulting from strategic commitments.
- Developmental expenses that are over and above the needs of existing businesses, such as R&D expenses for new products, sales promotions, development of management systems, and so forth.

A sound method of calculating strategic funds is first to forecast the sources and uses of funds by the firm. A procedure to make this computation follows.

SOURCES	USES

Earnings
Depreciation
New debt issuing
New equity issuing
Divestitures
Others
	Dividends
	Debt repayment
	Strategic funds:
	  New fixed assets and acquisitions
	  Increases in working capital
	  Increases in developmental expenses

Total Sources	= Total Uses
Strategic Funds	= Total Sources Less dividends Less debt repayment

Establishing a *debt policy* congruent with the company's financing requirements is another issue to be addressed at this point. The amount of strategic funds that can be invested and the maximum sustainable growth are clearly determined by the capital structure selected by the firm.

The *maximum sustainable growth* that can be obtained by using the internally generated resources and the recently defined debt policy can be estimated by using the relationship:

$$g = p\left[ROA + \frac{D}{E}(ROA - i)\right]$$

where

g = maximum sustainable growth expressed as a yearly rate of increase of the equity base (the debt-equity ratio is assumed to remain constant, so g represents also the increase in debt).

p = percentage of retained earnings

ROA = after-tax return on assets

$\dfrac{D}{E}$ = debt-equity ratio

i = after-tax interest on debt

Preliminary Evaluation of Proposed Action Programs and Assignment of Priorities for Resource Allocation to Each Business

There are two main tasks to be conducted at this stage of the planning process. One requires either the confirmation of the priority for resource allocation suggested by the business manager at stage 4 of the process, or an assignment of a different priority in light of the evidence gathered at the corporate level.

The second task is to assign the total available resources of the firm to SBUs. The two philosophies which have been developed around that issue are: either to assign resources to the SBUs according to their strategic priorities and let the SBU managers allocate those resources to specific projects; or directly assign those resources on a project-by-project basis. As we have indicated elsewhere, we favor the first approach.

The actual assignment of priorities and resources can be facilitated by using the market-to-book value model for each individual business, as explained in Chapter 15. The Aluminum Company of Martin Marietta can be used as an example. This business appeared in poor position in the three matrices. Divestment appears as a natural course of action, but selected economic and financial data would provide added information. The analysis conducted for evaluating the business is based on the four strategic alternatives recommended by Marakon (as discussed in Chapter 15): hold, build, harvest, and divest. in Figure 27–2 we present a summary of the basic parameters for the first three of these alternatives, as well as an estimate of the net cash flow for 1983. It can be observed, if the cash flow is a fair estimate, that none of the alternatives contributes a positive amount to the market value of the operation. All of them appear as subtracting value. Therefore, the divest strategy surges again as a most powerful alternative, which should be given careful consideration. In fact, we can at least say that liquidating will produce a positive value, mainly when considering that the company holds current assets of $428 million which are very liquid, and has a fairly modern plant which accounts for $776 million in fixed assets. On the other hand, current liabilities and long-term debt amount

FIGURE 27–2. The Basic Strategies for the Aluminum Company
of Martin Marietta

	HOLD	BUILD	HARVEST
Annual sales increase (%)	3	5	2
Return on sales (%)	4	3	5
Working capital/sales (%)	30	30	30
Net plant increase (%)	3	5	2
Maintenance investment/net plant (%)	11	11	11
Depreciation/net plant (%)	6	6	6
Deferred tax/net earnings (%)	6	6	6
Cash Flow Calculation (1983)			
Net Earnings	26	20	32
+ Depreciation	39	41	38
+ Deferred tax	2	1	4
− Capital expenditures	92	106	83
− Working capital	6	10	4
Net Operating Cash Flow 1983	− 31	− 54	− 13

SOURCE: Lily K. Lai, "Corporate Strategic Planning for a Diversified Company," 1983. Reprinted by permission of Lily K. Lai.

to $630 million. Therefore, to break even, the firm should sell the plant for only 26 percent of its net value, because we can assume that current assets are worth the same $428 million they are valued in the books.

Net proceeds from liquidating the firm:

Current assets	$428
Fixed assets (26% of $776)	202
Total	630
− Debt outstanding	630
NET TOTAL	0

It appears most likely that the fixed assets are worth more than $202 million, because not only is it a very modern plant, but the average M/B ratio for the industry is around 0.5.

CHAPTER 28

Steps 7 and 8: Specific Action Programs at the Business and Functional Levels

Specific action programs translate the broad action programs defined both at the business and functional levels into concrete tasks which can be evaluated and monitored. They constitute a structured, coherent, and timed continuum of actions, supporting each broad action program, with a clearly identified schedule of completion, in a relatively short time span, covering from six to eighteen months.

A normalized presentation of specific action programs facilitates their later evaluation and comparison at the corporate level, so we recommend the inclusion of the following items in that presentation:

- a verbal description
- a statement of priority indicating the desirability of the program for the competitive position of the firm: "absolutely first priority" (postponement will hurt the competitive position significantly), "highly desirable" (postponement will affect the competitive position adversely), "desirable" (if funds were to be available, the competitive position could be enhanced)
- the estimated costs and benefits
- the schedule of completion
- the identification of a single individual responsible for its implementation
- the procedure for controlling its execution (normally of the project control kind, like Critical Path Method and Gantt schedules).

This information helps evaluate the projects at the corporate level, which are approved based partly on the qualitative assessment of strategic position of the business, partly on the resources available to the firm, and partly on quantitative indicators of the specific project. The quantitative indicators usually include a Net Present Value project evaluation based on an incremental analysis. It is also common to prepare a cash-flow sensitivity analysis projection looking at the most likely, optimistic, and pessimistic scenarios.

Citibank Taipei: The Motorcycle Unit
Specific Action Programs at the Business and Functional Levels

A more precise definition of broad action programs at the business level is provided in Figure 28–1, to better delineate the meaning and scope of each program, and to help assign responsibilities for their execution. Also, Figure 28–2 on page 384 summarizes the main results obtained throughout the process of defining broad and specific action programs and illustrates the logic of its derivation.

FIGURE 28–1. Citibank Taipei: The Motorcycle Unit
Definition of Specific Action Programs

---

1. REFINE THE LENDING POLICY

The following issues should be included:

REDEFINE TARGET MARKET CRITERIA
The market was characterized by predominantly family-owned, highly leveraged, entrepreneurial, middle market business operating in a mature industry within a stagnant economic environment, which depends upon the U.S. as a trade partner. These factors underscore the need for a strong market process, that works down to the account officer level. The target market criteria should be redefined to weed out the existing weak accounts, including at least sales, profitability, leverage, and liquidity as factors in the analysis.

STRENGTHEN CREDIT INITIATION AND PROCESS
The market is full of under-capitalized business and is in a liquidity crunch. This makes timing an essential issue in identifying potential problems. Therefore, the depth and quality of the credit analysis and presentation should be strengthened.

Marketing-driven concepts do not apply in this industry. Attention should focus on credit issues to gain early problem recognition and to take the necessary remedial action.

ESTABLISH A RISK-RATING SYSTEM
Since the intensity of loan monitoring should be proportional to the perceived risk involved, the risk must be assessed at the time of credit approval. This assessment can be accomplished by the responsible loan officer, the credit department, or credit committee. Risk assessment must be stated in some tangible, quantifiable manner, and lead to one of the following risk categories:

Current	*Classified*
1. Grade A (highest quality)	I Weak
2. Grade B (good quality)	II Substandard
3. Grade C (fair quality)	III Doubtful
	IV Loss

STRENGTHEN MONITORING SYSTEM FOR EFFECTIVE LOAN MANAGEMENT
The process of loan monitoring must be strengthened to be responsive to changes in economic condition and industry maturity. In periods of recession, inflation, or uncertainty with industries facing a decaying maturity stage, the loan manager should change the monitoring guidelines to reflect a more defensive posture.

STAFFING: SELECT TALENTED PROFESSIONAL PEOPLE TO HANDLE CLASSIFIED ACCOUNTS AND PROVIDE THEM WITH ADEQUATE MOTIVATION AND REWARD

The classification of credits is designed to highlight problem credits for attention and action at all appropriate levels and to ensure corrective measures to reduce the bank's risk. In view of the gloomy outlook of the motorcycle industry, the more experienced people should be assigned to handle these weak credits to detect early signals and to take necessary remedial steps to rectify the problem. To cope with their heavy workload and severe pressure, appropriate motivation and reward systems should be in place.

IDENTIFY HIGHLY ATTRACTIVE INDUSTRY SEGMENTS AND BUILD MARKET SHARE SELECTIVELY THROUGH PRODUCT INNOVATION AND SERVICE DIFFERENTIATION

To reduce potential credit risks, the branch needs to focus on the top industry names and build market share through providing excellent service and innovative products. It is unwise to have a large customer base in a mature industry, like motorcycles; therefore, finding a niche to concentrate efforts on those attractive industry segments is a good strategy from both marketing and credit points of view.

TAKE HIGH PRICING STRATEGY

For the second- and third-tier clients in the industry, a strategy of walking away was formed. A high pricing strategy should be taken to skim this market segment, to increase return, and to accelerate phasing out the weakest accounts.

2. MANAGE SELECTIVELY OUTSTANDING LOANS

The specific action programs are:

SORT OUT EXCEPTIONAL ACCOUNTS

Use the refined target market criteria. Classify those unattractive industry segments into tenable, weak, and nonviable categories.

> For tenable names, credit extension should be made on asset based finance (ABF) basis

> For weak and nonviable accounts, security coverage should be improved to 100% and outstandings liquidated. Repayment schedule should be worked out as soon as possible.

> The appendix to this figure provides a primary classification of competitors.

INCREASE LIQUID SECURITY COVERAGE

Hold more certificates of deposit, time deposits, and receivables as security. For receivables, doublecheck bounced-back ratio and concentration ratio on a regular basis (at least monthly).

MONITOR CLASSIFIED LOANS CLOSELY

Prepare classified loan report on a monthly basis to monitor account's outstanding, performance, risk area, and progress of strategy implementation. Also ensure that all classified account documentations have been examined by legal counsel upon classification.

PREPARE CONTINGENT PLAN FOR CALLING THE LOAN

Assess the liquidation value of the collateral and evaluate the net worth of personal guarantors. Valuation of collateral should be made through an independent certified control service. The appraisal report should be carefully reviewed by a loan officer and an estimate made of the liquidation value by deducting the incremental taxes and applying an appropriate discount factor.

FIGURE 28–1. Continued

3. LOOK FOR OPPORTUNITIES TO INCREASE REVENUES AND REDUCE COSTS

The specific action programs are:

DESIGN NEW PRODUCTS AND SERVICES
Produce a list of new products and services that are nontraditional, and can effectively differentiate the bank from competitors. Emphasize product design, packaging service, and electronic products for top industry names.

INCREASE REVENUES
Increase fee-based revenue and self-liquidating trade transactions. Increase foreign exchange earnings through promoting third currency business.

REDUCE COSTS
Improve productivity through technology support, using telecommunication and data bases in different banking functions.

Appendix to Figure 28–1.   Primary classification of main competitors in the motorcycle industry.

The Taiwanese motorcycle industry is in a mature stage and the potential for profit making is below average. The industry shows limited product differentiation, small-scale manufacturing, eroding profitability, high exit barriers, falling sales, chronic overcapacity, saturated market, and tightening liquidity.

In the coming years, the focus of competition in this industry will be survival-market share. As the competition continues, there could be an industry reshuffle in the near future. Shake-out of some nonviable companies would be inevitable.

In cases like this, only strong competitors make money, while weak firms are forced out of the industry. The question is then, which competitors are in a relatively better situation? An analysis should be done, contrasting internal competencies in functional areas of all firms based on the following factors:

Area	Factors
1. Manufacturing	Productivity Quality Capacity utilization Logistic management system
2. Marketing	Dealer network Breadth of product line Price competitiveness After-sales service system Brand loyalty Market research
3. Finance	Capital structure Liquidity Leverage Profitability
4. Management	Management competence Planning and control system Reward system Capability for negotiating with government Delegation of authority Quality of corporate staff Stability of ownership R & D & Engineering

The conclusion is that, among the ten major manufacturers, only one (San Yang Ind.) has a strong competitive position, which gets reinforced because it has another SBU in the car manufacturing business, a growing market in Taiwan. Two makers (Kwang Yang Ind. and Vespa) are considered to have favorable competitive positions; three makers (Yuen Foong Ind., Tailung Ind., and Yeu Tyan Machinery) are tenable; two makers (Suzuki Ind. and KHS) are weak; and two (Wan Sun Machinery and Paijifa) are nonviable.

FIGURE 28-2. Citibank Taipei: The Motorcycle Unit
Derivation of Broad and Specific Action
Programs at the Business Level

Changes in Mission	Corporate Thrusts
• Provide core products to finance self-liquidating short-term transaction only • Focus on top industry names • Phase out shaky accounts and retain acceptable portfolio only	• Improve motivation and reward system • Maintain leading position as a low-cost, high-efficiency producer of financial services • Maintain good credit portfolio and reduce loss • Establish a mean whereby new earnings can be generated through innovation and new product development • Grow market selectively and eliminate weak accounts • Improve customer service quality

Strengths and Weaknesses	Opportunity and Threats
Strengths: • High integrity of management system • Good credit process/initiation system • Strong marketing team with innovative capability and favorable business image • Well-developed supportive system Weaknesses: • Below-average loan portfolio quality • Weak motivation and reward system • Inferior security position to local banks	Opportunities: • Profit contribution to SBU • Business potential for top industry names Threats: • Industry is in a declining maturity stage • Increasing credit risk • Limited growth and export potential for the industry • Overall unsatisfactory credit environment with economic crime

Broad and Specific Action Programs

1. Refine the lending policy
   Redefine target market criteria
   Strengthen credit initiation process
   Establish a risk-rating system
   Strengthen monitoring system for effective loan management
   Staffing: Select talented professional people to handle classified accounts and
       provide them with adequate motivation and reward
   Identify highly attractive industry segments and build market share selectively
       through product innovation and service differentiation
   Take high pricing strategy
2. Manage selectively outstanding loans
   Sort out exceptional accounts
   Increase liquid security coverage
   Monitor classified loans closely
   Prepare contingent plan for calling the loan
3. Look for opportunities to increase revenues and reduce costs
   Design new products and services
   Increase revenues
   Reduce costs

FIGURE 28–3. Definition and Evaluation of Specific Action Programs at the Business Level

Business:

Broad Action Program:

PROGRAM DESCRIPTION	PRIORITY*	$ COST	MANPOWER REQUIREMENTS	SCHEDULED COMPLETION	RESPONSIBILITY
1.					
2.					
3.					
4.					
5.					

*Categorize priorities in accordance with the following:
A = *Absolute First Priority*—postponement will significantly hurt our position
B = *Highly Desirable*—postponement will adversely affect our position in the market
C = *Desirable*—if funds were to be available to enhance our position

A comprehensive way of organizing additional information for the specific action programs is presented in Figure 28–3.

A sample form to be used in requests for capital appropriations is given in Figure 28–4. Much more detailed information could be collected, if so required by the corporate level, to identify the nature of cash flows through the planning horizon, as well as the breakdown of expenses implicit in the project.

The final allocation of strategic funds at the corporate level is based on the information provided by all SBUs in the form of specific action programs. To support the businesses of the firm, the corporation should consider the requests for capital investment, as well as the needs for an increase in working capital or in other strategic expenses.

FIGURE 28–4. Request for Capital Appropriation

A. Business Identification _____
B. Project Name _____
C. Responsible Manager _____
D. Type of Request
   1. Legal Requirements
   2. Cost Reduction and Productivity Improvements
   3. Maintenance of Existing Business
   4. Expansion of Existing Business
   5. New Business Development
   6. Energy Conservation
   7. Other (Explain) _____
E. Other Businesses Affected
   1. Business _____, _____ %
   2. Business _____, _____ %
   3. Business _____, _____ %
F. New Project?

   ☐ Yes   ☐ No
   If No, identify number _____ and year _____ of first capital appropriation.
G. Resources Requested

	Total Project	Current Budget	Current Year Forecast	Coming Year	Next Year
1. Property, Plant & Equipment	_____	_____	_____	_____	_____
2. Working Capital	_____	_____	_____	_____	_____
3. Total Capital	_____	_____	_____	_____	_____
4. Total Amount Requested from Corporation	_____	_____	_____	_____	_____

H. Description and Summary Justification of Project
I. Projected Cash Flows
   When information is available, and for all projects over $200,000, fill in this section:

FIGURE 28–4. Continued

	Pre-Operational Years			Operational Years				
Estimated Sales − Cost of Goods Sold								
Operational Profits − General Administrative and Marketing Expenses								
Profit before Taxes − Less Taxes								
Profit After Taxes + Depreciation − Investment − Increase in Working Capital ± Other Corrections to Determine Cash Flow								
Net Cash Flow								

Confidence in economic estimates:

☐ Solid Backing   ☐ Reasonable   ☐ Guess

J. Economic Indicators of the Project
   1. Cost of Capital   _____ %
   2. Time Horizon   _____ years
   3. NPV of Cash Flows $_____
   4. Internal Rate of return   _____ %
   5. Payback   _____ years

K. Key Milestone Schedule
   1. Appropriation Request Approved _____
   2. Start Engineering   _____
   3. Start Construction   _____
   4. Project Complete   _____

CHAPTER 29

Steps 9, 10, 11, and 12: The Final Cycle of Strategic Planning, Resource Allocation, and the Budgeting Process

Step 9 of the planning process involves allocation of resources and definition of performance measurements for management control. At this stage, a final commitment of strategic resources should be made. From the total funds appropriated for investments and strategic expenses, we have to deduct those which are required to fulfill legal obligations or correspond to approved commitments to ongoing projects.

The appropriation process for the remaining funds requires the completion of the following tasks:

- Collection and classification of all the information submitted by SBUs and functional units
- Analysis of the coherence between the strategic role assigned to SBUs and functional units, and the requests for funds
- Analysis of economic indicators, and value-creation potential of the proposed programs
- Final allocation of resources for the coming year
- Development of performance measurements to facilitate the controlling and monitoring of the broad and specific action programs supporting business and functional strategies in the short-run and over an extended planning horizon

There are three primary categories of information we find essential to be submitted by the SBU managers in order to guide the resource allocation process. First a brief narrative concerning the key descriptive elements of the SBU, generated from the previous stages in the planning process. Figure 29–1 provides a form containing suggestions for structuring this task.

Second, the SBU should provide basic financial information related not only to its operating base, but also to the strategic funds necessary for its future development. Figure 29–2 presents a simplified format to communicate this information.

FIGURE 29-1. Summary of Business Strategy by SBU

Business

Mission Statement _____

Industry Perspective

Market Overview	Competitive Environment
Narrative and Total Available Market	Narrative
Trends	Competitors Profile and Market Share

Business Description

Markets and Distribution	Products-Technology Scope	Manufacturing

Business Sales _____
After-Tax Profits _____

Industry Attractiveness and Business Strength (Current and Future)

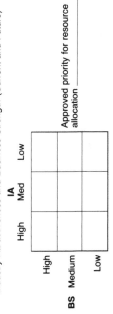

	Environmental Scan	Internal Security
Opportunities		*Strengths*
Threats		*Weaknesses*

Broad Action Programs	Specific Action Programs	Resources Requested	Statement of Benefits	Statement of Performance and Goals	Milestones	Responsible Manager

389

FIGURE 29–2. Summary of Financial Information and Strategic Funds by SBU

Business: _____

NUMBERS IN $, EXCEPT WHEN INDICATED	HISTORY					CURRENT YEAR		PROJECTIONS			
	19__	19__	19__	19__	19__	Actual	Budget	19__	19__	19__	19__
Total Market Market Share (%) Company Sales – Operating Cost of Goods Sold											
Gross Operating Margin – Operating Sales, General, & Administrative Expenses											
Operating Margin – Strategic Expenses											
SBU Margin – Taxes											
SBU Net Income + Depreciation – Capital Investments – Increases in Working Capital											
Contribution-Request of Funds to the Corporation											

Third, it is required to identify the key performance indicators for each SBU, with a statement of their historical realization, as well as projected targets. An example of this type of information is given in Figure 29–3. Notice that this constitutes one of the foundations for the subsequent control of the SBU.

We have alluded already to the two different philosophies regarding the degree of centralization in the resource allocation process. When the corporate level of a firm limits itself to a gross allocation of resources among SBUs, without intervening in the assignment of those resources within the SBU, it has already performed its key decisions in step 6 of the process. At that stage in the planning cycle, financial evaluation based on broad assessments of performance by SBU (such as the M/B model) should have provided the necessary assistance to allocate resources compatible with the strategic positioning of the SBU. What is left to be done in this case is simply a consolidation of all the information originated at the SBU level, checking for final consistency between the assigned priorities and requested funds. Figure 29–4 on page 394 suggests an approach to undertake this task.

The second philosophy for resource allocation advocates for total centralization in the assignment of resources at the corporate level, on a project-by-project basis. The information contained in the "Request for Capital Allocation" (Figure 28–4) is central in guiding those decisions. There are two further issues which need to be carefully addressed in this case. First, not every request for funds can necessarily be put in terms of a project that can be subjected to precise financial evaluation, as is the case with many of the strategic expenses needed to support the development of a business. Ordinarily, these requests are approved in the annual operating budget; however, we favor an explicit recognition of all strategic funds at this stage of the resource allocation process. Second, after having completed the approval of independent projects, one might detect inconsistencies between the resulting resources assigned to a business unit and its originally intended strategic priorities.

These considerations, together with the extraordinary demands for detailed involvement from the corporate level to pass judgment on matters which might not be totally grasped by those managers, have made many firms abandon these centralized practices of resource allocation in favor of a global assignment to SBUs. Also, as part of this step, we have to prepare a consolidation for the whole firm of the financial information and strategic funds presented by SBUs.

Finally, one should develop a set of performance objectives for the corporation, similar to those given in Figure 29–3 for each SBU. This should also include measures pertaining to the capital market (such as earnings per share, dividends per share, and market-to-book value), and other financial indices that can only be properly defined at the corporate level (such as return on equity, debt-equity ratio, and so forth).

Once all strategic programs have been approved and resources allocated accordingly, business and functional managers are left with the task of translating those commitments into detailed operational budgets and precise statements of strategic funds. Normally, this is accomplished with the help of the three conventional financial statements: balance sheet, profit and loss state-

FIGURE 29–3. Business Performance Objectives by SBU

Business Performance Objectives

INDICATORS OF PERFORMANCE		HISTORY				CURRENT YEAR		PROJECTIONS				
		19__	19__	19__	19__	Actual	Budget	19__	19__	19__	19__	19__
SIZE	Sales Assets Profits R&D expenses											
GROWTH	Sales Assets Profits R&D expenses											
PROFIT-ABILITY	Profit margin ROA											
TURN-OVER	Assets Inventory Accounts receivable											
HUMAN RESOURCES	Job satisfaction Job performance Turnover Absenteeism Motivation Job security Career prospects Psychological stress Safety/Health conditions Income											

FIGURE 29–3. Continued

TECHNOLOGICAL	Rate of technological innovation R&D productivity Rate of return in R&D investment Resources allocated to R&D Rate of new product introduction Technology-based diversification Other appropriate measures		
PROCUREMENT	Indicators for cost performance Indicators for service performance Indicators for quality performance Indicators for vendor relationships		
MANUFACTURING	Cost Delivery Quality Flexibility to volume changes Flexibility to new products introduction		
MARKETING	Product strategy Distribution strategy Price strategy Promotion and advertising strategy		

FIGURE 29–4. Resource Allocation Among Businesses According to the Strategic Positioning of SBUs

1. PORTFOLIO OF BUSINESSES AND FINAL PRIORITIES BY SBU

Industry Attractiveness

	H	M	L
H			
M			
L			

Business Strength

RESOURCE ALLOCATION PRIORITIES	LIST OF SBUs
Build Aggressively	
Build Gradually	
Build Selectively	
Maintain Aggressively	
Maintain Selectively	
Prove Viability	
Divest/Liquidate	

2. CHECKING CONSISTENCY BETWEEN SBU PRIORITY AND TOTAL FUNDS REQUESTED-APPROVED

LIST OF SBUs FROM HIGHER TO LOWER PRIORITY	CLASSIFICATION OF SPECIFIC ACTION PROGRAMS			TOTAL REQUESTED	TOTAL APPROVED
	A	B	C		
TOTAL REQUESTED					X
TOTAL APPROVED				X	

ment, and sources and applications of funds. Those statements exhibit historical as well as projected information, with the current year displayed in monthly figures. Moreover, a fourth document is used to present the operating performance indicators, again with historical and projected targets, constructed similarly to the financial statements just described.

These financial statements should be prepared at every operating level in the organization and aggregated upward for the final consolidation at the corporate level. Needless to say, most business firms look at the budget as the final element for planning and control, which drives, as a central thrust, the behavior of the key managers. This is why it is so important that the budget does not merely represent myopic operational commitments, but richly incorporates operational efficiency as well as strategic developmental efforts. It is to facilitate the accountability in these two modes that we have constantly insisted on separating operational from strategic funds, and ultimately, operational from strategic expenses and results. Since the preparation of budgets involves a well-known methodology, we do not address it here.

References

ADAMS, WALTER, *The Structure of American Industry* (7th ed.), New York: Macmillan, 1986.

AGUILAR, FRANCIS J., AND RICHARD G. HAMERMESH, *General Electric: Strategic Position—1981,* Case 381-174. Boston, MA: Harvard Business School, 1981.

ANALOG DEVICES, INC., *Corporate Objectives*. Norwood, MA:

ANDREWS, KENNETH R., *The Concept of Strategy*. Homewood, IL: Richard D. Irwin, 1980.

——— , "Corporate Strategy as a Vital Function of the Board," *Harvard Business Review,* 59, no. 6 (November–December 1981), 174–184.

ANSOFF, H. IGOR, *Corporate Strategy*. New York: McGraw-Hill, 1965.

——— , *Implanting Strategic Management*. Englewood Cliffs, NJ: Prentice Hall, 1984.

ANTHONY, ROBERT N., and JOHN DEARDEN, *Management Control Systems*. Homewood, IL: Richard D. Irwin, 1980.

——— , and ROBERT H. KAPLAN, *General Electric Company,* Harvard Business School, Case 6-113-121 in Robert N. Anthony and John Dearden, *Management Control Systems*. Homewood, IL: Richard D. Irwin, 1980.

ARTHUR D. LITTLE, INC., *Discovering the Fountain of Youth: An Approach to Corporate Growth and Development*. San Francisco, CA: 1979.

——— , *A Management System for the 1980s*. San Francisco, CA: 1980.

——— , *A System for Managing Diversity*. Cambridge, MA: December 1974.

BAROCCI, THOMAS A., and THOMAS A. KOCHAN, *Human Resources Management and Industrial Relations*. Boston, MA: Little Brown and Company, 1985.

BASS, B. M., *Leadership and Performance Beyond Expectations*. New York: The Free Press, 1985.

BEARDSLEY, SCOTT, and KENJI SAKAJAMI, *Advanced MicroDevices: Posed for Chip Greatness*. Unpublished student paper. Sloan School of Management, MIT, 1988.

BEER, MICHAEL, BERT SPECTOR, PAUL R. LAWRENCE, D. QUINN MILLS, and RICHARD E. WALTON, *Managing Human Assets*. New York: The Free Press, 1984.

BENNIS, WARREN, and BERT NANUS, *Leaders: The Strategies of Taking Charge*. New York: Harper and Row, 1985.

BOUTBOUL, ALAIN C., *A Framework for Analyzing Acquisition and Divestitures Decisions*. Unpublished Masters thesis. Sloan School of Management, MIT, 1986.

BOWER, JOSEPH L., and YVES DOZ, "Strategy Formulation: A Social and Political Process," in *Strategic Management: A New View of Business Policy and Planning*, eds. C. W. Hofer and Dan Schendel. Boston, MA: Little Brown and Co., 1979.

BREALEY, RICHARD A., and STEWART C. MYERS, *Principles of Corporate Finance* (3rd ed.). New York: McGraw-Hill Book Co., 1988.

BUFFA, EDWOOD S., *Meeting the Competitive Challenge—Manufacturing Strategy for U.S. Companies*. Homewood, IL: Richard D. Irwin, 1984.

BURGELMAN, ROBERT A., and MODESTO A. MAIDIQUE, *Strategic Management of Technology and Innovation*. Homewood, IL: Richard D. Irwin, 1988.

BURGNER, DAVID A., *Global Strategy: A Systematic Approach*. Unpublished Masters thesis, Sloan School of Management, MIT, 1986.

BURNS, JAMES B., *Leadership*. New York: Harper and Row, 1968.

CASH, JAMES I. JR., and BENN R. KONSYNSKI, "IS Redraws Competitive Boundaries," *Harvard Business Review*, (March–April 1985), 134–142.

CAVES, RICHARD E., *American Industry: Structure, Conduct, Performance* (6th ed.). Englewood Cliffs, NJ: Prentice Hall, 1987.

CHANDLER, ALFRED D., JR., *Strategy and Structure: Chapters in the History of the American Industrial Enterprise*. Cambridge, MA: The MIT Press, 1962.

CHARLES, DEXTER H., *International Commercial Banks Take on Wall Street, An Analysis and Evaluation*. Unpublished Masters thesis. Sloan School of Management, MIT, 1986.

CHIU, CHIN-TAIN, *Commercial Lending Strategy for Mature Industry: The Case of the Motorcycle Industry in Taiwan*. Unpublished Masters thesis. Sloan School of Management, MIT, 1986.

COOPER, ROBIN, and ROBERT S. KAPLAN, "Measure Costs Right: Make the Right Decisions," *Harvard Business Review*, 66, no. 5 (September–October 1988), 96–103.

COUNCIL FOR ECONOMIC PLANNING AND DEVELOPMENT, *1985 Taiwan Statistical Data Book*, ROC.

CRAVENS, DAVID W., *Strategic Marketing*. Homewood, IL: Richard D. Irwin, 1987.

CYERT, RICHARD M., and JAMES G. MARCH, *A Behavioral Theory of the Firm*. Englewood Cliffs, NJ: Prentice Hall, 1963.

DANIEL, D. RONALD, "Management Information Crisis," *Harvard Business Review*, 39, no. 5 (September–October 1961), 111–121.

DAVIS, STAN M., and PAUL L. LAWRENCE, *Matrix*. Reading, MA: Addison Wesley, 1977.

DAY, GEORGE S., *Strategic Market Planning*. St. Paul, MN: West Publishing, 1984.

DEMING, WILLIAM E., *Quality, Productivity, and Competitive Position*. Cambridge, MA: MIT CAES, 1983.

DYER, GIBB W., JR., *Culture in Organizations: A Case Study and Analysis*.

Unpublished Masters thesis. Alfred P. Sloan School of Management, MIT, 1982.

FINE, CHARLES H., "Quality Control and Learning in Productive Systems," Sloan School of Management Working Paper, #149483. Cambridge, MA: MIT, 1983.

_____ , and DAVID M. BRIDGE, "Managing Quality Improvement," Sloan School of Management Working Paper, #1607-84. Cambridge, MA: MIT, 1984.

_____ , and ARNOLDO HAX, "Manufacturing Strategy: A Methodology and an Illustration," *Interfaces,* 15, no. 6 (November–December 1985), 28–46.

FOMBRUM, CHARLES J., NOEL M. TICHY, and MARY ANNE DEVANNA, *Strategic Human Resources Management.* New York: John Wiley, 1984.

FORBES ANNUAL REPORT in the January 11, 1988 issue.

FOSTER, GEORGE, *Financial Statement Analysis* (2nd ed.). Englewood Cliffs, NJ: Prentice Hall, 1986.

FRUHAN, WILLIAM E., *Financial Strategy.* Homewood, IL: Richard D. Irwin, Inc., 1979.

GALBRAITH, JAY, *Organization Design.* Reading, MA: Addison Wesley, 1977.

_____ , and ROBERT K. KANZANJIAN, *Strategy Implementation: Structure, Systems, and Process.* St. Paul, MN: West Publishing and Co., 1986.

GARVIN, DAVID A., *Managing Quality: The Strategic and Competitive Edge.* New York: The Free Press, 1988.

GENERAL ELECTRIC COMPANY, "Background Note on Management Systems." Case No. 181-111. Boston, MA: Harvard Business School, 1981.

GLUECK, WILLIAM F., *Business Policy, Strategy Formation, and Management Action* (2nd ed.). New York: McGraw-Hill, 1976.

GRANT, EUGENE L., and RICHARD S. LEAVENWORTH, *Statistical Quality Control.* San Francisco, CA: McGraw-Hill, 1980.

GRAY, JOHN C., *The Strategic Planning Process Applied to a Natural Resource-Based Firm.* Unpublished Masters thesis. Sloan School of Management, MIT, 1984.

GUNN, THOMAS G., *Manufacturing for Competitive Advantage: Becoming a World Class Manufacturer.* Cambridge, MA: Ballinger Publishing, 1987.

HARRIGAN, KATHRYN RUDIE, *Strategic Flexibility: A Management Guide for Changing Times.* Lexington, MA: Lexington Books, 1985.

HAX, ARNOLDO C., "A New Competitive Weapon: The Human Resources Strategy," *Training and Development Journal,* 39, no. 5 (May 1985), 76–82.

_____ , and NICOLAS S. MAJLUF, "The Concept of Strategy and the Strategy Formation Process," *Interfaces,* 18, no. 3 (May–June 1988), 99–109.

_____ , "The Corporate Strategic Planning Process," *Interfaces,* 14, no. 1 (January–February 1984), 47–60.

_____ , "Organizational Design: A Case Study on Matching Strategy and Structure," *Journal of Business Strategy,* 4, no. 2 (Fall 1983), 72–86.

_____ , "Organizational Design: A Survey and an Approach," *Operations Research,* 29, no. 3 (May–June 1981), 417–447.

_____ , *Strategic Management: An Integrative Perspective.* Englewood Cliffs, NJ: Prentice Hall, 1984.

HAYES, ROBERT H., and KIM B. CLARK, *Dynamic Manufacturing: Creating the Learning Organization.* New York: The Free Press, 1988.

——, and STEVEN C. WHEELWRIGHT, "Link Manufacturing Process and Product Life Cycles," *Harvard Business Review,* 57, no. 2 (January–February 1979), 133–140.

——, *Restoring Our Competitive Edge: Competing through Manufacturing.* New York: John Wiley & Sons, 1984.

HEINRITZ, STUART F., PAUL V. FARRELL, and CLIFTON L. SMITH, *Purchasing: Principles and Applications* (7th ed.). Englewood Cliffs, NJ: Prentice Hall, 1986.

HORNGREN, CHARLES T., and GEORGE FOSTER, *Cost Accounting: A Managerial Emphasis* (6th ed.). Englewood Cliffs, NJ: Prentice Hall, 1987.

HORWITCH, MEL, ED., *Technology in the Modern Corporation: A Strategic Perspective.* New York: Pergamon Press, 1986.

JURAN, JOSEPH M. ED., *Quality Control Handbook* (3rd ed.). New York: McGraw-Hill, 1974.

——, and FRANK M. GRYNA, *Quality Planning and Analysis.* New York: McGraw-Hill, 1980.

KANTER, R. M., *The Change Masters: Innovation and Entrepreneurship in the American Corporations.* New York: Simon and Schuster, 1983.

KAPLAN, ROBERT S., "Measuring Manufacturing Performance: A New Challenge for Managerial Accounting Research," *The Accounting Review,* 58, no. 4 (October 1983), 686–705.

——, "One Cost System Isn't Enough," *Harvard Business Review,* 66, no. 1 (January–February 1988), 61–66.

——, and ANTHONY A. ATKINSON, *Advanced Management Accounting* (2nd ed.). Englewood Cliffs, NJ: Prentice Hall, 1989.

——, and H. THOMAS JOHNSON, *Relevance Lost: The Rise and Fall of Management Accounting.* Boston, MA: Harvard Business School Press, 1987.

KOH, LYNNET, *Strategic Analysis of the Worldwide Telecommunications Industry.* Unpublished Masters thesis. Sloan School of Management, MIT, 1986.

KOTTER, JOHN P., *Power and Influence—Beyond Formal Authority,* New York: The Free Press, 1985.

KUNSCHAK, MARIANNE, and LUIS F. TENA-RAMIREZ, *Strategic Management for a Pharmaceutical Company: A Case Study.* Unpublished Masters thesis. Sloan School of Management, MIT, 1983.

LAI, LILY K., *Corporate Strategic Planning for a Diversified Company.* Unpublished Masters thesis. Sloan School of Management, MIT, 1983.

LAWRENCE, PAUL R., and JAY W. LORSCH, *Organizations and Environment: Managing Differentiation and Integration.* Homewood, IL: Richard D. Irwin, 1967.

LEARNED, EDMUND P., C. ROLAND CHRISTENSEN, KENNETH R. ANDREWS, and WILLIAM D. GUTH, *Business Policy: Text and Cases.* Homewood, IL: Richard D. Irwin, 1965.

LEWIS, WALKER, "The CEO and Corporate Strategy in the 80's: Back to Basics," *Interfaces,* 14, no. 1 (January–February 1984), 3–9.

LIKERT, RENSIS, *The Human Organization: Its Management and Value*. New York: McGraw-Hill, 1967.

LINDBLOM, CHARLES E., "The Science of Muddling Through," *Public Administration Review,* (Spring 1959), 79–88.

MACEDA, EMMANUEL P., *Strategic Analysis: Du Pont Company, Engineering Polymers Divisions*. Unpublished student paper. Sloan School of Management, MIT, 1988.

MACMILLAN, IAN C., "Seizing Competitive Advantage," *The Journal of Business Strategy,* (Spring 1982), 43–57.

MALONE, THOMAS W., and STEPHEN A. SMITH, "Modeling the Performance of Organizational Structures," *Operations Research,* 36, no. 3 (May–June 1988), 421–436.

MALONE, THOMAS W., JoANNE YATES, and ROBERT I. BENJAMIN, "Electronic Markets and Electronic Hierarchies," *Communications of the ACM,* 30, (1987), 484–497.

MARAKON ASSOCIATES, *Criteria for Determining an Optimum Business Portfolio*. San Francisco, CA: 1980.

_____ , *The Marakon Profitability Matrix,* Commentary No. 7. San Francisco, CA: 1981.

MARSHALL, PAUL W., ET AL., *Operations Management: Text and Cases*. Homewood, IL: Richard D. Irwin, 1975.

McFARLAN, F. WARREN, "Information Technology Changes the Way You Compete," *Harvard Business Review,* (May–June 1984), 98–103.

McGREGOR, DOUGLAS, *The Human Side of the Enterprise*. Cambridge, MA: The MIT Press, 1960.

McTAGGART, JAMES M., "The Ultimate Takeover Defense: Closing the Value Gap," *Planning Review,* (January–February 1988), 27–32.

MINTZBERG, HENRY, "Crafting Strategy," *Harvard Business Review,* 65, no. 1 (July–August 1987), 66–75.

_____ , "Patterns in Strategy Formation," *Management Science,* (1976), 934–948.

_____ , *Power In and Around Organizations*. Englewood Cliffs, NJ: Prentice Hall, 1983.

_____ , *The Structuring of Organizations*. Englewood Cliffs, NJ: Prentice Hall, 1979.

_____ , and JAMES A. WATERS, "Of Strategy Delivered and Emergent," *Strategic Management Journal,* 6, no. 3 (July–September 1985), 257–272.

MYERS, STEWART C., "Finance Theory and Financial Strategy," *Interfaces,* 14, no. 1 (January–February 1984), 126–137.

ORTEGA, LUIS A., *Analysis of the Development of a Strategic Planning System*. Unpublished Masters thesis. Sloan School of Management, MIT, Cambridge, MA, 1985.

OUCHI, WILLIAM G., *Theory Z*. Reading, MA: Addison Wesley, 1981.

PARSONS, GREGORY L., "Information Technology: A New Competitive Weapon," *Sloan Management Review,* (Fall 1983), 3–14.

PASCALE, R. T., and A. G. ATHOS, *The Art of Japanese Management: Applications for American Executives*. New York: Simon and Schuster, 1981.

PORTER, MICHAEL E., *Competition in Global Industries*. Boston, MA: Harvard Business School Press, 1986.

———, *Competitive Advantage: Creating and Sustaining Superior Performance*. New York: The Free Press, 1985.

———, *Competitive Strategy: Techniques for Analyzing Industries and Competitors*. New York: The Free Press, 1980.

———, and VICTOR E. MILLAR, "How Information Gives You Competitive Advantage," *Harvard Business Review,* (July–August 1985), 149–160.

QUINN, JAMES BRIAN, "Formulating Strategy One Step at a Time," *The Journal of Business Strategy,* 1, no. 3 (Winter 1981), 42–63.

———, *Strategy for Changes—Logical Incrementalism*. Homewood, IL: Richard D. Irwin, 1980.

———, HENRY MINTZBERG, and ROBERT M. JAMES, *The Strategy Process: Concepts, Context, and Cases*. Englewood Cliffs, NJ: Prentice Hall, 1988.

RAPPAPORT, ALFRED, *Creating Shareholder Value: The New Standard for Business Performance*. New York: The Free Press, 1986.

———, "Executive Incentives vs. Corporate Growth," *Harvard Business Review,* 56, no. 4 (July–August 1978), 81–88.

ROBERTS, EDWARD B., ED., *Generating Technological Innovation*. New York: Oxford University Press, 1987.

ROCKART, JOHN F., "Chief Executives Define Their Own Data Needs," *Harvard Business Review,* 57, no. 2 (March–April 1979), 81–92.

———, and CHRISTINE V. BULLEN, EDS., *The Rise of Managerial Computing*. Cambridge, MA: MIT, 1986.

———, and DAVID W. DeLONG, *Executive Support Systems: The Emergence of Top Management Computer Use*. Homewood, IL: Dow Jones-Irwin, 1988.

———, and MICHAEL S. SCOTT MORTON, "Implications of Changes in Information Technology for Corporate Strategy," *Interfaces,* 1, no. 14 (January–February 1984), 84–95.

———, and MICHAEL E. TREACY, "The CEO Goes On-Line," *Harvard Business Review,* 60, no. 1 (January–February 1982), 82–88.

ROTHSCHILD, WILLIAM E., "How to Insure the Continuous Growth of Strategic Planning," *The Journal of Business Strategy,* 1, no. 1 (Summer 1980), 11–18.

SCHEIN, EDGAR H., *Career Dynamics*. New York: Addison Wesley, 1976.

———, "Coming to a New Awareness of Organizational Culture," *Sloan Management Review,* 25, no. 2 (Winter 1984), 3–16.

———, "Does Japanese Management Style Have a Message for American Managers?" *Sloan Management Review,* 23, no. 1 (Fall 1981), 55–67.

———, *Organizational Culture and Leadership: A Dynamic View*. San Francisco, CA: Jossey-Bass, 1985.

SCHERER, F. M., *Industrial Market Structure and Economic Performance* (2nd ed.). New York: Houghton Mifflin, 1980.

SCHONBERGER, RICHARD J., *World Class Manufacturing: The Lessons of Simplicity Applied*. New York: The Free Press, 1986.

———, *Japanese Manufacturing Techniques*. New York: The Free Press, 1982.

SCHWARTZ, HOWARD, and STANLEY M. DAVIS, "Matching Corporate Culture and Business Strategy," *Organizational Dynamics,* 10, (Summer 1981), 30–48.

———, *Organizational Dynamics,* AMACOM, New York, (Summer 1981).

SHAPIRO, ALAN S., "Corporate Strategy and the Capital Budgeting Decision," *Midland Corporate Finance Journal,* 3, no. 1 (Spring 1985), 22–36.

SIMON, HERBERT A., *Administrative Behavior: A Study of Decision-Making Processes in Administrative Organizations.* New York: The Free Press, 1976.

SKINNER, WICKHAM, *Manufacturing: The Formidable Competitive Weapon.* New York: John Wiley & Sons, 1985.

———, "The Focused Factory," *Harvard Business Review,* 52, no. 3 (May–June 1974), 113–121.

SOLOMONS, DAVID, *Divisional Performance: Measurement and Control.* Homewood, IL: Richard D. Irwin, 1965.

STEINER, GEORGE A., and JOHN B. MINER, *Management Policy and Strategy.* New York: Macmillan, 1977.

STONICH, PAUL J., "How to Use Strategic Funds Programming," *The Journal of Business Strategy,* 1, no. 2 (Fall 1980), 35–50.

———, "Using Rewards in Implementing Strategy," *Strategic Management Journal,* 2, no. 4 (October–December 1981), 345–352.

———, ET AL., *Zero-Base Planning and Budgeting.* Homewood, IL: Dow Jones-Irwin, 1977.

SUZAKI, KIYOSHI, *The Manufacturing Challenge: Techniques for Continuous Improvement.* New York: The Free Press, 1987.

TEECE, DAVID J., ED., *The Competitive Challenge: Strategies for Industrial Innovations and Renewal.* Cambridge, MA: Ballinger Publishing Co., 1987.

TICHY, NOEL M., and MARY ANNE DEVANNA, *The Transformational Leadership.* New York: John Wiley and Sons, 1986.

TWISS, BRIAN, *Management of Technology," in Studies in Operations Management,* ed. Arnoldo C. Hax. New York: North Holland Publishing, 1978.

VANCIL, RICHARD F., "Better Management of Corporate Development," *Harvard Business Review,* 50, no. 5 (September–October 1972), 53–62.

———, *Decentralization: Managerial Ambiguity by Design.* Homewood, IL: Dow Jones-Irwin, 1978.

———, and PAUL BROWNE, *General Electric Company, Background Note on Management Systems,* Case 9-181-111. Boston, MA: Harvard Business School, 1981.

———, and RONALD HALL, *Texas Instruments, Inc.: Management Systems, 1972,* Case 9-172-054. Boston, MA: Harvard Business School, 1972.

———, and PETER LORANGE, "Strategic Planning in Diversified Companies," *Harvard Business Review,* 53, no. 1 (January–February 1975), 81–90.

VON HIPPEL, ERIC, *The Sources of Innovation,* New York: Oxford, 1988.

WALKER, GORDON, "Strategic Sourcing, Vertical Integration and Transaction Costs," *Interfaces,* 19, (May–June 1988), 62–73.

WATERMAN, R. H., JR., "The Seven Elements of Strategic Fit," *The Journal of Business Strategy,* 2, no. 3 (Winter 1982), 69–73.

WEBSTER, MARK A., *Strategic Analysis of AT&T, NYNEX and IBM in the Telecommunications Industry*. Unpublished student paper. Sloan School of Management, MIT, 1988.

WESTON, J. F., and M. B. GOUDZWAARD EDS., *The Treasurer's Handbook*. Homewood, IL: Dow Jones-Irwin, 1976.

WHEELWRIGHT, STEVEN C., "Japan, Where Operations Really Are Strategic," *Harvard Business Review*, 59, no. 4 (July–August 1981), 67–74.

WILLIAMS, ANTOINETTE M., "A Strategic Planning Process: The Case of Citicorp and Its Commercial Finance Subsidiary." Unpublished Masters thesis, Sloan School of Management, MIT, 1983.

WILLIAMSON, OLIVER E., *Market and Hierarchies*, New York: The Free Press, 1975.

WRAPP, H. EDWARD, "Good Managers Don't Make Policy Decisions," *Harvard Business Review*, 62, no. 4 (July–August 1984), 8–21.

YAVITZ, BORIS, and WILLIAM H. NEWMAN, *Strategy in Action: The Execution, Policies and Payoff of Business Planning*, New York: The Free Press, 1982.

ZAKON, ALAN J., "Capital Structure Optimization," in *The Treasurer's Handbook*, eds. J. F. Weston and M. B. Goudzwaard. Homewood, IL: Dow Jones-Irwin, 1976.

Glossary

An *italicized term* in the glossary text has its own heading that can be referenced to get its precise definition.

Action programs. Action programs are well-defined activities that emanate from broader definitions of strategy (at business and functional levels). They correspond to a pragmatic expression of strategy. Action programs should respond to the desired changes in the mission, address properly the opportunities and threats revealed by the environmental scanning process, and reinforce the strengths as well as neutralize the weaknesses uncovered in the internal scrutiny. The action programs are defined at two different levels of specificity: broad action programs typically covering a multiyear planning horizon, normally understood to represent long-term strategic objectives; and specific action programs, covering six to eighteen months, which represent the necessary tactical support to realize strategic objectives.

Administrative systems. (See integration approaches.)

Alternative Boston Consulting Group matrix. (See portfolio matrices.)

Balance. The process of establishing congruency between the chosen organizational structure and the managerial processes that go with it: planning, management control, communication and information, and human resources management and reward systems. This process amounts to a search for a proper fit among all the formal-analytical managerial systems in the strategic management framework. The full-fledged operation of these systems provides a background of integrative relationships that the simple organizational structure fails to represent. Moreover, these systems must be designed both to reinforce the primary foci chosen by the organization, and to support those activities relegated to a secondary level in the definition of the organizational structure. (See integration approaches.)

Basic organizational structure. The basic structure represents the major segmentation of the businesses the firm is engaged in through a hierarchical order which reveals the priorities managers assign to the firm's central activities. The definition of a basic structure requires the full recognition of the businesses of the firm and their further segmentation into manageable units. Only the primary echelons of the organizational chart that are intimately linked to the strategic positioning of the firm are recognized in this definition.

Breadth of vertical integration. The breadth of vertical integration measures how broadly or narrowly the firm depends on its own internal sources for all of its important inputs and outputs. Breadth can be measured as the fraction of value provided by the internal inputs or outputs of the firm with regard to the total value of its internal and external transactions, for a given organizational unit.

Broad action programs. (See action programs.)

Budgets. They represent projections of financial data normally covering one or more years.

Business segmentation. It is the identification of the businesses the firm is in or intends to be in. (See strategic business unit.)

Business strategy. A well-coordinated set of *action programs* aimed at securing a long-term sustainable advantage. Business managers are supposed to formulate and implement strategic actions congruent with the general corporate directions, and constrained by the overall resources assigned to the particular business unit.

Business strength. It is the result derived from the *internal scrutiny* at the business level expressed in terms of major strengths and weaknesses in the current and future standing of the business, in relation to its most relevant competitors. A common procedure to perform this scrutiny is based on the *value chain*. (See internal scrutiny at the business level.)

Calendar-driven planning process. A formal planning process that stipulates the completion of major tasks and steps in the planning cycle by well-defined dates.

Common-size financial statements. A technique for carrying out the financial statement analysis of firms of different size that starts with the standardization of their financial figures to a common base (usually, total sales revenues are defined as 100 percent).

Communication system. It is an activity that allows managers to transmit the messages they think should be given to interested parties at all organizational levels, as well as the relevant external stakeholders. (See information system.)

Competitive advantage. It is the distinct way a business or a firm is positioned in the market in order to obtain an advantage over competitors, which means an ability to maintain sustained levels of profitability above the industry average. At the heart of achieving a long-term sustainable competitive advantage is the identification of opportunities to create conditions of disequilibrium which can legitimately allow a firm to claim economic rents beyond those resulting from perfect competition, and then to protect and sustain those conditions for as long as possible. (See generic competitive strategies.)

Competitive leadership. (See competitive advantage.)

Competitor interrelationships. (See horizontal strategy.)

Concept of strategy. Strategy is a coherent, unifying, and integrative pattern of decisions that determines and reveals the organizational purpose in terms of long-term objectives, action programs, and resource allocation priorities. A firm's strategy selects the businesses the organization is in or is to be in, attempts to achieve a long-term sustainable advantage in each of its businesses by responding properly to the opportunities and threats in the firm's environment and the strengths and weaknesses of the organization. The strategic concept engages all the hierarchical levels of the firm (corporate, business, functional) and defines the nature of the economic and noneconomic contributions it intends to make to its stakeholders.

Configuration. It refers to the location of each one of the activities of the *value chain* across the different areas of the firm's operation. It is particularly relevant for global firms with different operations in many countries.

Coordination. It refers to the design of the organizational and administrative systems put in place to achieve a state of adequate coordination among the different activities of the *value chain*, mainly when their *configuration* is dispersed among many different countries. (See integration approaches.)

Corporate, business, and functional planning challenges. Planning challenges correspond to the assignment of responsibilities and priorities for the proper execution of *corporate strategic thrusts* addressed at corporate, business, and functional levels.

Corporate culture. (See organizational culture.)

Corporate performance objectives. Corporate performance objectives are quantitative indicators of the overall performance of the firm. Typically, companies choose to express corporate objectives via a very selective number of indices. Although there is no universal set of such indices, we can classify them into two major categories. The first includes quantitative financial measures that relate to size, growth, profitability, capital markets, and a host of other financial variables. The second is oriented at measuring the overall efficiency of the managerial functions of the firm; in particular human resources, technology, procurement, manufacturing, and marketing. Incorporating these functional measures at the corporate level is relevant whenever we deal with centralized functions. Otherwise, the functional measure should become part of either divisional or business performance indicators, depending on where the function resides within the organization.

Corporate philosophy. Corporate philosophy is a rather permanent statement, articulated primarily by the chief executive officer, addressing the following issues: (1) the relationship between the firm and its primary stakeholders—employees, customers, shareholders, suppliers, and the communities in which the firm operates; (2) a statement of broad objectives of the firm's expected performance, primarily expressed in terms of growth and profitability; (3) a definition of basic corporate policies with regard to issues such as management style, organizational policies, human resources management, financial policies, marketing, and technology, and (4) a statement of corporate values pertaining to ethics, beliefs, and rules of personal and corporate behavior. The corporate philosophy has to provide a unifying theme and a vital challenge to all organizational units, communicate a sense of achievable ideals, serve as a source of inspiration for confronting the daily activities, and become a contagious, motivating, and guiding force congruent with the corporate ethic and values.

Corporate strategic thrusts. Strategic thrusts are the primary issues the firm has to address during the next three to five years to establish a healthy competitive position in the key markets in which it participates. The corporate strategic thrusts constitute a powerful mechanism to translate the broad sense of directions the organization wants to follow into a practical set of instructives to all key managers involved in the strategic process.

Corporate tasks. (See strategic corporate tasks.)

Cost center. (See responsibility center.)

Cost of capital. It is a benchmark defining the minimum rate of return that must be required of an investment, if it must generate a positive contribution to the *economic profitability* of a firm. The cost of capital is estimated by adding two components: a risk-free rate of return, and a positive risk premium to compensate for the inherent risk in the investment.

Critical success factors. The limited number of areas in which satisfactory results will ensure a successful competitive performance for a business unit. These indicators are specific to each business, and they reflect managerial preferences with regard to key variables at a given point in time. Therefore, they must be constantly adapted to reflect changes taking place in the organization or its environment. (See key performance indicators.)

Cultural audit. A systematic process to uncover the basic underlying principles at the core of an *organizational culture.*

Cultural risk. A measure of the compatibility between the strategy being considered for a firm and the *organizational culture.*

Cultural risk assessment. A methodology to determine the *cultural risk* of the different *action programs* of a strategy, and to suggest a way to go when a high-risk situation is detected.

Culture. (See organizational culture.)

Detailed organizational structure. The process of fleshing out the *basic organizational structure* with numerous specific details that pertain to the operational domain of the firm. The definition of a detailed organizational structure has two objectives: to identify all the major operational tasks the organization should undertake in the pursuit of its daily activities, and to assign those tasks to the organizational segments identified in the basic structure previously defined. The basic structure brings the selected strategy into the design process, while the detailed analysis recognizes the operational functional activities.

Differentiation. The tendency by individuals and units of an organization to create their own culture and distinctive approach to deal with different situations, due to the conceptual imprinting produced when conducting their normal activities in their specific environments. (See generic competitive strategies.)

Direction of vertical integration. The direction of vertical integration recognizes two different ways of adding value to the inputs and outputs of the firm: backward—which means getting closer to suppliers by incorporating into the firm a given input to the current core, and forward—which involves a greater proximity to customers by putting a given output of the core under the firm's umbrella. These two forms of vertical integration are sometimes referred to as upstream and downstream extensions, respectively.

Discretionary cost center. It is a *cost center* characterized by the inability to measure delivered outputs in a strict financial way, or by the lack of a clear association between inputs and outputs. Such is the case with most of the administrative activities of a firm (for example, legal, human resources, accounting departments), the research and development function, and marketing activities such as promotion and advertising.

Divisional organization. The divisional form is structured according to the outputs generated by the organization. The most common distinction of the outputs is in the terms of the products delivered. However, other types of outputs could serve as a basis for divisionalization, such as services, programs, and projects. Markets, clients, and geographical locations also could serve as criteria for divisionalization. This is a decentralized form of organization because many conflicts and decisions can be resolved at the divisional manager's level, preventing an overburdened top hierarchy.

Economic profitability. A measure of profitability that includes, among the cost of resources, the total cost of the capital used (including equity capital, which is normally omitted in the commonly used measures of accounting profitability).

Economic-to-book value model (E/B). It is equivalent to the *market-to-book value model*, in which the assessment of market value is done as a direct projection into the future of past trends for all financial indicators.

Environmental scan at the business level. The environmental scan at the business level attempts to identify the degree of attractiveness of the *industry* in which the business belongs, in terms of its potential for a sustainable long-term profitability.

Environmental scan at the corporate level. It attempts to diagnose the general health of the industrial sectors relevant to the businesses in which the corporation is engaged. It concentrates on assessing the overall economic, political, technological, and social climates that affect the corporation as a whole. This assessment has to be conducted, initially from a historical perspective to determine how well the corporation has mobilized its resources to meet the challenges presented by the external environment. Then, with a futuristic view in mind, future trends in the environment must be predicted and a repositioning of the internal resources sought to adapt the organization to those environmental trends. The main components of this scan are the economic scenario; the projection of global trends in the primary markets in which the firm competes; the analysis of emerging technologies; the availability and quality of the supply of human resources; and issues pertaining to the political, social, and legal environments.

Executive information system (EIS). (See information system.)

Extended performance evaluation approach. A system of *managerial compensation* that rewards managers for achieving certain performance levels over a multiyear period, by awarding them with deferred stock or stock options according to each one's ability to fulfill various strategic goals over the agreed-upon planning horizon.

Extent of integration. The extent of integration refers to the length of the *value chain* housed by the firm; whether it is limited to just a few stages or covers the whole array. One way of measuring the extent of integration is through the fraction of the final value of a product or service that is added by the firm.

External-factors analysis. A methodology to perform the environmental scan at the business level based on the identification of those critical external factors considered to be the central determinants of *industry attractiveness* in the opinion of key managers of the business. Managers are required to engage in an exercise for probing the identification of those issues which are considered truly significant, and to concentrate their efforts in assessing their influence on industry attractiveness.

Financial performance. Broadly understood, it refers to the performance of a firm or business unit in terms of the different dimensions included in the *financial ratio analysis*. Narrowly understood, it refers exclusively to the firm profitability, which can be measured in a score of different indicators, particularly return on assets, return on equity, return on investment, margin of sales, and *spread*.

Financial ratio analysis. The financial ratio analysis is aimed at characterizing the firm in a few basic dimensions considered fundamental to the financial health of a company. They are usually categorized in five types: (1) liquidity ratios (ability to meet short-term financial obligations); (2) leverage/capital structure ratios (ability to fulfill long-term commitments with debtholders); (3) profitability ratios (ability to generate profits); (4) turnover ratios (efficiency or productivity ratios); and (5) common stock security ratios (performance from the point of view of shareholders).

Financial statement analysis. A technique that makes use of public financial information (balance sheet, income statement, statement of changes in the financial position, and 10K reports) for gaining an understanding of the relative financial standing of different firms. In this book it is used as a methodology for determining the competitive position of firms participating in an industry. There are two basic procedures to make financial figures more easily comparable among different competitors: define *common-size financial statements*; and perform a *financial ratio analysis*.

Fit. (See balance.)

Five-forces model. A model proposed by Michael Porter to determine *industry attractiveness* by performing an analysis of the industry structure. The five forces which typically shape the industry structure are intensity of rivalry among competitors, threat of new entrants, threat of substitutes, bargaining power of buyers, and bargaining power of suppliers. These five forces delimit prices, costs, and investment requirements which are the basic factors that explain long-term profitability prospects and industry attractiveness. The generic structure of an industry is represented by the main players (competitors, buyers, suppliers, substitutes, and new entrants), their interrelationships (the five forces), and the factors behind those forces accounting for industry attractiveness. (See Figure 5–1).

Flexible budgets. They are *budgets* that allow for the modification of the parameters used to define them, when the actual level of operations changes.

Focus. (See generic competitive strategies.)

Formal-analytical approaches. (See integration approaches.)

Formal planning process. (See strategic planning process.)

Full integration. A firm which is fully integrated backward on a given input satisfies all the needs for that particular input from internal sources. Likewise, when a firm is fully integrated forward for a given output, it is self-sufficient in providing internally the demand for that product or source. Fully integrated companies have complete ownership of their assets.

Functional environmental scanning process. This is a process aimed at obtaining an understanding of critical industrial trends and the present and future standing of key competitors. A critical component in this process is functional intelligence, whose purpose is to generate all the relevant information concerning the current and future states of development of each individual function. It is not only the existing managerial practice and state of technological progress that are important to detect, but even more critical is the recognition of future trends and state-of-the-art developments, and its embodiment in actions by competitors.

Functional intelligence. (See functional environmental scanning process.)

Functional internal scrutiny. It is an effort aimed at the recognition of overall strengths and weaknesses typical of the analysis at the business level, and the determination of specific skills that could be built for each individual function in order to gain *competitive advantage*.

Functional organization. The functional form is structured around the inputs required to perform the tasks of the organization. Typically, these inputs are functions or specialties such as finance, marketing, production, engineering, research and development, and personnel. It is a centralized form of organization because only at the top is there a confluence of all the inputs required for conflict resolution and final decision making.

Functional strategy. Functional strategies are sets of well-defined *action programs* aimed at consolidating the functional requirements demanded by the composite of businesses of the firm, and also at developing unique competencies to exceed or at least match competitors' unique capabilities. The six major foci for strategic functional analysis are financial strategy, human resources strategy, technology strategy, procurement strategy, manufacturing strategy, and marketing strategy.

Generic competitive strategies. The general approach a business follows to compete in an industry to attain a sustainable level of profitability above the industry average. Michael Porter suggests three generic strategies: (1) Overall cost leadership requires aggressive construction of efficient-scale facilities, vigorous pursuit of cost reductions from experience, tight costs and overhead control, avoidance of marginal customer accounts, and cost minimization in areas like R&D, service, sales force, advertising, and so on. (2) Differentiation calls for creating something that is perceived industry-wide as being unique. Approaches to differentiation can take many forms: design of brand image, technology, features, customer service, dealer network, or other dimensions. (3) Focus consists of concentrating on a particular buyer group, segment of the product line, or geographic market. As with differentiation, focus may take many forms. Although the low-cost and differentiation strategies are aimed at achieving those objectives industry-wide, the entire focus strategy is built around servicing a particular market target very well, and each functional policy is developed with this in mind.

Growth-share matrix. (See portfolio matrices.)

Growth strategies (for the firm). (See Figure 9–2.)

Growth strategies (product-market segments). There are four major alternatives for growth strategies: (1) market penetration, when based on existing products and existing markets (like expansion in sales volume, geographical extensions, and market-share improvements), (2) product development, when based on the introduction of new product lines into existing markets, (3) market development, when based on the introduction of existing products into new markets, and (4) diversification, when based on the introduction of new products into new markets, which amounts to an entry into a new business.

Hierarchical levels of planning. There are three basic conceptual hierarchical levels which have been recognized as the essential layers of any formal planning process: corporate, business, and functional. (See strategic corporate tasks; business strategy; functional strategy.)

Horizontal strategy. Horizontal strategy is a set of coherent long-term objectives and action programs aimed at identifying and exploiting interrelationships across distinct but related business units. The types of possible interrelationships are: tangible interrelationships, arising from opportunities to share activities in the value chain; intangible interrelationships, involving the transference of management know-how among separate value chains; and competitor interrelationships, stemming from the existence of rivals that actually or potentially compete with the firm in more than one business unit.

Human resources management of key personnel. (See management of key personnel.)

Hybrid organization. An organizational structure that does not follow a unique criteria to segment activities, as in the case of a *functional organization* or a *divisional organization*, but mixes these two models, though a dominant pattern can be traced back to one of them. For example, most divisional organizations have a number of functional specialties centralized at the corporate level.

Imprinting the vision of the firm. The process of internalizing the *vision* in the organization via a number of formal-analytical approaches (appealing to the rational self to generate calculated reactions), and power-behavioral approaches (appealing to the affective self to generate intuitive reactions) in a way that is congruent with the culture of the firm. This process is at the heart of *strategic management*.

Industry. A group of firms offering products or services which are close substitutes for each other. Thus, the boundaries of the industry are determined from a user's point of view. Close substitutes are products that, in the eye of the individual, perform approximately the same function. Technically speaking, this means that they have high cross elasticities of demand.

Industry attractiveness. It is the result derived from the environmental scan at the business level and is expressed in terms of opportunities (factors that affect favorably) and threats (factors which constitute adverse impacts) to long-term profitability prospects in the industry. A common procedure to perform this scan is the structural analysis of the industry based on the use of the *five-forces model*. Another useful procedure is the *external-factors analysis*.

Information system. The formal process and administrative system of gathering, digesting, filtering, and distributing the information relevant to managers at all hierarchical levels. (See communication system.)

Intangible interrelationships. (See horizontal strategy.)

Integration approaches. A number of different managerial processes that are designed to provide incentives so that all individuals within the organization work in a harmonious way while seeking the achievement of the organizational vision. There are two major categories of integration approaches that we have recognized in the *strategic management* framework. The first one results from the formal-analytical approaches and is represented by the lateral coordinating mechanisms (mainly the creation of liaison roles, task forces, committees, integrating managers, and matrix relations), and by the central administrative systems of the firm (planning, control, communications and information, and human resources management and reward systems). The character of these formal-analytical mechanisms is dependent on the kind of strategy they are intended to support. The second one is generated from power-behavioral approaches to management, and they are basically informal, political, and psychological mechanisms intended to affect behavior in the desired strategic direction.

Intelligent budgets. They are *budgets* that are not a mere extrapolation of the past into the future but are instead instruments that contain both strategic and operational commitments.

Internal scrutiny at the business level. A systematic and disciplined approach to guide a manager through all the necessary steps to perform the *internal scrutiny* at the business level. The process attempts to identify the major strengths and weaknesses of the firm against its most relevant competitors (*business strengths*). The internal scrutiny is supported by the following tasks: identification of the most relevant *SBU's* competitors; determination of critical success factors; that is, those capabilities controllable by the firm in which it has to excel for the SBU to achieve a long-term sustainable competitive advantage and a profitability level above industry standards; development of a competitive profile for the SBU, by measuring the business strengths and weaknesses against each of the most relevant competitors; and preparation of the summary assessment and identification of overall strengths and weaknesses associated with the SBU.

Investment center. (See responsibility center.)

Issue escalation. The formal process by which critical disagreement among members of a firm located at similar hierarchical levels in the organizational structure of a firm is moved to the next higher level in the managerial hierarchy for final sanctioning.

Key performance indicators. A stable set of indicators, considered to be key to follow up the operation and performance of a business unit, that allow managers to detect and monitor the competitive position of all businesses the firm is engaged in. These indicators tend to be permanent and uniformly applied to all business units of a firm. (See critical success factors.)

Life-cycle matrix. (See portfolio matrices.)

Linking-pin. An integrating role aimed at coordinating the activities of two different units of the firm.

Logical incrementalism. A strategy formation process proactively guided by managers that builds strategy at disaggregated levels, later integrating these subsystem strategies step by step for producing the strategy for the overall firm. This process of strategy formation is fragmented, evolutionary, and largely intuitive.

Major tasks of a planning cycle. Tasks that need to be updated and revised at every planning cycle: *strategy formulation, strategic programming*, and *strategic and operational budgeting*. Each one of these major tasks is composed of a number of steps that progressively defines the different levels of the strategy of a firm (corporate, business, and functional) in terms of a hierarchy of objectives that moves from broad to very specific.

Management accounting approach. A system of *managerial compensation* based on the adjustment of the financial accounting model, in order to reflect both strategic and operational results of the firm. One way of achieving this is by breaking down expenses into strategic and operational, and maintaining a *strategic funds* accountability.

Management control. Management control is a structured process, quantitatively oriented, that is based on the definition of performance standards for the entire firm and each one of its units, and on the comparisons of planned with actual results obtained from operations. In this way, top managers can derive an opinion on the effectiveness of the implementation of strategic directions and the efficiency achieved in the use of its primary resources and then act accordingly, taking corrective action whenever needed. Management control is a major system for managing day-to-day operational and strategic activities with a unitary sense of direction imprinted in the quantitative benchmarks selected as standards for comparison. Finally, management control, mainly when coupled with the compensation and reward system, becomes a driver of individual behavior in the organizational setting.

Management of key personnel. One of the key corporate tasks that calls for the management of human resources in a strategic manner; that is, in a way that allows firms to establish and sustain a long-term advantage over competitors. A human resources strategy must be comprehensive in the sense of addressing all the diverse personnel and human resource activities central to the long-term development of the businesses of the firm. Its foundation lies in the proper recognition of the major categories of human resource strategic decision making: (1) selection, promotion, and placement—managing the flow of people in, through, and out of the organization; (2) appraisal—evaluation of the performance of people within the organization; (3) rewards—providing adequate compensation, fringe benefits, and motivational support to employees at all levels; (4) management development—creating mechanisms to enhance skills, promotional opportunities, and career paths; and (5) labor/employee relations and voice—establishing a cooperative climate among managers and employees.

Managerial compensation. The monetary reward received by managers for their individual and group performance as judged from their contribution to short-term and long-term results. (See rewards systems; extended performance evaluation approach; strategic factors approach; management accounting approach.)

Managerial infrastructure. A set of corporate tasks more directly related to the implementation of strategy: the design of the *organizational structure* and *administrative systems*, and the *management of key personnel*.

Market attractiveness-business strength matrix. (See portfolio matrices.)

Market-to-book value model (M/B). The M/B model is a blend of two different perspectives of the firm. In the denominator, the book value of the firm's shares provides the accountant's perspective, which corresponds to the historical measurements of resources contributed by shareholders. In the numerator, the market value of the firm's shares gives the investor's perspective, which corresponds to an assessment of future payments generated from the assets the firm has already in place and from the investments the firm would have the opportunity to make at some time in the future. Therefore, the M/B ratio can be equated to:

$$\frac{\text{Expected future payments}}{\text{Past resources committed}}$$

Master budget. It is a collection of *budgets* that includes all those activities whose monitoring is judged to be important for a healthy development of the firm's businesses. Among them are sales, manufacturing, administrative activities, investment, and cash management.

Matrix organization. Matrix organizations are structured around two (or more) design concepts. *Functional organizations* are structured around inputs and *divisional organizations* around outputs. Matrix organizations are a fundamental departure from this unitary notion because both inputs and outputs are considered equally important as criteria for segmentation of the organizational activities.

Maximum sustainable growth. The maximum growth of the assets of a firm that can be financed by maintaining a stable debt-equity ratio and dividend-payout policy.

Mission of the business. It is a statement of the current and future expected business scope and a definition of the way to attain *competitive leadership*. Business scope is expressed as a broad description of products, markets, and geographical coverage of the business today, and within a reasonably short time frame, commonly three to five years. For some businesses, technology is added as another dimension of its scope. (See competitive advantage.)

Mission of the firm. The mission of the firm is a statement of the current and future expected product scope, market scope, and geographical scope as well as the unique competencies the firm must develop to achieve a long-term sustainable advantage.

Mobility barriers. An assessment of the degree of difficulty that a *strategic group* within an industry has to penetrate into an adjacent strategic group.

Motivational and rewards system. (See rewards system.)

Natural strategy. The normal course of action suggested by the positioning of a business in *portfolio matrices*, commonly expressed in terms of a thrust for market share, using categories like the following: build aggressively, build gradually, build selectively, maintain aggressively, maintain selectively, prove viability, and divest-liquidate.

Nonconcurrence. A vote cast by functional managers when they do not agree with a proposed business plan because it is judged to contain inadequate or unrealistic commitment in a functional area. The conflict thus generated is solved by *issue escalation*.

Nonintegration. A firm which decides not to integrate on a given input or output and depends completely on external providers for its necessary support. The commitments that facilitate the reliance on those external parties are normally drafted in terms of contracts which represent joint responsibilities but no internal integration. Common forms of contracts are competitive bids, long-term contracting, and rent of assets.

Operational funds. They are expense items required to maintain the business in its present position (funds to keep up the momentum).

Opportunistic planning. A flexible form of planning to meet unexpected events not properly anticipated in the formal planning process. It is normally concentrated in a more narrow segment of corporate activities, and prompt answer rests on the provision of financial and organizational slack to absorb additional duties without experiencing a severe organizational constraint.

Organization. Organizations are groups of people seeking the achievement of a common purpose via division of labor, integrated through formal-analytical administrative systems and power-behavioral managerial approaches congruent with its organizational culture continuously through time.

Organizational archetypes. Different templates to guide the designs of the organizational structure. They are the *functional organization, divisional organization,* and *matrix organization*. A combination of these is the *hybrid organization*.

Organizational culture. Organizational culture is a complex set of basic underlying assumptions and deeply held beliefs shared by all members of the group that operate at a preconscious level and drive behavior in important ways.

Organizational structure. (See basic organizational structure; detailed organizational structure; balance.)

Overall cost leadership. (See generic competitive strategies.)

Performance measurements. They are quantitative indicators of the performance of the firm defined at different hierarchical levels: corporate, business, and functional. They are basically oriented at measuring the financial soundness of a firm or a business, and the overall efficiency of each one of the managerial functions of a firm, in particular: human resources, technology, procurement, manufacturing, and marketing. (See Figure 14–2, corporate performance objectives; financial statement analysis; financial performance; key performance indicators; critical success factors; strategic measures of functional performance.)

Planning cycle. A formal strategic planning process that is periodically conducted in a firm. (See structural conditioners of a planning cycle; major tasks of a planning cycle.)

Planning guidelines. They specify the different steps and responsibilities in the formal planning process through time and define the basic parameters, mainly economic assumptions, to be used by all the managers involved in this effort.

Portfolio management. Portfolio management is a major responsibility of the corporate level geared at the analysis of the basic characteristics of the portfolio of businesses of a firm, in order to assign priorities for *resource allocation. Portfolio matrices* can be used toward this end.

Portfolio matrices. A set of graphic displays developed by leading consulting firms to help managers in reaching a better understanding of the competitive position of the overall portfolio of businesses, to suggest strategic alternatives for each of the businesses, and to develop priorities for resource allocation. Each matrix positions the business units of the firm in accordance with two dimensions: one is an external dimension which attempts to capture the overall attractiveness of the industry in which the business participates; the other is an internal dimension that relates to the strength of the business within its industry. The factors that describe industry attractiveness are normally uncontrollable by the firm; those that contribute to business strength are largely under the control of the firm. The most popular portfolio matrices are: (1) the growth-share matrix developed by the Boston Consulting Group, which pioneered this concept; (2) the industry attractiveness-business strength matrix, conceived jointly by General Electric and McKinsey and Company, which was the first one to introduce multidimensional criteria in the external and internal dimensions; (3) the life-cycle matrix developed by Arthur D. Little, Inc., which contains a fairly comprehensive methodology that leads to a wide array of broad action programs to support the desired strategic thrust of each business; (4) the alternative Boston Consulting Group matrix that enriches the original BCG matrix by bringing in broader descriptions of industry structure ; and (5) the profitability matrix proposed by Marakon, which captures the three most central strategic objectives of each business—profitability, growth, and cash-generation capabilities. The position of a business in a matrix suggests a strategic course of action, called generic or natural strategy, and a priority for resource allocation.

Power-behavioral approaches. (See integration approaches.)

Primary structure. (See basic organizational structure.)

Principle of integration. Managers should create the conditions that will allow the members of an organization to achieve their own goals best by directing their efforts to the success of the enterprise.

Profit center. (See responsibility center.)

Profitability matrix. (See portfolio matrices.)

Program-period planning process. A formal planning process that allows for program initiatives to be generated at any time during the year (as opposed to calender-driven planning process that prescribes a timing for it). But at a given point in time, all programs are consolidated through a formal process called period planning.

Quasi-integration. Quasi-integrated firms do not have full ownership of all assets in the value chain related to a given input or output. Rather, they resort to several mechanisms to assure steady relationships with external constituencies. These reside somewhere in between long-term contracts and full ownership. Prevalent forms of quasi-integrations are joint ventures or alliances, minority equity investments, loans, loan guarantees, licensing agreements, franchises, R&D partnerships, and exclusivity contracts.

Resource allocation. A corporate task that requires discrimination among the wide array of requests for funding of the corporate, business, and functional programs defined in the strategic planning process. This is necessary because the financial, technological, and human resources available to the firm are not sufficient to support every proposed activity.

Responsibility center. A responsibility center is an organizational unit with a clearly identified scope of activities that has been entrusted to a responsible manager. It may be pictured in terms of three main factors: its inputs such as materials, parts, components, and labor; its outputs such as the different kinds of products and services generated by the unit; and the fixed resources assigned to the manager as total assets or net investment. Depending on the nature of managerial control, the responsibility center may be defined as: cost centers where managers are accountable for expenses generated from the input streams; revenue centers where accountability stems from revenues generated from the output streams as well as expenses from the input streams; profit centers where accountability is judged by ability to generate profits (revenues minus expenses); and investment centers where accountability is measured in terms of profit as percentage of the total investment base.

Revenue center. (See responsibility center.)

Rewards system. It is a formal definition of the different components considered in the performance evaluation of managers and the assignment of monetary and nonmonetary rewards to them.

SBU. (See strategic business unit.)

Segmentation. The process of conceptualizing the purpose of an organization and translating it in terms of a variety of specific tasks, whose execution is located in different units of the organization.

SFU. (See strategic functional unit.)

Shared common resources (among business units). *Horizontal strategy* defined for resources shared among business units, like manufacturing facilities, distribution channels, technology, or other functions support.

Shared concerns (among business units). *Horizontal strategy* defined for concerns shared among business units, like common geographical areas and key customer accounts.

Sources of value creation. Sources of value creation are the different mechanisms a firm uses to create *competitive advantages* and the ways to exploit them.

Special strategic issues. One of the strategic corporate tasks that calls for managers at this level to be specially alert to those environmental developments that are deeply transforming the traditional ways of conducting businesses in a given industry. Among them globalization, technological innovations, and the requirement of a new form of executive leadership are issues that are having a profound impact on business practices.

Specific action programs. (See action programs.)

Standard cost center. It is a *cost center* characterized by having well-defined output measures and clean relationships between the required inputs and the resulting outputs. Such is the case with manufacturing operations where standards can be computed to the amount of inputs—labor, raw materials, supplies, and additional supporting services—needed to produce a unit of a specific product.

Strategic and operational budgeting. One of the major tasks of the planning cycle that includes the formulation and consolidation of *budgets* at the business and functional levels, and the approval of *strategic funds* and *operational funds*.

Strategic business unit (SBU). An SBU is an operating unit or a planning focus that groups a distinct set of products or services which are sold to a uniform set of customers, facing a well-defined set of competitors. The external (market) dimension of a business is the relevant perspective for the proper identification of an SBU. Therefore, an SBU should have a set of external customers and not just serve as an internal supplier.

Strategic categories of decisions (linked to functional strategies). The set of specific skills related to each managerial function of a firm that could be built in order to gain *competitive advantage*.

Strategic corporate tasks. At the corporate level reside the decisions which, by their nature, should be addressed with full corporate scope. These are decisions that cannot be decentralized without running the risks of committing severe suboptimization errors. The central issue behind the strategic corporate tasks is how to add value at the corporate level. These tasks are: (1) *Mission of the firm*—choosing competitive domain and the way to compete; (2) *Business segmentation*—selecting planning and organizational focuses; (3) *Horizontal strategy*—pursuing synergistic linkages across business units; (4) *Vertical integration*—defining the boundaries of the firm; (5) *Corporate philosophy*—defining the relationship between the firm and its stakeholders; (6) *Special strategic issues*—identifying current key subjects of strategic concern; (7) *Strategic posture of the firm*—identifying strategic thrusts; corporate, business, and functional planning challenges; and corporate performance objectives; (8) *Portfolio management*—assigning priorities for resource allocation and identifying opportunities for diversification and divestment; (9) *Organization* and *managerial infrastructure*—adjusting the organizational structure, managerial processes, and systems in consonance with the culture of the firm to facilitate the implementation of strategy; and (10) *Human resources management of key personnel*—selection, development, appraisal, reward, and promotion.

Strategic factors approach. A system of *managerial compensation* that involves the identification of the critical success factors governing the future profitability of the business, and the assignment of proper weights depending on the inherent characteristics of the business unit and its agreed-upon strategy. This approach allows for establishing congruency in terms of the performance measurements to be used and the position of the business within the corporate portfolio.

Strategic functional unit. It is the focus of attention that drives all functional strategic analysis for all key functional areas. (See Figure 18–2.)

Strategic funds. They are expense items required for the implementation of strategic action programs whose benefits are expected to be accrued in the long term beyond the current budget period. There are three major components of strategic funds: (1) investment in tangible assets, such as new production capacity, new machinery and tools, new vehicles for distribution, new office space, new warehouse space, and new acquisitions; (2) increases (or decreases) in working capital generated from strategic commitments—such as the impact of increases in inventories and receivables resulting from an increase in sales, the need to accumulate larger inventories to provide better services, increasing receivables resulting from a change in the policy of loans to customers, and so on; and (3) developmental expenses that are over and above the needs of existing business—such as advertising to introduce a new product or to reposition an existing one—R&D expenses of new products, major cost-reduction programs for existing products, introductory discounts, sales promotions, and free samples to stimulate first purchases, development of management systems—such as planning, control, and compensation—certain engineering studies, and so on.

Strategic group analysis. A procedure to define *strategic groups* within an industry and the different degrees of *industry attractiveness* of each one of these groups. For the definition of strategic groups, Michael Porter suggests the following dimensions to identify differences in firm strategies within an industry: specialization, brand identification, push-versus-pull marketing approach, channel selection, product quality, technological leadership, vertical integration, cost position, service, price policy, financial and operating leverage, relationship with parent company, and relationship to home and host government. The industry attractiveness at the group level may be assessed using the *five-forces model*, in a process referred to as industry analysis within an industry.

Strategic groups. They correspond to aggregations of firms within an industry that include, in a unique set, competitors that follow a common or similar strategy along well-defined dimensions. Groups collect firms which are relatively homogeneous according to the way they compete. (See strategic group analysis.)

Strategic mapping. A useful tool that can guide the separation of *strategic groups* in an industry. It is a two-dimensional display that helps to explain the different strategies of firms. Those dimensions should not be interdependent because otherwise the map would show an inherent correlation. The two most common dimensions used for a strategic mapping purpose are the breadth of the product line and the degree of vertical integration. They allow us to separate firms which, on the one extreme, have a full coverage of product lines and, at the same time, are fully self-reliant from those firms which are focusing on a very narrow line and concentrating in a short range of the value-added chain.

Strategic management. Strategic management is a way of conducting the firm that has as an ultimate objective the development of corporate values, managerial capabilities, organizational responsibilities, and administrative systems which link strategic and operational decision making, at all hierarchical levels, and across all businesses and functional lines of authority in a firm. Institutions which have reached this stage of management development have eliminated the conflicts between long-term development and short-term profitability. Strategies and operations are not in conflict with one another, but they are inherently coupled in the definition of the managerial tasks at each level in the organization. This form of conducting a firm is deeply anchored in managerial style, beliefs, values, ethics, and accepted forms of behavior in the organization, which makes strategic thinking congruent with the *organizational culture*.

Strategic measures of functional performance. A collection of categories of variables that can be used as measures of performance to assess the quality of the final outputs of a functional strategy, in terms of the ability to achieve *competitive advantage*.

Strategic planning process. The strategic planning process is a disciplined and well-defined organizational effort aimed at the complete specification of a firm's strategy and the assignment of responsibilities for its execution. A formal planning process should recognize the different roles to be played by the various managers within the business organization in the formulation and execution of the firm's strategies.

Strategic posture. The strategic posture of the firm is a set of pragmatic requirements developed at the corporate level to guide the formulation of corporate, business, and functional strategies. It is expressed primarily through: *corporate strategic thrusts; corporate, business, and functional planning challenges; and corporate performance objectives.*

Strategic programming. One of the major tasks of the planning cycle that includes the following steps: definition and evaluation of specific *action programs* at the business and functional levels; and *resource allocation* and definition of *performance measurements* for *management control.*

Strategic thrusts. (See corporate strategic thrusts.)

Strategy formation process. The relevant dimensions that should be considered in delineating a strategy formation process responsive to the firm's needs are:
Explicit versus implicit strategy
1. The openness and breadth to communicate strategy, both internally in the organization and to all relevant external constituencies
2. The degree to which different organizational levels participate
3. The amount of consensus built around intended courses of action, especially the depth of CEO involvement in this effort
Formal-analytical process versus power-behavioral approach
4. The extent to which formal processes are used to specify corporate, business, and functional strategies
5. The incentives provided for key players to negotiate a strategy for the firm
Pattern of past actions versus forward-looking plan
6. The linkage of strategy to the pattern of action in the past
7. The use of strategy as a force for change and as a vehicle for new courses of action
Deliberate versus emergent strategy
8. The degree to which strategy is either purely deliberate or purely emergent.

Strategy formulation. One of the major tasks of the planning cycle that includes the following steps: *strategic posture* and *planning guidelines*; formulation of a *business strategy* and broad *action programs*; formulation of *functional strategy* and broad *action programs*, and consolidation of business and functional strategies, *portfolio management*, and definition of priorities for *resource allocation.*

Structural analysis of industries. A procedure for environmental scanning at the business level based on the tenet that an attractive industry is one that has a favorable structure which enhances long-term profitability projects. (See five-forces model; industry attractiveness.)

Structural conditioners of a planning cycle. Certain basic conditions that being more permanent are not altered in each planning cycle. They are the *vision of the firm*, the *managerial infrastructure, corporate culture, human resources management of key personnel*, and the *mission of the business.*

Tangible interrelationships. (See horizontal strategy.)

Tapered integration. Tapered integration represents a partial integration, backward or forward, that makes the firm dependent on external sources for the supply of a portion of a given input, or for the delivery of a portion of a given output. For the fraction of the input or output that the firm handles internally, it can resort to either a full integration or a quasi-integration mode of ownership.

Transfer prices. The internal prices set by a firm to determine the cash value of transfers of goods and services among its units. The most common criteria to establish transfer prices are: market prices; cost measured either as total cost, marginal cost or standard cost; cost plus a profit margin, where cost is measured according to the same alternatives just stated; and negotiated prices, either directly by the parties involved, via a mediator designated by both parties, or determined by top managers.

Value chain. A framework proposed by Michael Porter to conduct an *internal scrutiny* at the business level in order to assess the *business strength*. The tasks performed by the business are classified into nine broad categories. Five of them are the so-called primary activities, and the other four are support activities. The primary activities are those involved in the physical movement of raw materials and finished products, in the production of goods and services, and in the marketing, sales, and subsequent services of the outputs of the business firm. The support activities are much more pervasive. As the name indicates, their essential role is to provide support not only to the primary activities but to each other. They are composed by the managerial infrastructure of the firm—which includes all processes and systems to assure proper coordination and accountability—human resource management, technology development, and procurement. (See Figures 6–1 and 6–2.)

Value creation. A financial concept that expresses in quantitative terms the ability of an economic entity (a firm, business unit, or project) to create value; that is, to generate a profitability that exceeds its *cost of capital*.

Value gap. A diagnostic tool to determine if a business or firm is making adequate use of all available opportunities to create value. (See value creation.)

Vertical integration. Vertical integration involves a set of decisions that by the nature of their scope reside at the corporate level of the organization. These decisions are threefold: (1) defining the boundaries a firm should establish over its generic activities on the value chain (the question of make versus buy or integrate versus contract); (2) establishing the relationship of the firm with its constituencies outside its boundaries, primarily its suppliers, distributors, and customers; and (3) identifying the circumstances under which those boundaries and relationships should be changed to enhance and protect the firm's competitive advantage. This set of decisions is of critical importance in defining what the firm is and is not, what critical assets and capabilities should reside irrevocably within the firm, and what type of contracts the firm should establish to deal with its external constituencies. (See direction of vertical integration; full integration; quasi-integration; tapered integration; nonintegration; breadth of vertical integration; extent of integration.)

Vision of the firm. The vision of the firm is a permanent statement to communicate the nature of the existence of the organization in terms of corporate purpose, business scope, and competitive leadership; to provide the framework that regulates the relationships among the firm and its primary stakeholders; and to state the broad objectives of the firm's performance. It is described in terms of the *mission of the firm*, its *business segmentation*, *horizontal strategy*, *vertical integration*, *corporate philosophy*, and whatever other *special strategic issues* are regarded as critical.

Zero-base budgeting (ZBB). It is a budgeting process that establishes a set of comprehensive rules to force managers to justify their budgetary allocations from ground zero, rather than defining the new budget in an incremental way. (See budgets.)

Index